PARALLEL AND DISTRIBUTED SIMULATION SYSTEMS

Richard M. Fujimoto, PhD
Georgia Institute of Technology

A WILEY-INTERSCIENCE PUBLICATION

JOHN WILEY & SONS, INC.

New York • Chichester • Weinheim • Brisbane • Singapore • Toronto

Library of Congress Cataloging-in-Publication Data:

Fujimoto, Richard M.
    Parallel and distributed simulation systems / Richard M.
Fujimoto.
        p.   cm.
    "A Wiley-Interscience publication."
    Includes bibliographical references.
    ISBN 0-471-18383-0 (alk. paper)
    1. Computer simulation.   2. Parallel processing (Electronic
computers)   3. Electronic data processing—Distributed processing.
I. Title.
QA76.9.C65F84   2000
003′.3435—dc21   99-25438

PARALLEL AND DISTRIBUTED SIMULATION SYSTEMS

WILEY SERIES ON PARALLEL AND DISTRIBUTED COMPUTING

EDITOR:

ALBERT Y. ZOMAYA

FUJIMOTO • Parallel and Distributed Simulation Systems

SAPATY • Mobile Processing in Distributed and Open Environments

XAVIER AND IYENGAR • Introduction to Parallel Algorithms

To
Jan, Emily, and Alex

CONTENTS

Preface   **xv**

PART I   INTRODUCTION

1   Background and Applications   **3**

    1.1   Why Parallel/Distributed Simulation?   4

    1.2   Analytic Simulations versus Virtual Environments   6

    1.3   Historical Perspective   8
        1.3.1   High-Performance Computing Community   8
        1.3.2   Defense Community   9
        1.3.3   Interactive Gaming and Internet Communities   10

    1.4   Applications   11
        1.4.1   Military Applications   12
        1.4.2   Entertainment   13
        1.4.3   Social Interactions and Business Collaborations   13
        1.4.4   Education and Training   14
        1.4.5   Telecommunication Networks   14
        1.4.6   Digital Logic Circuits and Computer Systems   15
        1.4.7   Transportation   16

    1.5   Underlying Technologies   16

    1.6   Hardware Platforms   17
        1.6.1   Parallel versus Distributed Computers   17
        1.6.2   Shared-Memory Multiprocessors   19
        1.6.3   Distributed-Memory Multicomputers   20
        1.6.4   SIMD Machines   21
        1.6.5   Distributed Computers   22

    1.7   Summary   23

    1.8   Additional Readings   24

2   Discrete Event Simulation Fundamentals   **27**

    2.1   Time   27

    2.2   Real-Time, Scaled Real-Time, and As-Fast-As-Possible Execution   28

2.3 State Changes and Time Flow Mechanisms 30

    2.3.1 Time-Stepped Execution 31

    2.3.2 Event-Driven Execution 32

2.4 Discrete-Event Simulation Programs 34

2.5 An Example Application 36

2.6 Starting and Stopping the Simulation 39

2.7 Parallel/Distributed Simulation Example 39

2.8 World Views and Object-Oriented Simulation 41

    2.8.1 Simulation Processes 41

    2.8.2 Object-Based and Object-Oriented Simulations 45

    2.8.3 Query Events and Push versus Pull Processing 46

    2.8.4 Event Retraction 47

2.9 Other Approaches to Exploiting Concurrent Execution 48

2.10 Additional Readings 48

PART II PARALLEL AND DISTRIBUTED DISCRETE-EVENT SIMULATION

3 Conservative Synchronization Algorithms **51**

3.1 Synchronization Problem 52

3.2 Deadlock Avoidance Using Null Messages 54

3.3 Lookahead and the Simulation Model 58

3.4 Deadlock Detection and Recovery 60

    3.4.1 Deadlock Detection 60

    3.4.2 Deadlock Recovery 63

3.5 Synchronous Execution 65

    3.5.1 Centralized Barriers 66

    3.5.2 Tree Barrier 67

    3.5.3 Butterfly Barrier 68

    3.5.4 Transient Messages 70

    3.5.5 A Simple Synchronous Protocol 74

    3.5.6 Distance between Logical Processes 75

3.6 Bounded Lag 79

3.7 Conditional versus Unconditional Information 81

3.8 Dynamic Processes and Interconnections 82

3.9   Repeatability and Simultaneous Events   84

    3.9.1   Using Hidden Time Stamp Fields to Order
          Simultaneous Events   85
    3.9.2   Priority Numbers   85
    3.9.3   Receiver-Specified Ordering   86

3.10   Performance of Conservative Mechanisms   87

3.11   Summary and Critique of Conservative Mechanisms   91

3.12   Additional Readings   94

4   Time Warp   **97**

4.1   Preliminaries   98

4.2   Local Control Mechanism   98

    4.2.1   Rolling Back State Variables   100
    4.2.2   Unsending Messages   102
    4.2.3   Zero Lookahead, Simultaneous Events, and Repeatability   106

4.3   Global Control Mechanism   108

    4.3.1   Fossil Collection   110
    4.3.2   Error Handling   110

4.4   Computing Global Virtual Time   112

    4.4.1   Transient Message Problem   113
    4.4.2   Simultaneous Reporting Problem   114
    4.4.3   Samadi's GVT Algorithm   116
    4.4.4   Mattern's GVT Algorithm   117

4.5   Other Mechanisms   122

    4.5.1   Dynamic Memory Allocation   122
    4.5.2   Infrequent State Saving   123
    4.5.3   Specifying What to Checkpoint   126
    4.5.4   Event Retraction   128
    4.5.5   Lazy Cancellation   129
    4.5.6   Lazy Re-evaluation   132

4.6   Scheduling Logical Processes   133

4.7   Summary   135

4.8   Additional Readings   135

5   Advanced Optimistic Techniques   **137**

5.1   Memory Utilization in Time Warp   138

5.1.1 Preliminaries: State Vectors and Message Send
Time Stamps 139

5.1.2 Memory Management Mechanisms and Message
Sendback 140

5.1.3 Storage Optimality 142

5.1.4 Cancelback 145

5.1.5 Artificial Rollback 145

5.1.6 Pruneback 147

5.1.7 Memory-Based Flow Control 148

5.1.8 Trading Off Performance and Memory 149

5.2 Performance Hazards in Time Warp 151

5.2.1 Chasing Down Incorrect Computations 151

5.2.2 Rollback Echoes 152

5.3 Other Optimistic Synchronization Algorithms 154

5.3.1 Moving Time Window 155

5.3.2 Lookahead-Based Blocking 156

5.3.3 Local Rollback 156

5.3.4 Breathing Time Buckets 157

5.3.5 Wolf Calls 159

5.3.6 Probabilistic Rollbacks 160

5.3.7 Space-Time Simulation 160

5.3.8 Summary 160

5.4 Putting It All Together: Georgia Tech Time Warp (GTW) 161

5.4.1 Programmer's Interface 161

5.4.2 I/O and Dynamic Memory Allocation 162

5.4.3 GTW Data Structures 163

5.4.4 Direct Cancellation 165

5.4.5 Event-Processing Loop 166

5.4.6 Buffer Management 166

5.4.7 Flow Control 168

5.4.8 GVT Computation and Fossil Collection 168

5.4.9 Incremental State Saving 169

5.4.10 Local Message Sends 169

5.4.11 Message Copying 169

5.4.12 Batch Event Processing 169

5.4.13 Performance Measurements 170

5.5 Summary 171

5.6 Comparing Optimistic and Conservative
Synchronization 172

5.7 Additional Readings 174

6 Time Parallel Simulation   **177**

6.1   Time Parallel Cache Simulation Using Fix-up Computations   179

6.2   Simulation of an ATM Multiplexer Using Regeneration Points   183

6.3   Simulation of Queues Using Parallel Prefix   188

6.4   Summary   190

6.5   Additional Readings   191

PART III   DISTRIBUTED VIRTUAL ENVIRONMENTS (DVEs)

7 DVEs: Introduction   **195**

7.1   Goals   195

7.2   Contrasting DVE and PDES Systems   196

7.3   Server versus Serverless Architectures   197

7.4   Distributed Interactive Simulation   199

      7.4.1   DIS Design Principles   200
      7.4.2   DIS PDUs   202
      7.4.3   Time Constraints   203

7.5   Dead Reckoning   204

      7.5.1   Dead Reckoning Models   206
      7.5.2   Time Compensation   208
      7.5.3   Smoothing   208

7.6   High Level Architecture   209

      7.6.1   Historical Perspective   210
      7.6.2   Overview of the HLA   211
      7.6.3   HLA Rules   213
      7.6.4   Object Models and the Object Model Template   213
      7.6.5   Interface Specification   218
      7.6.6   Typical Federation Execution   219

7.7   Summary   220

7.8   Additional Readings   221

8 Networking and Data Distribution   **223**

8.1   Message-Passing Services   223
      8.1.1   Reliable Delivery   223

		8.1.2	Message Ordering	224
		8.1.3	Connection-Oriented versus Connectionless Communication	224
		8.1.4	Unicast versus Group Communication	224
		8.1.5	Examples: DIS and NPSNet	225
	8.2	Networking Requirements		226
	8.3	Networking Technologies		227
		8.3.1	LAN Technologies	227
		8.3.2	WAN Technologies	231
		8.3.3	Quality of Service	233
	8.4	Communication Protocols		234
		8.4.1	OSI Protocol Stack	235
		8.4.2	ATM Protocol Stack	238
		8.4.3	Internetworking and Internet Protocols	240
	8.5	Group Communication		243
		8.5.1	Groups and Group Communication Primitives	244
		8.5.2	Transport Mechanisms	244
	8.6	Data Distribution		245
		8.6.1	Interface to the Data Distribution System	245
		8.6.2	Example: Data Distribution in the High Level Architecture	247
		8.6.3	Implementation Issues	251
		8.6.4	Dynamic Group Management	254
		8.6.5	Wide-Area Viewers and Fast-Moving Entities	255
	8.7	Summary		256
	8.8	Additional Readings		257
9	**Time Management and Event Ordering**			**259**
	9.1	The Problem		259
	9.2	Message-Ordering Services		261
		9.2.1	Causal Order	261
		9.2.2	Causal and Totally Ordered	265
		9.2.3	Delta Causality	267
		9.2.4	Time Stamp Order	268
	9.3	Synchronizing Wallclock Time		269
		9.3.1	Time and Time Sources	270
		9.3.2	Clock Synchronization Algorithms	271
		9.3.3	Correcting Clock Synchronization Errors	273
		9.3.4	Network Time Protocol	274

9.4   Summary   275

9.5   Additional Readings   275

References   **277**

Index   **293**

■ PREFACE

These are exciting times in the parallel and distributed simulation field. After many years of research and development in university and industrial laboratories, the field has exploded in the last decade and is now seeing use in many real-world systems and applications. My goal in writing *Parallel and Distributed Simulation Systems* is to give an in-depth treatment of technical issues concerning the execution of discrete event simulation programs on computing platforms composed of many processors interconnected through a network. The platform may range from tightly coupled multiprocessor computer systems confined to a single cabinet or room to geo-graphically distributed personal computers or specialized simulators (for example, video game systems) spread across the world. This technology can be used to speed up the execution of large-scale simulations, for example simulations of the next generation of the Internet, or to create distributed synthetic environments for training or entertainment.

My goal in writing this book was to bring together into one volume the fundamental principles concerning parallel and distributed simulation systems that today are scattered across numerous journals and conference proceedings. The intended audience includes managers and practitioners involved in research and/or development of distributed simulation systems. The book can serve as a textbook for an advanced undergraduate or a graduate level computer science course. The book might be of interest in other disciplines (for example, industrial engineering or operations research) although the principal emphasis is on issues concerning parallel and distributed computation. Prior knowledge of discrete event simulation parallel, or distributed computation would be helpful, but is not essential as the book will include brief introductions to these fields.

Contents

The book is divided into three parts. The first provides an introduction to the field. Chapter 1 describes typical applications where this technology can be applied, and gives an historical perspective to characterize the communities that developed and refined this technology. Background information concerning parallel and distributed computing systems is reviewed. Chapter 2 reviews fundamental concepts in discrete event simulation to provide a common basis and terminology that is used in the remainder of the book.

The second part is primarily concerned with parallel and distributed execution of simulations, primarily for analysis applications such as to design large, complex systems. Here the goal is to use multiple processors to speed up the execution. Much of the material in these four chapters is concerned with synchronization algorithms that are used to ensure a parallel execution of the simulation yields the same results as a sequential execution, but (hopefully!) much more quickly. Two principal approaches to addressing this issue are called conservative and optimistic synchronization. Chapter 3 is concerned with the former, and Chapters 4 and 5 with the latter. Chapter 6 is concerned with an altogether different approach to parallel execution called time parallel simulation that is only suitable for certain classes of simulation problems, but can yield dramatic performance improvements when it can be applied.

The third part is concerned with distributed virtual environments (DVEs). Here the emphasis is on real-time simulations, that is, to create virtual environments into which humans may be embedded, for example, for training or entertainment. Chapter 7 gives an introduction to this area, focusing primarily on two efforts within the defense community, namely Distributed Interactive Simulation (DIS) and the High Level Architecture (HLA) where much of this technology was developed and has been applied. Chapters 8 and 9 are concerned with two specific issues in DVEs. Chapter 8 covers the problem of efficiently distributing data among the participants of the DVE. The first half of the chapter is an introduction to computer networks which provide the underlying communication support for DVEs. The second half is concerned with techniques to effectively utilize the networking infrastructure, particularly for large-scale simulations with many interacting components. Finally, Chapter 9 revisits the problem of time synchronization in DVEs as well as the problem of ensuring that the different computers participating in the simulation have properly synchronized clocks.

Part I lays the groundwork for the remainder of the book, so should be read first. Parts II and III can be read in either order. I have used this book as the text in a 10-week course in parallel and distributed simulation taught at Georgia Tech, and plan to use it when we transition to 15-week semesters. Alternatively, this book could be used for part of a course in discrete event simulation. When used in this manner, instructors may wish to skip Chapters 5 and 6, and the first half of Chapter 8 to obtain a more abbreviated treatment of the subject material.

Software

Interested readers may wish to try out some of the algorithms discussed in this book. Although software is not included with the text, it is available. In particular, the Georgia Tech Time Warp (GTW) software discussed in Chapter 5 and an implementation of a subset of the High level Architecture Run Time Infrastructure are freely available for education and research purposes. Information concerning this software is available at http://www.cc.gatech.edu/computing/pads. To obtain a copy of either or both of these software packages, you may contact me via electronic mail at fujimoto@cc.gatech.edu.

Acknowledgments

Obviously, this book would not be possible without the many technical contributions by numerous individuals in both academia and industry. I have attempted to recognize as many of these contributors as possible in the bibliography and references to additional reading materials. Regrettably, the field has expanded to the extent that anything approaching a complete listing of the contributors is impossible.

I am in debt to many individuals who contributed directly to the development of this book. In particular, many useful comments on early drafts were provided by students in my graduate class on parallel and distributed simulation taught at Georgia Tech. Specific detailed comments from Glenn Oberhauser and Katherine Morse are also appreciated. I am grateful to several funding agencies that sponsored my research in parallel and distributed simulation; some of the results of this work are included in this text. These agencies include the Ballistic Missile Defense Organization, the Defense Advance Research Projects Agency, the Defense Modeling and Simulation Office, the National Science Foundation, SAIC, Mitre Corporation, Bellcore, Army Research Office, the Office of Naval Research, and the Strategic Missile Defense Command.

Finally, I owe the greatest gratitude to my family, who provided continued support and understanding despite the countless evenings and weekends of dealing with my absence due to this project which came to be known simply as "the book." This manuscript would never have been completed were it not for their love and devotion.

PARALLEL AND DISTRIBUTED SIMULATION SYSTEMS

PART I

INTRODUCTION

CHAPTER 1

Background and Applications

Imagine that you are responsible for monitoring commercial air traffic in the United States and providing recommendations to air traffic controllers across the country. Your objective is to ensure that the air transportation system remains safe and efficient, and to minimize traveler delays. Severe storms unexpectedly develop in Chicago, causing the flow of traffic in and out of O'Hare airport to be reduced to only a fraction of its normal capacity. How does this situation affect air traffic across the country? Should aircraft about to take off be allowed to depart, potentially creating backlogs of planes that are forced to circle, wasting enormous quantities of fuel? Or should these aircraft be held on the ground, at the risk of causing traveler delays and frustrations that might not have been really necessary? What about aircraft already in flight? Should they be rerouted to alternate destinations? Computer simulations of the national air traffic space provide a means to "test out" different strategies in order to determine which will be the most effective. But, existing air traffic simulations may require hours to complete, while decisions must be made in minutes.

Consider a second scenario. You are an engineer working on designs for the next generation of the Internet. Specifically, you are responsible for designing communication protocols that will be used to carry multimedia traffic for a wide variety of users with vastly different requirements, for example, real-time video teleconferences requiring low latency transmissions of compressed video frames, electronic mail that can tolerate higher, more variable transmission delays, or web surfers transferring large data files, voice and audio transmissions. There are many important design issues and cost/performance trade-offs you need to consider that will play an important role in determining the success of your designs in a competitive marketplace. Again, computer simulation tools are available to evaluate different designs, but because of the size and complexity of the networks you are considering, even a single execution of the simulation program that models only a few minutes of network operation will require hours, or even days, to complete.

Consider still another scenario. You are the commander of a large military operation. You must prepare a variety of officers and enlisted personnel for combat in an engagement that is breaking out in another part of the world. In particular, you must perform multinational joint mission rehearsals including tank commanders stationed in the United States, aircraft pilots stationed in England, and naval commanders at sea. It is critical that individuals within each group gain experience using their equipment in situations they may encounter, as well as experience working with personnel from other units in coordinated military strikes. Time and budgetary restrictions preclude large-scale field exercises to practice maneuvers. How can you properly prepare individuals at geographically distinct locations when limited time and resources are at your disposal?

These scenarios describe real-world situations that exist today where parallel and distributed simulation technologies can, and in many cases are playing a critical role. We will return to these scenarios momentarily to discuss how such technologies can help. First, let us define what is meant by "parallel/distributed simulation" and examine why it has attracted so much interest in recent years.

1.1 WHY PARALLEL/DISTRIBUTED SIMULATION?

What is parallel/distributed simulation technology? Simply stated, this is a technology that enables a simulation program to be executed on parallel/distributed computer systems, namely systems composed of multiple interconnected computers. As this definition suggests, there are two key components to this technology: (1) simulation, and (2) execution on parallel or distributed computers.

A *computer simulation* is a computation that models the behavior of some real or imagined system over time. Simulations are widely used today to analyze the behavior of systems such as air traffic control and future generation telecommunication networks without actually constructing the systems and situations of interest. Constructing a prototype may be costly, infeasible, and/or dangerous. Another important use of simulations today is to create computer-generated "virtual worlds" into which humans and/or physical devices will be embedded. An aircraft flight simulator used to train pilots is one such example.

Parallel simulation and distributed simulation refer to technologies that enable a simulation program to execute on a computing system containing multiple processors, such as personal computers, interconnected by a communication network. Later we discuss the distinction between *parallel* and *distributed* simulation based on the type of computing system used to execute the simulation. For now, suffice it to say that parallel simulations execute on a set of computers confined to a single cabinet or machine room, while distributed simulations execute on machines that are geographically distributed across a building, university campus, or even the world.

There are primarily four principal benefits to executing a simulation program across multiple computers:

1. *Reduced execution time.* By subdividing a large simulation computation into many sub-computations, and executing the subcomputations concurrently across, say, ten different processors, one can reduce the execution time up to a factor of ten. This is not unlike subdividing your lawn into ten equally sized strips, and hiring ten people each with their own lawn mower to work on a different strip. In principle, you can mow the entire lawn in only one-tenth

the time it would have taken using only one lawn mower. In computer simulations it may be necessary to reduce execution time so that an engineer will not have to wait long periods of time to receive results produced by the simulation. Alternatively, when used to create a virtual world into which humans will be immersed, multiple processors may be needed to complete the simulation computation fast enough so that the simulated world evolves as rapidly as real life. This is essential to make the computer-generated world "look and feel" to the user just like the real thing.

2. *Geographical distribution.* Executing the simulation program on a set of geographically distributed computers enables one to create virtual worlds with multiple participants that are physically located at different sites. For example, consider a simulated air battle composed of flight simulators executing on computers at distinct geographical locations, such as London, New York, and Paris. Participants in this simulation exercise can interact with each other as if they were located together at a training facility at a single site, but without the time, expense, and inconvenience of traveling to that site.

3. *Integrating simulators that execute on machines from different manufacturers.* Suppose that flight simulators for different types of aircraft have been developed by different manufacturers. Rather than porting these programs to a single computer, it may be more cost effective to "hook together" the existing simulators, each executing on a different computer, to create a new virtual environment. Again, this requires the simulation computation to be distributed across multiple computers.

4. *Fault tolerance.* Another potential benefit of utilizing multiple processors is increased tolerance to failures. If one processor goes down, it may be possible for other processors to pick up the work of the failed machine, allowing the simulation computation to proceed despite the failure. By contrast, if the simulation is mapped to a single processor, failure of that processor means the entire simulation must stop.

Returning to our first scenario involving air traffic control, parallel simulation techniques can reduce the execution time of simulation tools for modeling air traffic from hours to minutes, or even seconds, enabling these tools to be used "on-line" in time critical decision-making processes. Similarly, in the Internet design scenario, parallel simulation techniques can enable much more extensive, detailed analyses of networks to be performed before a new product is brought to market, thereby resulting in improved performance, reliability, and/or reduced cost. In these two applications, reduced execution time is the principal benefit. Fault tolerance is also a potential benefit, but, a substantial amount of effort is required to recover and restart the computation from failed processors in order for the results of the simulation to be valid.

In the scenario involving the training of military personnel, geographic distribution and integrating simulators that execute on different hardware platforms are important benefits in utilizing a distributed simulation approach. Fault tolerance is also more straightforward, because one often does not need to recover the computation on failed processors unless they are critical to the entire exercise. Reduced execution time may be important, particularly as one expands the exercise to include more and more participants. As mentioned earlier, a training simulation must be able to complete its computations and advance "time" in the simulated world as rapidly as time progresses in the real world, or the simulation will not appear realistic. This becomes impossible if the number of entities in the simulated world increases, unless additional computing resources can be brought together to execute the simulation computations.

In the remainder of this first chapter we set the stage of the rest of this book. In particular, we introduce terminology, applications, and certain background information such as hardware platforms and underlying technologies that are important to understand the chapters that follow.

1.2 ANALYTIC SIMULATIONS VERSUS VIRTUAL ENVIRONMENTS

Historically two classes of simulation applications have received the most attention: *analytic simulations* and *virtual environments*. Characteristics that distinguish these different domains are summarized in Table 1.1.

Analytic simulations usually attempt to capture detailed quantitative data concerning the system being simulated. For example, in the air traffic simulation, one might be interested in the average "circling time" for each aircraft when it arrives at a busy airport. In a telecommunication network simulation, one might be interested in statistics such as the average delay to perform a file transfer or the amount of data per second transmitted through a typical connection. Analytic simulations require that the model reproduce as exactly as possible actual system behaviors so that the generated statistical results are valid. Analytic simulation is the

TABLE 1.1 Analytic simulations and virtual environments

	Analytic Simulations	Virtual Environments
Execution pacing	Typically as-fast-as-possible	Real-time
Typical objective	Quantitative analysis of complex systems	Create a realistic and/or entertaining representation of an environment
Human interaction	If included, human is an external observer to the model	Humans integral to controlling the behavior of entities within the model
Before-and-after relationships	Attempt to precisely reproduce before-and-after relationships	Need only reproduce before-and-after relationships to the extent that humans or physical components embedded in the environment can perceive them

"classical" approach to simulation; it has been used as long as electronic computers have been in existence. For example, the earliest machines were used to compute artillery shell trajectories.

Analytic simulation typically includes limited, or no interaction, with human participants or physical devices during the execution of the simulation program. In many cases users may merely analyze the statistics produced by the simulator after execution has been completed. Alternatively, the user may view an animation of the system being modeled, perhaps with an ability to pause the execution and change certain parameter settings. Analytic simulations typically execute "as-fast-as-possible," meaning that the simulation attempts to complete its computations as quickly as it can. This could mean that the simulator advances faster than real-time (for example, it might simulate hours of system behavior in only minutes of elapsed time to the user) or that it runs slower than real-time.[1]

A more recent phenomenon in simulation has been to create virtual environments into which humans or devices are embedded. Perhaps the most familiar use of simulations for this purpose are video arcade games where the player, often represented by a character or *avatar* on the game's display, is placed in a computer-generated world representing a medieval castle or a modern race track. This world may be populated by other characters representing other humans or by computer-generated characters whose behaviors and actions are represented by programs within the simulator. The battlefield training exercises alluded to earlier are an example of a multiple user virtual environment simulation widely used by the military today. A variation on this theme is to embed into the virtual environment actual physical components, possibly in addition to human participants. This is often used to test the component, for example, to test a missile defense system for scenarios that might be difficult and/or expensive to create with live range tests. Virtual environment simulations with human participants are sometimes referred to as *human-in-the-loop* (or *man-in-the-loop*) simulations, and simulations including embedded physical devices are also called *hardware-in-the-loop* simulations.

Virtual environment simulations differ from traditional analytic simulations in several important ways. First, they almost always include human participants or actual physical devices as entities *within* the simulation itself, as opposed to external users viewing or artificially manipulating the simulation as described earlier for analytic simulations. Thus it is important that the simulated world advance in time at approximately the same rate that time advances are perceived by the human participants. The central goal in most virtual environment simulation to date has been to give users the look and feel of being embedded in the system being modeled. As such, it is not always essential for these simulations to exactly emulate the actual system. If the differences between the simulated world and the actual world are not perceptible to human participants, this is usually acceptable. For example, if two events occur "close enough" in time that the human cannot perceive which occurred

---

[1]More precise meanings of terms such as simulated time, real-time, and wallclock time will be given in Chapter 2. For now, suffice it to say that simulated time is the simulation's representation of time in the system being modeled, and real-time corresponds to time during the *execution* of the simulation program.

first, it may be acceptable for the simulated world to model these events as occurring in an order that differs from that in which they would actually occur in the real system.

On the other hand, analytic simulations usually require that the simulator correctly reproduce the orderings of events, especially if there is a causal relationship between them, for example, an observer should see a weapon fire before it sees that the target has been destroyed. Failing to do so may compromise the statistics that are collected, especially if there is a bias in the outcomes that one observes. For example, if tanks for the red army are always observed to fire first when a red and a blue tank fire at approximately the same time, the "kill" statistics will be biased in favor of the red army.

In summary, it is useful to distinguish between analytic and virtual environment simulations because they have different objectives, leading to different requirements and constraints. To some extent, this dichotomy is historic, as much of the basic research in these applications has been conducted by different communities. We use this dichotomy here because these two areas have given rise to different problems and solutions.

1.3 HISTORICAL PERSPECTIVE

The bulk of the research in parallel and distributed simulation has evolved from three separate communities. Work in parallel and distributed simulation techniques for analytic simulation applications grew largely out of the high-performance computing community, which maintained the goal of reducing the execution time of simulation computations. Work in distributed virtual environments (DVEs) grew largely from two separate camps. On one hand, the military establishment can be credited with the development of sophisticated, though costly, geographically distributed virtual environments for training applications. At approximately the same time, much of the work originating in the interactive gaming and Internet communities was focusing on more economical DVEs that could be used by players on personal computers linked via public networks.

1.3.1 High-Performance Computing Community

Parallel and distributed simulation technologies for *analytic* simulation applications originated largely from basic research conducted in universities and research laboratories in the late 1970s and throughout the 1980s. This research has flourished in the 1990s. Work in this field began with the development of *synchronization algorithms* to ensure that when the simulation is distributed across multiple computers, the same results are produced as when the simulation is executed on a single machine. Although the first of these synchronization algorithms were published in 1977, few implementations on parallel and distributed computers appeared over the next ten years, perhaps due to limited availability of suitable hardware platforms and primitive software development environments on the few platforms that were available. Simulation of queuing networks (an example of which will be presented in Chapter 2) was popular for many years. To some extent, this continues to be a popular benchmark for evaluating the performance of parallel simulation techniques. Queueing network simulations remain popular benchmarks because they require little knowledge of a specific problem domain, they can be coded very quickly, and they are representative of many important application domains, for example, simulation of telecommunication networks and commercial air traffic.

Results from other applications began to appear in 1990. Noteworthy among these was work in the TWOS project at the Jet Propulsion Laboratory (JPL) in developing parallel war game simulations for the United States Department of Defense. As elaborated upon below, subsequent work has also focused on applications such as telecommunication networks, transportation systems, and digital logic circuits. At the time of this writing, work in the field has largely been confined to universities and industrial research laboratories, with application to a handful of real-world military and commercial simulation problems reported. With inclusion of these techniques in the U.S. Department of Defense (DoD) High Level Architecture (HLA) effort, which will be discussed below and in greater depth in Part III of this book, impact of this technology is accelerating in the late 1990s, especially for military applications.

1.3.2 Defense Community

Much of the work in distributed simulation for virtual environments began in the 1980s, largely independent of the work described above concerning analytic simulations. Compared to the sluggish infiltration of parallel/distributed simulation technology for analytic applications into real-world usage, technology transfer of distributed simulation for virtual environments has been rapid, and perhaps most notably, has gained widespread acceptance in military establishments and the entertainment industry. A key factor driving the development and adoption of distributed simulations for synthetic environments has been the need for the military to develop more effective and economical means of training personnel prior to deployment. Field exercises are extremely costly activities, and thus can only be utilized rather sparingly. It is clear that embedding personnel in a virtual environment provides a much more cost-effective, not to mention safer and environmentally friendlier, training facility. This has driven a large amount of R&D effort in the United States, Western Europe, and other parts of the world toward development of the technologies to realize such a capability.

Early work in distributed simulation for virtual environments for the military began with the SIMNET (SIMulator NETworking) project that extended from 1983 to 1989. Sponsored by the Defense Advanced Research Projects Agency (DARPA) in the United States, SIMNET demonstrated the viability of interconnecting autonomous simulators (for example, tank simulators) in training exercises, and it has since been deployed for use in actual (as opposed to experimental) training. The success of the SIMNET experiment has had far-reaching effects throughout the defense modeling and simulation community in the United States. SIMNET was replaced by what came to be known as Distributed Interactive Simulation (DIS) where standards were defined to support interoperability among autonomous training simulators in geographically distributed simulation environments.

A second major development springing from SIMNET was the Aggregate Level Simulation Protocol (ALSP) work that applied the SIMNET concept of interoperability to war game simulations. ALSP enabled war game simulations from the Army, Air Force, and Navy, for example, to be brought together in a single exercise to analyze joint military operations. ALSP used synchronization protocols discussed earlier for analytic simulations; it represents perhaps the most extensive application of that technology to date. Work in the ALSP community proceeded concurrently with work in the DIS community that was focused primarily (though not exclusively) on training.

The next major milestone in the evolution of this technology was the development of the High Level Architecture (HLA) which began in 1995 and resulted in the so-called *baseline* definition in August 1996. HLA is important for several reasons. From a practical standpoint, HLA was mandated in September 1996 as the standard architecture for all modeling and simulation activities in the Department of Defense in the United States. All DoD simulations are required to become *HLA compliant* (or obtain approval for an exception to this requirement) by 1999. From a technical standpoint, HLA is important because it provides a single architecture that spans both analytic and virtual environment simulations. In some respects it can be viewed as a merging of DIS and ALSP into a single architecture. Prior to the HLA effort, work in the parallel/distributed analytic simulation community and the distributed virtual environment communities proceeded largely independent of each other. HLA was a landmark effort in that it began integrating these technologies in a significant way. At the time of this writing, the initial baseline definition of the HLA and its realization in prototype versions of the Runtime Infrastructure (RTI) have been completed and standardization activities are in progress. Migration of DIS standards to the HLA is also under way.

1.3.3   Interactive Gaming and Internet Communities

A second major thread of activity in distributed virtual environments for nonmilitary applications grew from the interactive gaming and Internet communities. Just as defense simulations originated from "platform-level" simulators for tanks and aircraft, nonmilitary DVE work originated in "immersive" games such as *Adventure* and *Dungeons and Dragons*. Adventure was a fantasy computer game created at Xerox Palo Alto Research Center (PARC) in California in the mid-1970s. In it a user/player explored a rich computer-generated fantasy world, most of which was underground in a maze of caves and hidden passage ways. Adventure was a text-based game where users typed short phrases to describe their actions (for example, "move up"), and were given word descriptions of objects and rooms they encountered in their journey. This fantasy world was complete with a rich variety of hidden treasures and a wide assortment of other computer-generated creatures, both friend and foe, that could help or hinder the player from finding and obtaining the treasures. A skilled player could slay harmful adversaries such as dragons with various weapons, such as swords and magic potions giving the partaker special abilities for a limited amount of time. These weapons could be found in different areas of the virtual world. Adventure was developed in the 1970s and 1980s before powerful personal computers were widely available. Yet despite the limited interaction allowed by a text-oriented program, it was a very popular game among the college students who were lucky enough to have computer access. Computer and video games of this nature continue to thrive today, greatly enhanced with audio effects and computer graphics.

Adventure was a *single-player* game. A second, key ingredient in the development of DVEs was the introduction of multiple players to the virtual world. Though not initially computerized, the popular game of *Dungeons and Dragons*, also from the mid-1970s, is credited with being the catalyst for this development. This was a pencil and paper role-playing game where players gathered to play out roles as knights and sorcerers in a made-up world created by one of the players, referred to as the dungeon master. The actual environment could be as simple as a written description of the various portions of the virtual world, or as elaborate as scale models.

Computer-generated fantasy games and multiple users/players came together in the early 1980s with the MultiUser Dungeon (MUD) game developed at the University of Essex in England. Today, the term MUD is associated with multiplayer games of this sort in general, as opposed to any particular game. Further the applications for DVEs extend far beyond games, and a substantial amount of work has been geared toward nongaming applications.

In addition to computer-generated virtual worlds and the inclusion of multiple players, a third critical ingredient in the development of DVEs was the unprecedented expansion and growth of the worldwide network of computer networks known as the Internet. With the Internet a virtual environment can support multiple users who may be scattered around the globe. Multiplayer games with geographically distributed players are flourishing in the 1990s, despite limited bandwidth (for example modem lines with as little as 9600 bits per second) and relatively high network latencies. Continued increases in modem bandwidth (at the time of this writing in the late 1990s, 50 Kbits/second modems are becoming widely available) and megabit per second bandwidths (for example, via cable modems or other technologies) are on their way. The communication bottlenecks that have hitherto restricted widespread use of distributed virtual environments may be a thing of the past.

1.4 APPLICATIONS

With the above historical context, we now survey some of the applications where parallel and distributed simulation technologies have been applied. While far from being complete, this list gives a flavor of some of the current and potential uses of the technology.

1.4.1 Military Applications

It is clear that the military establishment has had a major role in developing distributed simulation technology for virtual environments, and to a lesser though still significant extent, parallel simulation technology for analytic simulation applications. Some of the most prominent military applications utilizing this technology are as follows:

1. *War gaming simulations*. These simulations are often used to evaluate different strategies for attacking or defending against an opposing force, or for acquisition decisions to determine the number and type of weapon systems that should be purchased to be prepared for future engagements. The simulation is typically composed of models for battalions, divisions, and so forth. Because these simulations usually model groups of units rather than individual platforms (for example, aircraft and tanks), they are sometimes also referred to as *aggregated simulations*. Two noteworthy examples of the application of parallel discrete event simulation techniques to war game simulations are the *Concurrent Theater Level Simulation* (CTLS) (Wieland, Hawley et al. 1989) and *Aggregate Level Simulation Protocol* (ALSP) (Wilson and Weatherly 1994) discussed earlier. The underlying execution mechanism for CTLS was a parallel simulation executive using a synchronization algorithm called *Time Warp*. ALSP used another algorithm called the Chandy/Misra/Bryant null message protocol. These algorithms will be discussed in detail in Chapters 4 and 3, respectively.

2. *Training environments*. As discussed earlier, these simulations embed pilots, tank operators, commanding officers and their staffs, and the like, into an environment to train personnel for actual combat. In contrast to aggregated simulations, many training environments use platform-level simulations that do model individual tanks, aircraft, and so forth.

3. *Test and evaluation (T&E)*. While training simulations embed humans into a synthetic battlefield, T&E simulations embed physical components (for example, a new sensor for detecting missile launches) into a virtual environment, often to evaluate the effectiveness of proposed new devices or to verify that manufactured devices operate at reported specifications. The T&E simulation community has sometimes been referred to as the "Consumer Reports" for the military because they evaluate new products before they are manufactured and eventually deployed.

As discussed earlier, the High Level Architecture effort attempts to integrate simulations from these three domains in order to facilitate reuse of simulation models in new contexts, thereby reducing the cost of developing new simulators.

1.4.2 Entertainment

The number of real F-15 pilots that can benefit from immersion into a computer-generated dogfight is dwarfed by the number of wannabe pilots that are looking for recreation on a Saturday night. Application of distributed simulation technology to the entertainment industry will (and already is) leading to the most significant impact of this technology on the average citizen. Single-player video arcade games cannot provide the same kind of entertainment as interactively competing with friends (or strangers) in a computer-generated virtual world.

Distributed simulation technology can be applied in amusement park and arcade centers where players are co-located but interact with each other and computer-generated entities over a local area network. These systems sometimes use costly custom-designed hardware that can only be justified economically by repeated use by many users. Another emerging market is the multi-user home entertainment industry where video game machines or personal computers are interconnected through the Internet.

Entertainment and training systems employing distributed simulation technologies have much in common, but they also differ in many important respects. Obviously, entertainment systems must be engaging. Unlike training simulators, one does not have a captive audience where players must return to fulfill job requirements. Thus the "realism" of the virtual environment may take second place to pure excitement and artistic effects. Economic factors play a much more dominant role in the design of entertainment systems, sometimes requiring compromises that would not be necessary in a multimillion dollar training system. Interoperability among separately developed simulations is a fundamental goal in DIS, but it may be viewed as undesirable by some in the entertainment industry. This would be true, for example, when a company marketing proprietary entertainment systems has control, as a single vendor, over the simulations that will be included in the system.

1.4.3 Social Interactions and Business Collaborations

Another potentially far-reaching impact of distributed virtual environments is in creating new means for people to interact socially on the Internet. The Internet has already made fundamental changes in the way people interact both in the office and at home. Many believe DVEs represent the next logical step in electronic social interactions. Already users around the world can "meet" without ever leaving their own home through Internet newsgroups and "chat rooms." Beyond this, a DVE application can create more realistic social settings such as the one known as *Diamond Park* developed by Mitsubishi Electric Corp's MERL research laboratory. Diamond Park provides a virtual park atmosphere where users can meet and interact in various settings such as the park's cafe, walkways, or meeting areas (Waters and Barrus 1997). Users can navigate through the park on foot or on bicycle and can even race against each other! Virtual environments like this may be the norm in the future for social interaction via the Internet.

Virtual environments can also provide a new means for interactions in the business world between colleagues and clients. Entire "virtual corporations" could be created, composed of employees who are based physically at different locations or different companies but who are working together on a joint venture. For example, one can envision building designers and engineers at different locations walking through a virtual design of a product (a building) to discuss and evaluate design changes.

1.4.4 Education and Training

Nonmilitary applications for DVEs in education and training abound. Much work has been accomplished in the medical community using virtual environments for training as well as treatment of patients. Computer-generated environments can provide a more cost-effective (and safe!) means for doctors to practice surgical techniques. Experimental studies have been performed/conducted using virtual environments to treat patients with various phobias such as a fear of heights. Patients are exposed gradually and in a controlled way to (virtual) situations that cause them anxiety. While much of the work to date in these areas has been focused on single-user virtual environments (i.e., *not* distributed), extensions to DVEs to allow for users to remain in different geographic locations are clear. Work has also focused on using DVE technology developed under DIS for nonmilitary applications, such as training air traffic controllers, or performing exercise drills for emergency procedures, such as recovery from earthquakes or major accidents.

1.4.5 Telecommunication Networks

Analytic simulations have long been used in the telecommunications industry to evaluate networking hardware, software, protocols, and services. The widespread deployment of fiber optics technology has had important impacts on the use of simulation in modeling networks. First, this technology has brought about increased use of telecommunication networks for applications other than voice communications, namely transmission of still images, data, and video. So-called Broadband Integrated Services Digital Networks (B-ISDN) provide a single networking infrastructure to carry these diverse types of traffic. Network designers have had to totally rethink their designs, and turn toward simulation tools to aid them. Networking technologies such as *Asynchronous Transfer Mode* or ATM[2] have emerged to meet the challenge of supporting these diverse types of traffic on a single network infrastructure, (for example, see Partridge 1993).

Second, because the underlying network is based on fiber optic links that can carry orders of magnitude more traffic than copper cables, simulations become more time-consuming. This is because one must often model the network for at least the duration of a conversation to collect useful data; that is, simulations of minutes to

---

[2] An unfortunate acronynm, this technology has nothing to do with Automated Teller Machines used in the baking industry.

hours of network operation are required. Because B-ISDN networks carry orders of magnitude more traffic during this time period, the computation time to complete the simulation increases in proportion. Parallel simulation techniques offer one approach toward alleviating this problem.

A typical problem in telecommunications that calls out for the use of parallel simulation is that of analyzing cell losses in ATM networks. A cell is a 53-byte block of data that is the basic unit transmitted through an ATM network. Each ATM switch contains buffers to hold cells waiting to be transmitted on links. If a link becomes congested and the buffers become full, subsequent cells that require use of that link are discarded. The cell loss probability is an important metric that indicates how frequently this happens. ATM switches often target cell loss probabilities to be 10^{-9}; that is, only one in 10^9 cells is lost under anticipated traffic conditions. This requires simulation of at least 10^{11} cell arrivals to obtain reliable statistical data. As of the late 1990s, fast sequential simulation will execute on the order of 10^5 events per second, so (optimistically) equating simulation of each cell arrival with a single event, such a simulation will require more than 11 days, just to simulate a single switch!

A second major area where parallel simulation may have a significant impact is in the simulation of large networks such as the Internet. Here, high-performance simulation engines are required because of the large number of entities that must be simulated. Simulations of millions of mobile subscribers are sometimes needed.

1.4.6 Digital Logic Circuits and Computer Systems

Like telecommunication networks, simulations of digital electronic circuits and computer systems is a second area where parallel simulation can play a significant role. Fast simulation of logic circuits is of considerable interest to the electronic computer-aided-design community because simulation is a major bottleneck in the design cycle. Final verification of a computer system may require weeks using conventional sequential simulation techniques.

Much of the work in applying parallel simulation techniques to logic circuits has been focused on the VHDL hardware description language that has become widely used in industry. Several prototype parallel simulation systems have been developed that execute VHDL programs on multiple processor computers, with varying degrees of success reported in the literature. Successful demonstrations typically report up to an order of magnitude reduction in execution time.

While so-called gate-level logic simulations focus on modeling individual circuits for implementing primitive Boolean functions and storage elements, higher-level simulations of computers using models for switches, processors, memories, and so forth, are also used extensively in preliminary investigations of design alternatives. These higher-level simulations often include simulated executions of benchmark programs on the modeled machine to evaluate it under realistic workloads. Direct execution is a technique where the benchmark program is executed directly on the machine used to perform the simulation rather than use a (much slower) software interpreter. Prototype parallel simulation systems using techniques such as these have been demonstrated to yield very accurate simulation results, within a few percent of measurements from a realized system, while delivering up to an order of magnitude reduction in computation time.

1.4.7 Transportation

Simulation can play an important role in designing and managing road and air transportation systems. It can be used as an analysis tool to evaluate the effectiveness of adding a new runway to an airport, or rerouting vehicular traffic after the completion of a major sporting event. As alluded to earlier, it may be used "on-line" in developing strategies to respond to an unexpected event, for example, congestion resulting from adverse weather conditions.

1.5 UNDERLYING TECHNOLOGIES

Parallel and distributed simulation is made possible by the confluence of three essential, underlying technologies:

- *Integrated circuits*. The first key ingredient is an inexpensive computer, thereby making systems composed of tens, hundreds, or even thousands of computers economically feasible. Fundamental to this development are steadily decreasing costs of integrated circuits, driven largely by an increasing ability to squeeze more and more circuits onto a single silicon chip. For example, the cost of random access memory (RAM) that accounts for a significant portion of the cost of a personal computer or workstation has, over the long term, decreased by 40% per year (Hennessy and Patterson 1996).

- *High-speed intercomputer communications*. There are two flavors of technology at work here. On the one hand, high-speed switches enable one to construct systems containing tens to hundreds or even thousands of processors that reside *within a single cabinet or computer room*. On the other hand, advances in fiber optics technology is fueling a revolution in the telecommunications industry, making possible computing systems *distributed across continents*. These advances enable one to consider developing computer applications utilizing many geographically distributed machines.

- *Modeling and simulation*. The final ingredient are technologies to enable construction of models of actual or envisioned real-world systems that can (1) be represented in the internal storage of a computer, and (2) be manipulated by computer programs to emulate the evolution of the actual system over time. Here, we are primarily concerned with *discrete event simulation*, where changes in the state of the simulation are viewed as occurring at distinct points in time.

In many applications other technologies such as graphics, human-computer interfaces, and databases clearly play a critical role. However, these technologies are somewhat tangential to the focus of this book, and are not discussed further here.

1.6   HARDWARE PLATFORMS

The hardware platforms of interest here contain a potentially large number of processors interconnected through a communication network. In most cases the processor is a general purpose CPU (central processing unit), often identical to those commonly found in personal computers and engineering workstations. The switching network may be as specific as a customized switch for a particular multi-processor system, or as general as the Internet.

1.6.1   Parallel versus Distributed Computers

Multiple-CPU hardware platforms can be broadly classified into two categories: parallel and distributed computers. Differences between these platforms are summarized in Table 1.2. Parallel and distributed computing platforms are distinguished by the physical area occupied by the computer. The processors in *parallel computers* are in close physical proximity, usually within a single cabinet, or a small number of adjacent cabinets in a machine room. These are usually *homogeneous* machines, using processors from a single manufacturer. These machines normally provide switching hardware tailored to the parallel computer, so the delay in transmitting a message from one computer to another (referred to as the *communication latency*) is relatively low. This latency is typically a few microseconds to tens of microseconds for a message containing a few bytes in contemporary machines. Latency is important because it has a large impact on performance; if latencies are large, the computers may spend much of their time waiting for messages to be delivered. Here, communication latency is perhaps the single most important technical aspect differentiating parallel and distributed computers. There are three principal classes of parallel computers that are in use today: *shared-memory multiprocessors*, *distributed memory multicomputers*, and *SIMD machines* (see Fig. 1.1), as will be elaborated upon momentarily.

Distributed computers cover a much broader geographic area. Their extent may be confined to a single building, or may be as broad as across an entire nation or even the world. Unlike parallel computers, each node of a distributed computer is usually a stand-alone machine that includes its own memory and I/O devices. Commercial off-the-shelf personal computers or engineering workstations, often from different manufacturers, are usually used. Communication latencies are usually

TABLE 1.2   Contrasting parallel and distributed computers

	Parallel Computers	Distributed Computers
Physical extent	Machine room	Single building to global
Processors	Homogeneous	Often heterogeneous
Communication network	Customized switch	Commercial LAN or WAN
Communication latency	Less than 100 microseconds	Hundreds of microseconds to seconds

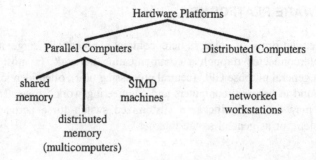

Figure 1.1   Taxonomy of important classes of parallel and distributed computers.

on the order of a few hundreds of microseconds for distributed computers with processors in close proximity (for example, a single building), but they may be as large as hundreds of milliseconds or even seconds for machines covering large geographical areas. In the latter case, satellites may be used for some communication links, contributing to increased latency. The latency of distributed computers is much higher than parallel machines because (1) signals must traverse large physical distances and (2) complex software protocols designed for interconnecting autonomous computers from different manufacturers are usually used rather than customized hardware and software designed for a specific interconnection scheme. While technological advances may be able to substantially reduce software overheads for communication, latency between geographically distributed machines is fundamentally limited by the speed of light, which is approximately 2.1×10^8 meters per second in optical fiber, or 210 kilometers (131 miles) per millisecond. A modern microprocessor such as that included in personal computers can execute *tens to hundreds of thousands* of machine instructions (where each instruction can perform a simple operation such as an integer addition) in one millisecond, so this is a substantial amount of time from a computing perspective.

Recently the distinction between parallel and distributed computers has become blurred with the advent of the *network of workstations*, which is a cluster of workstations interconnected through a high-speed switch usually confined to a single room. Through the use of new switching techniques that bypass traditional communication protocols, communication latency of these machines approach that of conventional parallel computers. Are these parallel or distributed computers? Here, because of the close physical proximity of the machines, they are characterized as parallel computers, though often these systems are classified as distributed machines. Because these machines often include aspects common to both parallel and distributed computers, the characterization is perhaps not so important.

Simulations that execute on shared memory multiprocessors, multicomputers, or SIMD machines are referred to as *parallel simulation* programs. The focus of this book with respect to parallel simulations is on discrete event simulations (discussed in Chapter 2) used for analysis. The field concerned with this subject is called *parallel discrete event simulation (PDES)*. Here, the terms *parallel simulation* and *parallel discrete event simulation* will be used synonymously.

Simulations executing on distributed computers are referred to as *distributed simulations*. Distributed simulations may be used for analytic purposes, or more commonly for constructing distributed virtual environments. The latter is perhaps the more common application for distributed simulation technology, and the term *distributed simulation* in the literature sometimes refers exclusively to distributed virtual environments.

1.6.2 Shared-Memory Multiprocessors

Shared-memory multiprocessors, distributed memory multicomputers, and SIMD machines provide different programming models to the application. The distinguishing property of the programming model for shared-memory multiprocessors is one may define variables that are accessible by different processors. Thus one can define a variable X that can be autonomously read or modified by one processor without the intervention of another.

Shared variables and message passing are the two dominant forms of interprocessor communications used in parallel and distributed simulation. Message-passing mechanisms, widely used in parallel simulation, can be implemented using shared memory by defining shared data structures (queues) to hold incoming or outgoing messages.

One type of shared-memory machine, the *symmetric multiprocessor (SMP)*, has become increasingly popular. A typical shared-memory machine is depicted in Figure 1.2. These systems consist of off-the-shelf microprocessors connected to memory through a high-speed switch, such as a bus. Frequently accessed instructions and data are stored in a high-speed *cache memory* that is attached to each processor. Typically the multiprocessor hardware automatically moves data and instructions between the cache and "main" memories, so the programmer need not be concerned with its operation, except perhaps to tune the program to maximize performance. Consistency protocols are required to ensure that multiple copies of any shared variable residing in different caches remain up-to-date if one copy is modified; this is often realized in the hardware by either invalidating or updating copies residing in other caches when one copy is changed. The Sun Enterprise system is an example of a contemporary SMP. Personal computers (PCs) containing

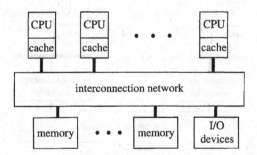

Figure 1.2 Block diagram of a typical shared-memory multiprocessor.

multiple CPUs in an SMP organization are also becoming common. Most SMPs only support a limited number of processors (for example, up to 20 or 30), although larger shared-memory machines containing hundreds of processors have been constructed in the past.

A second class of shared-memory multiprocessor is the so-called *nonuniform memory access (NUMA)* machine. These machines are typically constructed by providing memory with each processor (as opposed to separate memory modules as shown in Fig. 1.2) but allow each processor to directly read or write the memory attached to another processor (as well as its own memory). Unlike symmetric multiprocessors, the programmer's interface to these machines distinguishes between "local" and "remote" memory, and provides faster access to local memory. This makes these machines more difficult to program than so-called *uniform memory access (UMA)* machines where the average access time to any memory location is the same. This is because in a NUMA machine the programmer must carefully map program variables to memory modules in order to minimize remote references, or else pay a severe performance penalty in making frequent accesses to remote memory. Access to remote memory typically takes an order of magnitude (or more) longer than an access to a local memory location. The Silicon Graphic's Origin multiprocessor is one example of a NUMA machine.

1.6.3 Distributed-Memory Multicomputers

Multicomputers do not support shared variables. Rather, all communications between processors must occur via message passing. Message-passing libraries are provided to send and receive messages between processors. Examples include the Cray T3D, NCube/Ten, and Intel Paragon. Large multicomputers may contain hundreds of processors.

A block diagram for a typical distributed memory multicomputer is shown in Figure 1.3. Each "node" of the network is not unlike that found in personal computers; it includes a CPU, cache memory, and a communications controller that handles interprocessor communication. Unlike the cache used in shared-memory multiprocessors, the cache in each multicomputer node only holds instructions and data for the local processor, so no cache coherence protocol is needed. The memory

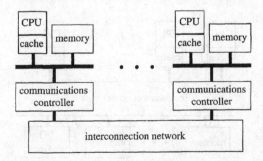

Figure 1.3 Block diagram of a typical distributed-memory multicomputer.

in each node can only be accessed by the CPU in that node. The communications controller is responsible for sending and receiving messages between nodes, and typically transfers messages directly between that node's memory and the interconnection network. Such transfers that usually do not require the intervention of the CPU, except to initiate the transfer or to be notified when the transfer is completed, are referred to as *direct memory access* (DMA) operations.

In principle, one could implement shared-memory operations in software on top of a distributed-memory architecture, providing the illusion to the programmer of having shared memory. For example, read and write operations could be implemented by sending messages to and from the processor on which a program variable resides, and copies of frequently referenced remote memory locations can be kept in the local processor with software used to maintain coherence. Software systems that support this capability are often referred to as *distributed shared-memory (DSM)* systems. Because these mechanisms must be implemented in software, however, the overhead associated with managing the memory system in this way may be prohibitive.

The distinction between shared-memory multiprocessors and multicomputers is important because the common address space provided by shared memory machines allows global data structures referenced by more than one processor to be used; these are not so easily implemented in distributed-memory multicomputers. Also, different memory management techniques may be used in shared-memory machines. For example, as will be seen in Chapter 5, it is possible to define memory management protocols in shared-memory computers that use, to within a constant factor, the same amount of memory as a sequential execution of the program. Such techniques have not yet been developed for distributed-memory machines.

1.6.4 SIMD Machines

SIMD stands for *single-instruction-stream, multiple-data-stream*. The central characteristic of these machines is that all processors must execute the same instruction (but using different data) at any instant in the program's execution. Typically these machines execute in "lock-step," synchronous to a global clock. This means *all* processors must complete execution of the current instruction (some may choose not to execute that instruction) before any is allowed to proceed to the next instruction. Actually lock-step execution need not be strictly adhered to so long as the machines appears to the application that it operates in this fashion. Lock-step execution and the constraint that all processors must execute the same instruction distinguish these machines from the others, so-called MIMD (multiple-instruction-stream, multiple-data-stream) computers that are described here.

A block diagram for a typical SIMD machine is depicted in Figure 1.4. The control unit fetches instructions from the control memory, and then broadcasts that instruction to each of the processing elements. Each processing element contains an ALU, registers, and control logic to implement machine instructions (LOAD, STORE, ADD, etc.). Upon receiving an instruction from the control unit, the processing element executes that instruction, possibly accessing its local data

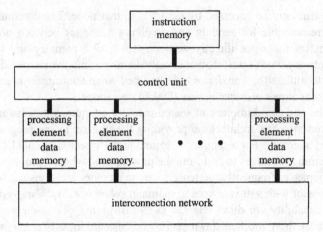

Figure 1.4   Block diagram of a typical SIMD machine.

memory or the interconnection network depending on the type of instruction. For example, a vector ADD operation might be performed by distributing the vector across all of the data memories, then having each processing element execute two LOAD instructions to fetch an element from each of the arrays into its local registers, next an ADD instruction to add the data values and store the result into another local register, and finally a STORE instruction to write the result into a location in the data memory.

SIMD machines typically contain more, albeit simpler, processors (processing elements) than either multiprocessors or multicomputers. Because they are simpler than complete microprocessors, custom-designed components are usually used rather than off-the-shelf parts.

Because all processors in an SIMD machine must execute the same instruction, these machines are more specialized than MIMD machines. The bulk of the effort in parallel simulation has been on MIMD machines, but some techniques are applicable on SIMD machines as well.

1.6.5   Distributed Computers

Two characteristics that distinguish distributed computers from parallel machines are *heterogeneity* and the network used to interconnect the machines. Unlike parallel computers, distributed systems are often composed of stand-alone computer workstations from different manufacturers. Unix-based workstations (for example, Sun, Silicon Graphics, DEC, or IBM workstations), and personal computers are most commonly used for distributed simulations today. Heterogeneity is important because many distributed simulators are constructed by interconnecting existing sequential simulators (for example, tank simulators in DIS) operating on specific workstations. Heterogeneity eliminates the need to port existing simulators to new platforms, and it enables participation of users with different computing equipment in distributed simulation exercises.

While parallel computers use interconnection switches customized for the processors that they are interconnecting, distributed computers use general interconnects based on widely accepted telecommunication standards such as asynchronous transfer mode (ATM) or Ethernet for interconnecting equipment from different manufacturers. The price of generality is performance, as complex software protocols inflate communication latencies to be one to two orders of magnitude larger than that of parallel machines, even for equipment in close physical proximity of each other. One can expect that this gap will be reduced in the future, however, blurring the distinction between parallel and distributed machines.

Different distributed computers are distinguished by the geographical extent covered by the system, which in turn dictates the type of network used to interconnect the machines. Local area network (LAN) based systems consist of a collection of machines in a limited geographic area, such as within a single building or a university campus, interconnected through a high-speed network or switch. MAN (metropolitan area network) based systems have the physical extent of a city, and a WAN (wide area network) based systems may be distributed across a nation or the world.

1.7 SUMMARY

Parallel and distributed simulation technology can provide substantial benefit in situations such as the following:

1. Time critical applications where simulations are used as decision aids (for example, how do I re-route air traffic?), and results are needed on very short notice.
2. Design of large and/or complex systems where execution of the simulation program is excessively time-consuming.
3. Virtual environments such as for training, where participants and/or resources are at geographically distant locations.

A variety of applications ranging from training to entertainment to the design of the next generation of the Internet are identified as targets for this technology.

Simulation applications were broadly divided into two categories: analytic simulations and distributed virtual environments. This distinction is important because each domain presents different requirements and technical challenges. Dividing simulations applications in this way also provides a convenient means for separating work in parallel and distributed simulation technology. Part II of this book focuses on analytic applications, while part III focuses on distributed virtual environments. Finally the underlying computing platform can be broadly classified as being a parallel or distributed computer, with geographical distribution of the processors used as the distinguishing characteristic. This distinction is important because different communication latencies are implied, leading to different problems and solutions. The distinction between "parallel simulation" and "distributed simulation" that is used here is based on this latter categorization.

1.8 ADDITIONAL READINGS

Numerous conferences report recent advances in the parallel and distributed simulation field. The *ACM/IEEE/SCS Workshop on Parallel and Distributed Simulation (PADS)* is the premier conference in the parallel discrete event simulation area (for analytic simulation applications) and has been operating since its inception in 1985, but results also appear in a variety of other conferences, including the *Winter Simulation Conference*, and the *Summer Computer Simulation Conference* and the *Annual Simulation Symposium*. The *ACM Transactions on Modeling and Computer Simulation* is a journal that includes articles concerning parallel and distributed simulation technology.

The literature contains numerous studies of applying parallel discrete event simulation techniques to specific applications. A few relevant references are listed below:

- Battlefield simulation (Wieland, Hawley et al. 1989; Morse 1990; Rich and Michelsen 1991; Steinman and Wieland 1994; Hiller and Hartrum 1997).
- Computer architectures (Konas and Yew 1992; Bailey, Pagels et al. 1993; Reinhardt, Hill et al. 1993; Agrawal, Choy et al. 1994; Konas and Yew 1994; Shah, Ramachandran et al. 1994; Chandrasekaran and Hill 1996; Dickens, Heidelberger et al. 1996); direct execution is described in (Fujimoto 1983).
- Digital logic circuits (Su and Seitz 1989; Chamberlain and Franklin 1990; Lin, Lazowska et al. 1990; Briner 1991; Chung and Chung 1991; Soule and Gupta 1991; Nandy and Loucks 1992; Willis and Siewiorek 1992; Manjikian and Loucks 1993; Sporrer and Bauer 1993; Chamberlain and Henderson 1994; Costa, DeGloria et al. 1994; Kapp, Hartrum et al. 1995; Hering and Haupt 1996; Keller, Rauber et al. 1996; Kim and Jean 1996; Krishnaswamy and Bannerjee 1996; Chen, Jha et al. 1997; Frohlich, Schlagenhaft et al. 1997; Krishnaswamy, Banerjee et al. 1997); see (Bailey, Briner et al. 1994) for a survey of this area.
- Ecological systems (Ebling, DiLorento et al. 1989; Deelman and Szymanski 1997; Glass, Livingston et al. 1997).
- Petri networks (Kumar and Harous 1990; Nicol and Roy 1991; Thomas and Zahorjan 1991; Baccelli and Canales 1993).
- Telecommunication networks (Mouftah and Sturgeon 1990; Phillips and Cuthbert 1991; Tallieu and Verboven 1991; Earnshaw and Hind 1992; Turner and Xu 1992; Chai and Ghosh 1993; Ronngren, Rajaei et al. 1994; Carothers, Fujimoto et al. 1995; Unger, Gomes et al. 1995; Bagrodia, Chen et

al. 1996; Hao, Wilson et al. 1996; Kumaran, Lubachevsky et al. 1996; Cleary and Tsai 1997).

- Transportation systems (Merrifield, Richardson et al. 1990; Wieland, Blair et al. 1995; Mitre Corp. 1997; Wieland 1997).

A readable introduction to DIS is provided in DIS Steering Committee (1994). The August 1995 issue of the *Proceedings of the IEEE* includes several articles concerning DIS, and the March 1997 issue of *IEEE Spectrum* concerning distributed virtual environments. A historical look at DIS is presented in Voss (1993). Several conferences include papers on recent work in the field. The *Simulation Interoperability Workshop (SIW)* meets every six months in Orlando, Florida, and focuses on distributed simulation for military applications. An important subject of this workshop concerns definition of standards to facilitate interoperability of simulations; previously called the DIS Workshop, the IEEE standards were developed in association with the forerunner to this meeting. The Defense Modeling and Simulation Office's web cite (http://www.dmso.mil) is the best source of information concerning the High Level Architecture, though numerous papers on the HLA appear in the SIW workshop. In a nonmilitary setting the bimonthly journal *Presence: Teleoperators and Virtual Environments* published by The MIT press includes numerous articles concerning the development of virtual environments, human factors issues, and applications. Recent developments in the field appear in the IEEE's *Virtual Reality Annual International Symposium (VRAIS)*.

There are several good textbooks on parallel and distributed computer architectures. For example, Hennessy and Patterson (1996) covers shared-memory and message-passing multicomputers as well as networked workstation platforms. Reed and Fujimoto (1987) is devoted to message-based multicomputer networks and includes a chapter on parallel discrete event simulation. Other books providing broad coverage of parallel computer architecture include Stone (1990), Hwang (1993), and Flynn (1995), among others. A survey of techniques for implementing shared-memory operations on distributed-memory computers is presented in Nitzberg and Lo (1991).

CHAPTER 2

Discrete Event Simulation Fundamentals

A simulation is a system that represents or emulates the behavior of another system over time. In a *computer simulation* the system doing the emulating is a computer program. The system being emulated is called the *physical system*. The physical system may be an actual, realized system, or it may only be a hypothetical one, for example, one of several possible design alternatives that only exists in the mind of its inventor.

A physical system contains some notion of state that evolves over time, for example, the number of aircraft waiting to land at an airport. The simulation must provide (1) a representation of the state of the physical system, (2) some means of changing this representation to model the evolution of the physical system, and (3) some representation of time. To address (1), computer simulations define a collection of *state variables*, namely program variables specified in some high-level programming language such as C or Java that represents the state of the physical system. To address (2), changes in the state of the physical system are realized by the simulation program writing new values into these state variables. Finally, time in the physical system is represented through an abstraction called *simulation time*. This is discussed next.

2.1 TIME

There are several different notions of time that are important when discussing a simulation. It is imperative to keep these concepts distinct, since this is perhaps one of the greatest sources of confusion when beginning to learn about parallel and distributed simulations.

The following definitions will be used throughout:

1. *Physical time* refers to time in the physical system.
2. *Simulation time* is an abstraction used by the simulation to model physical time. A more precise definition will be given momentarily.
3. *Wallclock time* refers to time during the execution of the simulation program.

A simulation program can usually obtain the current value of wallclock time (accurate to some specifiable amount of error) by reading a hardware clock maintained by the operating system.

To illustrate these different notions of time, consider a simulation of the transportation system in Atlanta during the 1996 summer Olympic games. Physical time for this simulation extends from July 19 to August 4, 1996. Simulation time might be represented in the simulation program by a double precision floating point number with each unit corresponding to a single day. In this case, simulation time advances from 0.00 to 17.00 during each execution of the program. If the simulation program ran for three hours on the afternoon of February 25, 1995, while planning for the Olympics, wallclock time might extend from 3:00 PM to 6:00 PM on that day.

All three definitions of time make use of *scales* or *axes* to represent specific instants of time and to define before and after relationships among these instants. Physical time and wallclock time are essentially the same as "time" used in the conventional sense, so we do not dwell upon their meaning here. Simulation time is a new concept that only exists in simulated worlds, and is defined as follows:

Definition *Simulation time* is defined as a totally ordered set of values where each value represents an instant of time in the physical system being modeled. Further, for any two values of simulation time T_1 representing physical time P_1, and T_2 representing P_2, if $T_1 < T_2$, then P_1 occurs before P_2, and $(T_2 - T_1)$ is equal to $(P_2 - P_1) * K$ for some constant K. If $T_1 < T_2$, then T_1 is said to occur *before* T_2, and if $T_1 > T_2$, then T_1 is said to occur after T_2.

The linear relationship between intervals of simulation time and intervals of physical time ensures durations of simulation time have a proper correspondence to durations in physical time.

For any given simulation, one common, global simulation time scale is used that is recognized by all components of the simulation, just as all countries in the world recognize Greenwich Mean Time. This ensures that all parts of the simulation have a common understanding of before and after relationships among simulated actions that occur at specific instants of simulated time.

2.2 REAL-TIME, SCALED REAL-TIME, AND AS-FAST-AS-POSSIBLE EXECUTION

The progression of simulation time during the execution of the simulation may or may not have a direct relationship to the progression of wallclock time. In simulations used for virtual environments, simulated time must be made to advance in synchrony with wallclock time, or the simulated environment will appear unrealistic. For example, if simulated time advanced more slowly than wallclock time, the virtual environment would appear to be sluggish and unresponsive to user actions. In a training exercise, tasks would appear to human participants as being too easy because more time is allowed for the human to perform operations than would be provided in the actual (physical) system. Similarly, if simulated time advanced more rapidly than wallclock time, human participants would be at a disadvantage. Simulation executions where advances in simulation time are paced by wallclock time are often referred to as *real-time executions*, and simulators designed to operate in this mode are called *real-time simulators*. Because of this relationship between simulation time and wallclock time in real-time simulations, the two are sometimes viewed as being synonymous in the distributed simulation literature. It is important to keep these two concepts distinct, however.

A variation on the above is *scaled real-time execution*. Here, simulation time advances faster or slower than wallclock time by some constant factor. For example, the simulation may be paced to advance two seconds of simulation time for each second of wallclock time, making the simulation appear to run twice as fast as the real world, not unlike pressing the fast-forward button on a VCR. This might be done in a training session to skip over uninteresting parts of the exercise. Similarly one might slow down the simulation by a certain constant factor to provide more detailed (slow motion) views of other parts. A real-time execution is a special case of a scaled real-time execution where the scale factor is set to one.

Real-time and scaled real-time simulations use a mapping function to translate wallclock time to simulation time. Specifically, the following function can be used to convert wallclock time to simulation time:

$$T_s = W2S(T_w) = T_{\text{start}} + Scale * (T_w - T_{w\text{Start}}),$$

where T_w is a value of wallclock time, T_{Start} is the simulation time at which the simulation begins, $T_{w\text{Start}}$ is the wallclock time at the beginning of the simulation, and *Scale* is the scale factor. If *Scale* is 2, then the simulation runs twice as fast as wallclock time, namely advancing one second in wallclock time corresponds to advancing two seconds in simulation time.

In analytic simulations that do not include humans or physical devices as components within the simulation, the progression of simulated time is usually *not* paced by wallclock time; a unit of advance in simulated time could require a few seconds in wallclock time during one part of the simulation, minutes in another part, or even hours in a third. These simulations are sometimes referred to as *as-fast-as-possible simulations* because one wishes to complete the execution of the simulation as quickly as possible, without any concern for maintaining a fixed relationship between advances in simulation time and wallclock time. The relationship between the rate of advance in simulation time with advances in wallclock time bears no significance, except to the extent that it provides a metric of how long the user has to wait to get the results of the simulation.

One can design simulation programs that can be used for *either* real-time or as-fast-as-possible executions. To accomplish this, one must augment an as-fast-as-possible simulation with a mechanism to pace its execution with wallclock time. This assumes, of course, that the unpaced execution advances simulation time faster than wallclock time advances; it is easy to slow down a simulation, but often difficult to speed one up! The pacing mechanism merely introduces a waiting mechanism to prevent the simulation from advancing simulation time ahead of wallclock time by more than some prescribed amount. This will be illustrated in the next section.

2.3 STATE CHANGES AND TIME FLOW MECHANISMS

The discussion thus far has focused on temporal aspects concerning the execution of the simulation. A second, independent classification corresponds to the manner in which the state of the model changes as simulation time is advanced, sometime referred to as the *time flow mechanism*. This classification of simulation models is depicted in Figure 2.1. Simulation models may be broadly classified as continuous or discrete. In a continuous simulation, the state of the system is viewed as changing continuously over time. The behavior of the system is typically described as a set of differential equations that describe how the system state changes as a function of simulation time. Typical examples of continuous simulation problems include modeling weather or climatic conditions, airflow around an aircraft wing, or changes in voltage on wires in an electronic circuit. Continuous models of the motion of vehicles (for example, aircraft, ships, robots) were used in some of the earliest distributed simulation applications for virtual environments. An extensive literature has developed concerning the use of parallel and distributed computers for continuous simulation problems, primarily to reduce execution time. A good introduction to the use of parallel computing in this field is described in Bertsekas and Tsitsiklis (1989).

In a discrete simulation, the simulation model views the physical system as only changing state at discrete points in simulation time. Conceptually the system is viewed as "jumping" from one state to the next, much like moving from one frame to another in a cartoon strip.

A simulation program defines a collection of state variables, and then defines the rules to modify these variables across simulation time. This concept can be represented via a space-time diagram such as that depicted in Figure 2.2. The y-axis of this graph represents the state variables and the x-axis denotes simulation

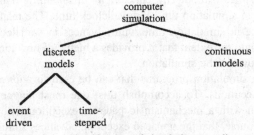

Figure 2.1 Classification of simulation paradigms.

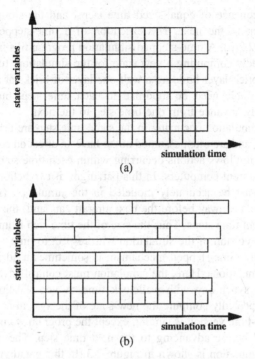

Figure 2.2 Space-time diagram for (*a*) time-stepped and (*b*) event-driven discrete-event simulations.

time. A horizontal "strip," namely all points $(*, X)^3$ represents the evolution of the variable X across simulation time. A change to state variable X at simulation time T is represented by a vertical line in the space-time diagram at coordinate position (T, X). A vertical strip, namely all points $(T, *)$ represents the state of the simulation model at simulation time T. The task of the simulation program is to "fill in" the space-time diagram by computing the values of each of the state variables across simulation time. In a discrete simulation, each change to a state variable occurs at a specific instant in simulation time.[4]

2.3.1 Time-Stepped Execution

The two most common types of discrete simulations are called *time-stepped* and *event-driven* (or sometimes called event-stepped) simulations. These two categories of simulation are distinguished by the time flow mechanism used by the simulation to advance simulation time. In a time-stepped simulation, simulation time is

---

[3] The character $*$ denotes all values.

[4] In practice, this is also true for *continuous* simulations because, even though the state variables are viewed as changing continuously over time, the simulation program will define time steps and typically compute new values only at time step boundaries.

subdivided as a sequence of equal-sized time steps, and the simulation advances from one time step to the next. The execution of a time-stepped simulation is depicted in Figure 2.2(*a*). A time-stepped simulation program fills in the space-time diagram by repeatedly computing a new state for the simulation, time step by time step, much like a brick layer building a wall one layer of bricks at a time. Actually not every state variable need be modified in each time step, but the execution mechanism can only advance from one time step to the next.

Actions in the simulation occurring in the same time step are usually considered to be simultaneous, and are often assumed not to have an effect on each other. This is important because it allows actions occurring within each time step to be executed concurrently by different computers. In this paradigm, if two actions have a causal relationship that must be accurately modeled in the simulation (for example, an aircraft must vacate a runway before the next aircraft can land) the actions must be simulated at different time steps. Thus the size of the time step is important because it determines the precision of the simulation with respect to time.

A variation on the time-stepped mechanism is sometimes used in real-time and scaled real-time simulations. Here, the simulation must control advances in simulation time to be in synchrony with wallclock time. A non-real-time time-stepped simulation must repeatedly compute the new state of the system at the end of each time step. The real-time version is similar, except the program waits until wallclock time has advanced before advancing to the next time step. The main loop for a typical real-time simulation is shown in Figure 2.3. In this paradigm, the computation for each time step should be completed before wallclock time advances to the next time step, or else the simulation will lag behind wallclock time.

2.3.2 Event-Driven Execution

Rather than compute a new value for state variables each time step, it may be more efficient to only update the variables when "something interesting" occurs. The "something interesting" that occurs is referred to as an *event*. This is the key idea behind *discrete event simulations*. An event is an abstraction used in the simulation to model some instantaneous action in the physical system. Each event has a time stamp associated with it that indicates the point in simulation time when the event occurs. Each event usually results in some change in one or more state variables defined by the simulation.

```
while (simulation in progress)

      wait until (W2S(wallclock time) ≥ simulation time)

      compute state of the system at the end of this time step

      advance simulation time to the next time step
```

Figure 2.3 Main loop in a time-stepped simulation where execution is paced to wallclock time. The *W2S* function converts wallclock time to simulation time.

For example, consider a simulation of an aircraft flying from New York to Los Angeles. A time-stepped simulation with time step size of ten minutes might compute the aircraft's new position every ten minutes. A more efficient approach is to compute the total flight time, and only update the aircraft's position variable when simulation time advances to the time the aircraft reaches Los Angeles. The aircraft arriving in Los Angeles is modeled by an event. In an event-driven simulation, changes in state variables only occur as the result of some event. This approach assumes intermediate positions of the aircraft are not needed, or if they are needed, they can be computed from the time the flight left New York and other state information, for example, the speed and direction of the aircraft.

Figure 2.2(b) shows a space-time diagram for an event driven simulation. In this figure, updates to state variables occur at irregular points in simulation time, namely the simulation time of the events.

In an event-driven simulation, simulation time does not advance from one time step to the next but, rather, advances from the time stamp of one event to the next. From a computational standpoint, the simulation can be viewed as a sequence of computations, one for each event, transforming the system across simulated time in a manner representing the behavior of the actual system. For example, Figure 2.4 depicts the execution of a discrete-event simulation of air traffic in a single airport, with events denoting the arrival, landing, and departure of different aircraft.

An event-driven simulation can emulate a time-stepped simulation by defining events that happen at each time step, for example, events can be defined with time stamp 1, 2, 3, ..., assuming a time step size of one. In principal, a time-stepped simulation may emulate an event-driven simulation by defining a time step size that is the greatest common divisor among all the time stamps assigned to events in the simulation. This will ensure that no event lies between two time steps. This may be rather inefficient in practice, however, because many time steps may not contain any computation to be performed.

A variation of the event-driven paradigm can also be used for real-time simulations. One approach is to prevent simulation time from advancing to the time stamp of the next event until wallclock time has advanced to the time of this event, that is, if the time stamp of the next event is T_s, simulation time is not advanced to T_s until $W2S(T_w)$ reaches T_s, where T_w is the current value of wallclock time.

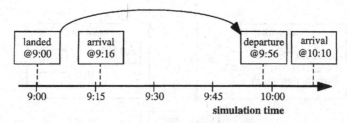

Figure 2.4 Sequence of events in a discrete-event simulation. The arrival at 9:00 schedules the departure event at 9:56.

2.4   DISCRETE-EVENT SIMULATION PROGRAMS

This book is primarily concerned with discrete event simulations. A *sequential* discrete event simulation program typically utilizes three data structures (see Fig. 2.5):

1. The *state variables* that describe the state of the system (for example, Fig. 2.5 shows variables that will be used later in an example for simulating an airport; briefly, these variables indicate counts of the number of aircraft that are flying overhead and are on the ground, and the state of the runway).

2. An *event list* containing events that are to occur some time in the simulated future (Fig. 2.5 shows the events depicted in Fig. 2.4; the event with time stamp 9:56 is absent because it has not been created yet).

3. A *global clock* variable to denote the instant on the simulation time axis at which the simulation now resides (in Fig. 2.5 the simulation has advanced to simulation time 8:45).

If the clock variable contains a value T, then this denotes the fact that all activities in the physical system up to the time represented by T have been simulated, and activities later than T have not yet been simulated. All events in the event list must have a time stamp greater than or equal to T.

Operationally, an event is usually implemented by a data structure that includes the event's time stamp (for example, 9:16 AM), some indication of the type of event (for example, an aircraft arriving at an airport) and various parameters elaborating more details of the event (for example, flight 396 arriving at LAX).

In the physical system, "events" such as an aircraft arrival "just happen." In the simulated world, nothing happens unless the simulation computation makes it happen. In other words, a mechanism is required to create new events. The mechanism for creating a new event in the simulation is called *scheduling* an event. For example, suppose that the simulation depicted in Figure 2.4 and Figure 2.5 now advances to simulation time 9:00 and the event at that time indicates flight 200 has landed. The simulation might now schedule a new departure event to denote the fact that this aircraft departs again at 9:56. "Scheduling an event" in the simulator is implemented by allocating memory for a new event, filling in the fields for the time stamp, event type, and the associated parameters, and adding the event

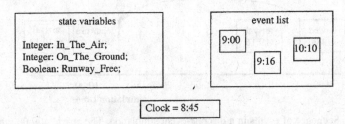

Figure 2.5   Principal data structures in a discrete-event simulation program.

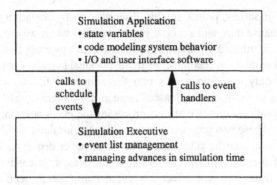

Figure 2.6 Separation of the simulation program into the simulation application and executive components.

to the event list data structure. Event scheduling is one way that simulation programs can model causal relationships in the physical system.

We are now ready to describe the simulation program. This program can be divided into two components (see Fig. 2.6). The lower piece is the *simulation executive* that maintains the event list and clock variable. This portion is independent of the physical system. Commercial vendors often sell the simulation executive as a "general purpose" component that can be used to simulate a variety of systems. The upper portion includes the state variables and the software for modeling the physical system. This part is called the *simulation application*, and it is intimately tied to the physical system. In its simplest form, the simulation executive need only provide a single primitive to the simulation application: a procedure for scheduling events.

The program executed by the simulation executive is shown in Figure 2.7. The heart of the simulation executive is the *event-processing loop* that repeatedly removes the event containing the smallest time stamp from the event list, advances the simulation time clock to the time stamp of this event, and then calls a procedure defined in the simulation application that processes the event. This procedure for processing the event may do two things:

1. Modify state variables to model changes in the state of the physical system that result from this event.
2. Schedule new events into the simulated future.

```
while (simulation is in progress)

        remove smallest time stamped event from event list

        set simulation time clock to time stamp of this event

        execute event handler in application to process event
```

Figure 2.7 Main event-processing loop in a discrete-event simulation program.

There are two important points in this discrete event simulation that are worth highlighting, because they will become very important when we consider execution on parallel and distributed computers. Both relate to ensuring that the simulation faithfully reproduces causal relationships in the physical system. First, the simulation application can only schedule events into the simulated future, namely the time stamp of any new event must be at least as large as the current time of the simulation. Second, the simulation executive always processes the event containing the smallest time stamp next. These two properties ensure that the simulation will process events in time stamp order, and the simulation time clock never decreases in value during the execution of the simulation. This is important because it ensures that an event computation at time T cannot affect any event computation with a smaller time stamp. This is certainly a good thing, because, if this were not the case, it would be possible for future events to affect those in the past!

2.5   AN EXAMPLE APPLICATION

Consider a simulation of air traffic arriving and departing at an airport. Assume that the airport contains a single runway for incoming aircraft. Such a simulation might be used to collect statistics such as the average number of aircraft waiting to land or the average amount of time each aircraft must wait; however, we will ignore the computation of such statistics here in order to focus on the event processing mechanism. In this example, the state of the airport is characterized by three state variables:

1. In_The_Air indicates the number of aircraft that are in the process of landing, or are circling, waiting to land.
2. On_The_Ground indicates the number of aircraft that have landed and are either at a gate, or traveling to or from a gate.
3. Runway_Free indicates whether or not the runway is currently being used by a landing aircraft.

These state variables and the observation that the state of the simulation can only change when an event occurs suggest the types of events that are needed. Specifically, In_The_Air is incremented by one when a new aircraft arrives at the airport, and is decremented by one when an aircraft lands. Similarly On_The_Ground is incremented when an aircraft lands, and is decremented when an aircraft departs. Finally Runway_Free will become FALSE when an aircraft arrives if the runway was not already in use, and becomes TRUE when an aircraft lands and there are no additional aircraft waiting to land. Departing aircraft are not included in the In_The_Air state variable. Thus three types of events are defined for this simulation:

1. An arrival event denotes the arrival of a new aircraft at the airport.
2. A landed event denotes that an aircraft has landed.
3. A departure event denotes an aircraft leaving to travel to another airport.

Arrival and departure events represent, respectively, the introduction and removal of aircraft in the simulation.

Upon arrival, each aircraft must: (1) wait for the runway and land (assume that the aircraft uses the runway for R units of time while landing), (2) travel to the gate and unload and load new passengers (assume that this requires G units of time), and (3) depart and travel to another airport. Assume that R and G are fixed, known quantities. To simplify the model, queuing at the runway for *departing* aircraft will not be considered here.

```
/*
 * Constants and other values:
 * Now: current simulation time (from simulation executive)
 * R = time runway in use to land aircraft (constant)
 * G = time required at gate (constant)
 *
 * State Variables:
 * Integer In_The_Air: number landing/waiting to land
 * Integer On_The_Ground: number of aircraft within airport
 * Boolean Runway_Free: TRUE if runway is not being used
 * Initialize these variables to 0, 0, and TRUE, respectively
 */

Arrival Event:
    In_The_Air := In_The_Air + 1;
    /* compute time aircraft landed and done using runway */
    If (Runway_Free)
        Runway_Free := FALSE;
        Schedule Landed Event at time Now+R;

Landed Event:
    /* update state for the aircraft that has landed */
    In_The_Air := In_The_Air - 1;
    On_The_Ground := On_The_Ground + 1;
    Schedule Departure Event at time Now+G

    /* land next aircraft if there is one */
    if (In_The_Air > 0)
        Schedule Landed Event at time Now + R;
    else
        Runway_Free := TRUE;

Departure Event:
    On_The_Ground := On_The_Ground - 1;
```

Figure 2.8 Simulation application program for a single airport.

The simulation application consists of the definitions of the state variables and constants, and three procedures, `Arrival`, `Landed`, and `Departure`, one to handle each of the three different types of events. As discussed previously, the simulation executive repeatedly removes the smallest time-stamped event from the event list, and calls the appropriate procedure for the type of event that was removed. The simulation executive also defines a function called Now that returns the current value of the Clock variable.

The code for this simulation application is shown in Figure 2.8. This program closely follows the behavior of the airport that was just described. When an arrival event occurs, `In_The_Air` is incremented, and if the runway is free, the aircraft begins to land. This is accomplished by setting `Runway_Free` to FALSE and scheduling a `Landed` event R time units into the future. If the runway is not free, no further action is taken. The `Landed` event procedure decrements `In_The_Air` and increments `On_The_Ground` to reflect the new status of the aircraft, and schedules a `Departure` event to represent the final departure of the aircraft from the airport. If there are additional aircraft waiting to land, the `Landed` event procedure also schedules a new `Landed` event to model the next aircraft landing. If there are no more aircraft waiting to land, the runway is marked as being free by setting `Runway_Free` to TRUE. Finally the Departure event procedure simply decrements `On_The_Ground` to represent the fact that the airport has one fewer aircraft.

It may be noted that in this simple example, no queueing of departing aircraft is modeled. It is straightforward to extend the model to include this aspect, so this is left as an exercise for the reader.

The above program models the movement of aircraft through the airport but does not provide any means for generating new aircraft, that is, generating new `Arrival` events. This could be accomplished by augmenting the `Arrival` event handler procedure so that each arrival event schedules a new arrival event *I* time units into the future, where *I* is the interarrival time, or time between arriving aircraft. *I* might be selected by invoking a random number generator, that is, a procedure that selects a number in accordance to some probability distribution. Rather than scheduling new arrival events in this fashion, here, we will assume that the event list is initialized to contain an arrival event for each aircraft that will pass through the airport in the entire simulation. This will facilitate discussions later when we expand this sequential simulation program to one that can execute on parallel or distributed computers.

A sample execution of this program is depicted in Figure 2.9. This figure shows a space-time diagram to illustrate how the state variables are modified by the different events. For example, the computation for the Arrival event increments the `In_The_Air` variable and sets `Runway_Free` to FALSE. It then schedules a Landed event R time units into the future. The Landed event decrements `In_The_Air`, increments `On_The_Ground`, sets `Runway_Free` to TRUE, and schedules a Departure event. Finally the departure event decrements `On_The_-Ground`.

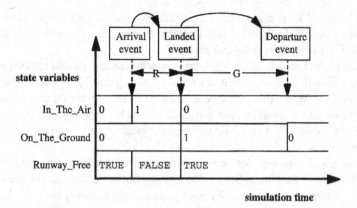

Figure 2.9 Space-time diagram depicting an aircraft arriving, landing, and then departing at an airport using the simulation application shown in Figure 2.8.

2.6 STARTING AND STOPPING THE SIMULATION

There are two remaining aspects of the simulation execution that need to be discussed: starting and stopping the simulation. The simulation begins by initializing the state variables, and generating initial events. Initialization of variables is accomplished by traditional programming techniques. The initial events may be created by defining an "initialization event" with time stamp equal to a simulated time prior to the beginning of the actual simulation. The simulation application provides a procedure that processes this initialization event by scheduling all other initial events required by the simulation.

There are several techniques for terminating the execution of the simulation. A "stop simulation" event may be used that is defined to be the last event processed by the simulation, even if there are other scheduled events remaining in the event list. Alternatively, an "end simulation time" may be defined that indicates the simulation is terminated when the simulation clock is about to exceed this time; that is, the simulation ends when the next event removed from the event list carries a time stamp larger than this time. In either case, the simulation will always terminate after an event computation if there are no events in the event list.

2.7 PARALLEL/DISTRIBUTED SIMULATION EXAMPLE

A parallel or a distributed simulation is typically composed of a collection of sequential simulations, each modeling a different part of the physical system and (at least potentially) executing on a different processor. Borrowing terminology from the parallel discrete event simulation community, let us refer to each sequential simulation as a *logical process* or *LP*. In other contexts, each sequential simulation might be referred to as a *simulator*. Thus the physical system can be viewed as a collection of *physical processes* that interacts in some fashion with each physical process being modeled by a logical process.

As each logical process executes, it processes events and generates new events. It may be the case that an event that is generated within one LP is relevant to one or more other LPs. When this happens, a *message* is sent to the other LPs to notify them of the event.[5] Viewed another way, interactions between physical processes are modeled in the distributed simulation by passing messages among the corresponding logical processes.

For example, let us consider extending the airport simulation described earlier to model air traffic in the United States. The U.S. air traffic network can be viewed as a collection of airports that interact by having aircraft fly between them. An actual air traffic system might also include other interactions such as radio transmissions between aircraft and airports, but these interactions will be ignored here to simplify the discussion.

The physical system consists of three airports: JFK in New York, LAX in Los Angeles, and ORD in Chicago. In this example, each airport is modeled by a logical process identical to that shown in Figure 2.8, except the departure event procedure is modified as described next.

The original model shown in Figure 2.8 assumed that once an aircraft departed, it left the simulation and was never heard from again. Here, we modify this simulation by observing that an aircraft departure results in a subsequent arrival event at another airport. To realize this change, only the procedure for processing departure events needs to be modified. The modified procedure is shown in Figure 2.10. Rather than discarding departing aircraft, each departure event generates a new arrival event for another airport. This is accomplished by sending a message to the LP modeling the destination airport requesting that it schedule a new arrival event with time stamp equal to the time of departure plus the amount of time required to fly between the two airports.

This completes our example for now. With the small change described above, we have now constructed a simple distributed simulation program for modeling a collection of airports. This example was intended to illustrate that distributed simulation is a direct extension of well-known concepts in the sequential simulation world. One can view a parallel/distributed simulation as a collection of sequential simulation programs that exchange messages to notify other simulations of events. While in this example each logical process in the distributed execution was a discrete event simulation program, one could easily replace each LP with a time stepped or a continuous model.

At this point we should alert the reader to the fact that the above example is deceptively simple. As will be seen in later chapters, extending the underlying

---

[5]The parallel discrete event simulation literature often views events and messages as being synonymous. This view is not taken here because it may be that a single event may be relevant to several other logical processes. It is more natural to view this situation as a single event resulting in several LPs being notified of the event via messages.

```
Departure Event:

    On_The_Ground := On_The_Ground - 1;

    /*

    * notify next airport of a new arrival event.

    * Source = ID of this airport

    * Dest = ID of destination airport

    * Flight_Time[S,D] = time to fly from S to D

    */

    Send Message to Dest to schedule an arrival event at

    time Now+Flight_Time[Source,Dest]
```

Figure 2.10   Modified departure event procedure for distributed simulation.

simulation *executive* to parallel and distributed environments introduces many nontrivial problems.

2.8 WORLD VIEWS AND OBJECT-ORIENTED SIMULATION

The approach discussed above for modeling air traffic is known as the *event-oriented* world view. In this approach the focus of the model is on events, and how they affect 'the state of the simulation. Simulation programs using this world view consist of procedures or event handlers, one for each different type of event that can occur in the simulation. The event-oriented world view will be used throughout much of this book because it is, in many respects, the "machine language" of discrete-event simulation. By this we mean it defines the fundamental mechanisms, specifically the mechanisms for handling events and advancing simulation time that are used by the other techniques described later in this chapter. We conclude this section with a discussion of another important world view, the so-called process-oriented approach, and a programming approach called object-oriented simulation.

For completeness we mention one other world view, known as the *activity-scanning* approach, that is also sometimes used. This is a variation on the time-stepped mechanism. The simulation program consists of a collection of procedures, with a predicate associated with each one. At each time step, each predicate is evaluated, and the associated procedure is executed if its predicate evaluates to TRUE. This process repeats until no predicate evaluates to TRUE. When this happens the simulation advances to the next time step.

2.8.1 Simulation Processes

Consider the air traffic simulation described earlier in this chapter. Imagine that you are employed by a commercial airline company to modify this simulation program to include more detail concerning actions performed by the pilot of an aircraft (for example, details concerning procedures for takeoff and landing or for changing altitude during a flight). While this is a manageable task for the simple simulation shown in Figure 2.8, this would be much more challenging if the simulation were much larger and more complex (for example, containing tens or hundreds of thousands of lines of code and hundreds of different event procedures). In order to make modifications such as those suggested above, you must locate all of the code describing the aircraft's behavior (for example, take off, landing and travel between airports, and modify these portions of the program). The problem is the behavioral description for a single aircraft is scattered across the entire program in the different event procedures, and it is not immediately clear from the code what sequence of events describes the behavior of a single aircraft. It is difficult to understand and modify the model for a single aircraft because the simulation program is not organized in a way to allow one to separate the aircraft's behavior from that of other types of aircraft (for example, flown by different airlines) and other activities that go on in the airport.

A process-oriented simulation attacks this problem through an abstraction called the simulation process. A simulation process is intended to model a specific entity in the simulation with a well-defined behavior (for example, an aircraft in the air traffic example). The behavioral description of the entity is encapsulated by the process. This description describes the actions performed by the process throughout its lifetime.

For example, in the simulation for a single airport, the lifetime of an aircraft can be described as follows: First it waits for the runway to become free. Then it lands, using the runway. It next moves to the gate to load and unload passengers, and then it departs. The simulation program for an aircraft process is depicted in Figure 2.11, where it can be seen that the program directly reflects this word description of the aircraft's behavior. This is in sharp contrast to the event-oriented description described previously. The simulation program uses two key primitives:

1. `Wait_Until (predicate)`. This construct causes the process to be suspended (blocked while simulation time advances) until the specified predicate, in this case the runway becoming free, evaluates to TRUE.
2. `Advance_Time (T)`. This construct causes simulation time for the process to advance by T units of simulation time. This construct is invoked to signify that the entity is "busy" performing some activity for T units of time.

A key point is that the *Wait_Until* and *Time_Advance* primitives cause simulation time to advance. This is critical because the lifetime of the entity modeled by the process is over a certain period of simulation time. By contrast, the "lifetime" of an event procedure is a single *instant* in simulation time.

In addition to processes, process-oriented simulations often utilize the concept of a *resource*. A resource is an abstraction that represents a shared entity for which one or more processes compete. The runway in the air traffic simulation is an example of a resource. The scenario described in Figure 2.11 where the aircraft waits until the

```
/*
 * Constants and other values:
 * R = time runway in use to land aircraft (constant)
 * G = time required at gate (constant)
 *
 * State Variables:
 * Integer In_The_Air: number of landing or waiting to land
 * Integer On_The_Ground: number of aircraft within airport
 * Boolean Runway_Free: TRUE if runway is not being used
 * Initialize these variables to 0, 0, and TRUE, respectively
 */


Process Aircraft:
      /* simulate aircraft arrival, circling, and landing */
1     In_The_Air := In_The_Air + 1;
2     Wait_Until (Runway_Free); /* circle */
3     Runway_Free := FALSE;        /* land */
4     Advance_Time(R);
5     Runway_Free := TRUE;

      /* simulate aircraft on the ground */
6     In_The_Air := In_The_Air - 1;
7     On_The_Ground := On_The_Ground + 1;
8     Advance_Time(G);

      /* simulate aircraft departure */
9     On_The_Ground := On_The_Ground - 1;
```

Figure 2.11   Process-oriented simulation of airport.

resource becomes available (the `Wait_Until(Runway_Free)` statement), acquiring the resource (the `Runway_Free := FALSE;` statement) and releasing the resource (the `Runway_Free := TRUE;` statement), is sufficiently common that primitives for performing these functions are often included in a library, or built into the simulation language itself. Conceptually a process-oriented simulation can be viewed as collections of processes, each advancing in a somewhat autonomous fashion through simulation time and interacting with other processes by competing for shared resources.

As mentioned earlier, process-oriented simulations are typically implemented "on top of" event-oriented simulation mechanisms. Specifically, process-oriented simulations use the same event list and time advance mechanism defined for the event-oriented paradigm but provide additional mechanisms for managing simulation processes. The lifetime of a simulation process can be viewed as a kind of miniature event-oriented simulation in that it consists of a *sequence* of event computations. Simulation time for the process only advances *between* these event computations. The key difference is that in an event-oriented simulation, the event computation is encapsulated into a procedure (i.e., the event handler). In a process-oriented simulation the event computations are blocks of statements *within* the code for the simulation process, and they are terminated by a call to a primitive to advance simulation time, i.e., the `Wait_Until` and `Advance_Time` statements. In the simulation in Figure 2.11, there are four event computations:

1. Statements 1 and 2 modeling the aircraft waiting to land.
2. Statements 3 and 4 modeling the aircraft landing.
2. Statements 5, 6, 7, and 8 modeling the aircraft on the ground.
3. Statement 9 modeling the departure.

The event-oriented paradigm provides a very straightforward mapping of the simulation program to standard programming language constructs; that is, each event handler could be simply implemented as a procedure. The mapping of a simulation process to language constructs is somewhat more complex. One could partition the simulation code into separate procedures and revert back to the event-oriented style of execution. For example, a compiler or preprocessor could translate the simulation code in Figure 2.11 into four procedures, P1, P2, P3, and P4, with each procedure terminated by a call to a simulation primitive that results in simulation time to advancing. This ensures that simulation time only advances between calls to the procedures, which is identical to an event-oriented simulation. The compiler could create an event handler for each process that is called whenever an event pertaining to that process is removed from the event list. This event handler calls P1 the first time it is invoked, P2 the second time, and P3 and P4, respectively, on the final two invocations. The `Advance_Time` (T) primitive schedules a new event T time units into the future, thereby guaranteeing the event handler for the process will be called again at the precise simulation time when the process should resume execution. The `Wait_Until` primitive updates a data structure within the simulation executive to indicate the condition on which the process is waiting. Prior to processing each event, the simulation executive must check to determine which waiting processes are now able to resume execution, and schedules an event (at the current simulation time) to "wake up" one such process. If there are several that are eligible to execute (for example, there may be several processes waiting for a resource that has now become free), the simulation executive must use some prioritization rule to determine which process should be resumed. Of course, this is something that the modeler must have control over, since it will usually affect the simulation results, so a queueing discipline may be specified (for example, first-come-first-serve) to address this issue.

The above discussion describes a typical implementation of a process-oriented simulation paradigm, with one exception. Suppose that a `Wait_Until` or `Advance_Time` primitive is called within a loop, or within a procedure called by the simulation process. In this case, decomposing the code for the process into a sequence of procedure calls is not so simple. For situations such as these, a co-routine mechanism (or equivalently, a "threading mechanism") is needed to transfer execution in and out of the process code. A co-routine mechanism is a facility that allows a computation (for example, a simulation process) to stop and transfer execution to another computation (the simulation executive). Later, the simulation process can resume execution at exactly the point at which it had been stopped.

To summarize, the principal points concerning process-oriented simulations are as follows:

1. They provide a more convenient paradigm for developing simulation applications for certain types of applications.
2. They can be implemented on top of the basic event-oriented style of execution that was described earlier.
3. They incur a certain amount of additional computational overhead to control and manage the execution of simulation processes.

2.8.2 Object-Based and Object-Oriented Simulations

Many physical systems can be viewed as collections of components (aircraft, controllers, airports, etc.) that interact in some fashion. Thus it is natural to model these systems as collections of interacting *objects*. For this reason, object-based and object-oriented paradigms have become popular modeling paradigms.

An *object* consists of a collection of fields (state variables or attributes) and a set of *methods*, typically implemented as procedures, that model the behavior of the component. Objects are created (*instantiated*) dynamically during the execution of the program, enabling one to easily model the creation of new components (for example, aircraft in an air traffic simulation) during the execution of the simulation. Objects may initiate execution (invoke methods) of other objects or request (query) the current value of another object's fields. Logically, invoking a method can be viewed as sending a message to the object requesting that the method be executed. When executed on a single computer, invoking an object's method can be implemented by a simple procedure call. On a parallel or distributed computer, messages are used to invoke methods for objects that reside on another computer.

The fields of an object can only be modified by that object's methods. This principal, called encapsulation, greatly simplifies software maintenance and debugging. Systems that require the simulation to be structured as collections of interacting objects are often referred to as *object-based* systems. Object-oriented systems go a step further by providing a capability called *inheritance* to characterize relationships among collections of similar, but not identical objects.

A key aspect of object-oriented languages is that they allow one to define new types of objects in terms of already defined object types. The new object type is said to inherit the properties (fields and methods) of the original. However, the new object type, called the *derived type*, may replace these properties with new ones, or extend the object type to include entirely new fields and methods. This allows, for instance, one to define a generic object type and define specific object types that elaborate upon the original, *base*, type. For example, the base type might be vehicle objects with fields indicating the vehicle's current position, direction, and velocity. An aircraft object can be derived from this base type that extends this definition to include an altitude field.

The derived type may replace or *overload* methods in the base object type. Both the derived type and the base type use the same name for the method. Thus an object can invoke the "move" method for a vehicle object without being concerned whether the vehicle is an aircraft or an automobile. The move method for an aircraft might cause it to climb 1000 feet, while that of the automobile causes it to travel another 10 minutes down the freeway. The underlying system ensures that the correct method is invoked at runtime. Replacing methods in this fashion allows one to extend existing libraries and tailor them to suit the purposes of the user. The fact that different object types can use the same name for their move method is important because it allows new object types to be defined and incorporated into the simulation program without modifying the object that invokes the method, thereby simplifying the addition of new types of objects to the program. The ability to have different methods with the same name is called *polymorphism*.

It should be obvious that object-based and object-oriented languages are natural vehicles for implementing discrete-event simulations. This should come as no surprise because many of the ideas in object-oriented simulation can be traced back to a language called Simula that was designed for discrete event simulation. Methods can be used to implement event procedures. Encapsulation of the state of an object supports parallel and distributed simulations because it discourages the use of global variables that may be difficult to implement on parallel and distributed computers which do not provide shared memory. Moreover the approach of constructing simulation programs as collections of objects that interact in some fashion is a natural way to view systems of interacting components.

2.8.3 Query Events and Push versus Pull Processing

When simulating collections of interacting objects, such as aircraft and airports, it is common for one object to need to collect state information from other objects. For example, in the simulation of the three airports discussed earlier, one might define a fourth object that monitors traffic conditions at all three airports, and dispatches recommendations (for example, rescheduling of flights) to these airports. This monitor object might request the current value of the In_The_Air state variable at each of the other airports to determine which airports are congested. This might be implemented by invoking an "Ask" method at each of the airport objects requesting the value of this variable. In a sequential simulation, this could be implemented by a simple procedure call for each airport. In a distributed simulation, the monitor object and the airport objects may reside on different processors, so messages must be sent to retrieve the requested information. Adhering to our paradigm of logical processes exchanging time-stamped events, requesting the value of the In_The_Air state variable is viewed as scheduling an event (called a *query* event) for each airport process with time stamp equal to the current simulation time of the monitor object. The event handler for this event (a method in the airport object) generates a reply by scheduling a new event at the monitor object containing the requested value. The time stamp of this reply is the same as the query.

The approach described above using query events is sometimes referred to as "pull processing" because each LP is responsible for "pulling" in the information it needs when it needs this information. The drawback with pull processing in distributed simulations is that two message transmissions are required to collect information from another processor. Further the process requesting the information must usually block until the query has been satisfied.

An alternative approach is to have the airport processes automatically provide the monitor process the value of the required state information whenever the variable changes. This is sometimes called "push processing" because the LP that holds the state variable "pushes" changes to the variable to other processes. This reduces the two messages required for each transmission of state information in the pull approach to only one, and it eliminates forcing the monitor process to block while waiting for the response of its queries. Push processing may require more message transmissions than are really needed, however, because the source of the data cannot know if the user of this information requires each new value of the state variable.

2.8.4 Event Retraction

Another commonly used mechanism is to *retract* (sometimes called "cancel" in the discrete-event simulation literature; however, event cancellation is used to denote an entirely different mechanism here, as will be discussed in Chapter 4) previously scheduled events. Fundamental to the discrete event simulation paradigm described earlier is the notion of scheduling events into the simulated future. This is, in essence, predicting what will happen (for example, once an aircraft lands, we can predict that it will later depart again). In some circumstances this may be difficult to do with absolute certainty. In that case the simulation program may schedule events that it *believes* will occur when the event is scheduled, but later it will retract the scheduled event should this belief turn out to be incorrect.

For example, again consider the air traffic example described earlier. Suppose that we now introduce a "gremlin" process that generates airport closings (for example, because of bad weather) at randomly selected points in time. An airport closure could be easily implemented by the gremlin process scheduling a "closing" event at an airport with a time stamp indicating when the airport closes. When an airport closing event is processed by an airport, it may have other events already scheduled, based on the assumption that the airport did not close. For instance, there may be departure events scheduled for aircraft that have recently landed. The event retraction mechanism can be used to "unschedule" these departure events, and reschedule new departure events based on the re-opening time of the airport. Without the ability to retract previously scheduled events, the simulator would need to devise a way to ignore the now invalid departure events when they are processed. It is possible to do this, though somewhat cumbersome.

2.9   OTHER APPROACHES TO EXPLOITING CONCURRENT EXECUTION

This book is primarily concerned with parallel and distributed simulation techniques that are composed of simulation models for different parts of the system executing concurrently on different processors. For completeness, other approaches to exploiting concurrency in simulation problems are mentioned. One approach that has been proposed is to use dedicated functional units to implement specific *sequential* simulation functions, for example, event list manipulation and random number generation. This method does not scale to large simulation models, however, because no provision is made to partition large models into smaller submodels executing concurrently on different processors.

Another well-known approach is to execute independent, *sequential* simulation programs on different processors. This *replicated trials* approach is useful if one is performing long simulation runs to reduce variance, or if one is investigating the behavior of a system across a large number of different parameter settings. The replicated trials approach is a very simple and useful technique to exploiting multiple processors, and one that is widely used today. A disadvantage of this approach is that each processor must have enough memory to hold the entire simulation program. Also this approach is obviously not well suited for interactive virtual environments. Finally it is not suitable if results of one experiment are needed to determine the experiment that should be performed next.

2.10   ADDITIONAL READINGS

Discrete-event simulation is a mature field that dates back at least to the 1950s. The field includes numerous areas such as model design and development, programming languages, experimental design, analysis of output, and random number generation, to mention a few. The focus of this book is limited to one aspect of this field, namely model execution on parallel and distributed computing systems. Several good textbooks giving broader coverage of the field are available; for example, see Law and Kelton (1991); Fishwick (1994); and Banks, Carson II et al. (1996).

The space-time view of simulation programs, and different execution mechanisms (both sequential and parallel) for "filling in" the graph is described in Chandy and Sherman (1989) and elaborated upon in Bagrodia, Liao et al. (1991). The functional decomposition approach where different processors of a parallel computer are used to execute different portions of a sequential simulation (event list processing, random number generation, etc.) is described in Comfort (1984), and Davis, Sheppard et al. (1988). Use of the replicated trial approach to reduce the time of long simulation runs are described in Biles, Daniels et al. (1985), Heidelberger (1986), Glynn and Heidelberger (1991), and Sunderam and Rego (1991).

PART II

PARALLEL AND DISTRIBUTED DISCRETE-EVENT SIMULATION

CHAPTER 3

Conservative Synchronization Algorithms

This chapter and the three that follow are concerned with the execution of analytic simulation programs on parallel and distributed computers with the principal goal of reducing execution time. The emphasis is on as-fast-as-possible execution; however, as was described in the previous chapter, the simulation program could be paced to execute as a real-time (or scaled real-time) simulation if the execution is fast enough to keep up with (scaled) wallclock time.

As discussed in the previous chapter, the physical system is viewed as being composed of some number of physical processes that interact in some fashion. Each physical process is modeled by a logical process (LP), and interactions between physical processes are modeled by exchanging time-stamped messages between the corresponding logical processes. The computation performed by each LP is a sequence of event computations, where each computation may modify state variables and/or schedule new events for itself or other LPs.

At first glance this paradigm would seem to be ideally suited for parallel/distributed execution; one can simply map different logical processes to different processors and let each LP execute forward, event by event, and exchange messages (that schedule events for other LPs) as needed. Unfortunately, there is a catch. Each logical process must process *all* of its events, both those generated locally and those generated by other LPs, in time stamp order. Failure to process the events in time stamp order could cause the computation for one event to affect another event in its past, clearly an unacceptable situation. While we saw in Chapter 2 that time stamp ordered event processing was easily accomplished on a sequential computer by using a centralized list of pending events, this is not so easily accomplished when execution is distributed over more than one processor. Errors resulting from out-of-order event processing are referred to as *causality errors*, and the general problem of ensuring that events are processed in a time stamp order is referred to as the *synchronization problem*.

This chapter describes one major class of algorithms for addressing the synchronization problem, namely conservative synchronization protocols where each LP strictly avoids processing events out of time stamp order. The two chapters that follow describe an alternative approach called optimistic synchronization where errors are detected during the execution, and some mechanism is used to recover from them.

3.1 SYNCHRONIZATION PROBLEM

Consider a simulation program composed of a collection of logical processes exchanging time-stamped messages. Consider the execution of this program on a *sequential* computer. The sequential execution ensures that all events across all of the logical processes are processed in time stamp order. When the simulation is distributed over multiple processors, a mechanism is required for the concurrent execution to produce exactly the same results as the sequential execution. The goal of the synchronization algorithm is to ensure that this is the case. It is important to realize that the synchronization algorithm does not need to actually guarantee that events in different processors are processed in time stamp order but only that the end result is the same as if this had been the case.

Consider parallelization of a simulation program that is based on the logical process paradigm discussed above. The greatest opportunity for parallelism arises from processing events from different LPs concurrently on different processors. However, a direct mapping of this paradigm onto (say) a shared-memory multi-processor quickly runs into difficulty. Consider the air traffic example discussed in the previous chapter with three LPs that model LAX, ORD, and JFK. Consider the concurrent execution of two arrival events in this example. Specifically, E_{10} at the LP for ORD has a time stamp of 10, and E_{20} at LAX with time stamps 20. If E_{10} affects E_{20} (for example, E_{10} might write into a state variable that is read by E_{20}), then E_{10} must be executed before E_{20}.

To avoid scenarios such as this, the restriction is made that there *cannot be any state variables that are shared between logical processes*. The state of the entire simulator must be partitioned into state vectors, with one state vector per LP. Each logical process contains a portion of the state corresponding to the physical process it models, as well as a local clock that denotes how far the process has progressed in simulation time.

Although the exclusion of shared state in the logical process paradigm avoids many types of causality errors, it does not prevent others. Again, consider two arrival events, E_{10} at logical process LP_{ORD} with time stamp 10, and E_{20} at LP_{LAX} with time stamp 20 (see Fig 3.1). If E_{10} schedules a new event E_{15} for LP_{LAX} that contains time stamp 15, then E_{15} could affect E_{20}, necessitating sequential execution of all three events. For example, E_{15} might denote the arrival of an aircraft at LAX, delaying the landing of the flight arriving at time 20.

We impose the following *local causality constraint* on each logical process to avoid errors such as this:

Local Causality Constraint A discrete-event simulation, consisting of logical processes (LPs) that interact exclusively by exchanging time stamped messages obeys the local causality constraint if and only if each LP processes events in nondecreasing time stamp order.

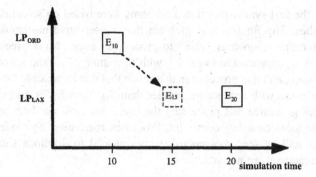

Figure 3.1 Event E_{10} affects E_{20} by sheduling a third event E_{15} which modifies a state variable used by E_{20}. This necessitates sequential execution of all three events.

It is clear that if one violates the local causality constraint, causality errors may occur. However, one could ask the opposite question. If each LP in the parallel simulation adheres to the local causality constraint, is this sufficient to guarantee that the simulation is "correct"? It turns out that the answer to this question is yes, as stated in the following observation:

Observation If each LP adheres to the local causality constraint, then the parallel/distributed execution will yield exactly the same results as a sequential execution of the same simulation program provided that events containing the same time stamp are processed in the same order in both the sequential and parallel execution. Events containing the same time stamp are referred to as *simultaneous events*.

Note that this observation does not guarantee that the simulation produces useful or even meaningful results. Any simulation model must be validated before its results can be trusted. From the standpoint of synchronization, "correctness" only goes so far as to say that the parallel execution will produce identical results as a sequential execution of the same program. Also it should be pointed out that adherence to this constraint is sufficient, but not always necessary, to guarantee that no causality errors occur. It may not be necessary because two events within a single LP may be independent of each other, in which case processing them out of time stamp sequence is acceptable.

Operationally one must decide whether or not E_{10} can be executed concurrently with E_{20}. But how does the simulator determine whether or not E_{10} affects E_{20} without actually performing the simulation for E_{10}? This is the fundamental dilemma that must be addressed. The scenario in which E_{10} affects E_{20} can be a complex sequence of events, and it is critically dependent on event time stamps.

Assume that the simulation consists of N logical processes, $LP_0, \ldots, LP_{N-1}$. $Clock_i$ refers to the current simulation time of LP_i: when an event is processed, the process's clock is automatically advanced to the time stamp of that event. If LP_i sends a message to LP_j during the simulation, a *link* is said to exist from LP_i to LP_j.

Historically the first synchronization algorithms were based on so-called conservative approaches. The fundamental problem that conservative mechanisms must solve is to determine when it is "safe" to process an event. More precisely, if a process contains an unprocessed event E_{10} with time stamp T_{10} (and no other with smaller time stamp), and that process can determine that it is impossible for it to later receive another event with time stamp smaller than T_{10}, then E_{10} is said to be *safe* because one can guarantee that processing the event now will not later result in a violation of the local causality constraint. Processes containing no "safe" events must block. As will be seen momentarily, this can lead to deadlock situations if appropriate precautions are not taken.

3.2 DEADLOCK AVOIDANCE USING NULL MESSAGES

Let us assume that one *statically* specifies the links that indicate which logical processes may communicate with which other logical processes. Further assume that (1) the sequence of time stamps on messages sent over a link is nondecreasing, (2) the communications facility guarantees that messages are received in the same order that they were sent (software to re-order messages is necessary if the network does not guarantee this property), and that (3) communications are reliable (i.e., every message that is sent is eventually received). This implies that the stream of messages arriving on a given link will have nondecreasing time stamp values. It also guarantees that the time stamp of the last message received on an incoming link is a lower bound on the time stamp of any subsequent message that will later be received on that link.

Messages arriving on each incoming link can be stored in a first-in–first-out (FIFO) queue, which is also time stamp order because of the above restrictions. Here, we ignore "local" events that are scheduled by an LP for itself. In practice, processing of these events must be interleaved with the processing of messages from other LPs so that all events are processed in time stamp order, however, this is easy to accomplish.[6] Each link has a clock associated with it that is equal to the time stamp of the message at the front of that link's queue if the queue contains a message, or the time stamp of the last received message if the queue is empty. For example, a snapshot of the queues for the JFK logical process in our airport example is shown in Figure 3.2. This logical process is guaranteed that any subsequent message sent to it from ORD has a time stamp of at least 5 and that any subsequent message from LAX has a time stamp of at least 9.

A program for executing incoming messages in time stamp order is shown in Figure 3.3. Because messages in each FIFO queue are sorted by time stamp, the LP can guarantee adherence to the local causality constraint by repeatedly processing the message containing the smallest time stamp, *so long as each queue contains at least one message*. If one of the FIFO queues becomes empty, the LP must wait until

---

[6] Local events could be placed in a separate FIFO queue that is similar to the others except the LP should not block if this queue becomes empty.

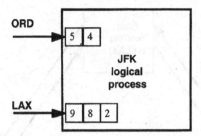

Figure 3.2   Snapshot of the logical process modeling JFK.

a new message is added to this queue because a message could later arrive that contains a time stamp as small as the message it just removed and processed from that queue. The LP could process messages in other queues containing the same time stamp as the one it just processed; however, it cannot process any messages containing a larger time stamp. In this way the protocol shown in Figure 3.3 guarantees that each process will only process events in nondecreasing time stamp order, thereby ensuring adherence to the local causality constraint.

For example, consider the air traffic simulation described earlier. As shown in Figure 3.2, each airport LP will have one queue to hold incoming messages from each of the other airports that are simulated. Again, assume that there are only three airports: LAX, ORD, and JFK. Consider the queues in the JFK process. The queue-holding messages from ORD contains messages with time stamps 4 and 5, and the queue for LAX has messages with time stamp 2, 8, and 9. The JFK process will now process arrival messages in the following order: 2 (LAX), 4 (ORD), and 5 (ORD). Assuming that no new messages have been received, the JFK simulator will block at this point, even though there are unprocessed messages with time stamps 8 and 9 from LAX. The LP must block because of the possibility that a new message will later arrive from ORD with time stamp less than 8. As mentioned earlier, we can only guarantee the next message has a time stamp of at least 5.

A cycle of empty queues could develop such as that shown in Figure 3.4 where each process in that cycle must block. The simulation is now deadlocked. In Figure 3.4 the JFK LP is waiting to receive a message from ORD, ORD is waiting for LAX, and LAX is waiting for JFK. Because no logical process can safely process any event, the simulation is frozen in this state, unable to advance forward, even though

```
while (simulation is not over)

    wait until each FIFO contains at least one message

    remove smallest time stamped message M from its FIFO

    clock := time stamp of M

    process M
```

Figure 3.3   Initial version of central event processing loop for a logical process.

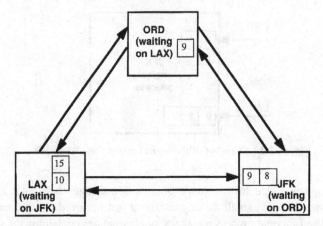

Figure 3.4   Deadlock situation. Each process is waiting on the incoming link containing the smallest link clock value because the corresponding queue is empty. All three processes are blocked, even though there are event messages in other queues that are wating to be processed.

there are several events that have not yet been processed. In general, if there are relatively few unprocessed event messages compared to the number of links in the network, or if the unprocessed events become clustered in one portion of the network, deadlock may occur frequently.

This deadlock situation can be broken as follows: Suppose that the minimum amount of time to fly from one airport to another is 3 units of simulation time, and JFK is at simulation time 5. This implies that any message JFK sends to LAX in the future must have a time stamp of at least 8 (i.e., its current time plus the minimum flight time to reach LAX). This information is not sufficient for LAX to safely process its next message (with time stamp 10). However, because LAX now knows its next event must have time stamp of at least 8, any message sent from LAX to ORD must have a time stamp of at least 11 (i.e., 8 plus the minimum flight time to reach ORD, or 3 units of simulation time). Because ORD is now guaranteed any future message that it will receive from LAX must have a time stamp of 11, it can safely process its message with time stamp 9, thus breaking the deadlock.

Some mechanism is required for an LP to indicate to other LPs a lower bound on the time stamp of messages it will send that LP in the future. *Null* messages can be used for this purpose. Null messages are used only for synchronization, and do not correspond to any activity in the physical system. In general, a null message with time stamp T_{null} that is sent from LP_A to LP_B is essentially a promise by LP_A that it will not send a message to LP_B carrying a time stamp smaller than T_{null}. How does a process determine the time stamps of the null messages it sends? The clock value of each *incoming* link provides a lower bound on the time stamp of the next unprocessed event that will be removed from that link's buffer. When coupled with knowledge of the simulation performed by the process (for example, the minimum time for an aircraft to fly from one airport to another), this incoming bound can be used to determine a lower bound on the time stamp of the next *outgoing* message on each output link. Whenever a process finishes processing an event, it sends a null message on each of its output ports indicating this bound; the receiver of the null message can then compute new bounds on its outgoing links, send this information on to its neighbors, and so on. It is typically up to the application programmer to determine the time stamps assigned to null messages.

This is the essential idea behind the "null message" or Chandy/Misra/Bryant algorithm (named after its inventors). One question that remains is when should null messages be sent? One approach is to send a null message on each outgoing link after processing each event. This guarantees that processes always have updated information on the time stamp of future messages that can be received from each of the other processes. Using this approach, the algorithm shown in Figure 3.3 can be revised to yield the algorithm shown in Figure 3.5. It should be observed that incoming null messages are processed exactly the same as other messages; that is, the LP's clock is updated, but no application code is executed to process the message.

An alternative approach to sending a null message after processing each event is a *demand-driven* approach. Whenever a process is about to become blocked because the incoming link with the smallest link clock value has no messages waiting to be processed, it requests the next message (null or otherwise) from the process on the sending side of the link. The process resumes execution when the response to this request is received. This approach helps to reduce the amount of null message traffic, though a longer delay may be required to receive null messages because two message transmissions are required.

As mentioned earlier, the air traffic example relied on the fact that the minimum amount of time for an aircraft to fly from one airport to another was 3 units of time in order to determine the time stamp of null messages. More generally, this algorithm relies on a quantity called *lookahead*, defined below.

Lookahead If a logical process at simulation time T can only schedule new events with time stamp of *at least* $T + L$, then L is referred to as the lookahead for the logical process.

```
while (simulation is not over)

        wait until each FIFO contains at least one message

        remove smallest time stamped message M from its FIFO

        clock := time stamp of M

        process M

        send null message to neighboring LPs with time stamp

                equal to lower bound on time stamp of future

                messages (clock plus lookahead)
```
Figure 3.5 Chandy/Misra/Bryant null message algorithm.

In general, the lookahead for a logical process may change during the execution of the simulation. Here, we define lookahead in terms of a single logical process. This concept can easily be extended to define lookahead for all messages sent from one LP to another. As will be discussed later, lookahead depends on the semantics of the simulation model.

Returning to the null message algorithm, the time stamp of null messages can be set to the current time of the LP plus its lookahead. Continuing the air traffic example, the lookahead of each LP is 3. When the JFK LP completes processing its event at time 5, it sends a null message to both LAX and ORD with time stamp 8. LAX will then process this null message, advance to simulation time 8, and send a null message to ORD (and JFK) with time stamp 11. ORD can now process the time stamp 9 (non-null) message.

The above example illustrates a very important point: The performance of the null message algorithm depends critically on the lookahead value. Suppose that the lookahead were 0.5 instead of 3. Then the following sequence of null messages would be sent: JFK to LAX (time stamp 5.5), LAX to ORD (time stamp 6.0), ORD to JFK (time stamp 6.5), JFK to LAX (time stamp 7.0), LAX to ORD (time stamp 7.5). Additional null messages would be generated because the LP must send one to *both* LPs with each time advance. Five null messages must be transmitted in order to process a single event! It is clear that smaller lookahead values would create even longer sequences of null messages before a non-null message can be processed.

Further suppose that the lookahead is zero; that is, an LP at time T could schedule a new event with time stamp T. The null message algorithm will fail in that case because an endless sequence of null messages will be sent, all containing a time stamp of 5, cycling from JFK to LAX to ORD, back to JFK, and so on. *Thus an important limitation of the null message algorithm is that there cannot be any cycle of logical processes with zero lookahead.* It can be shown, however, that the null message algorithm will avoid deadlock if no such cycle exists.

The restriction that there not be any zero lookahead cycles implies that certain types of simulations cannot be easily performed. One problematic situation is in simulations where LPs can request (query) other LPs for state variables. A query is usually implemented by the logical process requesting the state information LP_A sending a message to the process holding the desired state LP_B with time stamp equal to T, LP_A's current time (i.e., zero lookahead is used). When LP_B's receives the message, it will have advanced to time T, and it will send a reply containing the desired value with time stamp T (i.e., again with zero lookahead). This creates a zero lookahead cycle. A simple solution is to include a small time stamp increment with each message. However, while this avoids the zero lookahead cycle, as explained earlier, small lookahead often leads to very poor performance for the null message algorithm.

3.3   LOOKAHEAD AND THE SIMULATION MODEL

The notion of lookahead is fundamental to conservative synchronization mechanisms. Consider the logical process with the *smallest* clock value at some instant in the execution of a parallel simulation program. Let the current simulation time of this LP be T. This LP could generate events relevant to every other LP in the simulation with a time stamp of T. This implies that no LP can process any event with time stamp larger than T, or it may violate the local causality constraint. Similarly no LP can advance beyond simulation time T because it is then prone to receiving notification of an event in its past.

Lookahead is used to solve this problem. Let T_S be the current time of the LP with the *smallest* clock value in the entire simulation. If each LP has a lookahead of L, then this guarantees that any new message sent by an LP must have a time stamp of at least $T_S + L$. This in turn implies that all events with time stamp in the interval $[T_S, T_S + L]$ can be safely processed. L is referred to as the lookahead for the LP because it must be able to "look ahead" L time units into the future and schedule the events at least L time units prior to when they actually happen.

Lookahead is clearly very intimately related to details of the simulation model. Some examples of where lookahead may be derived are described below.

- *Limitations concerning how quickly physical processes can interact with each other.* In the air traffic example, the minimum amount of time for an aircraft to fly from one airport to another determined the minimum amount of simulation time that must elapse for one logical process to affect another. This minimum flight time was used to define a lookahead value.

- *Physical limitations concerning how quickly one LP can react to a new event.* Consider again the air traffic simulation. Suppose that the minimum amount of time an aircraft must remain on the ground to exchange passengers is one unit of simulation time. Then, if the smallest time stamp of any arrival event that will be received in the future is T, no new aircraft will depart until $T + 1$, and the minimum time stamp of any arrival event it will schedule for another process is $T + 1 + \text{minimum\_transit\_time}$. Thus the minimum amount of time any aircraft remains on the ground further enhances that LP's lookahead.

- *Tolerance to temporal inaccuracies.* Suppose that an LP produces an event at time T, but errors of up to 1 unit in simulation time can be tolerated by the receiver while still producing sufficiently accurate results. Then the LP may schedule events 1 time unit into the future, providing a lookahead of this amount.

- *Non-preemptive behavior.* In the air traffic example, once an aircraft departed from one airport, nothing in the simulation model could prevent that aircraft from arriving at its destination airport at the assigned arrival time. If the model included other events that preempted this behavior, such as at midflight, JFK could divert an LAX-bound aircraft to ORD, and arrive at ORD only 0.5 time units after the "divert flight" event, then JFK's lookahead would be reduced to only 0.5. Thus the non-preemptive nature of the original air traffic simulation enhances its lookahead.

- *Precomputing simulation activities.* If the events produced by an LP over the next L units of time do not depend on external events but only on internal computations, these computations can be performed in advance, enhancing lookahead. For example, if the time for an aircraft to fly to another airport were drawn from a random number generator, the flight time could be selected in advance, and this value rather than the smallest number that could be selected from the generator can be used as the lookahead value.

Lookahead can change dynamically during the execution. However, lookahead cannot instantaneously be reduced. At any instant, a lookahead of L indicates to the simulation executive that the LP will not generate any new event with time stamp less than $T + L$, where T is the LP's current time. If the lookahead is reduced by K units of simulation time, the LP must first advance K units before this changed lookahead can take effect, so no events with time stamp less than $T + L$ are produced.

3.4 DEADLOCK DETECTION AND RECOVERY

As discussed earlier, the principal disadvantage of the Chandy/Misra/Bryant algorithm is that a large number of null messages can be generated, particularly if the lookahead is small. Recall that the approach used in this algorithm is to *avoid* deadlock situations. Another approach is to use the original algorithm shown in Figure 3.3 that is prone to deadlock but provide a mechanism to detect and recover from deadlock situations. This approach is described next.

3.4.1 Deadlock Detection

The simulation computation depicted in Figure 3.3 is one example of a *diffusing computation*. This means the distributed computation consists of a set of processes, and processes only perform computations upon receiving one or more messages. Once initiated, the process continues with its local computation, sending and receiving additional messages to other processes, until it again stops. Once a process has stopped, it cannot spontaneously begin new computations until it receives a new message. The computation can be viewed as spreading or diffusing across the processes much like a fire spreading through a forest.

A single controller process is introduced to the distributed simulation. The distributed simulation computation cycles through the following steps:

1. The computation is initially deadlocked.
2. The controller sends message(s) to one or more LPs informing them that certain events are safe to process, thereby breaking the deadlock. More will be said about this later.
3. The LP(s) process the event(s) that have been declared safe. This typically generates new messages that are sent to other LPs that (hopefully) cause them to process still more events, and generate additional messages to still other LPs. The spreading of the computation to previously blocked processes is

viewed as constructing a tree. Every process that is not blocked is in the tree. Whenever a message is sent to a process that is not in the tree, that process is added to the tree, and (logically) a link is established from the process sending the message to the process receiving the message. LPs that are in the tree are referred to as being *engaged*. Processes that are not in the tree are referred to as being *disengaged*.

4. Just as the tree expands when the diffusing computation spreads to new LPs, it also contracts when engaged LPs become blocked. Specifically, if an LP becomes blocked, *and that LP is a leaf node in the tree*, the LP removes itself from the tree and signals its parent (the LP that originally sent it the message that caused it to become engaged) that it is no longer in the tree. An LP becomes a leaf node in the tree when all of the LPs it added to the tree signal that they have removed themselves from the tree.

5. If the controller becomes a leaf node in the tree, then the computation is again deadlocked, completing the cycle.

A signaling protocol is used to implement the paradigm described above. Specifically, each LP adheres to the following rules:

- When an engaged process (a process already in the tree) receives a message, it immediately returns a signal to the sender to indicate the message did not cause the tree to expand.
- When a disengaged process receives a message, it becomes engaged; it does not return a signal to the sender until it becomes disengaged.
- Each LP maintains a count indicating the number of messages that it has sent without receiving a signal. When this count is zero, the LP is a leaf node in the tree. If the LP is blocked and its count becomes zero, it becomes disengaged, so it sends a signal to the process that originally caused it to become engaged.

An example depicting a scenario with four logical processes is shown in Figure 3.6. In (*a*) the computation is initially deadlocked and all four processes are disengaged. The controller sends a message to process 3 to break the deadlock. In (*b*) process 3 is now engaged (i.e., is in the tree) and the computation "diffuses" to the other three processes as process 3 sends a message to each of them. Figure 3.6(*c*) shows the engagement tree including all four processes. In (*d*) several independent actions occur. Process 2 sends a message to process 4; however, process 4 is already in the tree, so process 4 immediately returns a signal to process 2 (not shown). Processes 1 and 3 both become blocked because of an empty FIFO queue. At this point, process 1 is a leaf node in the tree, so it sends a signal to process 3, the process that originally caused 1 to become engaged. Process 3, however, is an interior (nonleaf) node of the tree, so it does not send any signal. The end result of these actions is process 1 becomes disengaged, as shown in Figure 3.6(*e*). In this figure, processes 2 and 4 also become idle and send signals to process 3, since they are leaf nodes of the tree. As shown in (*f*), both 2 and 4 become disengaged. Process 3 is

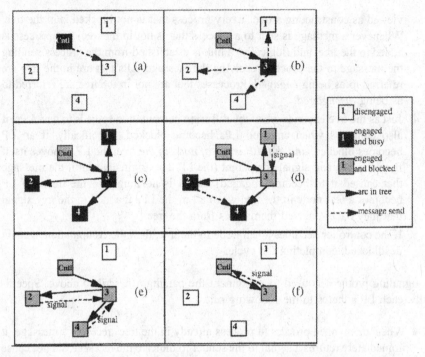

Figure 3.6   Example of deadlock detection algorithm. (*a*) Controller initiates process 3 after deadlock, (*b*) 3 is added to engagement tree, 3 sends messages to 1, 2, and 4 to spread computation, (*c*) engagement tree includes all processors, (*d*) 1 and 3 become idle, 2 sends a message to 4, but 4 is already in tree, (*e*) 2 and 4 become idle, (*f*) 3 becomes idle and the computation is deadlocked.

now a leaf node of the tree and is idle, so it sends a signal to the controller process, indicating that the entire computation is again deadlocked.

To implement this signaling protocol, each LP must be able to determine whether it is engaged or disengaged, and if it is engaged, whether or not it is a leaf node of the tree. Two variables are defined for this purpose:

- C is defined as the number of messages received from neighbors that have not yet been signaled.
- D is defined as the number of messages sent to other processors from which a signal has yet to be returned (the number of descendants in the tree).

The approach used in the signaling protocol is the following: An LP assumes that each message it sends causes the receiver to become engaged. The receiver returns a signal if either (1) it is already engaged or (2) it is becoming disengaged because it is a leaf node of the tree and it is blocked. An LP is engaged if C is greater than zero. If C is equal to 0, the process is disengaged, and D must also be zero. An LP is a leaf node of the tree if its C value is greater than zero (i.e., it is engaged) and its D value is zero.

Sending a message to another process causes D in the sender to be incremented by one. C in the receiver is also incremented by one when the message is received. When a process sends a signal to another process, C in the sender is decremented by 1, and D in the receiver is decremented by 1. It must always be the case that either C is greater than zero (the process is engaged and hasn't returned a signal for the message that caused it to become engaged), or D is equal to zero. If C is zero, then it must be the case that D is also zero, and the process is disengaged. When C and D in the controller are both zero, the simulation is deadlocked.

3.4.2 Deadlock Recovery

The deadlock can be broken by observing that the message(s) containing the smallest time stamp in the entire simulation is (are) always safe to process. This is the event that would be processed next in a sequential execution of the simulation program. Thus, to break the deadlock, the simulation executive need only identify the event containing the smallest time stamp and send a message to the LP(s) holding the event to indicate that the event can now be safely processed.

Locating the smallest time-stamped event is relatively straightforward because the computation is deadlocked, so no new events are being created while the smallest time stamped event is being located. The controller can broadcast a message to all of the LPs requesting the time stamp of the event within that processor containing the smallest time stamp. After receiving a message from each processor, the controller determines the smallest time-stamped event(s) in the entire simulation, and instructs the processors(s) that hold them to process the events(s). This approach assumes that there are no messages in transit in the network while the deadlock is being broken. Depending on details of the communication subsystem, which in turn depends on the hardware architecture, this may or may not be the case. We will return to this subject later.

The broadcast could be performed by having the controller directly send a message to every other processor in the system, or by constructing a spanning tree, that is, a tree with processors as the tree nodes and the controller at the root that includes all processors in the system as shown in Figure 3.7. The links of the tree can be defined arbitrarily; they need not correspond to links between logical processes. The controller initiates the broadcast by sending a "request minimum time stamp" message to each descendent processor in the tree. Upon receiving this message, each processor forwards the message to each of its descendants in the tree. Processors that are leaf nodes in the tree do not forward the request to other processors. Instead, each leaf node processor returns a message to its parent in the tree indicating the time stamp of the smallest time-stamped event in that processor. Each processor that is not a leaf node of the tree waits until it has received such a "reply" message from each descendant in the tree, and computes the minimum among (1) the time stamp of local events within that processor and (2) the time stamp value in each of the reply messages it receives from descendants in the tree. Thus each processor computes the

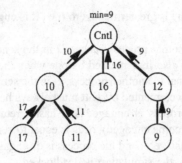

Figure 3.7 Example of deadlock recovery mechanism. Each node of tree represents a processor, and the number in each node indicates the time stamp of the smallest time-stamped even in that processor. Arrows indicate communications in the second round to compute the global minimum.

minimum among all processors in the subtree rooted by that processor. This minimum time stamp value is reported by that processor to its parent in the tree in its reply message, as shown in Figure 3.7. In this way the global minimum computation propagates up the tree, and the controller computes the global minimum. The controller can then broadcast this global minimum back down the spanning tree, indicating that all processors with an event(s) with time stamp equal to this global minimum can safely process that event(s). Thus the tree-based algorithm uses three rounds of messages to break the deadlock: (1) messages initiating the global minimum computation flowing down the tree, (2) reply messages to compute the global minimum flowing up the tree, and (3) restart messages to instruct processors which events are safe to process again flowing down the tree.

One drawback of the algorithm described above is that it is overly conservative in that it only specifies the smallest time stamped event(s) as being safe to process. Using lookahead information, a larger set of safe events can usually be obtained. In general, any algorithm that is able to define a set of safe events among a collection of blocked logical processes can be used. One such algorithm based on a concept called "distance between processes" is described later in this chapter.

The deadlock detection and recovery approach described above also relies on the *entire* computation becoming deadlock before it attempts to break the deadlock. An alternative approach is to detect deadlock among a subset of logical processes, and then break these "local deadlocks" as they occur. Detecting partial deadlocks is more complex than detecting deadlocks of the entire system, however, and the extra complexity required to perform this computation may not result in a significant performance improvement. Although some parallel simulation systems have been proposed using this approach, few have been realized, so this subject will not be pursued further.

Unlike the null message algorithm, the deadlock detection and recovery algorithm described above allows the lookahead of the simulation application to be zero. Cycles of zero lookahead LPs are permitted with this algorithm. If lookahead is available, this information can be used to expand the set of safe events when the deadlock is broken. For example, if the lookahead of each LP is L and the LP furthest behind in the execution has a clock value of T, then all events in the interval $[T, T + L]$ are safe and can be processed.

An important observation in the deadlock detection and recovery algorithm is that it utilizes the time stamp of the next unprocessed event. This information was not used in the null message algorithm. Consider a set of logical processes, each with lookahead of 1, all blocked at simulation time 10. Suppose that the time stamp of the next unprocessed event is 100. Unless this information is used, there is no means to immediately advance all of the LPs to time 100. Instead, the LPs are doomed to advance only in increments of the lookahead value until they reach 100.

3.5 SYNCHRONOUS EXECUTION

In the deadlock detection and recovery algorithm the processors repeatedly cycle through "phases" of (1) one or more processors processing simulation events and (2) deadlock resolution. Several conservative synchronization algorithms utilize this approach of cycling between phases, but they explicitly control when the entire computation stops rather than relying on the system becoming deadlocked. To control the latter, these algorithms rely on a mechanisms called *barrier synchronizations*.

A barrier is a general parallel programming construct that defines a point in (wallclock) time when all of the processors participating in the computation have stopped. As shown in Figure 3.8, when a processor executes the barrier primitive, it blocks, and remains blocked until all of the processors have executed the barrier primitive. The barrier operation is completed when all of the processors have executed the barrier primitive; each processor is then allowed to resume execution, starting at the statement immediately following the barrier.

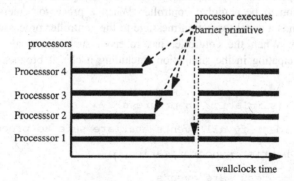

Figure 3.8 Sample execution of processors entering a barrier. The solid horizontal line indicates that the processor is executing; the white space indicates that the processor is blocked, waiting for the barrier to complete.

The barrier synchronization is a useful primitive because it defines a point in wallclock time where all the processors are at a known point in their execution. One typical use is to divide the execution of a parallel program into a sequence of steps, where each step involves a parallel computation that must be completed before execution moves on to the next step so that successive steps do not interfere with each other. Barriers will be used for this purpose here. Specifically, the parallel simulation program executing on each processor can be structured as shown in Figure 3.9.

The barriers ensure that no events are being processed, and thus no new events are being created, while the simulation executive is trying to determine which events are safe to process.

In Figure 3.9 "processing safe events" is identical to what was done before: Each processor executes simulation application code to model the occurrence of each event. The principal question concerns the method for determining which events are safe to process. As discussed earlier in the context of deadlock recovery, the smallest time stamped event in the entire simulation is clearly safe to process. Lookahead is used to identify other events that are safe to process.

We next describe techniques for implementing the barrier primitive, particularly on distributed-memory computers. Two approaches for determining the set of safe events are then discussed.

3.5.1   Centralized Barriers

There are two important issues that must be addressed in implementing the barrier primitive. The first concerns controlling the blocking of processors entering the barrier, and releasing the processors after the barrier has been achieved. The second concerns ensuring that there are no messages lingering in the network, referred to as *transient messages*, when the processors are released from the barrier. Three approaches are described next.

A simple approach to implement the barrier is to designate one of the processors in the simulation to be a global controller. When a processor enters the barrier primitive, it sends a synchronization message to the controller processor, and waits for a response. When the controller has received such a message from every processor participating in the simulation (including itself), it broadcasts a *release*

```
while (simulation in progress)

        identify all events that are safe to process

        barrier synchronization

        process safe events

        barrier synchronization
```

Figure 3.9   Parallel simulation program using barrier synchronizations.

message indicating the global synchronization point has been reached. Upon receiving the release message, each processor continues execution starting at the statement immediately following the barrier.

In a shared-memory multiprocessor, the equivalent to the central controller approach is to utilize global synchronization variables. For example, two counters can be maintained. A variable called Blocked indicates the number of processors that have reached the barrier point. The second counter called Released indicates the number of processors that have (1) reached the barrier point, (2) detected that all of the processors have reached the barrier point, and (3) proceeded beyond the barrier. Both counters are initialized to zero. Assume that there are N processors in the system. The condition Blocked equal to N (for any value of Released) indicates that all processors have reached the barrier point, and it is used to signal that processors can proceed beyond the barrier. Before a processor can initiate a barrier operation, it must wait until Released is equal to 0. This is necessary to avoid starting a new barrier operation before all processors have been released from the previous one. Once Released is equal to 0, the processor enters the barrier by incrementing Blocked. This must be done as an atomic operation to avoid race conditions. The processor then waits until Blocked becomes N. When the last processor to reach the barrier point increments Blocked to N, the processors can be released from the barrier. At this instant, Released will still be equal to zero. Each processor that is released from the barrier increments Released (again as an atomic operation) and resumes execution beyond the barrier. The last processor to be released from the barrier detects that it is setting Released to become equal to N, so it resets both variables to zero. Setting Released equal to 0 "arms" the barrier for the next operation.

The principal drawback with the centralized approach is that it does not scale to large numbers of processors, since the central controller, or the shared variables in a shared-memory machine, become a bottleneck. The controller must perform $N - 1$ message sends and receives on each barrier operation.

3.5.2 Tree Barrier

The bottleneck problem is easily solved by organizing the processors as a balanced tree with each node of the tree representing a different processor (see Fig. 3.10 for the case of fourteen processors). When a leaf processor reaches the barrier point, it sends a message to its parent processor. Each interior node of the tree waits until it receives a synchronization message from each of its children. When it has received such a message from each child, and has itself reached the barrier point, it sends a message to its parent. The barrier is achieved when the root of the tree is at the barrier point and has received a synchronization message from each child node. Once the root detects the achieved barrier, it broadcasts a release message to all of the other processors. This can be done by propagating the release messages down the tree, reversing the flow of messages used to detect the achievement of the barrier. This tree-based barrier mechanism requires approximately time $2 \log_k N$ where k is the degree of the tree, and $2(N - 1)$ messages for N processors; each processor

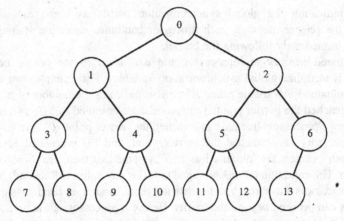

Figure 3.10   Processors organized into a tree to implement the barrier primitive.

except the root sends one message up the tree to its parent and receives one broadcast message coming down the tree. Although Figure 3.10 shows a binary tree, in general, any node degree can be used. In fact the centralized approach described earlier is an $N-1$ ary tree, with the controller at the root node, and the remaining $N-1$ nodes the children of the controller.

3.5.3 Butterfly Barrier

Another approach that eliminates the broadcast to notify the processors that a global synchronization has been achieved is the *butterfly barrier*. Assume that an N-processor barrier is performed, and the processors are numbered $0, 1, 2, \ldots, N-1$. To simplify the discussion, assume that N is a power of 2; it is straightforward to extend the approach to arbitrary N. The communication pattern among processors for this barrier mechanism for the case of eight processors is shown in Figure 3.11(*a*). Each processor executes a sequence of $\log N$ *pairwise* barriers with a different processor at each step. A pairwise barrier between processors i and j is accomplished by simply having i (or j) send a message to j (i) when it has reached the barrier point, and then wait for a message from j (i) indicating that processor has also reached the barrier point. In the first step, processors whose binary addresses differ only in the least significant bit perform a pairwise barrier; for example, processors 3 (01<u>1</u>) and 2 (01<u>0</u>) perform a pairwise barrier. In the second step, processors whose addresses differ only in the second least significant bit; for example, processor 3 (0<u>1</u>1) and 1 (0<u>0</u>1) synchronize. In general, in step k processor i synchronizes with the processor whose address differs in only the kth bit (where bits are numbered $1, 2, \ldots, \log N$ from least significant to most significant). These pairwise synchronizations continue for $\log N$ steps until all of the address bits have been scanned. This communication pattern is referred to as a butterfly. Each processor is released from the barrier once it has completed the $\log N$ pairwise barriers.

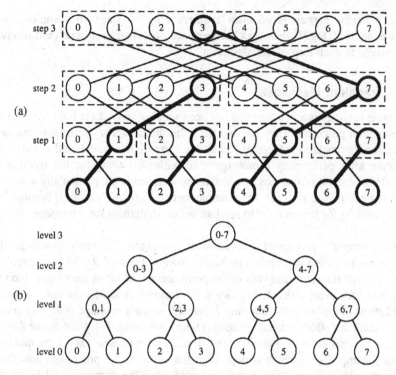

Figure 3.11   Eight-processor Butterfly barrier. (*a*) Communications pattern, and illustration of barrier from the perspective of processor 3; (*b*) tree abstraction of barrier mechanism.

To see why this algorithm works, consider the operation of the barrier mechanism from the perspective of a particular processor. The highlighted nodes and arcs in Figure 3.11(*a*) illustrate the barrier from the perspective of processor 3. After step 1 has completed, processor 3 knows that processor 2 (as well as itself) has reached the barrier point. This is illustrated by the dashed box around processors 2 and 3 in step 1 of Figure 3.11(*a*). After step 2, processor 3 receives a message from processor 1, so it knows processor 1 has also reached the barrier. However, processor 1 must have synchronized with processor 0 in step 1 before it could have synchronized with processor 3 in step 2, so processor 3 can conclude 0, 1, 2, and 3 have all reached the barrier point. This is represented by the dashed box around these four processors in step 2. Continuing this analysis, after step 3 is completed, processor 3 infers from receiving a synchronization message from processor 7 that processors 4, 5, 6, and 7 have also reached the barrier, so it can safely conclude that all eight processors have reached the barrier point. In effect, as shown in Figure 3.11(*b*), a tree is constructed in bottom-up fashion with processors at the leaves. Intermediate nodes of the tree indicate the set of processors that are known to have reached the barrier when that step of the algorithm has been completed.

The butterfly barrier mechanism requires $\lceil \log N \rceil$ steps to complete, and transmission of $N \lceil \log N \rceil$ messages because each processor must send (and receive) one message in each step of the algorithm.[7]

3.5.4 Transient Messages

A *transient message* is a message that has been sent but has not yet been received by the destination processor. They are, in effect, "in the network." Transient messages are an issue if asynchronous message sends are allowed; that is, the sender is allowed to execute after performing a message send without waiting for the receiver to acknowledge receipt of the message. Asynchronous sends are particularly useful in distributed computing systems (for example, networks of workstations) because the delay in waiting for the receiver to send an acknowledgment for a message may be large.

Unless properly accounted for, transient messages can cause errors in the synchronous execution mechanism protocol shown in Figure 3.9. The basic problem is that transient messages may not be properly accounted for in the computation to determine which events are safe to process. For example, consider the case where all of the LPs advance to simulation time T, one LP sends a message with time stamp $T + 1$, and all the others generate messages with time stamp $T + 10$. Assume that all of these messages are transmitted to their destination processor except the message with time stamp $T + 1$, which is delayed in the network. All processors now enter the barrier primitive, are subsequently released from the primitive, and begin the computation to determine the events that are safe to process. Because the time stamp $T + 1$ message has not been received, it is not taken into account in this computation. This would result in the processors erroneously believing the time stamp $T + 10$ events are all safe to process, since there are none with a smaller time stamp. It may be noted that this problem does not exist if synchronous message sends are used, since the processor sending the time stamp $T + 1$ message would block until this message is received at its destination. This prevents each processor from entering the barrier until all messages it has sent have been received.

This problem can be solved without giving up asynchronous message sends by using message counters. Each processor maintains two local counters indicating (1) the number of messages it has sent, and (2) the number of messages it has received.[8] There are no transient messages in the system when (1) all of the processors have reached the barrier point and thus are not producing new messages, and (2) the sum of all of the send counters across all of the processors is equal to the sum of the receive counters across all of the processors.

Tree Barriers The mechanism for ensuring that the total of the send and receive counters match can be combined with the barrier primitive. Consider the tree barrier. When a leaf processor sends a message up the tree to indicate that it has reached the

[7] $\lceil X \rceil$ (pronounced ceiling of X) denotes the smallest integer greater than or equal to X.

[8] A simple optimization to this approach is to maintain one variable indicating the difference between these two quantities.

barrier point, it also transmits its send and receive counters. Each processor at an interior node of the tree sums the counters it receives from the child processors in the tree with its own counters, and sends the two sums to its parent in the tree. Using this approach, the root will hold the total sum of the send and receive counters across all of the processors. These counters may not match at the root, however, because a processor may not have received one or more transient messages when it added the values of its local counters into the sum. To address this problem, if any processor receives a message after it has sent its counters to its parent in the tree, it sends a separate message to the root denoting this fact, causing the total count of the number of received messages to increase by one. When the root detects that the total send and receive counters match, it broadcasts a message indicating that the barrier has been reached and that there are no more transient messages in the system.

Butterfly Barriers   A more complex mechanism is required when the butterfly barrier is used. The butterfly barrier can be viewed as a sequence of barriers, each covering a successively larger set of processors. For example, as shown in Figure 3.11(b), from processor 3's perspective the barrier is achieve by first performing a barrier among processors $(2, 3)$, next among processors $(0, 1, 2, 3)$, and then among $(0, 1, 2, \dots, 7)$. The path up the tree dictates the sets of processors that must synchronize in order to achieve global synchronization. Define $G_k(i)$ as the group of synchronizing processors at level k of the tree that includes processor i, or equivalently, the kth level node of the tree that includes leaf node i as a descendent. For example, $G_1(3) = (2, 3)$, $G_2(3) = (0, 1, 2, 3)$, and $G_3(3) = (0, 1, 2, \dots, 7)$. To accomplish synchronization at level k of the tree, processor i communicates with the processor with the same binary address as i except in bit position k to accomplish synchronization with half of the processors in $G_k(i)$. Define this set of "sibling" processors with which processor i is attempting to achieve synchronization in step k as $S_k(i)$. For example, $S_1(3) = (2)$, $S_2(3) = (0, 1)$, and $S_3(3) = (4, 5, 6, 7)$. This notation is illustrated in Figure 3.12 (each shaded box represents a processor). In

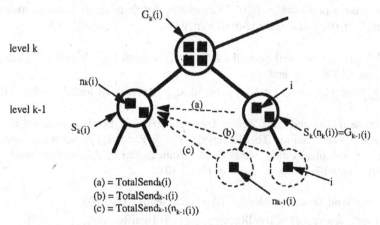

(a) = TotalSend$_k$(i)
(b) = TotalSend$_{k-1}$(i)
(c) = TotalSend$_{k-1}$(n$_{k-1}$(i))

Figure 3.12   Notation for detecting transient messages in the butterfly barrier.

general, $S_k(i)$ is the sibling node to $G_{k-1}(i)$, where level 0 is the level containing the leaf nodes. Let $n_k(i)$ be the processor with the same binary address as i, except for bit position k ($k = 1, 2, \ldots$). $n_k(i)$ is referred to as the neighbor to processor i during step k of the algorithm. Thus, in step k of the algorithm (for example, step 2), processor i (for example, processor 3) must wait for a message from $n_k(i)$ ($n_2(3)$ is processor 1; see Fig. 3.11(b)) in order to synchronize with $S_k(i)$ ($S_2(3) = (0, 1)$), thereby ensuring synchronization among the processors in $G_k(i)$ ($G_2(3) = (0, 1, 2, 3)$). Observe that $G_{k-1}(i) = S_k(n_k(i))$ and that $G_k(i) = S_k(i) \cup S_k(n_k(i))$. Finally it can be seen that during step k of the barrier processor i is attempting to achieve synchronization among processors in sibling nodes of the tree; that is, $S_k(i)$ (which includes $n_k(i)$) and $S_k(n_k(i))$ (which includes i).

One can extend the butterfly barrier algorithm to accommodate transient messages by preventing a processor from advancing to the next step if there are any transient messages among the set of processors trying to synchronize in the current step. Specifically, a processor i is not allowed to advance beyond step k of the barrier algorithm unless

1. the processors in $G_k(i)$ have all reached the barrier point (just as before), and
2. there are no messages in transit between any two processors l and m where l, $m \in G_k(i)$.

When processor i reaches step k, there cannot be any transient messages among processors within $G_{k-1}(i)$ (i.e., $S_k(n_k(i))$; see Fig. 3.12) because processor i could not have completed step $k - 1$ if there were any. Similarly there cannot be any transient messages within $S_k(i)$ when $n_k(i)$ completes step $k - 1$. Therefore, to ensure that there are no transient messages among processors in $G_k(i)$, each processor $i \in G_k(i)$, must ensure that there are no transient messages traveling from $S_k(n_k(i))$ to $S_k(i)$ and vice versa. This is accomplished by maintaining four sets of counters. First, $\text{Send}_k(i)$ ($k = 1, 2, \ldots, \log(N)$) denotes the number of messages processor i has sent to a processor in $S_k(i)$, and $\text{Receive}_k(i)$ denotes the number of messages processor i has received from a processor in $S_k(i)$. To guarantee that there are no transient messages between $S_k(n_k(i))$ and $S_k(i)$, one must verify that

1. $\sum \text{Send}_k(i)$ summed over all $i \in S_k(n_k(i))$ is equal to $\sum \text{Receive}_k(j)$ summed over all $j \in S_k(i)$, and
2. $\sum \text{Send}_k(j)$ for all $j \in S_k(i)$ is equal to $\sum \text{Receive}_k(i)$ for all $i \in S_k(n_k(i))$.

To compute these conditions, define $\text{TotalSend}_k(i)$ as $\sum \text{Send}_k(i)$ summed over all $i \in S_k(n_k(i))$, and define $\text{TotalReceive}_k(j) = \sum \text{Receive}_k(j)$ summed over all $j \in S_k(i)$. A key observation is that these quantities can be defined recursively (see the dashed arcs labeled a, b, and c in Fig. 3.12):

1. $\text{TotalSend}_k(i) = \text{TotalSend}_{k-1}(i) + \text{TotalSend}_{k-1}(n_{k-1}(i))$,
2. $\text{TotalReceive}_k(j) + \text{TotalReceive}_{k-1}(j) + \text{TotalReceive}_{k-1}(n_{k-1}(j))$,

3. $TotalSend_1(i) = Send_1(i)$, and
4. $TotalReceive_1(i) = Receive_1(i)$.

Operationally each processor maintains the log N element Send and Receive arrays as it sends and receives simulation messages. Sending and receiving synchronization messages are not included in these counters. Consider the operation of processor 3 in executing the barrier algorithm. When it begins the barrier, it sends its arrays $Send_k(3)$ and $Receive_k(3)$ (for all k) which are equivalent to $TotalSend_k(3)$ and $TotalReceive_k(3)$, respectively, to its neighbor, processor 2, and waits to receive arrays $TotalSend_k(2)$ and $TotalReceive_k(2)$ from processor 2 if they haven't already been received. Processor 3 then compares the first elements of the arrays. If $TotalSend_1(3)$ is equal to $TotalReceive_1(2)$, and $TotalReceive_1(3)$ is equal to $TotalSend_1(2)$, then there are no messages in transit between processors 2 and 3, so each processor can advance to the next step in the algorithm. In particular, processor 3 adds $TotalSend_k(2)$ (and $TotalReceive_k(2)$) to its local array $TotalSend_k(3)$ (and $TotalReceive_k(3)$). At this point, the TotalSend and TotalReceive arrays in processors 2 and 3 are identical. Processor 3 then sends its new TotalSend and TotalReceive arrays to processor 1, its neighbor in step 2 of the algorithm. The above steps are repeated, except now, the second elements of each array ($TotalSend_2(3)$ and $TotalReceive_2(1)$, and $TotalReceive_2(3)$ and $TotalSend_2(1)$) are used to determine if transient messages remain between the sets $(0, 1)$ and $(2, 3)$. This process repeats for log N steps. After successfully completing the last step, each processor can advance beyond the barrier point, with the knowledge that all processors have reached the barrier point and no transient messages remain.

If in step p of the algorithm $TotalSend_p(i)$ and $TotalReceive_p(n_p(i))$ (or $TotalReceive_p(i)$ and $TotalSend_p(n_p(i))$) do *not* match, then there is at least one message in transit from processor i to $n_p(i)$ (or processor $n_p(i)$ to i). In this case, the barrier operation has failed, and the processor must wait for additional messages before it can proceed. Specifically, if a processor receives a new simulation message, then this indicates that the initial TotalReceive vector it sent in the first step of the algorithm was incorrect, so the processor aborts the barrier operation and starts over from the beginning (step 1). If a processor receives new TotalSend and TotalReceive arrays signaling that it was previously passed incorrect information in step k, then it must return to step k and repeat the barrier from step k onward. This requires a processor to maintain a copy of its TotalSend and TotalReceive vectors after each step, however. An alternative approach is to simply abort the barrier computation and restart it from the beginning. In either case, the barrier is, in effect, rolled back to an earlier point in time and restarted. Because of the use of rollback, this barrier mechanism is sometime called an *optimistic barrier*. It should be noted, however, that the simulation program is not rolled back, only the barrier computation itself.

These mechanisms enable one to define a barrier where it is guaranteed that there are no transient messages in the system when the processors are released from the barrier. We next describe algorithms for determining the set of events that are safe to process. We will return to the transient message problem again in the next chapter when we discuss algorithms for computing a quantity called Global Virtual Time in systems using optimistic synchronization.

3.5.5 A Simple Synchronous Protocol

A simple approach using lookahead to determine safe events can be derived by parallelizing the sequential event processing loop. Consider a sequential simulation that has advanced to simulation time T, which is the time of the next unprocessed event in the event list. If the constraint is made that an event must be scheduled at least L units of simulation time into the future, then it can be guaranteed that all new events that are later scheduled in the simulation will have a time stamp greater than or equal to $T + L$, so any event with time stamp less than $T + L$ can be safely processed.

In the parallel simulation, assume, as before, that the simulation is composed of some number of logical processes. Each logical process LP_i defines a lookahead value L_i. Let T_i be the smallest time stamp of any unprocessed event in LP_i. Let $T_M + L_M$ be the minimum of $T_i + L_i$ over all of the LPs in the simulation. This is the minimum time stamp of any new event that will be later generated in the execution. Then, as illustrated in Figure 3.13, all events with time stamp less than or equal to $T_M + L_M$ (those in the shaded rectangle in the figure) are safe to process because any new event must have a time stamp larger than $T_M + L_M$ (beyond the shaded rectangle).

The program executed by each processor using this protocol is shown in Figure 3.14. A computation is required to compute a global minimum across the simulation. This can be implemented by extending any of the barrier algorithms described earlier to compute a minimum value among the processors entering the barrier. For example, using the tree barrier algorithm, each processor in the tree would (1) compute the minimum among all child processors in the tree if there are any, and its own local minimum, and (2) report the minimum of these values to its parent in the tree. The minimum computed by the processor at the root of the tree is the global minimum, which is then broadcast to all of the other processors. Each processor would then process all events with time stamp less than $T_M + L_M$, the result of the global minimum computation.

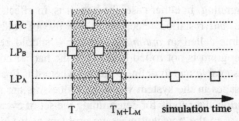

Figure 3.13 A simple synchronous protocol. Events in the shaded region are safe to process.

```
while (simulation in progress)

    T_Min = min (T_i + L_i) for all i

    S = set of events in the processor with time stamp ≤ T_Min

    process events in S

    barrier synchronization
```

Figure 3.14 Synchronous simulation protocol.

This approach requires few restrictions other than lookahead. The topology among logical processes is arbitrary, and can change during the course of the simulation. Further LPs need not schedule new events in time stamp order. The cost of avoiding these restrictions is that there is no opportunity to exploit such information when it is available. Extensions to the synchronous protocol to exploit topology information are described next.

3.5.6 Distance between Logical Processes

Consider application of the synchronous protocol described in the previous section to the air traffic simulation discussed earlier including LPs for LAX, ORD, and JFK. Suppose that a fourth airport is added, in San Diego, called SAN. Recall that lookahead is derived from the minimum amount of time required for an aircraft to fly from one airport to another. Suppose that the minimum flight time from SAN to Los Angeles (LAX) is 30 minutes; this is clearly the minimum lookahead of any airport in this example. Further suppose that at some point in the simulation there are only two unprocessed events, one in SAN with time stamp 10 : 00, and a second in JFK with time stamp 10 : 45. It is clear that the event in SAN cannot affect the event in JFK, since an aircraft requires several hours to fly from San Diego to New York, so one should be able to process these two events concurrently. Yet, using the protocol described earlier, no event in the system with time stamp larger than 10 : 30 can be processed in the current iteration of the algorithm, since the minimum time stamp of the next event that can be scheduled is 10:30. To circumvent this problem, additional information concerning which LPs can schedule events for which others must be provided.

To verify that the event in JFK cannot be affected by the event in SAN, we need to know the smallest amount of simulation time that must elapse for an event in SAN to affect JFK. Suppose that there is no link from SAN to JFK because the model does not include any direct flights between these two airports. SAN could affect JFK by scheduling an event in LAX, which then schedules another event in JFK. Consideration of all paths from SAN to JFK (specifically, SAN to ORD to JFK must also be considered) allows one to determine the minimum amount of simulation time that must elapse for an event in SAN to affect JFK.

This idea is captured in the notion of *distance between processes* which provides a lower bound in the amount of *simulated time* that must elapse for an event in one process to affect another. If the network of LPs is not fully connected, that is, if there is not a link between every pair of LPs, an event will have to propagate through one or more additional LPs before it can reach a specific LP. Distance information provides a means of exploiting information concerning the topology of logical processes to derive better bounds on the time stamp of events that can arrive in the future, and in principle, it allows one to derive larger numbers of events that are safe to process in the synchronous execution approach.

Here, it is assumed that there is a fixed network of logical processes. If logical process LP_A can send a message to LP_B, then there is a link from LP_A to LP_B. A lookahead L_{AB} is associated with each *link*; that is, messages sent from LP_A to LP_B must have a time stamp of at least L_{AB} larger than LP_As current time. For notational convenience, we assume that there is at most one link from LP_A to LP_B.

Distance is defined as follows:

- If a path exists from LP_A to LP_Z traversing in succession logical processes LP_A, LP_B, LP_C, ..., LP_Y, LP_Z, then $D_{ABC...YZ}$ is defined as $L_{AB} + L_{BC} + \cdots + L_{YZ}$.
- D_{AB}, the distance from LP_A to LP_B, is defined as the minimum of D_{path} over all paths from LP_A to LP_B.

The distance between pairs of processes can be encoded in a matrix called the *distance matrix*. The entry in row i and column j indicates the minimum distance D_{ij} from LP_i to LP_j. Figure 3.15(b) shows the distance matrix for the network shown in Figure 3.15(a). For example, there are two paths from LP_A to LP_D, of lengths 3 (via LP_C) and 4 (via LP_B). The distance from LP_A to LP_D is the minimum of these two values, or 3. In general, if there is no path from LP_i to LP_j, then the distance D_{ij} is defined as ∞.

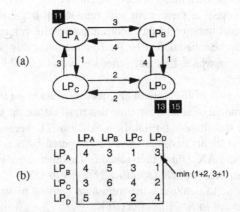

Figure 3.15 (a) Network of logical processes indicating lookahead on each arc. The boxes represent events with time stamp 11, 13, and 15; (b) distance matrix for this network of LPs.

In simulations containing a large number of logical processes relative to the number of processors there will be many LPs mapped to each processor. In this case it may be more efficient to consider distances between processors than processes. In essence the LPs mapped to a single processor can be viewed as a "superlogical process" that includes many LPs for the purpose of determining which events are safe to process. This has the disadvantage that it may be overly conservative in determining which events are safe to process. In other words, each LP implicitly assumes that all events within that LP must be processed in time stamp order, but this may not be necessary if the LP models several independent components.

The distance from an LP to itself is computed by determining the minimum length cycle that includes this LP. For example, for LP_A in Figure 3.15, there are four cycles including LP_A: $LP_A \rightarrow LP_B \rightarrow LP_A$ (length 7), $LP_A \rightarrow LP_C \rightarrow LP_A$ (length 4), $LP_A \rightarrow LP_B \rightarrow LP_D \rightarrow LP_C \rightarrow LP_A$ (length 9), and $LP_A \rightarrow LP_C \rightarrow LP_D \rightarrow LP_B \rightarrow LP_A$ (length 11), so D_{AA} is 4.

An event in LP_D with time stamp T_D *depends on* (can be affected by) an event in LP_A with time stamp T_A if $T_A + D_{AD} < T_D$. For example, in Figure 3.15(a) the time stamp 11 event in LP_A could cause a new event to be sent to LP_D with a time stamp as small as 14. Thus the time stamp 15 event in LP_D depends on the time stamp 11 event in LP_A. Conversely, the time stamp 13 event in LP_D does not depend on the time stamp 11 event in LP_A because the minimum distance from LP_A to LP_D is 3. An event E in LP_X is said to be *safe* if it is not possible for a new event to be generated and sent to LP_X that contains a time stamp smaller than E's time stamp.

Each logical process can determine which events within that LP are safe to process if it can determine a lower bound on the time stamp of any message that LP will later receive. Let $LBTS_i$ be the lower bound on the time stamp of any message LP_i can receive in the future. All events in LP_i with time stamp less than $LBTS_i$ are safe. Let T_i be the smallest time stamped event in LP_i. T_i is defined as ∞ if there are no events in LP_i. Then

$$LBTS_i = \min_{all\ j}(T_j + D_{ji}). \tag{3.1}$$

Note that the minimum computation includes the case where j is equal to i. This is necessary to account for the possibility of an event in LP_i causing a message to be sent to one or more other processors that results in another message that is sent back to LP_i. Also this equation assumes that there are no transient messages in the network. Thus it is assumed that this equation will be applied after a barrier mechanism has been used to ensure there are no such messages.

For example, in Figure 3.15, $LBTS_A$ is 15 ($T_A + D_{AA}$), $LBTS_B$ is 14 ($T_A + D_{AB}$), $LBTS_C$ is 12 ($T_A + D_{AC}$) and $LBTS_D$ is 14 ($T_A + D_{AD}$). This implies that the time stamp 11 even in LP_A and the time stamp 13 event in LP_D can be safely processed. The time stamp 15 event in LP_D is *not* safe, verifying the analysis that was performed earlier.

The approach described above requires each processor to communicate with every other processor in the system to obtain their T_i values to compute which events are safe to process. This generates N^2 messages each time the set of safe events must be computed. This limits the applicability of this algorithm to systems containing a modest number of processors. An approach using *time windows* will be discussed later to alleviate this problem.

Another drawback with this approach is the distance matrix must be recomputed if lookaheads change during the execution of the simulation program. This problem can be addressed by using an alternate method for computing LBTS values, depicted in Figure 3.16. An approach reminiscent of the null message algorithm (and similar to Dijkstra's algorithm for computing shortest paths) is to have each LP initialize its LBTS value to ∞. Then each LP sends a message to the other LPs to which it may send messages indicating the smallest time stamp on any message it may send in the future, assuming that it does not receive any new messages (initially, the time stamp of the next unprocessed event plus the link's lookahead). An LP receiving such a message will use this information to determine if its local LBTS value should be

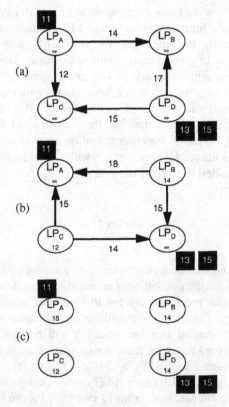

Figure 3.16 Computation for computing LBTS values. (*a*) Each LP sends messages indicating a lower bound on the time stamp of the sent messages (if this value is not ∞). (*b*) Each LP updates its LBTS, and if its value decreased, it sends messages indicating a new lower bound on the time stamp of these messages. (*c*) No new messages are generated; the final LBTS values have been computed.

updated (reduced). If the LPs LBTS value is reduced, and the LP now discovers that it could send a smaller time-stamped message than what it had previously reported to its neighbors, it sends new messages indicating a new lower bound on the time stamp of messages it could later send. This process continues until no additional messages are generated, at which time each LP has computed its LBTS value, and the computation completes.

For example, in Figure 3.16(a), LP_A may send messages with time stamp 14 and 12 to LP_B and LPC, respectively, because of its local event with time stamp 11, and its lookahead to LP_B is 3, and to LP_C is 1. Similarly LP_D may send messages with time stamp 17 and 15 to LP_B and LPC, respectively. No messages are sent by LP_B and LP_C because they cannot generate a lower bound on the time stamp of future messages other than ∞. In Figure 3.16(b) the LBTS values of LP_B and LP_C are updated to the smallest value among the messages they received. LP_B and LP_C now send additional messages indicating lower bounds on the time stamp of messages it may later send. Because LP_B may receive a message with time stamp 14 (its new LBTS value), it could generate messages with time stamp 18 to LP_A (lookahead 4) and 15 to LP_D (lookahead 1). Similarly LP_C could generate new messages with time stamp 15 to LP_A, and 14 to LP_D. These messages cause the LBTS values of LP_A and LP_D to change, as shown in Figure 3.16(c). However, this new LBTS value is *higher* than the time stamp of events already buffered in each LP, so the lower bound on future messages it might send is not reduced any further. Because no new messages are generated, the computation is now complete.

It is instructive to compare the synchronous style of execution with the deadlock detection and recovery approach described earlier. Both share the characteristic that the simulation moves through phases of (1) processing events and (2) performing some global synchronization function to decide which events are safe to process. The two methods differ in the way they enter into the synchronization phase.

In the best case the detection and recovery strategy will never deadlock, eliminating most of the clock synchronization overhead. In contrast, synchronous methods will continually block and restart throughout the simulation. On the other hand, the synchronous methods do not require a deadlock detection mechanism. However, an important disadvantage of the detection and recovery method is that during the period leading up to a deadlock when the computation is grinding to a halt, execution may be largely sequential. This can severely limit speedup.[9] Synchronous methods have some control over the amount of computation that is performed during each iteration, so, at least in principle, they offer a mechanism for guarding against such behavior.

3.6 BOUNDED LAG

Consider a large network of logical processes where the distance between pairs of logical processes varies widely from one pair to another. For instance, if we extend

---

[9] Amdahl's law states that no more than k-fold speedup is possible if $1/k$th of the computation is sequential.

the air traffic simulation described earlier to a simulation of the global air traffic network, there is a direct relationship between the physical distance between airports and the minimum distance in simulation time required for two airport LPs to interact, assuming as before that interactions occur through aircraft flying between the airports. Consider a parallel simulation where all LPs are at simulation time T. It is clear that air traffic now departing from Tokyo International airport cannot affect a flight arriving at LAX 30 minutes from now; however, a flight that just left San Diego airport destined for LAX could affect this incoming flight.

Thus it is curious that a simulation of the global air traffic network using the synchronous parallel simulation algorithm based on equation 3.1 must collect information from every other processor in the system (i.e., every other airport in the world) before it can determine which local events are safe to process. Specifically, in the above scenario where flights are converging on LAX, the simulation algorithm requires that LAX solicit information from Tokyo International before it certifies that the arrival event at LAX 30 minutes from now is "safe" to process. As mentioned earlier, requiring each processor to collect information in this way from every other processor prevents the algorithm from scaling to large numbers of processors. Thus a mechanism is needed that will reduce interprocessor communication so that one can determine which events are safe.

The reason that the algorithm using equation 3.1 must collect information from every other processor is because no consideration is made on how far into the future one should check for the safety of a local event. For example, while it is intuitively clear that a recent Tokyo departure cannot affect an arrival at LAX occurring 30 minutes from now, such a departure could affect LAX arrivals that occur 24 hours from now. Because the synchronization algorithm makes no distinction between "near-future" and "far-future" events, it must check all logical processes in the entire simulation to determine whether its far-future events are safe to process. Because far-future events are unlikely to be safe, expending much effort to determine if these events are safe to process is usually wasteful.

A simple approach to improving the efficiency of the synchronization algorithm is to introduce an interval (also commonly referred to as a "window") of simulation time extending from the time stamp of the smallest event in the simulation T_S to $T_S + T_W$, where T_W denotes the size of the window. Events with time stamp larger than $T_S + T_W$ are not considered for execution in this iteration of the algorithm. Thus the simulation executive need not determine the safety of "far-future" events; these are events with time stamp larger than $T_S + T_W$. Because events with time stamp beyond $T_S + T_W$ are never processed in the current iteration, no LP can advance its local simulation time clock more than T_W units of simulation time ahead of another LP. For this reason T_W is also referred to as a *bounded lag* in the simulation; it limits how far behind one LP can lag behind another.

Events with time stamp less than or equal to $T_S + T_W$ are called *near-future* events, and those with time stamp greater than $T_S + T_W$ are called *far-future* events. Far-future events are automatically assumed to be unsafe. The synchronization algorithm only attempts to determine the safety of near-future events.

If $D_{XY} > T_W$, then LP_Y need not check LP_X to determine if its near future events are safe. This is because LP_Xs next event must have a time stamp of at least T_S. This event cannot affect any event in LP_Y with time stamp less than $T_S + D_{XY}$, which is greater than $T_S + T_W$ since $D_{XY} > T_W$. But LP_Y is only considering the safety of near-future events that have a time stamp less than $T_S + T_W$. Thus LP_X is "too far" away to affect any events that LP_Y is considering for execution during this iteration, so LP_Y need not check LP_X when checking the safety of its events.

Using time windows, LP_Y need only check LP_X if $D_{XY} \leq T_W$. Thus equation 3.1 is modified to equation 3.2 below:

$$\text{LBTS}_i = \min_{\substack{all\ j\ where \\ D_{ji} \leq T_W}} (T_j + D_{ji}) \tag{3.2}$$

For example, in Figure 3.15, if T_W is 4 and D_{CB} is 6, then LP_B does not need to check LP_C in computing LBTS_B to determine which events are safe to process.

An important question concerns setting the size of the time window. If the window is too small, there will be too few events within the window that are available for concurrent execution. On the other hand, if the window is too large, the benefits afforded by the window are lost because the simulation mechanism will behave in much the same way as if no time window were used at all. In general, one must carefully tune the simulation executive for each application to set the window to an appropriate size that both achieves a reasonable amount of concurrent execution and limits the overhead in performing the LBTS calculations.

3.7 CONDITIONAL VERSUS UNCONDITIONAL INFORMATION

It is sometimes useful to distinguish between *conditional* and *unconditional* information in the simulation. Unconditional information is that which can be guaranteed to be true based on local information. For example, if an LP has advanced to simulation time T, and it has a lookahead of L, then the LP can unconditionally guarantee $T + L$ is a lower bound on the time stamp of messages that it may generate in the future. Only unconditional information was transmitted among logical processes via null messages in the Chandy/Misra/Bryant algorithm.

Conditional information is information provided by a logical process that is *only* guaranteed to be true if some predicate is true. In the example illustrated in Figure 3.16, each LP initially sends a message to neighboring LPs equal to the time stamp of its next event plus the lookahead for the link on which the message is sent. This information is a lower bound on the time stamp of future messages sent over that link *provided that LP does not receive any messages in the future with time stamp smaller than its next local event.* In this sense the lower-bound information sent by the LP is conditioned on the fact that it could receive a new message in the future with time stamp smaller than its next local event. As the algorithm proceeds, LPs may receive new information concerning events it could receive in the future that may cause it to reduce the conditional lower-bound information it had sent in previous messages. It is only when each LP has determined its true LBTS value that it can unconditionally guarantee the lower bound on time stamps of future messages it will send in the future.

The fact that the original Chandy/Misra/Bryant algorithm only transmits unconditional guarantees on the time stamp of future events, and the synchronous algorithm described above allows logical processes to transmit conditional information is a key distinction between these algorithms. It allows the simulation executive to avoid the "simulation time creep" problem where LPs only advance in lookahead increments to advance to the time stamp of the next unprocessed event.

3.8 DYNAMIC PROCESSES AND INTERCONNECTIONS

The discussion thus far has assumed a static topology; that is, the processes and links among processes are known prior to the execution and do not change during the execution of the simulation program. This is acceptable for certain classes of applications, such as a simulation of a wired telecommunication network utilizing some fixed topology. For other applications the interactions between logical processes may vary over time. For example, if an LP were used to model each aircraft in the air traffic simulation discussed earlier, interactions among LPs would depend on the physical proximity of aircraft to airports, which will change dramatically throughout the simulation.

One simple approach to allowing dynamic creation and destruction of logical processes and links is to initially create all logical processes and links that *may* be needed during the entire execution. This allows existing synchronization algorithms to be used more or less "as is." A pool of unused LPs is created at the beginning of the execution, and is used as new LPs are required. This approach requires one to be able to place an upper bound on the number of processes that will be required. Unless one can guarantee a priori that certain pairs of LPs will never need to exchange messages during the execution, a fully connected topology where each LP can send a message to any other LP must be used. This can lead to inefficiencies in certain synchronization algorithms. For example, each of the unused logical processes may be required to send null messages to the other LPs.

A more flexible approach is to allow new LPs and connections to be established and joined to the existing network of logical processes during the execution. With respect to synchronization, creation of new LPs does not produce problems so much as establishing new connections. The central problem that must be addressed is that any new connection to an existing LP provides a new source of messages for that LP. Let the "sending LP" refer to the LP on the sending side of the new connection, and the "receiving LP" be the LP on the receiving side. Precautions must be taken to ensure that no messages are sent on the new connection in the past of the receiving LP. Two approaches to preventing causality errors such as this are described below. The first constrains the behavior of the receiving LP, and the second constrains the behavior of the sending LP.

1. *Receiver constrained.* One can prevent the receiving LP from advancing "too far" ahead of all potential sending LPs in order to ensure that it does not receive messages in its past. For example, if the receiving LP is constrained so that it cannot advance more then L_i units of time ahead of each potential sending process LP_i, where L_i is the lookahead for LP_i, then it is guaranteed that the receiving LP will not receive any new messages in its past.

2. *Sender constrained.* One can constrain the sending LP so that it cannot send messages in the past of the receiving LP. If the sending logical process LP_S is at simulation time T_S and the receiving process LP_R is at simulation time T_R when a new connection is established from LP_S to LP_R, then the lookahead on the newly established connection must initially be set to be at least $T_R - T_S$ to prevent LP_R from receiving messages in its past.

The first approach described above is somewhat restricting in that it does not allow LPs to advance more than a lookahead amount ahead of other LPs. The second approach allows LPs greater flexibility to advance further ahead of others but provides less control because there is, in general, no limit on how large $T_R - T_S$ can be (the initial lookahead on the new connection) other than the lookahead values already in place on other existing links.

One example of the receiver constrained approach is called a *connection transfer protocol*. This approach is based on the assumption that logical process LP_S cannot send a message to logical process LP_R unless LP_S first obtains a handle (a reference) to LP_R. An important restriction is that logical processes cannot autonomously manufacture new handles. Rather, handles can only be obtained by either creating a new LP or receiving a handle from another LP via a message. It is assumed an LP can only send messages to LPs for which it holds a handle. The parallel simulation executive keeps track of which handles are owned by each LP in order to determine the topology among LPs.

To illustrate connection transfer, suppose logical process LP_A owns a handle to LP_R, indicating LP_A can send messages to LP_R. Assume LP_A is at logical time T_A, and it has a lookahead of L_A, and LP_A is *not* blocked waiting for a simulation time advance. This implies $T_R \leq T_A + L_A$ where T_R is the current logical time of LP_R. To establish a new connection from a third logical process LP_S to LP_R, LP_A can send LP_S a copy of its handle. In order to prevent LP_S from sending messages into the pat of LP_R, this new connection must first be recorded within the simulation executive to ensure LP_S is taken into account when computing LBTS values for LP_R. After this has been accomplished, a copy of the LP_R handle can be transmitted to LP_S. LP_S cannot start using this handle until it reaches simulation time $T_A + \max(0, L_A - L_S)$. This constraint guarantees that LP_S will not send a message into a past of LP_R.

A key observation in this transfer protocol is that LP_As existing connection with LP_R is used to prevent LP_R from advancing "too far ahead" and LP_As communication with LP_S, prevents LP_S from lagging "too far behind" when the new connection is established. This enables one to avoid causality errors when LP_S sends messages to LP_R. Thus, LP_A plays a critical role in this mechanism.

An alternate approach is to use time windows to establish new connections. Recall that a time window of size T_W prevents any LP from advancing more than T_W units of time ahead of any other LP. This constrains the advance of LPs but allows an LP to advance more than a lookahead amount ahead of other LPs because T_W may be larger than the lookahead. To prevent an LP from receiving a message in its past, the sender LP is required to use a lookahead of at least T_W when the new connection is first established. Specifically, if the sender is at time T_S when it establishes the new connection, the first message it sends on the new connection must have a time stamp of at least $T_S + T_W$. Because no LP can be more than T_W units of time ahead of another LP, this guarantees that the new message will not be in the past of the receiving LP. As the sending LP advances its simulation time past T_S, the lookahead for this new connection can be decreased by an equal amount.

The window-based approach described above provides a means for establishing new connections among existing LPs. When a new LP is created, one must ensure that the new LP is initialized to have a simulation time no less than T_L, the lower edge of the time window. This is easily accomplished by requiring that the logical process that created the new process do so by scheduling an event into its future. The time stamp of this "create process" event defines the initial simulation time of the new LP.

Finally a mechanism is required to ensure that proper destruction of LPs and/or connections. This is relatively straightforward. Destroying a connection is equivalent to setting the lookahead for the connection to infinity. This ensures that the receiving LP will not block on the connection. Destroying an LP can be accomplished by destroying all connections to and from the LP, thus removing the LP from the system.

3.9 REPEATABILITY AND SIMULTANEOUS EVENTS

In some cases it is important that repeated executions of the simulation program using the same external inputs (and initial state) produce exactly the same results on each execution. For example, the U.S. Department of Defense sometimes uses simulations to make acquisition decisions, so the General Accounting Office (GAO) may re-execute simulations to verify the results that are produced. Further, repeatability simplifies debugging the simulation program because errors can be reproduced. In addition, if the simulation should produce repeatable results but does not, this may immediately flag a bug in the simulation code or the simulation executive.

Recall that the synchronization protocols described thus far attempt to produce the same results as a sequential execution of the same simulation program where events are processed in time stamp order. If no two events contained the same time stamp, then the results of the simulation would always be repeatable if the computation performed by each event is repeatable. This latter condition is actually a nontrivial matter. For example, if the simulation program executes on different CPUs, differences in floating point round-off error could result in nonrepeatable executions. Here, it is assumed that individual event computations are repeatable. So, to ensure that executions of the parallel simulation produce exactly the same results, it is sufficient to ensure that events containing the same time stamp at any logical process are processed by that process in the same order from one execution to the next. Events containing the same time stamp are referred to as *simultaneous events*.

3.9.1 Using Hidden Time Stamp Fields to Order Simultaneous Events

One approach to ensuring that simultaneous events are processed in the same order from one execution to the next is to extend the time stamp field to include additional, lower-precision bits that are hidden from the application program. The simulation executive can automatically assign values to these bits to, in effect, ensure that no two events in the system contain the same time stamp. The simulation application is constrained to process events in increasing time stamp order, where the time stamp now includes these hidden bits. The value placed in these lower-precision bits must be assigned so that the time stamp values including the hidden bits are consistent for causally dependent events. For example, if the computation for an event E_1 schedules a new event E_2 to contain the same time stamp (excluding the hidden bits) as the original, the hidden bits in the time stamp of E_2 must be larger than those in E_1.

One can append two tie-breaking fields to the application defined time stamp called the *age* and *id*, with the age field given precedence (assigned to more significant bits) over the *id* field. Events that exist at the beginning of the simulation are assigned an age of 1. If an event with time stamp T and age A schedules another event with the same time stamp (ignoring the extra fields), the new event is assigned an age of $A + 1$. If the new event has a time stamp larger than T, the age of the new event is 1.

The *age* field ensures that events always schedule other events with higher time stamps, but it does not ensure uniqueness. For example, an event with time stamp T, and age 5 could schedule two new events also with time stamp T. In this case both events will have an age of 6. The *id* field ensures uniqueness. This field is actually a tuple with two components (S, i). S is an identifier that indicates the logical process scheduling the event. It is assumed that this identifier remains the same from one execution to the next. The i field is a counter indicating this is the ith event scheduled by the process.

3.9.2 Priority Numbers

While hidden bits can be used to ensure repeatable orderings of simultaneous events, a critical drawback with this approach is that it assigns the task of ordering simultaneous events to the simulation executive, which typically has no knowledge of the semantic meaning of the events. The proper ordering of simultaneous events should normally be controlled by the simulation application. For example, consider a simulation that is used to make acquisition decisions by comparing two competing weapons systems. If two simultaneous events denoting detonations at a target occur, the "kill" may be credited to the system associated with the first detonation event that is processed. The simulation executive might use a scheme for ordering simultaneous events that systematically favors one system over the other. This could lead to misleading results if many simultaneous events occur, which might be the case if a "coarse" timing model with limited temporal precision is used.

One approach to specifying the ordering of simultaneous events is to allow the simulation application to define a priority number for each event, with lower-priority numbered events processed before those with a higher-priority number. In effect the priority field serves as the low-precision bits of the time stamp. A potential drawback with this approach is that the sending process is responsible for assigning the time stamp of the event. It is often more convenient to have the receiving process prioritize events because, in general, only the receiver knows what other events occur at the same time stamp, and the appropriate priority might depend on the state of the receiver. If the priority depended on the state of the sender, the sender could always include such information as a data field within the event itself, but it is much more difficult to have the sender assign a priority based on state information within the receiver.

3.9.3 Receiver-Specified Ordering

Another approach to treating simultaneous events is to have the simulation executive deliver all such events to the simulation application, and then force the application to order the events in a manner consistent with the objectives of the simulation. For example, in the above example, a random number generator might be used to determine which system is credited with the destruction of the target. To ensure repeatability, the simulation application needs only to ensure that the algorithm used to order the simultaneous events is repeatable. It is noteworthy that if this approach is used to order simultaneous events, the simulation executive does not need to deliver the events to the simulation application in a repeatable fashion, since the application will order the events using its own criteria once the events are passed to it. The executive must only be able to guarantee to the application that it has delivered all simultaneous events, so that the application can then order and process these events.

One slight complication to the scheme described above is that the simulation executive cannot guarantee that it has delivered all simultaneous events to a logical process if zero lookahead is allowed. To see this, consider the following scenario: The simulation executive guarantees some logical process LP_1 that it has passed it all simultaneous events with time stamp T. LP_1 advances to time T to order and process these events. LP_1 now generates a new event E_1 at time T; this is possible because zero lookahead is allowed. A message for E_1 is received and processed by another process LP_2. LP_2 now returns a message to LP_1 with time stamp T. This contradicts the original claim that LP_1 had received all events with time stamp T! One solution to this dilemma is to require that a logical process temporarily have nonzero lookahead whenever it requests to receive all simultaneous events at a given time stamp. The lookahead may return to zero once the LP has advanced its simulation time.

3.10 PERFORMANCE OF CONSERVATIVE MECHANISMS

Lookahead plays a crucial role in the performance of conservative synchronization algorithms. Further the simulation application must be written in such a way as to maximize its lookahead. This often has a profound effect on the way the simulation program is developed.

To illustrate this, consider the simulation of a queuing network. Here, each station in the queuing network consists of a single server that services incoming jobs one at a time, and an unlimited capacity queue holding jobs waiting for service (see Fig. 3.17). For example, a runway in the air traffic example presented earlier can be

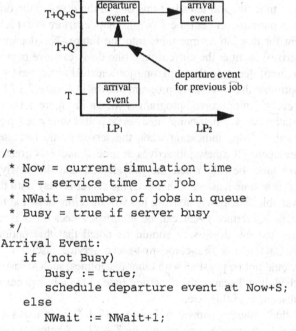

```
/*
 * Now = current simulation time
 * S = service time for job
 * NWait = number of jobs in queue
 * Busy = true if server busy
 */
Arrival Event:
    if (not Busy)
        Busy := true;
        schedule departure event at Now+S;
    else
        NWait := NWait+1;


Departure Event:
    schedule Arrival event at LP₂ at Now
    if (NWait>0)
        NWait := NWait-1;
        schedule departure event at Now+S;
    else
        Busy := false;
```

Figure 3.17 Classical approach to modeling a queuing network server using arrival and departure events.

modeled as a queue, with jobs representing aircraft and the server modeling the runway itself. If a job arrives while the server is busy with another job, the newly arriving job is placed into the queue where it waits to receive service. Here, assume that the server processes the jobs in the queue in first-come–first-serve order, or more precisely, the queue is a first-in–first-out buffer.

The classical approach to modeling a single queue is to use two types of events: arrival events to signify the arrival of a new customer at the station and departure events to represent a customer completing service, and leaving the station, typically to advance to another station. In the air traffic simulation presented in Chapter 2, the arrival and landed events are equivalent to the arrival and departure events that are used here, respectively. The sequence of events for a single job arriving at a station, receiving service, and departing from the station is shown in Figure 3.17. An arrival event occurs at time T. If the server is idle, the job immediately begins service and schedules a departure event S time units into the future, where S is the amount of time the job receives service. If the server is busy, the job is added to the queue. After Q units of time, the job ahead of this one in the queue will complete service (and process a departure event at time $T + Q$). That departure event schedules a new departure event for this job S time units into the future. The departure event also schedules an arrival event at the current time (the delay to move between stations is assumed to be zero) denoting the departing job's arrival at the next station.

One can optimize the simulation program shown in Figure 3.17 by eliminating the departure event. An optimized program is shown in Figure 3.18. Exploiting the fact that the station uses a first-come–first-serve policy, one need only maintain a state variable called Done indicating when the server would have served all jobs currently in the queue. If a new job arrives at time T and T is greater than Done, then the server must be idle when the job arrives, and the newly arriving job completes service at time Now+S. Otherwise, the server is busy until the time stored in the Done variable. The newly arriving job will therefore depart at time Done+S. In either case the departure event can be eliminated because it is not needed to determine when the job departs. It should be noted that this optimization relies heavily on the fact that a first-come–first-serve service discipline is used. The optimization would not be possible with other disciplines, such as last-in–first-out or preemptive scheduling, because the departure time of the job depends on what other jobs arrive subsequent to this one.

The simulation program shown in Figure 3.17 has poor lookahead properties because LP_1 must advance to simulation time $T + Q + S$ before it can generate the new arrival event with time stamp $T + Q + S$. The LP has zero lookahead with respect to scheduling this event. On the other hand, the simulation program shown in Figure 3.18 has good lookahead because the program attempts to schedule events far into the simulated future. One way of viewing lookahead is to observe that the arrival event at time $T + Q + S$ is invariant to any other events occurring in the interval $[T, T + Q + S]$. This allows the event to be generated at time T.

These two programs exhibit dramatically different performance. Performance measurements of the execution of each of these simulation programs in modeling the central server queuing network in Figure 3.19 are shown in Figure 3.20 and Figure

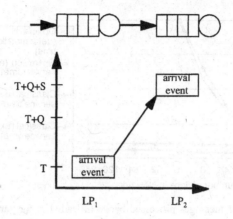

```
/*
 * Now = current simulation time
 * S = service time for job
 * Done = time server will become idle
 */
Arrival Event:
    if (Now ≤ Done)   /* if server busy */
        Done := Done+S;
        schedule arrival event at LP₂ at Done;
    else /* server is idle */
        Done := Now+S;
        schedule arrival event at LP₂ at Done;
```

Figure 3.18   Optimized queuing network simulator for first-come–first-serve queues.

3.21. These measurements show the performance of the parallel simulator using the deadlock detection and recovery algorithm executing on a shared-memory multiprocessor with five processors, one for each of the logical processes shown in Figure 3.19. A closed queuing network is simulated, with the number of jobs circulating among the queues left as a parameter.

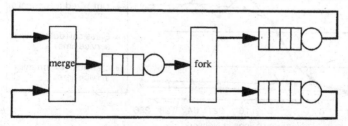

Figure 3.19   Central server queuing model. The fork module routes incoming jobs to one of its output ports. Here, jobs are equally likely to be routed to either port. The merge module joins incoming stream of jobs into a single output stream.

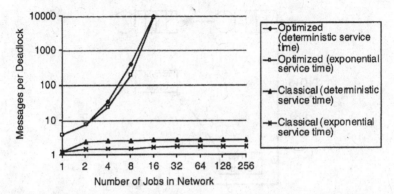

Figure 3.20 Number of messages processed between deadlocks for parallel simulation of central server queuing network for the simulation programs shown in Figure 3.17 and Figure 3.18.

Figure 3.20 gives the number of messages that are processed between deadlocks for different numbers of jobs. This number should be maximized, since deadlock represents an overhead that does not occur in a sequential execution. Shown are curves for the classical implementation using both arrival and departure events and the optimized version using only arrival events. The service time is selected either deterministically or from an exponentially distributed random variable. It can be seen that when there are more than a few jobs circulating through the network, the simulation application that is optimized to exploit lookahead is far more efficient than the unoptimized simulation; that is to say, deadlocks occur much less frequently. The speedup measurements in Figure 3.21 show that the optimized simulation executes two to three times faster than the sequential execution for reasonably large job populations, but the unoptimized version executes much more slowly than the sequential execution.

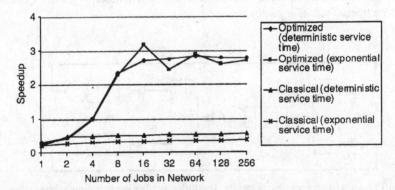

Figure 3.21 Speedup relative to a sequential execution of the parallel simulation of the central server queuing network.

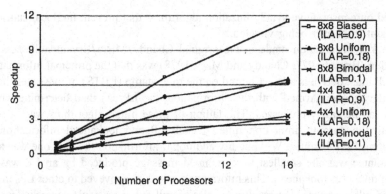

Figure 3.22 Performance of the null message algorithm for synthetic workloads with different degrees of lookahead.

The curves for the optimized simulation in Figure 3.20 illustrate a kind of "avalanche effect." This means that the efficiency of the simulator is poor for small-message populations but improves dramatically once the population reaches a certain critical level.

It should be highlighted that the simulation used in these experiments was one where it was possible to design the application to exploit lookahead. The resulting simulation program is somewhat "fragile" in that seemingly modest changes in the model, such as the addition of job preemption invalidate this optimization.

Figure 3.22 shows the speedup obtained for an experiment using the null message algorithm in executing a synthetic workload. The workload consists of a collection of LPs configured in a toroid topology. A fixed number of messages migrates at random throughout the network. Each event schedules exactly one new event. The distribution used to select the time stamp of the new event was a parameter in these experiments. Lookahead is characterized by a value called the Inverse Lookahead Ration (ILAR) which is defined as the minimum of the time stamp increment divided by its mean. High ILAR values (up to 1.0) correspond to good lookahead, while low values correspond to poor lookahead. As can be seen, dramatically different performance results are obtained depending on the ILAR value, which indicates the lookahead in the simulation.

3.11 SUMMARY AND CRITIQUE OF CONSERVATIVE MECHANISMS

This chapter introduced the synchronization problem which has been a focal point of much of the work to date concerning the execution of analytic discrete event simulation programs on parallel and distributed computers. The central goal of the synchronization algorithm is to satisfy the local causality constraint, namely to ensure that each LP processes events in time stamp order. Once this has been accomplished, one can ensure that the concurrent execution of the simulation program will produce the same results as a sequential execution. This chapter focused on conservative synchronization algorithms that prevent the local causality constraint from ever being violated.

The key observation made in the original Chandy/Misra/Bryant null message algorithm (Bryant 1977; Chandy and Misra 1978) was that the principal information each LP must derive is a lower bound on the time stamp (LBTS) of messages that it may later receive. Armed with this information, the LP can then determine which events can be safely processed. The failing of these initial algorithms was in only utilizing the current simulation time of each LP and lookahead information in computing LBTS values. Without any additional information the best one was able to guarantee was the smallest time stamped message produced by an LP was its current time plus lookahead. This information was then conveyed to other LPs in the form of null messages. The resulting cycles of null messages could severely degrade performance.

Newer algorithms circumvented this problem by also including information on the time stamp of the next unprocessed event in computing LBTS values. This allowed the synchronization protocol to immediately advance simulation time to the time stamp of the next unprocessed event, just as sequential simulators are able to do. Collecting next event information in this way is much more straightforward if the computation is stopped at a barrier because a snapshot of the entire simulation can be easily made, greatly simplifying the task of determining the smallest time-stamped event in the system. Synchronous algorithms such as Lubachevsky's bounded lag (Lubachevsky 1989), Ayani's distance between objects algorithm (Ayani 1989), and the synchronous algorithm described in Section 3.5.5, which is similar to Nicol's YAWNS protocol (Nicol 1993) and Steinman's Time Buckets protocol (Steinman 1991), all exploit this fact. Implementing a barrier, and making sure that there are no transient messages in the system when the barrier is realized then becomes important, at least on distributed memory machines where transient messages may arise and be difficult to detect. A barrier mechanism developed by Nicol provides a solution to this problem (Nicol 1995).

Underlying all of these techniques is the requirement that the simulation contain good lookahead properties, or there is little hope of achieving much concurrent execution, except in specialized cases such as when there are many events with the same time stamp. Different restrictions may be placed on the behavior of the parallel simulator in order to make lookahead information more easily known to the synchronization protocol. Examples include specifying the topology among logical processes, thereby restricting which LPs may send messages to which others, or specifying distances between LPs. While first-generation algorithms utilized restrictions such as no dynamic creation of processes or static network topologies, and required messages sent over a link to have nondecreasing time stamps, these limitations were *not* fundamental to conservative algorithms and could be overcome by various techniques. Similarly it was observed that techniques could be developed that ensure simulation executions could be repeated (Mehl 1992).

Conservative synchronization algorithms have advanced to a state where they are viable for use in real-world simulation problems. Nevertheless, some fundamental limitations of these algorithms exist. Perhaps the most obvious drawback of conservative approaches is that they cannot fully exploit the concurrency that is available in the simulation application. If it is possible that event E_A *might* affect E_B either directly or indirectly, conservative approaches must execute E_A and E_B sequentially. If the simulation is such that E_A seldom affects E_B, these events could have been processed concurrently most of the time. In general, if the worst case scenario for determining when it is safe to proceed is far from the typical scenario that arises in practice, the conservative approach will usually be overly pessimistic, and force sequential execution when it is not necessary. In this sense conservative algorithms use a "Murphy's law" approach to executing the simulation: any possible scenario that could lead to violation of the local causality constraint must be prevented.

Another way of stating this fact is to observe that except in a handful of special cases such as feed-forward networks without cycles, conservative algorithms rely on lookahead to achieve good performance. If there were no lookahead, the smallest time-stamped event in the simulation *could* affect every other pending event, forcing sequential execution no matter what conservative protocol is used. Consider a fully connected network topology. If the logical process furthest behind in the simulation is at time T_S and that LP has a lookahead of L, then the simulation executive can only guarantee the safety of those events whose time stamp lies in the interval $[T_S, T_S + L]$. In effect, the lookahead defines a time window where events with time stamp within this window can be safely processed concurrently. The larger that L is, the more events there are that can be processed concurrently. Characteristics such as preemptive behavior diminish the lookahead properties of the simulation. Conservative algorithms struggle to achieve good performance when the simulation application has poor lookahead, even if there is a healthy amount of parallelism available.

A related problem faced by conservative methods concerns the question of robustness. Seemingly minor changes to the application may have a catastrophic effect on performance. For example, adding short, high-priority messages that interrupt "normal" processing in a computer network simulation can destroy the lookahead properties on which the model relied to achieve good performance, leading to severe performance degradations. This is problematic because experimenters often do not have advance knowledge of the full range of experiments that will be required, so it behooves them to invest substantial amounts of effort to parallelize the application if an unforeseen addition to the model at some future date could invalidate all of this work.

Perhaps the most serious drawback with conservative simulation protocols is the requirement that the simulation program be designed to maximize its lookahead to achieve acceptable performance. A natural approach to programming an LP is to have it update state variables as the LP advances, and generate "state update" messages with time stamp equal to the LPs current simulation time for those variables of interest to other LPs. This leads to simulations with zero lookahead, which in turn may limit concurrent execution to only those events that have the same time stamp. To increase lookahead, the modeler must design the simulation program so that it can predict state updates at an earlier simulation time; then the messages can be generated in advance with a suitable lookahead value. Further it is up to the modeler to guarantee that it can generate events sufficiently far in advance so that lookahead guarantees made to the simulation executive can be maintained.

Ideally one would separate the development of the simulation application from the mechanisms used in the underlying simulation executive. For example, sequential simulation programs normally do not need to be concerned with the data structure used to implement the pending event list. Writing the application in a way to maximize its lookahead often leads to a complex, "fragile," code that is difficult to modify and maintain. Thus far, techniques to automatically determine the lookahead in the application or restructure the simulation code to improve lookahead have had only limited success.

3.12 ADDITIONAL READINGS

Independently Chandy and Misra (Chandy and Misra 1978) and Bryant (Bryant 1977) developed the original null message algorithm that bears their names. Early work in defining the synchronization problem and determining conditions for deadlock are also described in Peacock, Wong et al. (1979). Variations on the null message algorithm, including many aimed at reducing the number of messages that are generated are described in Misra (1986), Bain and Scott (1988), Su and Seitz (1989), Cai and Turner (1990), DeVries (1990), Preiss, Loucks et al. (1991), Yu, Ghosh et al. (1991), and Blanchard, Lake et al. (1994). Other early proposals for synchronization algorithms are described in Reynolds (1982), Nicol and Reynolds (1984), Groselj and Tropper (1988), Jones, Chou et al. (1989), and Zeigler and Kim (1996). A categorization of algorithms, both conservative and optimistic, is discussed in Reynolds (1988). The scheme to use hidden fields in the time stamp to order simultaneous events is taken from Mehl (1992).

The deadlock detection and recovery algorithm is described in Chandy and Misra (1981), and the Dijkstra/Scholton algorithm for detecting deadlock is described in Dijkstra and Scholten (1980). A variation on this algorithm that detects local deadlocks (deadlocks among a subset of the logical processes) is described in Liu and Tropper (1990). Limitations of the amount of parallelism that can be extracted by these algorithms in simulations of queueing networks are described in Wagner and Lazowska (1989).

Early experimental work discussing empirical performance evaluations of the null message and deadlock detection and recovery algorithms are described in Reed, Malony et al. (1988) and Fujimoto (1989), demonstrating the importance of lookahead in achieving speedup. Work in detecting and improving the lookahead properties of simulation applications, often with good success in speeding up the computation are described in Groselj and Tropper (1986), Nicol (1988), Cota and Sargent (1990), Lin and Lazowska (1990), and Wagner (1991).

The importance of utilizing information concerning the next unprocessed event, in addition to only considering the current simulation time of each LP, has been long recognized in the field. This is articulated in Chandy and Sherman (1989) where a synchronization algorithm called the *conditional event algorithm* is described.

Algorithms using global synchronizations to determine events that are safe to process began to appear in the late 1980s. Lubachevsky's bounded lag algorithm (Lubachevsky 1989) was perhaps the first, with the distance between objects algorithm appearing shortly thereafter (Ayani 1989). The synchronous protocol described in Section 3.5.5 is similar to the two protocols that appeared in 1990, the YAWNS protocol analyzed in Nicol (1993) and the Time Buckets protocol described in Steinman (1991). Barrier algorithms and mechanisms to eliminate transient messages are in the general parallel computation literature. The butterfly barrier algorithm described here is based on the algorithm described in Nicol (1995). Connection transfer protocols to dynamically change LP connections are described in Bagradia and Liao (1994) and Blanchard and Lake (1997).

CHAPTER 4

Time Warp

Conservative synchronization algorithms avoid violating the local causality constraint, whereas optimistic algorithms allow violations to occur but provide a mechanism to recover. Jefferson's Time Warp mechanism was the first and remains the most well-known optimistic synchronization algorithm. Although many others have been proposed, many of the fundamental concepts and mechanisms used by these algorithms such as rollback, anti-messages, and Global Virtual Time (GVT) first appeared in Time Warp. This chapter describes the fundamental ideas introduced in Time Warp and the associated algorithms for its efficient implementation.

The term *optimistic* execution refers to the fact that logical processes process events, "optimistically" assuming there are no causality errors. Optimistic execution has long been used in other computing applications, in some cases prior to it being proposed for simulation. Two other uses include:

- *Distributed database systems.* When several clients of a database system simultaneously initiate transactions on the database (for example, to update an inventory of spare parts), a *concurrency control* algorithm is required to ensure that the final result is the same as if the transactions were performed in some serial order. One approach to accomplishing this is to have transactions optimistically proceed as if no conflicts (read and write accesses to the same record) occur. If a conflict is later detected, one of the transactions is aborted, and restarted later. Database concurrency control is in many ways similar to synchronization of parallel simulations, with the important distinction that *any* ordering of transactions in database systems is usually acceptable. These systems need only to ensure that transactions appear to be *atomic*, namely that the result after concurrently processing the transactions is the same as if each were completed in sequence, one after the other. In parallel simulations causal relationships in the physical system dictate the order in which events must be completed, so it is definitely *not* the case that any order will do.

- *Microprocessors.* Most modern microprocessors use optimistic processing because of an implementation technique called *pipelining*. With pipelining, the microprocessor begins processing the next instruction (specifically, fetching the next instruction from memory) before completing the current instruction. This is problematic if the current instruction is a conditional branch, since it is not known which instruction should be fetched next until the current instruction has (almost) completed execution. Many modern microprocessors predict the result of the branch instruction (branch taken or not taken) and optimistically begin executing instructions according to this prediction. Of course, if the prediction proves to be incorrect, the CPU must have some way to "back out" of the incorrect sequence of instructions that it began to execute.

Returning to parallel simulation applications, recall that the central problem faced by a logical process is that it may have one or more messages that it has received from other processes but cannot be sure that it is safe to process these events because doing so might later result in violating the local causality constraint. Optimistic synchronization protocols process events even though their safety cannot be guaranteed, and they provide some mechanism to "back out" these computations should a causality error (out of order event processing) be detected.

4.1   PRELIMINARIES

Like the conservative synchronization algorithms, the simulation computation is again assumed to be composed of a collection of logical processes that communicates exclusively by exchanging time-stamped messages. There are no state variables that are shared between logical processes. Communications among logical processes are assumed to be reliable; that is to say, every message that is sent eventually arrives at the receiver. A logical process need *not* send messages in time stamp order, and the communication network need *not* guarantee that messages are delivered in the same order in which they were sent. Further, logical processes may be created or destroyed during the execution, and there is no need to explicitly specify which LPs communicate with which other LPs.

Initially, to simplify the discussion, it is assumed that the simulation has nonzero lookahead; namely an LP at simulation time T can only schedule events with time stamp strictly greater than T. It will be seen later that with some simple precautions, zero lookahead simulations can be allowed.

The Time Warp algorithm consists of two distinct pieces that are sometime called the *local control* and the *global control* mechanisms. The local control mechanism is implemented within each processor, largely independent of the other processors. The global control mechanism is used to commit operations such as I/O that cannot be rolled back and to reclaim memory resources; it requires a distributed computation involving all of the processors in the system.

4.2   LOCAL CONTROL MECHANISM

The behavior of each logical process in a Time Warp system can be described in relation to a sequential simulation. Recall that a sequential simulator contains a data

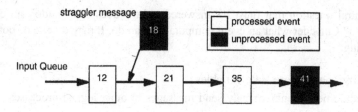

Figure 4.1   Events in Time Warp logical process when a straggler message arrives.

structure called the event list that includes all events that have been scheduled but have not yet been processed. A Time Warp logical process (TWLP) can be viewed in exactly the same way, except for two differences:

- The events in the TWLPs event set may result from messages sent to this LP from other LPs.
- The TWLP does not discard events after processing them but rather keeps the processed events in a queue. This is necessary because the TWLP may roll back, in which case previously processed events will have to be re-processed.

A TWLP showing both the processed and unprocessed events is depicted in Figure 4.1. Each event processed by the TWLP is placed at the end of the "processed" part of the event list. Because events are processed in time stamp order, events in this list will be sorted by time stamp. The white events in Figure 4.1 with time stamps 12, 21, and 35 have already been processed by the LP, and the black event with time stamp 41 has not yet been processed. The TWLP's clock is at simulation time 35 in this snapshot, and is about to advance to 41.

As in a sequential simulator, the TWLP will repeatedly remove the smallest time-stamped unprocessed event from the event list and process that event. Unlike a conservative simulation executive that must first verify that an event is safe, TWLP makes no such check, and blindly (optimistically) goes ahead and processes the next event. This means that the TWLP may later receive a message in its past, that is, a message with time stamp smaller than the clock value of the TWLP.[10] Such "late" arriving messages are referred to as *straggler messages*. Figure 4.1 shows a straggler message arriving at a TWLP, with time stamp 18, indicating that a violation of the local causality constraint has occurred.

Events with a time stamp larger than the straggler were processed incorrectly because the state of the LP did not take into account the processing of the straggler event. Thus in Figure 4.1 the events with time stamps 21 and 35 were processed incorrectly. Time Warp addresses this problem by rolling back or "undoing" the computations for the time stamp 21 and 35 events, and then re-processing these events (the straggler at time 18, and the rolled back events at times 21 and 35) in time stamp order.

---

[10] We assume for now that all events have unique time stamps. This issue will be discussed later.

The central question that must be answered is how does one "undo" an event computation? Consider what an event computation can do. It may do one or both of the following:

1. Modify one or more state variables.
2. Schedule new events, namely send messages to other logical processes.

Thus a mechanism is required to undo changes to state variables and to "unsend" previously sent messages. Each of these is described next.

4.2.1 Rolling Back State Variables

There are two widely used techniques to undoing modifications to state variables that are commonly used in Time Warp systems:

1. *Copy state saving.* The TWLP makes a copy of all of the modifiable state variables within the LP. Typically a copy is made *prior* to processing each event, but as will be discussed later, the copying could be performed less frequently. Figure 4.2(*a*) depicts the state-saving and restoration process for the rollback scenario shown in Figure 4.1. The LP's state in this example includes three variables, X, Y, and Z that hold the values 1, 2, and 3, respectively, after processing E_{12} (the event with time stamp 12). Event E_{21} writes a new value, 4, into X, and E_{35} writes 5 into X and 9 into Z. As shown in Figure 4.2(*a*), all three state variables are copied into memory associated with an event just before that event is processed. When the straggler message with time stamp 18 arrives, the LP's state is restored to the state of the LP at time 18, the state which existed prior to processing E_{21}. The rollback causes the snapshot associated with E_{21} to be copied back into the LP's state variables, effectively undoing the modifications to the state variables made by E_{21} and E_{35}.

2. *Incremental state saving.* A log recording changes to individual state variables is kept for each event computation. Each record in the log indicates (a) the address of the state variable that was modified, and (b) the value of the state variable prior to the modification. To roll back modifications to state variables performed by an event, the Time Warp executive scans the events being rolled back in the order of decreasing time stamps. For each event the Time Warp executive goes through that event's log, last record to first, and copies the value saved in the log entry to the corresponding state variable. For example, the rollback scenario shown in Figure 4.1 using incremental state saving is shown in Figure 4.2(*b*). The log for E_{21} contains the record (adr(X), 1) where adr(X) indicates the address of variable X, and the log for E_{35} contains the records (adr(X), 4) and (adr(Z), 3). As shown in Figure 4.2(b), rolling back these events will restore (1) Z to 3, (2) X to 4, and (3) X to 1, yielding the original values that existed prior to processing E_{21}.

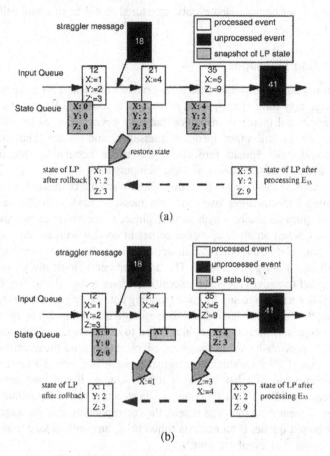

Figure 4.2 Undoing modifications to state variables. (*a*) Copy state method; (*b*) incremental state saving.

If most of the state variables are modified in each event, copy state saving is more efficient because one does not need to save the addresses of individual variables, and many machines are optimized to efficiently copy large blocks of data. On the other hand, if only a small portion of the state vector is modified on each event, incremental state saving will be more efficient because it only saves those state variables that were actually modified. These two techniques are *not* mutually exclusive. Some Time Warp systems use copy state saving for variables that are modified frequently, and incremental state saving for other variables that are modified infrequently, with the choice of state-saving technique for each variable typically left to the application programmer.

Whether copy state saving or incremental state saving is used, some amount of state information is associated with each event. The collection of state information for the events within an LP is referred to as the *state queue*. The events themselves, both the processed and unprocessed events, are stored in a data structure called the *input queue*.

4.2.2 Unsending Messages

At first glance, undoing a message send seems rather complex. This is because an incorrect message may have already been processed by another LP, resulting in the generation of additional incorrect messages that have been processed by still other LPs, which results in still other incorrect messages, and so on. The incorrect computation could have spread throughout the entire simulation, requiring a mechanism to undo all of the effects of these computations!

Perhaps the most elegant aspect of the Time Warp mechanism is a simple mechanism called *anti-messages* used to undo message sends. The name "anti-message" comes from an analogy with particle physics concerning matter and anti-matter. In physics, when an atom of matter comes in contact with an atom of anti-matter, the two annihilate each other and disappear. Similarly, for each message sent by a TWLP, an anti-message is created. The anti-message is logically an identical copy of the original (positive) message, except it contains a flag identifying it as an anti-message. When a message and its corresponding anti-message are both stored in the same queue, they are both deleted and their storage is reclaimed. The process of combining message/anti-message pairs is referred to as message annihilation.

To "unsend" a previously sent message, an LP need only send the matching anti-message to the same TWLP to which the original message was sent. This implies the TWLP must keep a log of what messages it has sent, so it can later send anti-messages, if necessary. Each TWLP defines a data structure called the *output queue* for this purpose. Whenever a message is sent, the corresponding anti-message is left in the sender's output queue. If an event is rolled back, any anti-messages stored in the output queue for that event are sent.

The example shown in Figure 4.1 is continued in Figure 4.3 to show the operations that take place when a rollback occurs. The straggler message causes E_{21} and E_{35} to be rolled back. The state of the LP is restored using the information stored in the state queue, and the memory used for this saved state information can now be reclaimed. E_{21} and E_{35} are marked as unprocessed events. In this example, E_{35} generated one message, E_{42}, so the anti-message for E_{42} is removed from the output queue and sent. The final state of the LP after the rollback has been processed is shown in Figure 4.3(*b*).

Now consider what happens when a logical process, LP_A, receives an anti-message. There are three cases to consider:

1. The corresponding positive message has not yet been processed. In this case the message and anti-message pair can both be annihilated, and removed from LP_A's input queue, and the storage used for these messages can be reclaimed (see Fig. 4.4).

2. The corresponding positive message has already been processed. In this case LP_A is rolled back to the point just prior to processing the about-to-be-

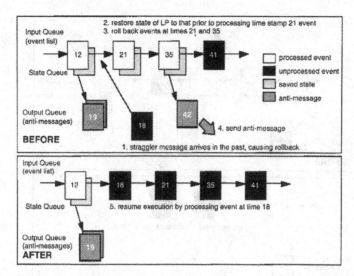

Figure 4.3 Rollback caused by receiving a straggler message. (Top) Actions performed to roll back the LP; (bottom) final state of the LP after the rollback.

canceled positive message (see Fig. 4.5). Once the rollback has been performed, the message and anti-message pair can be annihilated, just as in case 1. This rollback caused by receiving an anti-message in the TWLP's past is referred to as a *secondary rollback* (the initial rollback resulting from the original straggler message is called a *primary rollback*). The secondary

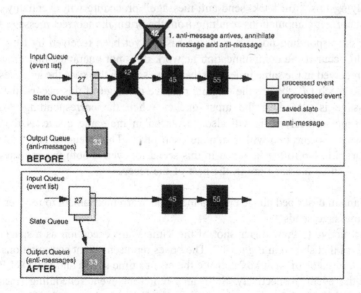

Figure 4.4 Receiving an anti-message, positive message has not yet been processed. (Top) Message/anti-message pair annihilated; (bottom) final state of queues after annihilation.

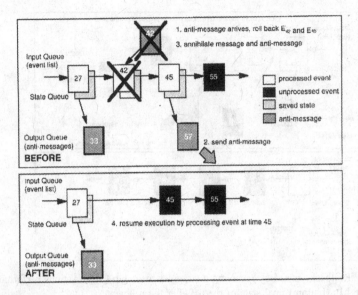

Figure 4.5 Receiving an anti-message, positive message has already been processed. (Top). Rollback action prior to processing message, annihilated message/anti-message pair; (bottom) final state of queues after annihilation.

rollback may generate additional anti-messages, which may in turn cause further rollbacks (and anti-messages) in other logical processes. Recursively applying this "roll back, send anti-message" procedure will eventually erase all incorrect computations resulting from the original, incorrect message send.

3. The corresponding positive message has not yet been received by LP_A. This could occur if the communication network does not guarantee that messages are received in the same order that they were sent; in this case the anti-message could reach LP_A before the original positive message. If this occurs, the anti-message is placed in the input queue. When the corresponding positive message is received, it will also be placed in the same queue as the anti-message, so the two will annihilate each other. This scenario is depicted in Figure 4.6. No rollbacks occur in this scenario, even if both the anti-message and positive message are in the past of the receiver.

The mechanism described above enables the Time Warp mechanism to recover from incorrect message sends.

It is instructive to view a snapshot of the Time Warp execution as a space-time graph such as that shown in Figure 4.7. The boxes represent event computations, and the X-Y coordinates of each box indicate the event's time stamp and the TWLP that processes the event, respectively. Solid arcs represent event scheduling (message sending) relationships; that is, an arc from event E_1 to E_2 denotes the fact that the computation for E_1 scheduled event E_2. Successive events within an LP are

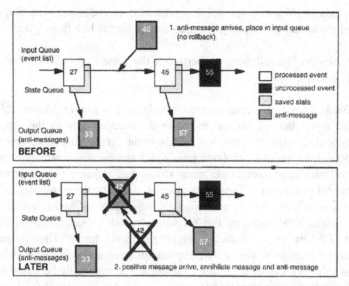

Figure 4.6 Receiving an anti-message when the positive message has not yet been received. (Top) Place anti-message in input queue (no rollback occurs); (bottom) when a positive message arrives, annihilate message/anti-message pair.

connected by dashed arcs indicating dependencies between events due to accesses to common state variables (it is assumed successive events within the same LP always depend on each other in this way). An event E_2 *is dependent on* another event E_1 if there is a path of arcs (using either state dependence and/or scheduling dependence arcs) from E_1 to E_2. When an event E is rolled back, all events that depend on E are either rolled back (if they have been processed) or canceled via the anti-message mechanism.

Assuming nonzero lookahead, scheduling arcs must always move from left to right in the space-time diagram. Similarly state dependence arcs also move from left

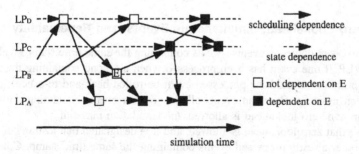

Figure 4.7 Space-time diagram depicting a snapshot of a Time Warp execution and dependencies among events.

to right.[11] This implies that the graph represented in the space-time diagram is acyclic, and traversing the dependence arcs always moves one from left to right in the graph.

One can observe the following properties of the Time Warp execution from the space-time diagram:

1. *Rollbacks always propagate into the simulated time future.* Because rollbacks spread along the scheduling and state dependence arcs in the graph, the rollback always spreads from left to right in the graph. Viewed another way, if a TWLP rolls back to simulated time T, all anti-messages sent as a result of this roll back must have a time stamp strictly larger than T (recall the nonzero lookahead assumption). Thus any rollbacks caused by these anti-messages will be to a simulation time greater than T. Subsequent rollbacks resulting from anti-messages generated by this secondary rollback must similarly roll back other TWLPs to successively larger simulated times. This property is important because it shows that one cannot have a *domino effect* where an initial roll back causes the entire computation to eventually be rolled back to the beginning of the simulation.

2. *At any instant during the execution, the computation associated with the smallest time-stamped message or anti-message in the system that has not yet been completed will not be later rolled back.* The computation associated with an anti-message is the annihilation of the message/anti-message pair. If there is more than one computation containing the smallest time stamp, the above statement applies to at least one of these computations. Intuitively the smallest time-stamped computation cannot be rolled back because rollbacks propagate from left to right in the space-time graph, and there is no computation to the left of the leftmost uncompleted computation in the graph. Thus there is nothing that can cause this computation to be rolled back. This property is important because it shows that so long as the Time Warp system has a scheduling mechanism that eventually executes the lowest time-stamped computation, the execution always make forward progress, so no deadlock situations can occur.

4.2.3 Zero Lookahead, Simultaneous Events, and Repeatability

Consider two simultaneous events (events containing the same time stamp) within a single TWLP. If one event has been processed when a second containing the same time stamp arrives, should the processed event be rolled back and re-executed? As will be seen momentarily, if an event rolls back other events containing the same time stamp and zero lookahead is allowed, the simulation may fail.

Suppose that zero lookahead is allowed, and it is designated that a straggler does roll back other already processed events containing the same time stamp. Consider

---

[11] In the case of events containing the same time stamp (simultaneous events), the LP places some ordering of these events which is used to preserve the left-to-right nature of the state dependence arcs.

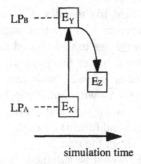

Figure 4.8 Cyclic dependence among three events containing the same time stamp.

the scenario shown in Figure 4.8. Event E_X at LP_A schedules E_Y at LP_B, which in turn schedules E_Z back to LP_A. Suppose that all three events contain the same time stamp. E_Z will roll back E_X, since they have the same time stamp. Rolling back E_X will cancel E_Y, which will in turn cancel E_Z. When E_X is re-executed, it will again generate E_Y, which will generate E_Z, this will again roll back E_X, causing the cancellation of E_Y and E_Z, and so on. The simulation will repeat this cycle indefinitely.

The unending rollback cycle occurs because there is a cycle in the dependence arcs in the space time diagram. Rolling back E_X when E_Z arrives implies that E_X is state dependent on E_Z. This means there is a cycle from E_X to E_Y to E_Z via scheduling dependence arcs (see Fig. 4.8), and then from E_Z back to E_X via a state dependence arc. Dependence cycles such as this must be eliminated to avoid unending rollback scenarios such as that described above.

One way to address this problem is to simply designate that a straggler message does *not* roll back other already processed events containing the same time stamp. This prevents rollback cycles.[12] In effect, simultaneous events are delivered to the LP in the order that they were received. The disadvantage of this approach is that the execution may not be repeatable, since the events may arrive in a different order during the next execution. To ensure repeatability, the TWLP must first collect all simultaneous events, and then order them itself in a repeatable fashion, such as by sorting on some characteristic of the event.

Another approach is to allow an event to roll back some events containing the same time stamp but to ensure that an event never rolls back another event on which it is either scheduling dependent or *indirectly* scheduling dependent. An event E_j is *indirectly scheduling dependent* on another event E_i if there is a path of *only* scheduling dependence arcs from E_i to E_j. This approach breaks the cycle in Figure 4.8 because E_Z is indirectly scheduling dependent on E_X, so using this rule, E_Z cannot roll back E_X. This approach can be realized by extending the time stamp of

---

[12] It might be noted that receiving an anti-message at time T could still cause another message in the same LP with time stamp T to be rolled back; however, because rollback cycles must begin with a straggler message that is regenerated within the rollback cycle, this does not lead to an unending cycle.

the event with an additional *age* field, like that described in Chapter 3, where the age was used to order simultaneous events. Like the time stamp field, the larger the age field, the later is the event. Thus the age can be viewed as an extension of the time stamp field that provides additional, lower precision digits. Recall that the age is assigned as follows: Suppose that an event E_X with time stamp T_X contains an age A_X, and E_X schedules another event E_Y with time stamp T_Y and age A_Y. If $T_Y > T_X$, then A_Y is 1. If $T_Y = T_X$, then A_Y is $A_X + 1$. Thus, if one considers the tree formed with simultaneous events as nodes and (direct) scheduling dependencies as arcs, the age indicates the level of the event in the tree.

In Figure 4.8, E_X, E_Y, and E_Z would be assigned ages 1, 2, and 3, respectively. Because E_Z has a larger (later) age than E_X; E_Z does not cause E_X to be rolled back. Note that there may be two or more events containing both the same time stamp and age; for example, if E_X also scheduled another event E_W with time stamp T_X, then both E_W and E_Y would have the same time stamp and age. An additional field is required if unique time stamps are required, for example, to guarantee repeatability of the execution. In the TWOS (Time Warp Operating System) developed at the Jet Propulsion Laboratory, the body of the message itself was used as the identifier; the only "ties" that can occur are when the messages themselves are identical, in which case, the order doesn't matter. Another approach, discussed in Chapter 3, is to use the tuple (LP_S, I) where LP_S identifies the logical process sending the message and I is a sequence number indicating the number of events scheduled by LP_S, excluding message sends that have been rolled back (i.e., canceled by sending the corresponding anti-message).

Using the approach with an age field, but no additional fields to specify an ordering among events with the same time stamp and age, one can still specify that an event rolls back a processed simultaneous event with the same (or greater) age. This allows the application to explicitly order simultaneous events with the same time stamp and age according to its own criteria. The system will automatically guarantee events that are directly or indirectly scheduling dependent on this event will not result in unending rollback cycles.

To summarize, these techniques enable the Time Warp system to schedule zero lookahead events. Unending rollback cycles can be prevented by either specifying that a straggler message does not roll back events containing the same time stamp or by using an age field. By itself, neither of these techniques guarantees repeatable executions. Repeatability can be obtained through the use of an additional, unique, identifier field in the time stamp, or by requiring the application to collect and order simultaneous events in a repeatable fashion.

4.3 GLOBAL CONTROL MECHANISM

The local control mechanism described above is sufficient to ensure that the execution yields the same results as if the simulation were executed sequentially and all events were processed in time stamp order. However, two problems must be addressed before this can be regarded as a viable mechanism:

1. The computation consumes more and more memory throughout the execution via the creation of new events, but it seldom releases memory! A mechanism is required to reclaim memory resources used for processed events, anti-messages, and state history information that is no longer needed. Reclamation of memory holding history information is referred to as *fossil collection*.
2. Certain operations performed by the simulation computation cannot be rolled back. Specifically, once I/O is performed, it cannot be easily undone.

Both of these problems can be solved if one can guarantee that certain events are no longer prone to roll back. For example, if one could guarantee that no roll back will occur to a simulated time earlier than T, the history information for events with time stamps smaller than T could be reclaimed. Similarly I/O operations generated by any event with a time stamp less than T could be performed without fear of the operation later being rolled back. Thus the solution to both of the problems cited above is to determine a lower bound on the time stamp of any future rollback. This lower bound is referred to as *Global Virtual Time* (GVT).

From the local control mechanism it becomes immediately apparent that a TWLP only rolls back as the result of receiving a message, which is either a positive message or an anti-message, in the TWLP's past. Observe that positive messages can only be created by unprocessed (or partially processed) events. Therefore, if one could capture a snapshot of the Time Warp system, the minimum time stamp among all anti-messages, positive messages, and unprocessed and partially processed events in the system represents a lower bound on the time stamp of any future rollback. Observe that a positive message in transit to a TWLP holds an unprocessed event. Therefore Global Virtual Time is defined as follows:

Definition Global Virtual Time at wallclock time T (GVT$_T$) during the execution of a Time Warp simulation is defined as the minimum time stamp among all unprocessed and partially processed messages and anti-messages in the system at wallclock time T.

Figures 4.2, 4.3, and 4.5 illustrate that if the TWLP is rolled back to time T, only the history information (specifically state information and anti-messages) for the events that are rolled back is needed. Therefore memory for events with time stamp strictly less than GVT and the anti-messages and state information associated with these events can be reclaimed. Memory associated with events with time stamp equal to the GVT value cannot be reclaimed, however, even if the Time Warp system is defined so that a straggler message with time stamp T does *not* roll back other events with time stamp equal to T. This is because GVT could be equal to the time stamp of an anti-message that has not been processed (i.e., annihilated), so such an anti-message could require one to roll back events with time stamp exactly equal to GVT (see Fig. 4.9).

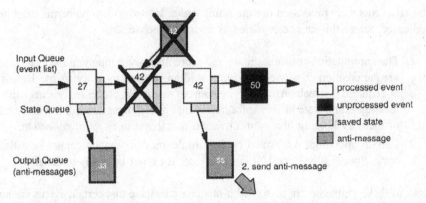

Figure 4.9 Example where the information in an event with time stamp equal to GVT is needed. Here, GVT is 42, and there are two processed events with time stamp 42. In the first, the TWLP processed is canceled by an anti-message with time stamp equal to GVT.

4.3.1 Fossil Collection

Most Time Warp systems compute GVT periodically (for example, every few seconds), or when the simulation runs out of memory. There are two common approaches to reclaiming memory:

- *Batch fossil collection.* When fossil collection is performed, the Time Warp executive in each processor scans through the event lists of all of the TWLPs mapped to that processor, and reclaims the memory used by events (and associated state information and anti-messages).
- *On-the-fly fossil collection.* When GVT is computed, the system does *not* immediately reclaim memory. Instead, processed events are placed into a list of events, typically managed as a FIFO queue. When memory for a new event is required, the Time Warp executive allocates memory from this list but only reallocates the storage for an event if the time stamp of that event is less than GVT. This approach avoids a possible time-consuming search through the event lists of the TWLPs in order to perform fossil collection.

4.3.2 Error Handling

Unlike conservative simulation systems, if a simulation program executing on a Time Warp executive produces an error (for example, performs a divide by zero operation), the program *cannot* simply be aborted. This is because the error may later be erased by a rollback operation. When an error occurs, it is flagged, and the TWLP is blocked so that it will not process any additional events. If the error is not erased by a rollback, it is committed when GVT advances past the simulation time at which the error occurred. The program can then be aborted and the user can be notified of the error.

The tricky aspect of error handling is to ensure that the error itself can be erased. Different countermeasures are required for different types of errors. Below we enumerate some possible errors and how they can be handled:

- *Program detected errors.* These are errors in logic and inconsistencies detected by the simulation program itself. For instance, it may be that a certain state variable should never take on a negative value (for example, the number of aircraft waiting to land at an airport). As a precautionary measure the program might periodically test this variable to make sure that it has not been assigned a negative value, as a check for a programming bug that could cause the simulation to reach an incorrect state. This is the most straightforward type of error to address. The Time Warp executive can provide an abort primitive that marks the logical process as being in an error state so that no more events are processed by that TWLP. As described earlier, if the error is erased by a rollback, the process can be returned to the "normal" state. If the error is committed, the program is then aborted.

- *Infinite loops.* If the program enters an infinite loop, a mechanism is required to break out of the loop if a message is received that would cause the event containing the infinite loop to be rolled back. This can be accomplished by using an interrupt mechanism to handle incoming messages. Alternatively, a call into the Time Warp executive might be placed in each loop of the application program that could become an infinite loop. This call must check to see if any messages were received that would roll back the event that is now being processed. If such an event is detected, the processing of the current event should be aborted, and the rollback processed.

- *Benign errors.* These are errors that do not result in the incorrect modification of any memory other than checkpointed state variables. Examples include arithmetic errors such as dividing by zero, taking the square root of a negative number, or an illegal memory reference (for example, to a location within the operating system) that is aborted by the operating system's memory protection mechanisms. A mechanism is required to pass control to the Time Warp executive when such errors occur. Support must be provided by the operating system or the language's runtime system. For example, the Ada language provides a mechanism to execute user (or in this case, Time Warp executive) code when such an error occurs. Similarly programs written for the Unix[TM] operating system can specify code that is executed when a signal is raised, denoting such exceptions. Once the error has been detected and control is passed to the Time Warp executive, the error can be handled in the same way as a program-detected error.

- *Destructive errors.* Destructive errors are those that result in the modification of state that is not checkpointed; for example, an errant pointer reference or running off the end of an array could modify internal data structures within the

Time Warp executive. Because the Time Warp executive is usually viewed by the operating system as part of the application program, such an error does not typically result in a trap, as would occur if (say) the program attempted to overwrite a memory location within the operating system. These are the most problematic types of errors because once the state has been erroneously modified, it is difficult to recover from such an error. A brute force solution is to checkpoint all memory that can be modified by the application without causing a trap in the operating system, such as all state used by the Time Warp executive. Another approach is to provide explicit runtime checks for such errors (for example, array bounds checks or adding code to check that memory writes only modify checkpointed state), effectively converting the error to a program detected error. Such checks are only required on references using memory addresses that are computed at runtime. Minimizing use of computed addresses (for example, not performing arithmetic on pointers to compute addresses) reduces the likelihood of destructive errors.

4.4 COMPUTING GLOBAL VIRTUAL TIME

GVT computation is a close cousin to the lower bound on time stamp (LBTS) computation discussed in Chapter 3 for conservative synchronization. GVT computes a lower bound on the simulation time of any future rollback. But as noted earlier, rollback only occurs when an LP receives a message or anti-message in its (simulation time) past, so the value relevant to each LP is a lower bound on the time stamp of messages/anti-messages that may arrive in the future. This is essentially the same as the LBTS value computed by conservative algorithms.

Differences between LBTS and GVT computations stem largely from (1) different underlying assumptions concerning topology among logical processes and lookahead, and (2) different performance requirements. Regarding the former, Time Warp systems usually assume that any LP can send messages to any other LP and that there is zero lookahead. Conservative algorithms usually make more stringent assumptions regarding topology and lookahead that they can then exploit to minimize blocking among LPs. An LBTS computation where one assumes a fully connected topology and zero lookahead is essentially the same as a GVT computation.

With respect to different performance requirements, LBTS in conservative systems must be computed often, and very rapidly, because processors may be idle and waiting for it to complete. This is typically *not* the case in optimistic systems where processors optimistically process events and need not wait for the GVT computation to complete, so long as they do not run out of memory or need to commit I/O operations very quickly. Thus simpler, but perhaps higher-latency algorithms may be adequate, or even preferred in optimistic systems. Here, we focus on algorithms developed specifically for computing GVT. These same algorithms can, in principle, be used to compute LBTS, and conversely, the LBTS algorithms discussed in the previous chapter can be used to compute GVT, provided that one adheres to their underlying assumptions.

From the definition of GVT, it is clear that if one could capture in a snapshot all unprocessed (and partially processed) events and anti-messages in the system at wallclock time T, computing GVT_T would be trivial. There are two challenging problems associated with making such a snapshot. They are referred to as the *transient message problem* and the *simultaneous reporting problem*. Each of these is described next, followed by a discussion of algorithms for efficiently computing GVT.

4.4.1 Transient Message Problem

Suppose that one could instantaneously "freeze" all processors in the system, have each report its local minimum among the unprocessed events and anti-messages within that processor, and then compute a global minimum from these values. This algorithm would *not* compute a correct value for GVT. The reason is that while all of the processors are "frozen," there may be one or more messages "in the network," namely messages that have been sent by one processor but have not yet been received at its final destination. As shown in Figure 4.10, such messages may result in rollbacks. Thus it is clear that these so-called *transient messages* must be included in the GVT computation, or an error results. This problem is referred to as the *transient message problem*.

There are essentially two approaches to solving the transient message problem: (1) Have the sender take into account the time stamp of transient messages when it reports its local minimum, or (2) have the receiver to take into account the time stamp of transient messages when they arrive. The latter approach requires one to provide a mechanism to determine when all relevant transient messages have been received. An approach using message counters will be described later. We first discuss solutions using the former approach.

One simple solution to the transient message problem is to use message acknowledgments. The key idea is to ensure that every transient message is accounted for by at least one processor when GVT is being computed. It is

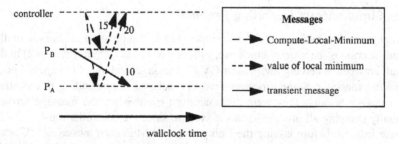

Figure 4.10 Transient message problem. Processors P_A and P_B compute their local minimums to be 15 and 20, respectively. If the transient message is not considered, GVT will be incorrectly computed as 15, when it should be 10.

acceptable for more than one processor to account for a single message because this would not affect the global minimum computation. If an acknowledgment is sent for every message, the sender of each message is responsible for accounting for the message in its local minimum until the acknowledgment is received. The receiver takes responsibility for the message as soon as it receives the message. This handshake between the sender and receiver ensures that no transient messages "fall between the cracks" during the GVT computation.

A simple, synchronous GVT algorithm using acknowledgments can now be described. This algorithm uses a central controller to initiate the GVT computation, compute the global minimum, and report the computed GVT to the other processors. Specifically, the algorithm takes the following steps:

1. The controller broadcasts a "Start-GVT" message, instructing each processor in the system to initiate a GVT computation.

2. Upon receiving the Start-GVT message, each processor stops processing events, and issues a "Received-Start message" to the controller. The processor blocks until receiving another message from the controller.

3. When the controller has received a "Received-Start" message from every processor, it broadcasts a "Compute-Local-Minimum" message.

4. Upon receiving the "Compute-Local-Minimum" message, each processor computes the minimum time stamp among (a) the unprocessed events and anti-messages within that processor and (b) the minimum time stamp of any message the processor has sent but has not yet received an acknowledgment. This minimum value is sent to the controller.

5. When the controller has received the local minimum from each processor, it computes a global minimum and broadcasts this value to each processor.

Using this approach, the scenario in Figure 4.10 will result in P_B reporting 10 instead of 15 as its local minimum because it will not have received an acknowledgment for the time stamp 10 message it has sent. Thus the controller will correctly compute the GVT to be the value 10.

4.4.2 Simultaneous Reporting Problem

An important drawback to the synchronous GVT computation described in the previous section is the need to block every processor in the system (see step 2) in the interval between receiving the "Start-GVT" message and the "Compute-Local-Minimum" message. Some processors may be delayed in responding to the Start-GVT message because they were processing an event when the message arrived, potentially delaying all processors in the system, since the controller must receive a response from all before issuing the Compute-Local-Minimum message.[13] A better approach would be to allow processors to continue processing events while the GVT

---

[13] This could be circumvented by using an interrupt mechanism, however.

computation is in progress, that is, to use an asynchronous computation that does not require global synchronization points.

One might suggest a simple asynchronous GVT algorithm where the controller simply broadcasts a Compute-Local-Minimum request to all of the processors, and then simply collects these values and computes a global minimum. Processors may process events asynchronously while the GVT computation is in progress. This simple approach does not work, however, because it introduces a problem known as the *simultaneous reporting problem*. Intuitively this problem arises because not all processors will report their local minimum at precisely the same instant in wallclock time. This can result in one or more messages "slipping between the cracks"; that is, one or more unprocessed messages may not be accounted for by either the processor sending or receiving the message.

A scenario illustrating the simultaneous reporting problem is depicted in Figure 4.11. The controller broadcasts the Compute-Local-Minimum message. Processor P_A receives this message and reports its local minimum is 35. The Compute-Local-Minimum message that is sent to processor P_B is delayed in the communications network, however, and does not arrive until some time later. In the mean time, P_B sends a message to P_A with time stamp 30 and then moves on to begin processing another event with time stamp 40. At this point P_B receives the Compute-Local-Minimum message and reports its local minimum is 40, the time stamp of its next local event. The controller computes an incorrect GVT value of 35 (minimum of 35 and 40) because it failed to take into account the time stamp 30 message. The scenario shown in Figure 4.11 could still occur even if message acknowledgments were used.

The basic problem is that accounting for all unprocessed messages in the system becomes more complicated if processors are allowed to process events and generate new ones while the GVT computation is in progress. In Figure 4.11, P_A cannot take into account the time stamp 30 message in its local minimum computation because it had not even received the event when its local minimum was computed. P_B does not take this event into account in its local minimum computation because it believes that the message is P_A's responsibility, since the message was generated (and acknowledged if message acknowledgments are used) well before it computed its

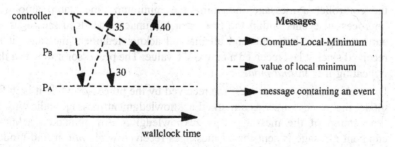

Figure 4.11 Simultaneous reporting problem. The time stamp 30 message is not accounted for, resulting in an incorrect GVT value of 35 being computed.

local minimum. Thus the time stamp 30 message is not accounted for by either processor.

4.4.3 Samadi's GVT Algorithm

This algorithm assumes that message acknowledgments are sent on every message and anti-message sent between processors. As discussed earlier, the sending processor is responsible for accounting for each message it has sent until it receives the acknowledgment, thereby solving the transient message problem.

The simultaneous reporting problem is solved by having processors tag any *acknowledgment* messages that it sends in the period starting from when the processor reported its local minimum until it receives the new GVT value. This identifies messages that might "slip between the cracks" and notifies the sender that it (the sender) is responsible for accounting for the message in its local minimum computation. Thus, in Figure 4.11, P_A will tag the acknowledgment it sends for the time stamp 30 message it received from P_B. P_B includes in its local minimum computation (1) the minimum time stamp among the unprocessed message or anti-message stored within the processor, (2) the minimum time stamp among the messages it has sent for which it has not yet received an acknowledgment (i.e., transient messages), and (3) the minimum time stamp among the tagged acknowledgment messages the processors received since the last GVT computation. Thus, in Figure 4.11, if the (tagged) acknowledgment for the time stamp 30 message reaches P_B before it reports its local minimum, this message will be included in the local minimum computation by (3) above. If the acknowledgment is received *after* P_B reports its local minimum, this message will still be included by P_B in its local minimum computation because the message was a transient (unacknowledged) message when P_B reported its local minimum. Either way, P_B will account for the message.

More precisely, Samadi's GVT algorithm operates as follows:

1. The controller broadcasts a Compute-Local-Minimum message to all processors to initiate the GVT computation.
2. Upon receiving the Compute-Local-Minimum message, the processor sends the controller a message indicating the minimum time stamp among all unprocessed events within the processor, all unacknowledged messages and anti-messages it has sent, and all marked acknowledgment messages it has received since it last received a new GVT value. The processor now sets a flag, indicating it is in *find mode*.
3. For each message or anti-message received by the processor while it is in find mode, the processor sends a marked acknowledgment message indicating the time stamp of the message it is acknowledging. An unmarked acknowledgment message is sent for all messages received while *not* in find mode.
4. When the controller receives a local minimum value from every processor in the system, it computes the minimum of all these values as the new GVT and broadcasts the new GVT to all processors in the system.

5. Upon receiving the new GVT value, each processor changes its status so that it is no longer in find mode.

It can be shown that this algorithm computes a new value of GVT that is no larger than the true GVT value at the instant the controller broadcast the Compute-Local-Minimum message to initiate the GVT computation.

4.4.4 Mattern's GVT Algorithm

One drawback with Samadi's algorithm is that it requires an acknowledgment message to be sent for each message and anti-message. The underlying communications software may automatically send acknowledgments for messages in order to implement the reliable message delivery service being used by the Time Warp executive; however, such acknowledgments are typically not visible to the Time Warp executive. Instead, a separate application-level acknowledgment message must be sent to implement Samadi's algorithm.

Like Samadi's algorithm, Mattern's GVT algorithm is also asynchronous. That is it avoids global synchronizations, but it does not require message acknowledgments. The basic idea in the algorithm is to cleanly divide the distributed computation by a "cut" that separates it into a "past" and "future." As shown in Figure 4.12, each processor defines a point in its execution called a *cut point*, with all actions (computations, message sends, and message receives) before a processor's cut point (in wallclock time) referred to as being in that processor's past, and all actions occurring after the cut point referred to as occurring in that processor's future. The set of cut points across all of the processors defines a cut of the distributed computation. A *consistent cut* is defined as a cut where there is *no* message that was sent in the future of the sending processor and received in the past of the receiving processor. Graphically, if each message is represented as an arrow, this means there is no message arrow extending from the future part of the graph to the past part. Figure 4.12(*a*) shows a consistent cut and Figure 4.12(*b*) shows an inconsistent cut. The latter cut is inconsistent because of the message sent from P_C's future to P_D's past.

A snapshot taken along a consistent cut includes the local state of each processor at its cut point and all transient messages crossing the cut—namely all messages sent in the past part and received in the future part of the computation. A key observation is that the snapshot of the computation taken along a consistent cut can be used to compute GVT. To see this, consider the execution of the *synchronous* GVT algorithm discussed earlier. Specifically, let each processor's cut point in Figure 4.12(*a*) represent the wallclock time at which it received a "Compute-Local-Minimum" message. Recall that in the synchronous GVT algorithm, this message causes the processor to "freeze," that is, not perform any new computations or send or receive any additional messages. The processors then compute GVT based on a cut defined at one instant in wallclock time after all the processors have been frozen; see Figure 4.12(*c*). It is clear the synchronous GVT algorithm correctly computes GVT_T, where T is the wallclock time of the cut points in Figure 4.12(*c*).

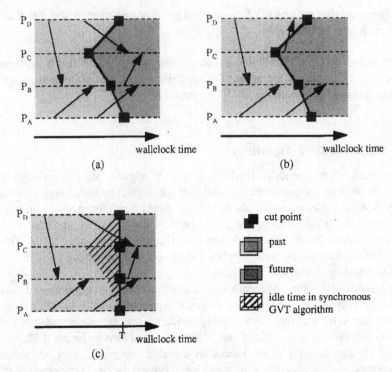

Figure 4.12 Cuts dividing the distributed computation into past and fugure parts. (*a*) A consistent cut; (*b*) an inconsistent cut; (*c*) cut for computation shown in (*a*) using the synchronous GVT algorithm so that all cut points correspond to the same point in wallclock time.

Now suppose that rather than freezing each processor at its cut point, we allow each processor to compute forward; that is to say, we compute GVT asynchronously, as in Figure 4.12(*a*). Assume that the cut in the asynchronous algorithm is a consistent one. The set of transient messages in the synchronous snapshot is exactly the same as the set of transient messages in the asynchronous one because (1) any message in the synchronous snapshot will (obviously) also appear in the asynchronous one and (2) the asynchronous snapshot cannot include any additional messages because any such message crossing the cut must have been sent by a processor after its cut point, which would cause the cut to become inconsistent. Similarly it is clear that the local snapshot taken by each processor in the asynchronous algorithm will be identical to that in the synchronous algorithm because the consistent nature of the cut prevents any new events appearing in the asynchronous snapshot that did not appear in the synchronous one. Thus an *asynchronous* algorithm that computes GVT based on the consistent cut in Figure 4.12(*a*) will compute GVT$_T$, the same value computed by the synchronous algorithm.

From the above discussion it is clear that if the asynchronous cut were *not* consistent, the snapshot based on that cut would not match that used in the corresponding execution using the synchronous algorithm. For example, in Figure 4.12(b), the snapshot defined by the inconsistent cut includes a message in P_D's local state that would not exist in the snapshot obtained by the synchronous GVT algorithm.

Happily, an asynchronous GVT algorithm need not construct a consistent cut. It can simply ignore all messages that would make the cut inconsistent. These messages can be ignored because they must have a time stamp larger than the GVT computed using the consistent cut. To see this, observe that the time stamp of any message (or anti-message) sent by a processor after its cut point at wallclock time T must be at least as large as the minimum of (1) the smallest time stamp of any unprocessed event in the processor at time T and (2) the smallest time stamp of any message received by the processor after time T. The computed GVT value must be less than or equal to both of these quantities, so the time stamp of any inconsistent message must be larger than the computed GVT value.

Thus, to compute GVT, one needs to only identify (1) the smallest time-stamped unprocessed event within each processor at its cut point and (2) the smallest time stamp of any transient message crossing the cut from the past to the future. The difficult part is determining the set of transient messages without using acknowledgments. This can be accomplished by utilizing *two* cuts, as shown in Figure 4.13, and computing the GVT along the second cut, C2. The purpose of the first cut is to notify each processor to begin recording the smallest time stamp of any message it sends; these messages *may* be transient messages that cross the second cut and must be included in the .GVT computation. The second cut is defined in a way to guarantee that there are no messages generated prior to the first cut that still have not been delivered to the destination processor. This guarantees that all transient messages in the system crossing the second cut must have been sent after the first cut and thus have been included in the GVT computation.

Processors are said to be colored to denote where they are with respect to the two cuts. Initially processors are colored white. After the first cut point is reached, the processor's color changes to red. After the second cut point, the processor returns to the white color. Messages that are sent while the processor is white are called *white*

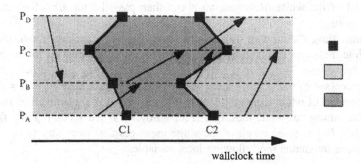

Figure 4.13 GVT computation using two cuts. GVT is based on the snapshot defined by the second cut, C2.

messages, and messages sent while the processor is red are called *red messages*. By design, all white messages must be received prior to C2. Thus, all transient messages crossing C2 must be colored red. The set of messages crossing C2 is a subset of all red messages. Thus the minimum time stamp among all red messages is a lower bound on the minimum time stamp of all transient messages crossing C2.

GVT is computed as the minimum among (1) all red messages, and (2) the minimum time stamp of any unprocessed message in the snapshot defined by C2. This can be done by each processor based on local information. Thus the only question that remains concerns defining C2 so no white message crosses C2.

C1 can be constructed by logically organizing the processors in a ring, and sending a control message around the ring. Upon receiving the control message, each processor changes color from white to red, and passes the control message to the next processor in the ring. Once C1 has been fully constructed, it is guaranteed that no new white messages are being created. C2 can be constructed one processor at a time by sending the control message around the ring again. However, a processor P_i will not forward the message to the next processor in the ring until it can guarantee that there are no more white messages destined for P_i. This can be determined as follows:

1. Compare the number of white messages sent to P_i.
2. Compute the number of white messages received by P_i.
3. Wait for these two numbers to be the same (i.e., wait until all sent messages have been received).

For 1 each processor keeps a counter indicating the number of white messages sent to P_i. These counters are accumulated within the control message as it circulates among the processors during the construction of C1. After the control token has visited every processor, the sum in the token indicates the total number of white messages that were sent to P_i. This total value is passed to P_i during the construction of C2, again via the control token. For 2, P_i keeps a counter indicating the number of white messages it has received (from any processor). When this second counter is equal to the number of messages sent to P_i received in the control token, P_i knows it has received all of the white messages, so it can then pass the token to the next processor in the ring.

Counters indicating the number of white messages sent to a processor, and the number of white messages received by the processor must be maintained for every processor in the system. Thus a *vector* of counters is required by each processor. Specifically, processor P_i maintains a local vector counter V_i such that $V_i(j)$ $(i \neq j)$ indicates the number of white messages sent by P_i to P_j. $V_j(j)$ is a negative number that denotes the number of white messages received by V_j. When $V_j(j) + \sum V_i(j)$, $(j \neq i) \leq 0$, then P_j has received all of the white messages that were sent to it.

Each processor maintains the following local variables:

1. T_{min} is defined as the smallest time stamp of any unprocessed message in the processor.

2. T_{red} is defined as the smallest time stamp of any red message sent by the processor.
3. V_i is the vector counter for processor P_i, as defined above.
4. Color is the current color of the processor, white or red.

The GVT algorithm can now be described. Each message includes a flag indicating its color (white or red). On each message send, processor P_i executes

```
send (Color, time_stamp) to P_j
if (Color = white)
    then V_i(j) := V_i(j) + 1;
    else T_red := min (T_red, time_stamp)
```

When a message is received by a processor P_i it executes

```
if (Msg.color = white)
    then V_i(i) := V_i(i) - 1;
```

The control message contains three fields:

1. CMsg_T_{min} recording the minimum time stamp value among unprocessed messages among processors that the control message has visited thus far.
2. CMsg_T_{red} recording the minimum time stamp of any red message sent by a processor (among the processors that the control message has visited thus far).
3. CMsg_Count is the cumulative vector counters among the processors visited thus far. CMsg_Count[i] indicates the number of white messages sent to P_i that have not yet been received (number of transient messages).

When the control message is received by P_i, it executes the following procedure:

```
if Color=white then
    T_red := ∞;
    Color := red;
wait until V_i[i] + CMsg_Count[i]≤0;
send (min(CMsg_T_min, T_min), min(CMsg_T_red, T_red),
                                    V_i + CMsg_Count)
    to next processor in ring;
V_i := 0;
```

The GVT computation can be initiated by a controller. When the controller receives the control message after the first round, it first checks if CMsg_Count is zero. If it is, there are no transient messages, so the GVT is the smaller of CMsg-T_{min} and CMsg_T_{red}. If not, the controller initiates a second round.

4.5 OTHER MECHANISMS

The local and global control mechanisms described above form the heart of the Time Warp mechanism. A number of additional mechanisms are often included in Time Warp systems to provide added functionality, such as to support dynamic allocation of memory or to optimize performance. Several such mechanisms are described next.

4.5.1 Dynamic Memory Allocation

The discussion thus far has implicitly assumed that all of the memory used for state variables in the simulation is allocated before execution begins and is not released until execution completes. Simulation programs often allocate additional memory for state variables *during* the execution of the simulation. For example, a simulation of a factory might require additional memory to hold information concerning new components created within the factory. Sequential simulation programs can obtain additional memory by calling a memory allocation procedure defined by the operating or runtime system for the program. For example, C programs may call the malloc() procedure to allocate additional memory. Similarly an additional procedure may be invoked by the program to return memory that is no longer used, for example, the free() procedure for C programs. To facilitate the presentation, the discussion that follows refers specifically to calls to malloc() to allocate memory and free() to release memory, however the mechanisms that are discussed apply generically to any dynamic memory allocation and release procedure.

Some precautions must be taken when using dynamic memory allocation and release procedures in Time Warp systems, or for that matter, any parallel simulation system using rollback for synchronization. Suppose that the application calls malloc() and free() directly without informing the Time Warp executive of calls to these procedures. Two problems may arise:

- An invocation of malloc() may be later rolled back. Since rollbacks are transparent to the application, it is impossible for the TWLP to call free() to release this memory. Further, assuming that the pointer to this memory was saved in checkpointed state variables, the rollback would have erased any pointers to the dynamically allocated memory so that memory could be referenced by the TWLP. Thus a "memory leak" occurs where memory has been allocated but cannot be referenced or returned to the system.

- An invocation of free() may be rolled back. The original call to free() will have released the memory to the system. This memory may have since been reallocated by malloc() to another logical process. When free() is rolled back, the first process in effect declares that it did not actually release this memory, leading to the awkward situation that two different logical processes are now using the same memory at the same time for completely different purposes! This will typically lead to unpredictable, and difficult to locate, bugs in the program.

The first problem resulting in a "memory leak" leads to an inefficient use of memory but does not cause incorrect results to be produced by the simulation. It could cause the program to prematurely exhaust all available memory resources, resulting in an aborted execution that would not have otherwise occurred. This problem can be solved by having the Time Warp executive note each call to malloc() and invoke free() whenever a call to malloc() is rolled back. This could be implemented by defining a new procedure called TWmalloc() that is called by the application instead of malloc(). TWmalloc() would simply call malloc(), and then note the call to malloc() in the data structure for the event that is now being processed. The Time Warp executive would call free() for any such calls to malloc() made by each event that it rolls back.

The second problem is perhaps more serious in that it can result in an execution error, or worse, the simulation to produce incorrect results but otherwise appear to be correct. Further this error may be difficult to reproduce because the same sequence of rollbacks may not appear on subsequent executions. This problem can be solved by treating calls to free() the same as calls to I/O procedures. Namely the memory is not actually returned to the system until GVT advances beyond the time stamp of the event that called free(). Operationally, this could be implemented by defining a new procedure called TWfree() that is called by the application rather than free(). The Time Warp executive maintains a list of calls to TWfree() that have been made by each TWLP but have not yet been committed. TWfree() adds a new entry to this list but does *not* call free() to release the memory. If the event calling TWfree() is rolled back, the corresponding call is removed from the list of uncommitted TWfree() calls. This list is scanned when fossil collection is performed, and the memory is reclaimed by calling free() for any call to TWfree() with time stamp less than GVT.

Finally, like any memory used to hold state variables, dynamically allocated memory must be checkpointed. This memory could be copy state saved by having the Time Warp executive maintain a list of dynamically allocated memory locations for each TWLP and automatically make a copy of this state prior to processing each event. Alternatively, incremental state saving can be used. Because the incremental state-saving mechanism does not need to distinguish between dynamically allocated memory and memory that was allocated before execution began, this mechanism operates no differently than what was described earlier.

4.5.2 Infrequent State Saving

The copy state-saving mechanism discussed earlier makes a copy of all of the modifiable state variables used by the logical process prior to processing *each* event. Making a copy of the state vector before each event may consume large amounts of time and memory. Incremental state saving provides an efficient mechanism to reduce these overheads if a relatively small portion of the state is modified by the event computation. However, incremental state saving becomes more expensive than copy state saving if most of the TWLPs state is modified by each event,[14] since copy state saving can perform block moves to save and restore state. Copy state saving does not need to store the address of each variable that is modified (only a single address must be stored) if the state variables are stored in contiguous memory locations.

An alternative approach is to use copy state saving, but save the state of the logical processes less frequently than prior to every event. For example, a copy state save operation might be performed every kth event. This approach is referred to as *infrequent state saving*. This technique is more attractive than incremental state saving if most of the state of the logical process is modified by each event.

The rollback mechanism defined earlier must be modified to accommodate infrequent state saving because the state of the logical process at the simulation time of the rollback may not have been saved. Instead, the process must be rolled back to an earlier simulation time where the state of the LP was saved, and the events reprocessed in order to recreate the desired state.

For example, Figure 4.14 depicts a rollback scenario where the state is saved after every third event. The state of the process prior to processing the time stamp 12 event was saved, but the state prior to processing the events with time stamp 21 and 35 was not saved. A straggler message containing time stamp 26 arrives. Since the state of the LP at simulation time 26 (the state prior to processing the time stamp 35 event) was not saved, the state of the LP must be restored to that at simulation time 12, prior to processing the time stamp 12 event. The events with time stamps 12 and 21 must be reprocessed to reconstruct the state at simulation time 26. Reprocessing events in order to reconstruct the desired state vector is referred to as the *coast-forward* phase, and is only required when infrequent state saving is used. The coast-forward computation increases the cost of state restoration, thereby increasing the time to perform a rollback, and it is an additional cost associated with infrequent state saving. The other computations associated with rollback, namely sending anti-messages, processing the straggler, and reprocessing other rolled-back events (besides those involved in the coast-forward computation), must still be performed just as was the case when a state save operation was performed prior to processing each event.

"Coast-forward" events such as those at time stamps 12 and 21 in Figure 4.14 must be treated differently from other events being rolled back. In particular, it is imperative that (1) no anti-messages be sent when rolling back coast-forward events and (2) no positive messages be sent when reprocessing events during the coast-forward phase. Thus, in Figure 4.14, the anti-message with time stamp 24 must not be sent. Suppose that the logical process were to send anti-messages for coast forward events. Then this scenario depicts a case where a rollback to time 26 causes

---

[14] Empirical measurements report that incremental state saving is slower than copy state saving when more than approximately 20% of the state variables are modified for certain simulations of telecommunication networks. In general, however, the "crossover point," where incremental state saving starts to become more expensive, is implementation and application dependent.

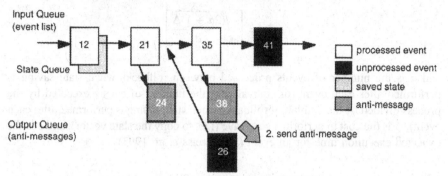

3. restore state of LP to that prior to processing time stamp 12 event
4. reprocess events with time stamp 12 and 21 (coast forward)

Figure 4.14 Rollback scenario using infrequent state saving. Note that the anti-message with time stamp 24 is not sent for this rollback, but the anti-message with time stamp 38 is sent.

an anti-message with time stamp 24 to be sent, which could cause a secondary rollback to time 24, a time earlier than the original rollback. This could produce a new wave of cancellations and rollbacks with even smaller time stamps, leading to a domino effect that could roll back the computation beyond GVT. This clearly cannot be allowed. Designating that no anti-messages be sent for coast-forward events, and discarding positive messages generated during the coast-forward phase, eliminates this problem.

How often should one checkpoint if using infrequent state saving? The above discussion correctly points out that infrequent state saving is double edged. On the one hand, it reduces the number of state save operations that must be performed, favoring very infrequent state saves. On the other hand, rollbacks become more time-consuming because of the need to recreate the required state, a cost that also increases the less frequently one performs state saving. It can be shown that if one assumes that the behavior of the Time Warp execution (i.e., the frequency of rollbacks and number of events that are rolled back, excluding coast forward events) does not change as the state-saving frequency is varied, then m_{opt}, the number of events processed between state-saves, should be set in the range:

$$m_{opt}^- < m_{opt} < m_{opt}^+,$$

where

$$m_{opt}^- = \left\lceil \sqrt{\frac{(\alpha - 1)\Delta}{e}} \right\rceil$$

and

$$m_{\text{opt}}^{+} = \left\lceil \sqrt{\frac{(2\alpha + 1)\Delta}{e}} \right\rceil$$

and α is the number of events processed between rollbacks when state saving is performed after each event (or equivalently, the number of events executed by the process divided by the number of rollbacks when state saving is performed after each event), Δ is the cost to perform a state save (i.e., to copy the state vector), and e is the expected execution time for an event (Lin, Preiss et al. 1993).

4.5.3   Specifying What to Checkpoint

For any checkpointing frequency, copy state saving can be realized transparent to the application program[15] once the Time Warp executive has determined which memory locations need to be saved. The Time Warp executive will automatically have this information if the storage for state variables is allocated within the Time Warp executive. Alternatively, if storage for the state variables is allocated within the application itself, the application must pass the location of its variables to the Time Warp executive. This latter approach is usually preferable if one is modifying an existing simulation program to operate on a Time Warp system because the memory allocation scheme used within the application can remain the same. Similarly the Time Warp executive must be notified whenever the set of checkpointed memory locations changes, such as if memory is dynamically allocated or released during the execution of the program. If copy state saving is used, this can be done transparent to the application for dynamic memory allocation and release because such mechanisms must be handled within the Time Warp executive, as discussed earlier.

Incremental state saving is more difficult to implement transparent to the application program. This is because unlike copy state saving, the Time Warp executive must checkpoint a variable *each time it is modified*. But how does the Time Warp executive know when a variable is modified? There are several approaches that can be used:

- *Manual checkpointing*. The application programmer can be required to insert a call to the Time Warp executive prior to each modification of each state variable. Actually, if a variable is modified many times while processing a single event, the Time Warp executive needs to be notified only on the first modification, though no harm is done (except with respect to efficiency) by checkpointing a variable more than once within an event. The call into the Time Warp executive must specify the address of the state variable and the contents of that variable prior to modifying it. This information is then entered

---

[15] This means the application program need not explicitly perform any action for state saving to be performed, once the Time Warp executive has determined which locations to state save.

into the incremental state save log. The primary advantages of this approach are that it simplifies the Time Warp executive and is easy to implement. The principal disadvantages are that introducing such state saving calls can be tedious and prone to errors.

- *Compiler/pre-processor checkpointing.* A variation on the manual checkpointing approach is to automate the process of inserting the calls to the Time Warp executive. This can be accomplished by a pre-processor that scans through the application program, inserting calls to the Time Warp checkpointing routine as necessary, or within the program compiler itself. To minimize the number of unnecessary checkpointing calls, a control flow analysis of the program can be performed so that a checkpoint call is only inserted the first time the variable is modified, but (ideally) not on subsequent modifications. It may not be possible to avoid all unnecessary checkpoint calls, however. The principal advantage of this approach is that it relieves the application programmer of the responsibility for inserting incremental state-saving calls. The principal disadvantage is the cost of developing and maintaining a specialized pre-processor or compiler.

- *Overloading the assignment operator.* Many languages, especially object-oriented programming languages, allow the application program to redefine primitives such as the assignment operator (= in many languages). This operator can be redefined to perform an incremental state-saving operation before modifying the program variable. It is more difficult to avoid unnecessary checkpoints to variables with this technique. One approach is to maintain some information with each state variable to indicate if it has already been modified by this event. For example, one could store the time stamp of the last modification with each variable and check this information prior to checkpointing it. The time required to check this information, however, could be almost as large as just blindly checkpointing the event, so the principal savings with this approach is reducing storage required to maintain the log, and reducing the time to restore the state after rollback. The principal advantages of overloading assignment operators are that it frees the application programmer from checkpointing each call and it is simpler to implement than building a compiler, preprocessor, or (as discussed next) a program for editing the executable. The principal disadvantage is this approach can only be applied to programming languages that support overloading of the assignment operator. C++ is perhaps the most well-known language that supports this capability. Other widely used languages such as C do not provide this facility.

- *Executable editing.* Another approach to inserting incremental state-saving calls is to edit the file containing the executable for the program. The executable contains a representation of the machine instructions for the program. Thus this approach is similar to the pre-processor approach, but it operates on the machine-level representation of the program rather than the high-level language. Many modern reduced-instruction-set-computers (RISC) use a "load-store" architecture where the only instructions accessing memory are load and store instructions. For these CPUs the program editing the executable needs only to examine store instructions, and if the store corresponds to a modification of a state variable, machine instructions are inserted to checkpoint the variable before it is modified. Some technique must be used to identify those store instructions modifying state variables. For instance, if the Time Warp system does not allow automatic variables stored on the stack to be state variables, all modifications made by event-processing procedures to nonstack variables can be checkpointed. The same techniques may be used for non-load-store machine architectures, but a wider variety of machine instructions must be examined to catch all modifications to state variables. Like the pre-processor/compiler approach, flow analysis can be used to eliminate unnecessary checkpointing operations. The central advantages of this approach are that it is less language dependent compared to the preprocessor/compiler and operator overloading approaches and can be applied to libraries of compiled code that must be checkpointed, but for which the source code is not available. The central disadvantages of this approach are that it is machine dependent and may not be easily ported to new architectures.

The principal advantages and disadvantages of these approaches to incremental state saving are summarized in Table 4.1. There is no one approach that is clearly superior to the others for all circumstances and situations. The manual and operator overloading approaches are perhaps the most commonly used techniques today.

4.5.4 Event Retraction

Recall that event *retraction* refers to a mechanism, *invoked by the application program*, to "unschedule" an event that had previously been scheduled. This might be used to implement unexpected events such as interrupts. For example, suppose that the air traffic simulation were augmented to model in-flight re-routing of aircraft. The logical process for the ORD airport may have scheduled an event

TABLE 4.1 Approaches to Incremental State Saving

Technique	Principal Advantage	Principal Disadvantage
Manual checkpointing	Easy to implement in a Time Warp executive	Manual insertion is tedious and error prone
Pre-processor/compiler	Portable	Cost to develop and maintain pre-processor or compiler
Operator overloading	Easy to implement	Only applicable to languages that support overloading the assignment operator
Executable editing	Not language specific, supports state-saving libraries where source-code is not available	Not easily ported to new machine architectures

denoting the arrival of an aircraft at JFK, and then receive a new message indicating the aircraft has been re-routed to Boston because of congestion at JFK. This could be modeled by having the ORD process retract the arrival event at JFK and schedule a new arrival event at the process modeling Logan Airport in Boston.

At first glance, retraction and cancellation of events appear to be one and the same. However, there is an important difference. Retractions are invoked by the application program, so there must be a mechanism to "undo" an event retraction if the event computation that invoked the retraction is rolled back. No such mechanism is necessary for event cancellation, because cancellation is an operation that is realized within the Time Warp executive.

Two approaches to implementing event retraction include:

- Implementing it at the application level, such as in a library, without providing any additional support in the simulation executive.
- Implementing a retraction primitive within the simulation executive.

Event retraction can be implemented "on top of" an existing Time Warp executive that does not support retraction by realizing the retraction primitive and scheduling an event with time stamp slightly smaller than the event being retracted. Let E denote the event being retracted, and E_R the event that retracts E. Both E and E_R must be processed by the same logical process. When E_R is processed, a variable is set in the state vector of the logical process that indicates that event E should be ignored when it is removed from the event list for processing. The central advantage of this approach is that it allows event retraction to be implemented with an existing Time Warp executive that does not support this facility. The disadvantage is that this mechanism may be somewhat less efficient than a retraction mechanism implemented within the simulation executive.

The second approach to implementing retraction is to provide a new mechanism to retract previously scheduled events. A straightforward technique is to have the application program send an anti-message for each event it is retracting. The Time Warp annihilation mechanism will guarantee the event is properly canceled, and computations depending on that event are rolled back and re-executed.

A retraction operation for an event E can be rolled back by simply re-sending the original positive message for E. A log of retractions can be kept by placing a positive copy of the each event that is retracted in the output queue. When the logical process is rolled back, positive messages stored in the output queue can be sent along with the other anti-messages.

4.5.5 Lazy Cancellation

When a rollback occurs, the Time Warp mechanism described earlier in this chapter will immediately cancel messages sent by rolled-back events by sending an anti-message for each one. It is sometimes the case that when an event is rolled back and

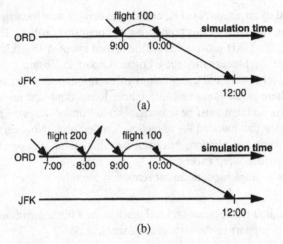

Figure 4.15 Scenario demonstrating lazy cancellation. (*a*) Scenario of events after simulating flight 100; (*b*) scenario after events for flight 200 are processed. Events for flight 200 do not affect the arrival of flight 100 at JFK at 12:00.

reprocessed, the same message that was produced (and subsequently canceled) during the original execution is again re-created when the event is reprocessed. In this case it was not really necessary to cancel the original message.

For example, let us consider an air traffic simulation like that discussed earlier, with aircraft arrival and departure events. Consider the scenario shown in Figure 4.15. An event is received, and processed, indicating that flight 100 arrived at ORD at 9:00 AM, exchanged passengers and subsequently departed for JFK at 10:00 AM, and arrived at JFK at noon. The ORD process will thus send a message to the JFK process modeling the arrival at noon. Later in the execution of the simulation, a straggler message is received at ORD with time stamp 7:00 AM modeling flight 200's arrival. Assume that these are the only two flights that arrive that morning.[16] Flight 200 then departs for another airport at 8:00 AM. Since flight 200 has come and gone before flight 100 arrived, it is quite likely the message sent by ORD denoting flight 100's arrival at JFK at noon will not be affected by flight 200.[17] However, Time Warp will still roll back the events for flight 100, cancel the message sent to JFK with time stamp 12:00, reprocess these events, and resend the same message back to JFK. The cancellation of the 12:00 message at JFK will cause a rollback if the JFK LP already processed that message. It is clear the cancellation of the 12:00 message was unnecessary.

Lazy cancellation is a technique that avoids canceling messages that are later recreated when the events are reprocessed. When a rollback occurs either from

---

[16] ORD only handling two aircraft in one morning is clearly unheard of, but it greatly simplifies the presentation of this example.

[17] This is not necessarily the case. For example, passengers arriving on flight 200 might then depart on flight 100, affecting the subsequent message to JFK if that message included a passenger count. However, the model presented here does not include information such as this in its messages.

receiving a straggler message or an anti-message in a process's past, *no anti-messages are sent*. Instead, the process only sends an anti-message if the original message was not again created when the events were reprocessed. Operationally this can be implemented by examining each message sent during the re-execution phase, and checking the output queue to see if that message was previously sent. If it was, the new message is discarded and the anti-message remains in the output queue. If it was not, the message is sent just as is done during "normal" Time Warp operation. An anti-message is removed from the output queue and sent if no matching positive message was generated during the recomputation phase, and the logical process advances to a simulation time larger than the simulation time when the anti-message was created. A field in the anti-message called the *send time stamp* is used to denote the simulation time of the logical process when the anti-message was created.

For example, in the scenario shown in Figure 4.15, the events in the ORD process for flight 100 will first be processed, resulting in the time stamp 12:00 message being sent to JFK. The ORD process will roll back when it receives the time stamp 7:00 straggler message for flight 200. However, unlike the scenario described earlier, the time stamp 10:00 and 12:00 events will *not* be canceled. This message, and the event at 8:00, will be processed. The 9:00 event denoting the arrival of flight 100 will be re-processed. It will again regenerate the same event with time stamp 10:00, so no new event is scheduled. Similarly, when the 10:00 event is re-processed, it will also regenerate the same 12:00 event, so again, no new event is scheduled. Lazy cancellation avoids canceling the 10:00 event, and more significantly, the 12:00 event. Had the 12:00 event generated by the re-execution been different from that produced during the initial processing, or if no event were re-generated at all, the anti-message for the 12:00 event would be sent once the ORD logical process advanced beyond simulation time 10:00.

The original mechanism presented earlier where anti-messages are sent as soon as the rollback occurs is called *aggressive cancellation*. Lazy cancellation offers the advantage that it avoids canceling messages that are recreated when rolled-back events are reprocessed. This will also eliminate secondary rollbacks that occur in aggressive cancellation when an anti-message is unnecessarily canceled. The principal disadvantages of lazy cancellation are as follows:

1. Cancellation of incorrect computations is delayed, compared to aggressive cancellation. In general, the sending of anti-messages is delayed until some rolled-back events are reprocessed. This delay allows the "damage" (i.e., incorrect computations) caused by the incorrect message to spread further than it would had the anti-message been immediately sent. Thus more computation may need to be rolled back when the anti-message is finally sent.

2. Reprocessing events using lazy cancellation requires some additional overhead computation relative to aggressive cancellation to compare messages that are sent with anti-messages in the output queue. Also the simulation executive must check if any anti-messages must be sent whenever the process's simulation clock is advanced.

3. Lazy cancellation requires some additional memory to hold anti-messages during the re-computation phase that would have been sent (allowing the memory they used to be reclaimed) if aggressive cancellation had been used.

Depending on the application, performance of Time Warp using lazy cancellation can be better or worse compared to aggressive cancellation. One can construct scenarios where lazy cancellation outperforms aggressive cancellation by as much as a factor of N when executing on N processors, and one can construct scenarios where aggressive cancellation executes N times faster than lazy cancellation. Only a limited amount of empirical data is available comparing aggressive and lazy cancellation; however, these data suggest that lazy cancellation typically performs marginally better than aggressive cancellation in queueing network benchmark programs. The difference in performance that has been reported is usually somewhat modest, however. For example, on the order of 10% to 15% relative to aggressive cancellation is typical.

The lazy cancellation optimization does point out a noteworthy characteristic concerning the Time Warp mechanism, and for that matter, most synchronization protocols that have been proposed thus far. Time Warp "conservatively" assumes that one event depends on a second event if they both are scheduled at the same logical process, and invokes the rollback mechanism based on this assumption. If two events occur with a single TWLP but do not depend on each other, there is no need to process them in time stamp order. Because Time Warp does not attempt to analyze dependencies between events within the same process, which in general is a very difficult problem, it cannot avoid such unnecessary rollbacks.

4.5.6 Lazy Re-evaluation

Another technique along similar lines as lazy cancellation is the *lazy re-evaluation or jump-forward* optimization. Again, consider the scenario depicted in Figure 4.15. Lazy cancellation avoided canceling and resending the time stamp 12:00 message to the JFK process. However, even with lazy cancellation, the two events at ORD for flight 100 with time stamp 9:00 and 10:00 will have to be reprocessed after the rollback. If the re-processing of these events for flight 100 is identical to that in the original execution (i.e., if flight 100s events are completely unaffected by those for flight 200), there is no reason to process them again after the rollback.

Lazy re-evaluation is an optimization that attempts to exploit this fact. The central question is how can the Time Warp simulation executive determine if the re-computation of an event will be the same as the original computation? The answer is if the state of the logical process before re-processing the event after a rollback is the same as what it was in the original execution of these events, then the recomputation will again be the same. This assumes, if course, that each event computation is repeatable.

To implement this technique, the saved state vector indicating the state of the logical process before each event was processed must *not* be discarded when an event is rolled back. During the re-execution phase, before reprocessing an event, the

Time Warp executive compares the state of the logical process with the state that existed before the event was last processed, which is saved in the state queue. If the two are equal and the set of unprocessed events is the same as the previous execution, the logical process can skip re-processing the events, and immediately jump back to its state prior to when the rollback was processed. For example, in Figure 4.15, assume again that the time stamp 9:00 and 10:00 events have been processed when the straggler at 7:00 is received. The ORD logical process rolls back, processes the straggler and the time stamp 8:00 event created by the straggler. The logical process then observes that the current state of the logical process is the same as the saved state of the process prior to processing the 9:00 event. The logical process can restore the state of the logical process to that which existed just prior to when the straggler arrived, mark the 9:00 and 10:00 events as processed, and resume processing events as if the rollback never occurred.

Lazy re-evaluation is similar to lazy cancellation, except it deals with state vectors rather than messages. It is useful when straggler events do not affect the state of the logical process. One situation where this might occur is the *query event*. Query events are intended to read state variables within a logical process and return those values to the scheduler of the event. The main drawback with lazy re-evaluation is the cost of comparing state vectors, and the fact that straggler events typically do modify state variables, so often processes are not able to benefit from this technique. If incremental state saving is used, comparison of state vectors may be cumbersome and time-consuming, since one must examine logs to recover a snapshot of the state of the process.

4.6 SCHEDULING LOGICAL PROCESSES

A processor will, in general, contain many logical processes. A scheduling policy is required to select the logical process that should be allowed to execute next. Two important questions are: When should execution change from one logical process to another? And, when execution changes to a new logical process, which one is allowed to execute next? While scheduling has been widely studied in general contexts (i.e., nonsimulation applications), it merits special attention in the design of a Time Warp simulation executive because selection of a poor scheduling algorithm can lead to extremely poor performance.

Nearly all existing simulation executives (both optimistic and conservative) only shift execution from one logical process to another between, as opposed to during, processing successive events. Possible approaches concerning when to switch execution from one logical process to another include the following:

- Process all unprocessed events for a logical process before changing execution to another logical process. This has the advantage that it minimizes the frequency of changing the process that is executing, which may entail context switch overheads if a process-oriented simulation paradigm is used, and yields better locality of memory references, improving the performance of cache memories.[18] However, this approach can cause some logical processes to execute far ahead of others in simulation time, and can lead to very poor performance. This is particularly true if a process schedules events for itself. This issue will be explored in much greater depth in the next chapter. Thus this approach is not well suited for Time Warp executives.

- Allow execution to change to a different logical process after processing each event. This approach is most commonly used in Time Warp executives today, and it provides the greatest control and ensures that the "most appropriate" logical process is executed at any instant. Selection of the "most appropriate" logical process will be discussed momentarily.

- Allow execution to change to a different logical process after processing some number of events. This approach is a compromise between the two approaches described above. The "trigger" that causes the Time Warp executive to consider switching execution to another logical process might be after the current TWLP has processed some number of events, after it has been allocated a certain amount of CPU time to execute, or perhaps when the current logical process has advanced in simulation time some threshold ahead of other logical processes.

When a scheduling decision is made, which logical process should be allowed to execute? In principal, one would like to execute the logical process that leads to the shortest overall execution time; however, this is impossible to predict because one cannot know what event computations will take place in the future. A related goal is to allow the logical process that is least likely to roll back to execute next. From a correctness standpoint, the scheduling mechanism must be fair in the sense that the smallest time-stamped event in the entire simulation system must eventually be allowed to execute, or Time Warp cannot guarantee forward progress and could enter a livelock situation where it continues to process and roll back events, but GVT does not advance.

A commonly used approach is to always process the event in the processor with the smallest time stamp next, by the rationale that this event is least likely to be rolled back. This *smallest time stamp first* (STF) policy has the advantages that it is simple and that it tends to let the logical process farthest behind in simulation time execute next. Further, if the Time Warp executive has no information on what messages will arrive in the future, the process with the smallest time-stamp is intuitively the process one would expect is least likely to be rolled back by messages that will arrive in the future. The smallest time-stamped event in the entire simulator will never be rolled back.

---

[18] A cache memory is a high-speed memory that holds recently referenced instructions and data. Virtually all general purpose microprocessors use some form of cache memory. If the program repeatedly accesses the same memory locations, the memory locations being referenced are more likely to be in the cache, improving performance.

4.7 SUMMARY

This chapter has focused on the Time Warp mechanism, by far the best-known optimistic synchronization protocol. Although many optimistic protocols have since been developed, Time Warp is important because it has introduced many new, fundamental concepts and mechanisms that are widely used in other protocols. For example, anti-messages, state saving, event rollback, Global Virtual Time, and fossil collection are utilized in most other optimistic synchronization mechanisms.

Further, use of rollback requires the introduction of new mechanisms to perform other commonly used operations such as I/O and dynamic memory allocation. Specifically, the new wrinkle that is added is that there must be the ability to roll back these operations. Thus the techniques discussed here to allow these operations to be rolled back are equally applicable to other synchronization mechanisms using rollback.

The discussion in this chapter has been focused on what might be termed "pure" Time Warp simulation executives. As will be discussed in the next chapter, a "pure" Time Warp system has certain deficiencies that can lead to very poor performance for some applications, and a variety of other optimistic synchronization protocols have since been developed to solve these problems.

4.8 ADDITIONAL READINGS

The Time Warp algorithm is described in Jefferson (1985). Prior to Time Warp, optimistic synchronization was proposed for database concurrency control (Kung and Robinson 1981), and it has long been used in computer architecture, such as in predicting the outcome of branch instructions (Hennessy and Patterson 1996). Conversely, Time Warp has also been proposed as a means to parallelize arbitrary sequential programs (Knight 1986; Cleary, Unger et al. 1988; Tinker and Katz 1988; Fujimoto 1989; Tinker 1989).

Implementation of incremental state saving using operator overloading and executable editing are described in Ronngren, Liljenstam et al. (1996), Chandrase-karen and Hill (1996), and West and Panesar (1996), respectively. Measurements of state-saving costs in a Time Warp system are reported in Cleary, Gomes et al. (1994). The optimal checkpointing interval for infrequent state saving is derived in Lin, Preiss et al. (1993), and performance evaluations using this technique are reported in Bellenot (1992), Preiss, MacIntyre et al. (1992); Palaniswamy and Wilsey (1993), Avril and Tropper (1995), and Fleischmann and Wilsey (1995). Adaptive selection of the checkpointing interval is described in Ronngren and Ayani (1994). A hybrid approach that combines copy and incremental state saving is described in Franks, Gomes et al. (1997).

Perhaps the first GVT algorithm using message acknowledgments is described in Samadi (1985) where the transient message and simultaneous reporting problems are discussed. The GVT algorithm based on distributed snapshots is described in Mattern (1993). Distributed snapshots, on which the Mattern algorithm is based, are discussed in Chandy and Lamport (1985) and Ahuja (1990). Other GVT algorithms are described in Bellenot (1990); Lin and Lazowska (1990); Concepcion and Kelly (1991), Tomlinson and Garg (1993), D'souza, Fan et al. (1994), Lin (1994), Varghese, Chamberlain et al. (1994), Xiao, Cleary et al. (1995), and Fujimoto and Hybinette (1998). The on-the-fly fossil collection technique is described in Fujimoto and Hybinette (1998).

Error-handling mechanisms for Time Warp were implemented in some of the earliest implementations. For example, JPLs Time Warp Operating System (Jefferson, Beckman et al. 1987) included facilities to catch non-destructive errors using signal handlers. More recently, the problem is discussed in Nicol and Liu (1997).

Extensions to Time Warp to realize shared-state variables and application-invoked event retraction are described in Fujimoto (1989), Ghosh and Fujimoto (1991), Mehl and Hammees (1993), Bruce (1995), and Lomow, Das et al. (1991). Lazy cancellation is described in Gafni (1988), and performance comparisons with aggressive cancellation are presented in Reiher, Fujimoto et al. (1990). Lazy re-evaluation is described in West (1988). Use of hidden fields in the time stamp to allow zero lookahead simulations are discussed in Reiher, Wieland et al. (1990) and Mehl (1992).

Several attempts to develop analytic models to predict Time Warp performance have been conducted. Early investigations were confined to analyzing two processors (Lavenberg, Muntz et al. 1983; Mitra and Mitrani 1984; Felderman and Kleinrock 1991). Later work extended this to arbitrary numbers of processors (Gupta, Akyildiz et al. 1991) and under limited memory constraints, as discussed in the next chapter (Akyildiz, Chen et al. 1993). In Lin and Lazowska (1990) it is shown that if state saving and rollbacks require zero time, Time Warp using aggressive cancellation will achieve execution time equal to the critical path through the computation if incorrect computation never rolls back correct computation, and Time Warp using lazy cancellation can reduce execution time even further. Lipton and Mizell (1990) show that Time Warp can outperform the Chandy/Misra null message algorithm by up to a factor of N using N processors, but the null message algorithm can only outperform Time Warp by a constant factor assuming constant rollback costs. Performance bounds for Time Warp and conservative protocols are derived in Nicol (1991). Finally, several empirical studies of Time Warp performance for a variety of applications have been performed. Among the earliest are Fujimoto (1989), Wieland, Hawley et al. (1989), Morse (1990), and Preiss (1990). The evaluation described in Fujimoto (1990) introduces a synthetic workload model called PHOLD that is sometimes used to benchmark different systems. Early implementations of Time Warp are described in Jefferson, Beckman et al. (1987) and Fujimoto (1989).

Hardware support for Time Warp has also been proposed. Support for state saving is described in Fujimoto, Tsai et al. (1992), and support for reduction networks to perform global minimum computations is described in Reynolds, Pancerella et al. (1993).

CHAPTER 5

Advanced Optimistic Techniques

In a "pure" Time Warp system there is no limit as to how far some logical processes can advance ahead of others in simulation time. This is problematic because it can lead to very inefficient use of computation and communication resources. First, the amount of memory required to execute the simulation can become unboundedly large. To see this, consider a simulation with two logical processes, each processing one event per unit of simulation time. Suppose that LP_A requires 1 millisecond of wallclock time to process each event but LP_B requires 10 milliseconds. LP_A will advance ten events in the time LP_B takes to advance only one event, so it requires sufficient memory to hold ten message buffers; see Figure 5.1(a). After LP_B has processed a second event, LP_A has processed ten more events; see Figure 5.1(b). Only one event can be fossil collected from each LP. It is clear that the memory requirements will grow without bound as the simulation progresses.

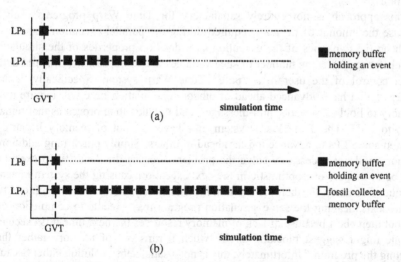

Figure 5.1 Example illustrating unbounded memory requirements of a Time Warp simulation. (a) Snapshot after 10 milliseconds; (b) snapshot after 20 milliseconds.

A second source of inefficiency with such "overoptimistic" execution is that it can lead to very long and/or frequent rollbacks. It is clear from Figure 5.1(b) that if LP_B now sends a message to LP_A, a long rollback will occur. Long rollbacks imply much time was wasted performing computations that were later thrown away. This is not so problematic if the processors have no other useful computations to perform and would otherwise be idle, but otherwise, it is a serious deficiency. Further, significant computation and communication resources may have to be expended to perform the rollback itself. As will be discussed later, a "rollback thrashing" behavior could result where logical processes spend most of their time processing rollbacks rather than performing useful simulation computations.

Building upon the Time Warp mechanism, this chapter discusses advanced topics concerning optimistic synchronization. Specifically, memory management mechanisms and other optimistic synchronization protocols that have been proposed since Time Warp first appeared are discussed. We conclude this chapter by examining the design of an operational Time Warp system; we discuss various optimizations included in this design to exploit shared-memory multiprocessors.

5.1   MEMORY UTILIZATION IN TIME WARP

Consider the execution of a Time Warp program where there is some fixed amount of memory available on the parallel computer. One might ask, What happens if the Time Warp system runs out of memory? In a sequential simulation one typically aborts the program, and informs the user that additional memory is required to complete the simulation run. Can a similar strategy be used for Time Warp programs?

This approach is not entirely satisfactory for Time Warp programs. This is because the amount of memory required during the parallel execution depends as much on the dynamics of the execution as it does on properties of the simulation model (for example, the number of state variables that are used), which is not under direct control of the user in a "pure" Time Warp system. Specifically, logical processes that have advanced ahead of others in simulation time will require more memory to hold past events, anti-messages, and the like, than processes that remain close to GVT. The Time Warp system may have run out of memory because it allowed some LPs to advance too far ahead of others. Simply purchasing additional memory will not necessarily solve the problem because the Time Warp executive may be even more overoptimistic in the next execution, causing the system to again run out of memory. Further, the amount of memory required will vary from one run to the next, meaning the same simulation program may execute to completion one day but then abort because of lack of memory resources the next time it is executed.

One might suggest blocking an LP when it runs out of memory rather than aborting the program. Unfortunately, this is not a satisfactory solution either because it can lead to deadlock situations. For example, in Figure 5.2, suppose that LP_B, the logical process executing at simulation time equal to GVT, has run out of memory in attempting to schedule a new event. If the LP blocks to wait for more memory, it may

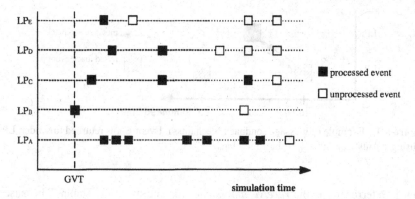

Figure 5.2   Snapshot of a Time Warp computation indicating memory required to store events.

wait forever because a GVT advance may be required to reclaim additional memory, but GVT cannot advance because LP_B is blocked.[19]

Solving this problem requires (1) a mechanism to either directly or indirectly control memory utilization and (2) a policy to judiciously invoke this mechanism to maximize performance without consuming too much memory. After introducing some additional terminology, we next discuss memory management mechanisms and policies, and a property known as storage optimality.

5.1.1   Preliminaries: State Vectors and Message Send Time Stamps

There are three types of memory used by the Time Warp system that are of concern here: memory used to hold (1) positive messages (stored in the input queue), (2) anti-messages (stored in the output queue), and (3) state vectors (stored in the state queue). The first two contain time-stamped event messages. For the purposes of memory management, it is convenient to view the third, state vectors, also as messages. Specifically, a state vector can be viewed as a message sent by an LP to itself containing information concerning the state variables within the LP. The time stamp of the state vector is that of the event that reads the state information, which is the next event that is processed by the LP. Viewing state vectors in this way allows us to discuss memory management in terms of only one type of memory object, time-stamped messages.

Many memory management protocols assign *two* time stamps to each message. In addition to the time stamp field discussed previously, a second one is defined that indicates the virtual time of the logical process when it scheduled the event. This is referred to as the *send time stamp* of the event. The time stamp field discussed up to

---

[19] Actually memory can also become available through the message annihilation procedure. However, there is no guarantee additional annihilations will occur, so this cannot be relied upon to break the deadlock situation.

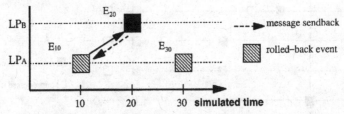

Figure 5.3   Example of message sendback mechanism. Event E_{20} is returned to sender, LPA, causing events E_{10} and E_{20} to be rolled back.

now is referred to as the *receive time stamp* (or simply "time stamp") because it indicates the simulation time of the logical process when it receives the message. The send time stamp of an event (for example, E_{20} in Fig. 5.3) is equal to the receive time stamp of the event that scheduled this event (E_{10}). For example, Figure 5.3 shows three events, E_{10}, E_{20}, and E_{30}. The send and receive time stamps of the message containing E_{20} are 10 and 20, respectively.

5.1.2   Memory Management Mechanisms and Message Sendback

There are several mechanisms that can be used to control memory usage or to reclaim memory once the system has run out:

1. *Blocking.* The Time Warp system can block certain logical processes to prevent them from advancing forward and allocating additional memory. Blocking prevents future allocations of memory but does not provide a means for reclaiming memory currently being used by the Time Warp system.

2. *Pruning.* The Time Warp system reclaims memory used by state vectors created via copy state saving. The net effect after reclaiming these state vectors is the same as if infrequent state saving had been used to avoid creating the state vectors in the first place.

3. *Rollback.* A logical process can be rolled back to reclaim memory used for state vectors in the rolled back events. In addition rollback will typically cause anti-messages to be sent, and the subsequent message annihilations and rollbacks will release additional memory resources.

4. *Message sendback.* This is a new mechanism to reclaim memory by returning a message back to its original sender.

Blocking and rollback have been discussed previously, and pruning is based on principles (infrequent state saving) that have also been discussed in Chapter 4. The message sendback mechanism is described next.

Message sendback is based on the observation that a logical process can recover memory used by a message in its input queue by removing the message from the queue, returning it to its sender, and reclaiming the memory.[20] The logical process receiving the returned message will usually roll back when it receives the returned message to a simulation time prior to when the message was sent.[21] For example, Figure 5.3 illustrates an example of the message sendback mechanism. Here, LP_B returns the message holding event E_{20} to its original sender, LP_A. Upon receiving the returned message, LP_A rolls back events E_{10} and E_{30}. Rolling back these events may result in sending anti-messages, which may in turn cause secondary rollbacks and reclaim additional memory. After the events have been rolled back LP_A will then reprocess E_{10} (and possibly E_{30}), resending E_{20} to LP_B. This cycle will repeat, creating a type of "busy wait loop" until sufficient memory is available for the computation to proceed forward.

Recall that GVT defines a lower bound on the time stamp of any future rollback. Therefore the message sendback mechanism cannot return a message whose send time stamp is less than or equal to GVT,[22] as this would result in a rollback beyond GVT. Further the definition of GVT itself must be modified to accommodate message sendback. This is because there may be a "sent-back" message in transit (referred to as a *backward transient* message), being returned to its sender while the GVT computation is in progress. If the GVT computation does not take into account this message, a rollback beyond GVT could occur through the following sequence of actions:

1. A message M is sent back with send time stamp equal to T ($T >$ GVT).
2. A new GVT computation is initiated and computes a new GVT value greater than T; M remains in transit while the new GVT value is computed.
3. M is received by its original sender, causing a rollback to T. However, GVT has advanced, so a rollback beyond GVT occurs.

To circumvent this problem, GVT is redefined as follows:

Definition: GVT with message sendback   Global Virtual Time at wallclock time T during the execution of a Time Warp simulation (GVT_T) is defined as the minimum among (1) the receive time stamp of all unprocessed and partially processed messages and anti-messages in the system and (2) the send time stamp of all backward transient message at wallclock time T.

The algorithms described in the previous chapter can still be used to compute GVT. One need only note messages that are being sent back, and modify the minimum computation to use the send time stamp of any such transient message rather than the receive time stamp.

---

[20] If the message that is sent back has already been processed, the LP must also roll back to prior to the time stamp of the message. If the "message" being sent back is actually a state vector (recall state vectors are viewed as messages here), no rollback is required.

[21] This will normally be the case. An LP may be at a point preceding the generation of the message if it was rolled back after sending the message.

[22] It can be shown an infinite loop can occur if messages with send time equal to GVT are returned.

5.1.3 Storage Optimality

It is clear that some minimal amount of memory is required to reasonably expect the Time Warp simulation to complete, just as some minimal amount of memory is required to execute a sequential simulation. The amount of storage required to execute a sequential simulation would seem to be a reasonable lower bound on the amount of memory required for a parallel execution. It is clear, however, that even if one were able to execute the simulation program using this little memory, performance would be poor because there is little latitude for processes to advance optimistically ahead of others. Thus one would like a memory management protocol that is able to guarantee that it can complete the simulation if given only the memory needed in a sequential execution but can utilize additional memory to exploit optimistic execution when it is available. This approach gives rise to *storage optimal* memory management protocols:

Definition: Storage Optimality   A memory management protocol is said to be storage optimal if it is able to guarantee that it can complete the execution of any simulation program using no more than K times the memory required to complete a sequential execution of the same program for some constant K.

Of course, K should be small for the algorithm to be practical. To see how a memory management protocol can achieve storage optimality, consider a Time Warp simulation where GVT is equal to T. Storage optimality can be achieved if the memory management protocol can reclaim all memory buffers that would not exist in a sequential execution of the simulation program that has advanced to simulation time T. To achieve this, the memory management system must be able to recognize those events that would exist in the sequential simulation at time T, and those that would not. Fortunately this is straightforward. The key observation is that the events that reside in the pending event list in a sequential simulation at time T are those that have a time stamp greater than or equal to T, and were scheduled prior to simulation time T.

To illustrate this concept, consider the snapshot of the execution of a Time Warp program shown in Figure 5.4. There are three types of events, differentiated by the position of the send and receive time stamps relative to GVT (equal to T):

1. *Past events.* Send time stamp $\leq$ receive time stamp $<$ GVT; these events can be fossil collected.
2. *Present events.* send time stamp $\leq$ GVT $\leq$ receive time stamp; these events match those that would exist in the pending event set in a sequential execution at time T.[23]
3. *Future events.* GVT $<$ send time stamp $\leq$ receive time stamp; these events have not yet been created in the sequential simulator at time T, and they can be

---

[23] Actually this definition includes all events scheduled at time T, not all of which may be in the pending event list at the same time during the sequential simulation.

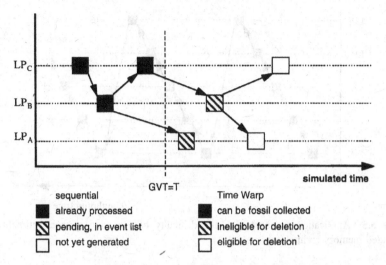

Figure 5.4 Snapshot of a Time Warp execution illustrating the different types of events with respect to memory management. Arcs in this figure indicate which events scheduled which other events.

reclaimed by the memory management protocol via message sendback or rollback.

The memory management protocol must locate and, if necessary, reclaim storage used by future events. The protocol will achieve the storage optimality property if it is able to reclaim all of the storage (or to within a constant factor) used by the future events.

The focus of the discussion here is on storage optimal memory management protocols for optimistic parallel simulations. Note that existing conservative simulation protocols are not storage optimal, though it is widely believed that memory usage is not as severe a problem in conservative simulation systems as it is in optimistic systems.

It may be mentioned that storage optimality is much more difficult to achieve on distributed-memory architectures than on shared-memory platforms. To see this, consider the simulation application depicted in Figure 5.5 consisting of five logical processes organized as a ring. Assume that each logical process executes on a different processor. This application initially contains a single message. When the message is processed, it creates one new message that it sends to the next process in the ring, with a certain time stamp increment. Because there is only one event in the pending event list at any time, a sequential simulator will only need two memory buffers: one to hold the current event being processed, and one to hold the new event that is scheduled by this event. A Time Warp execution of this program on a shared-memory multiprocessor using a storage optimal memory management protocol will also only require two buffers if they are stored in shared memory and can be allocated to any processor. Operationally the Time Warp program will process an

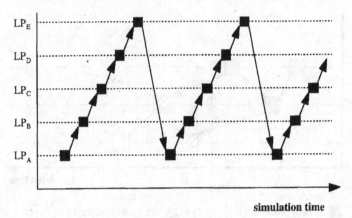

Figure 5.5 Application demonstrating the difficulty of achieving storage optimality in distributed memory architectures.

event E_1 at the LP where it currently resides, then schedule a new event E_2 for the next LP in the ring. Once E_1 has been processed, GVT can advance, and the storage used to hold E_1 can be reclaimed. This buffer can now be used to hold the new event schedule by E_2, so only two buffers are required.

When the same Time Warp program is executed on a distributed-memory platform, however, memory buffers cannot be shared among processors. Thus *each* processor must hold two memory buffers to implement this application, or a total of $2N$ buffers are needed where N is the number of processors in the system.[24] Thus the execution is *not* storage optimal, since it requires N times the number of buffers required in a sequential execution. In principal, this problem could be circumvented if logical processes are allowed to migrate between processors; however, process migration is a relatively time-consuming operation. Similarly one could implement shared-memory abstractions on top of a distributed memory architecture; however, the high cost of access to memory that physically resides on another machine currently makes this approach not very attractive from a performance standpoint.

Specific memory management protocols are described next. Four protocols are considered, each using a different mechanism to control memory utilization. The *Cancelback* protocol uses the message sendback mechanism. *Artificial Rollback* uses rollback. *Pruneback* uses state pruning, and *Memory-Based Flow Control* uses blocking. Among these, Cancelback and Artificial Rollback are storage optimal; they are designed for shared-memory machines. Pruneback and memory-based flow control are not storage optimal but are designed for distributed-memory machines.

---

[24] One could argue that in principal, each processor could release its memory buffers once it has completed processing the event, resulting in only two buffers being allocated in the entire system at any instant during the execution. This is not really a storage optimal execution, however, because the parallel computer must physically have memory for $2N$ buffers, even if only two are being used at one time.

Other optimistic synchronization protocols are described later in this chapter that provide mechanisms to limit the amount of "optimism" in the Time Warp execution. Although the principal motivation behind these protocols is reducing the amount of rolled-back computation, these protocols indirectly limit memory consumption.

5.1.4 Cancelback

Cancelback uses a global pool of memory to hold buffers that are not in use. All memory is allocated from this pool, and memory that has been released, such as via fossil collection or annihilation, is returned to this pool. After each memory allocation, the processor checks if additional memory (or some minimal amount) is available. If it is not, the fossil collection procedure is called to reclaim memory. If fossil collection fails to allocate additional memory, the processor uses the message sendback protocol to reclaim memory.

Any message with a send time stamp greater than GVT is eligible to be sent back. Because message sendback may roll back the sender LP to the send time stamp of the returned message, the message containing the largest send time stamp in the simulation is a good candidate for being sent back. This will tend to roll back LPs that have advanced ahead of the others. If no buffers with send time stamp greater than GVT are found, then there are no future events in the system (indicating all events in the Time Warp execution would also be required in a sequential execution), so the program is aborted due to lack of memory.

An example illustrating the Cancelback protocol is depicted in Figure 5.6. Figure 5.6(a) shows a snapshot of the execution when Cancelback is called. The memory buffer containing event E_C contains the largest send time stamp, so Cancelback selects this event for storage reclamation. As depicted in Figure 5.6(b), this event is sent back to LP_A, causing event E_S (the event that scheduled E_C) to be rolled back.

Each Cancelback call is a relatively time-consuming operation because it includes a GVT computation, fossil collection, and a procedure for locating the event containing the largest time stamp as well as the sendback mechanism itself. This cost can be reduced by performing message sendback on several messages in each Cancelback call. Operationally this can be done by applying the message sendback mechanism to several events, until at least some minimal amount of memory has been reclaimed. This minimal amount of memory that must be reclaimed is called the *salvage parameter*.

5.1.5 Artificial Rollback

The artificial rollback protocol is somewhat similar to Cancelback, except it uses a rollback mechanism to reclaim memory rather than sendback. Like Cancelback, artificial rollback also uses a salvage parameter that indicates the minimum amount of storage that should be reclaimed when this mechanism is invoked. If an LP runs out of memory and nothing can be reclaimed via fossil collection, the LP with the largest simulation time clock value is rolled back to the simulation time of the LP

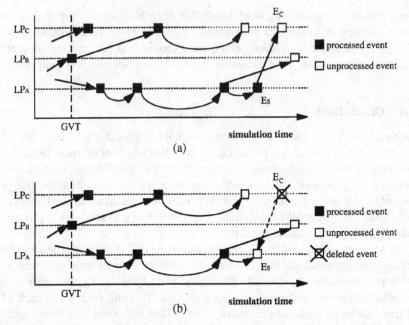

Figure 5.6 Cancelback example. (*a*) Snapshot of the simulation before Cancelback call; (*b*) snapshot after Cancelback operation; event E_C is sent back, causing event E_S to be rolled back.

with the second largest clock value. If insufficient memory is reclaimed, then the two LPs mentioned above are both rolled back to the simulation time of the LP with the third largest clock. This procedure continues until enough memory has been reclaimed, or until no additional buffers are eligible for recovery via rollback.

Figure 5.7 illustrates an invocation of the Artificial Rollback protocol (for the same situation as in Fig. 5.6). As shown in Figure 5.7(*a*), LP_A is the furthest ahead in the simulation, so it is rolled back to the current simulation time of LP_C, the second most advanced LP. This results in the rollback of events E_{R1} and E_{R2}. Rolling back these events results in the cancellation, and storage reclamation of events E_{C1}, E_{C2}, and E_{C3}.

Like Cancelback, Artificial Rollback is also storage optimal when implemented on a shared-memory multiprocessor with a global buffer pool. It is somewhat simpler to implement than Cancelback because there are no reverse transit messages. Thus there is no possibility of race conditions such as a positive message in reverse transit "passing by" an anti-message in forward transit and missing each other.

As discussed earlier, the use of global, shared memory allows Cancelback and Artificial Rollback to have the storage optimality property. Variations on these protocols can be defined that do not use a global memory pool (for example, each processor or even each LP can have a separate memory pool) but at the cost of losing the storage optimality property.

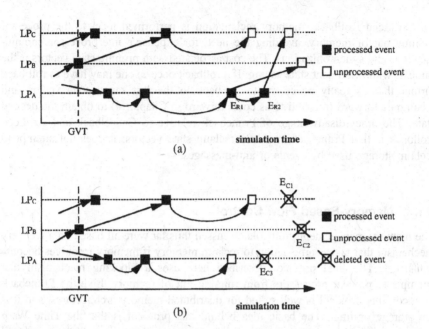

Figure 5.7 Artificial Rollback example. (*a*) Snapshot of system before invoking Artificial Rollback; (*b*) snapshot after the protocol rolls back events E_{R1} and E_{R2}.

5.1.6 Pruneback

The Pruneback protocol does not use rollbacks to reclaim memory. Instead, it uses the pruning mechanism described earlier where uncommitted state vectors are reclaimed. Pruneback was designed for distributed-memory architectures where there is a pool of free memory in each processor that can be used by LPs mapped to that processor. When a processor exhausts its supply of memory, and no additional memory can be obtained via fossil collection, the memory used for uncommitted state vectors created via the copy state saving mechanism is reclaimed.

The specific state vectors that are reclaimed is arbitrary, with the constraint that at least one copy of the state vector older than GVT must remain (as well as the events in the input queue with a time stamp larger than the state vector, even if the event time stamp is less than GVT) in case a rollback to GVT later occurs. The current state of the logical process (which may or may not reside in the state queue, depending on the implementation) also cannot be reclaimed by the pruning mechanism. From a correctness standpoint, any state vector can be reclaimed. The choice of which state vectors to reclaim will affect performance, however. A straightforward approach might be to reclaim every kth state vector, mimicking the strategy used in infrequent state saving. Another approach might be to try to reclaim states with small time stamp first, operating under the assumption that rollbacks to the "far past" are less likely than rollbacks to the "near past."

The pruning mechanism has the advantage that unlike rollback, no user computations are erased that have to be later repeated. Also, unlike Cancelback and Artificial Rollback, memory reclamation is performed local to the processor running out of memory, avoiding the need for expensive interprocessor communications and synchronizations. The cost associated with pruning state vectors is the same as with infrequent state saving. If a rollback occurs, one may have to roll back further than is really necessary to go back to the last saved state vector, and recompute forward (referred to as coast forward in Chapter 4) to obtain the desired state. The other disadvantage of Pruneback relative to Cancelback and Artificial Rollback is that Pruneback can only reclaim state vectors; it does not attempt to reclaim storage used by events or anti-messages.

5.1.7 Memory-Based Flow Control

The memory management protocols discussed thus far were all based on a recovery mechanism that takes some action to reclaim memory if memory resources become exhausted. The final protocol described here uses a blocking mechanism that attempts to prevent processors from running out of memory. Like the Pruneback protocol, this protocol is well suited for distributed-memory architectures, and it is not storage optimal. The basic idea behind this protocol is that the Time Warp system predicts the amount of memory the program will require until the next fossil collection and then only provides this amount of memory to the program. This estimate is computed by the Time Warp system, transparent to the application, by monitoring the program's execution, and it is updated throughout the execution so that the system can adapt to changes in program behavior. If a logical process requests memory and none is available, it blocks until additional memory is freed via rollbacks, message cancellations, or fossil collection.

The projected amount of memory that will be required is computed by (1) estimating the *instantaneous* amount of memory required by a sequential execution of the program, (2) inflating this amount to determine the amount that will be required until the next fossil collection, and (3) inflating the amount computed in (2) further to allow for optimistic event processing. To estimate (1), the allocation of message buffers during a sequential execution is modeled as a queueing network (see Fig. 5.8). Each buffer is viewed as a "job" that arrives at a server when it is allocated from the free pool. The buffer remains in service until the storage it uses is reclaimed, at which time it departs from the server and is returned to the free pool. The average number of jobs in the server (buffers "in use") at one time indicates the amount of memory required in a sequential execution.

In general, the average number of jobs in a server can be computed if one knows the rate at which buffers arrive, and the average amount of time each job remains in the server. Here, these quantities are computed per unit simulation time. Specifically, let

1. λ denote the average rate that buffers are allocated (jobs arrive at the server). Operationally λ can be computed as A/T, where A is the number of message sends occurring over a period of T units of simulation time.

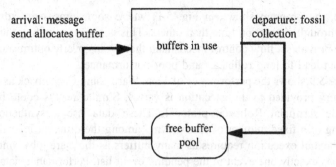

Figure 5.8 Model for estimating memory requirements for sequential simulation.

2. $1/\mu$ denote the amount of simulation time that the buffer remains in use; this is simply the average difference between the receive and send times of each event, and it can be computed as L/A, where L is the sum of the differences in send and receive time, computed over A message sends.

Little's Law is a well-known result from queueing theory. It says that the average number of jobs that will be in service at one time is λ/μ. Intuitively λ jobs arrive per unit simulation time, so over $1/\mu$ units of simulation time, λ/μ new jobs arrive, displacing the λ/μ jobs in the server at the start of the observation period. Thus the average number of buffers required in the sequential execution is L/T. One additional modification is required to estimate the amount of sequential memory during the execution of a Time Warp simulation: If an event is canceled by sending an anti-message, this is erased from the measured statistics by assigning the anti-message a negative time stamp increment and negative count.

To provide enough memory between successive fossil collections, this memory size is increased by $\lambda T'$ buffers, where T' is the expected increment in GVT at the next fossil collection (measured from previous fossil collections). The resulting number of buffers, $L/T + \lambda T'$ is multiplied by a scaling factor m (greater than 1.0) that is constantly varied during the execution; m is increased (decreased) from one fossil collection to the next so long as it increases performance.

5.1.8 Trading Off Performance and Memory

The memory management protocols discussed thus far provide a means to execute Time Warp programs with limited amounts of memory. It is clear that if only a minimal amount of memory is provided, performance will be poor. This section addresses the question of how performance varies as the amount of memory provided to the Time Warp program varies.

Consider the Cancelback and Artificial Rollback protocols. Intuitively, as the memory is increased beyond that required for sequential execution, one would expect performance to increase. As the amount of memory is increased further, performance may actually decrease, particularly for poorly balanced workloads (for example, the program shown in Fig. 5.1) where some processors advance more rapidly through simulation time than others. This is because limiting the amount of memory provides a flow control mechanism that avoids overly optimistic execution, which can lead to long rollbacks and poor performance.

Figure 5.9 shows the performance of Time Warp using Cancelback as the amount of memory provided to the execution is varied. Similar results could be expected using the Artificial Rollback protocol. These data use a synthetic workload consisting of a fixed number of jobs moving among the different logical processes. The sequential execution requires as many buffers as there are jobs, since each job always has exactly one event in the pending event list. Performance data are shown for the cases of four, eight, and twelve processors as the number of buffers beyond sequential execution is varied. Each processor contains one LP. The number of buffers needed in the sequential execution are 128, 256, and 384, or 32 buffers per logical process. Two curves are plotted for a given number of processors. One shows performance predictions computed from an analytic model for Cancelback. The second shows experiments performed on the Georgia Tech Time Warp (GTW) simulation executive, with Cancelback, described later in this chapter. These experiments were performed on a Kendall Square KSR-1 multiprocessor. In this implementation each memory buffer includes information concerning a single event, a state vector holding copy state saved variables (state saving is performed prior to the processing of each event), and information concerning the messages that were sent while processing the event.

It is seen that performance rises rapidly as the number of memory buffers is increased beyond the minimum. A well-defined knee is formed, beyond which performance improves only slightly or not at all. This program does not experience poor performance for very large amounts of memory because of the balanced nature of the synthetic workload. Overall, for these experiments, if the Time Warp program provides from 25% to 75% additional buffers beyond that required for sequential execution, performance is about the same as if unlimited memory were provided. The reader should be cautioned, however, that these results are heavily dependent on

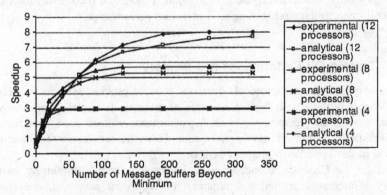

Figure 5.9 Performance of Time Warp using Cancelback as the amount of memory is varied.

details of the application program, so better or worse performance could occur for other applications.

5.2 PERFORMANCE HAZARDS IN TIME WARP

The previous section focused on mechanisms and policies to ensure that Time Warp makes effective usage of memory resources. Let us now turn our attention to ensuring effective utilization of the CPU. As was pointed out earlier in this chapter, Time Warp may produce inefficient executions due to long rollbacks if no constraints are placed on how far some processes can advance ahead of others. Severe performance degradation can result in other situations as well.

This section focuses on specific scenarios that can lead to very poor performance in Time Warp executions, and countermeasures that should be taken in implementing Time Warp to minimize the probability that they occur. The next section discusses a variety of other optimistic synchronization protocols that have been developed to circumvent these potential problems.

5.2.1 Chasing Down Incorrect Computations

At any instant in the execution of Time Warp there will usually be incorrect computations that will be later rolled back and intermixed with correct ones which will eventually be committed. It is important to realize that while the rollback/anti-message mechanism is canceling incorrect computations, this incorrect computation is spreading throughout the simulation system. It is essential that the Time Warp system be able to cancel erroneous computations more rapidly than they propagate throughout the system. Stated another way, if the disease spreads faster than the cure, the patient dies!

A scenario illustrating this phenomenon is shown in Figure 5.10. This scenario consists of three logical processes, LP_A, LP_B, and LP_C, each mapped to a different processor. Initially an incorrect computation in LP_C generated an erroneous event in LP_B, which in turn generated an erroneous event in LP_A; see Figure 5.10(a). The event in LP_C is about to be canceled by an anti-message. Figure 5.10(b) shows the state of the system after the cancellation in LP_C has occurred, which has also generated a new anti-message which is sent to LP_B. While this is going on, LP_A schedules a new, erroneous event for LP_C. This set of actions (cancellation and send anti-message, and propagate the wrong computation to another processor) is repeated again and again, yielding the snapshots shown in Figure 5.10(c) and (d). As can be seen, the incorrect computation remains a step ahead of the cancellation operations and is never completely canceled, much like a dog chasing its own tail.

Time Warp is more likely to encounter situations such as this when there is little computation required to process incorrect events, and the amount of parallelism in the application is less than the number of processors. Having little computation per event hastens the spread of incorrect computations. If the degree of parallelism is

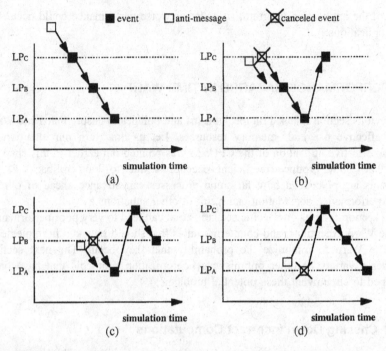

Figure 5.10   Scenario illustrating the "dog chasing its tail" effect in Time Warp. (*a*) Initial snapshot of system; (*b*) snapshot after message cancellation and propagation of incorrect computation to one more processor; (*c*) and (*d*) successive snapshots showing the cancellation "wave" failing to catch up to the spread of the incorrect computation.

low, there will be processors available to spread the erroneous computation as soon as they arrive.

This scenario suggests that anti-messages must be able to rapidly "outrun" the incorrect computations that they are intended to cancel. Canceling a message and sending an anti-message must consume less time than processing an event and scheduling a new event in order to avoid the scenario depicted in Figure 5.10. Further, anti-messages should be given higher priority than positive messages. An alternative approach is to always give highest priority to the computation associated with the smallest time stamp, whether processing positive messages or performing annihilation and rollback.

5.2.2 Rollback Echoes

If the time to perform a rollback is high, very poor performance may result. Rollback requires the following computations to be performed:

1. Anti-messages must be sent for all of the events that are to be canceled.

2. The state of the logical process must be restored; this requires copying a state vector from the copy state save queue, and undoing all modifications to state variables stored in the incremental state saving log.

3. Pointers within the input queue must be updated; details depend on the specific data structure used to implement this queue.

Step 1 and the incremental state restoration portion of step 2 suggest that the rollback overhead is proportional to the number of events being rolled back. Suppose that rolling back a computation T units of simulated time takes twice as long as forward progress by the same amount. Consider the case of two logical processes LP_A and LP_B that are mapped to different processors, and LP_A is 10 units of simulation time ahead of LP_B; see Figure 5.11(a). LP_B sends a message to LP_A, causing the latter to roll back 10 units of simulation time. While LP_A is rolling back 10 units of time, LP_B advances forward 20 units of time according to our assumption that rollback is more time-consuming than forward progress; see Figure 5.11(b). Later, LP_A sends a message back to LP_B, causing LP_B to roll back 20 units in simulation time. While LP_B is rolling back, LP_A advances forward 40 units of time, leading to a rollback of this length; see Figure 5.11(c). One can see that this is an

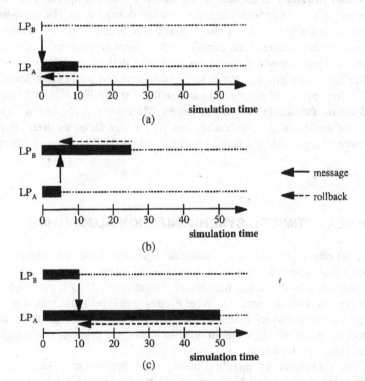

Figure 5.11 Echo example. (a) LP_B sends a message to LP_A, causing LP_A to roll back. (b) While LP_A rolls back, LP_B advances forward. (c) Sequence repeats, with the length of rollback expanding at an exponential rate.

unstable situation where the length of each rollback (and thus the time spent rolling back logical processes) is doubling with each round in this scenario. The net rate of progress in simulation time (as measured by GVT advances) decreases as the simulation proceeds! This scenario is referred to as an "echo" in the parallel simulation literature.

Fortunately, under normal circumstances, rolling back T units of simulation time should not be more time-consuming than forward progress by the same amount. Sending a positive message during forward execution should be less time-consuming than sending an anti-message during rollback. The reason is that sending a positive message requires allocation of a memory buffer, specifying its contents, and creating the anti-message copy, which are steps not required during rollback. Logging state changes during incremental state saving will similarly be about as time-consuming, if not less, than restoring state after ə rollback. Forward execution also entails other computations, such as selecting the event to be processed next, copy state saving for each event, processing incoming positive and negative messages, and the simulation computation itself.

On the other hand, infrequent state saving does increase the cost of rollback. This is because when infrequent state saving is used, one may have to roll back further than is strictly necessary to go back to the last saved state of the process, and then compute forward (coast forward) to regenerate the desired state. The coast-forward step must be included as part of the rollback cost because forward computation beyond the simulation time of the causality error cannot proceed until coast forward is completed. Thus a disadvantage of the infrequent state-saving technique is that it pushes the Time Warp program closer to unstable scenarios such as that described in Figure 5.1. In general, techniques that increase the cost of rollback must be carefully weighed against the benefit that will be gained. Moreover this discussion highlights the fact that implementation overheads can play a key factor in determining the performance of a parallel simulation system based on the Time Warp protocol.

5.3 OTHER OPTIMISTIC SYNCHRONIZATION ALGORITHMS

A number of other optimistic synchronization algorithms have been proposed since Time Warp first appeared. They were motivated to a large extent by the potential performance hazards discussed throughout this chapter. Thus a common theme among these protocols is a policy to avoid excessive rollbacks and logical processes executing too far ahead of others in simulation time. Most algorithms provide parameters to "tune" the algorithm in order to control the behavior of the algorithm and to maximize performance.

Like the discussion of memory management mechanisms, each optimistic synchronization protocol can be characterized by the mechanism used to control the execution, and the policy or the rules governing when the mechanism(s) is applied. Control mechanisms that have been widely explored include the following:

1. *Blocking*. The progress of one or more logical processes is blocked in order to *avoid* inappropriate optimistic execution.
2. *Rollback*. Inappropriate optimistic execution is controlled by selectively rolling back one or more logical processes.

Three of the four memory management protocols discussed earlier in this chapter are examples of synchronization protocols that can be used to control optimistic execution. The memory-based flow control mechanism uses a blocking mechanism: memory utilization is used as the metric to control blocking. Cancelback and Artificial Rollback use rollback. The fourth protocol, Pruneback, does not provide a mechanism for directly controlling optimistic execution.

A second, orthogonal axis by which protocols can be classified is according to whether the control policy is *static* or *adaptive*. Static control mechanisms set control parameters (for example, the amount of memory for the memory-based control mechanisms) at the beginning of the execution and do not vary these parameters during the course of the execution. Adaptive protocols monitor the execution of the program and attempt to adaptively change the control parameters during the execution. The memory-based flow control mechanism described earlier is an example of an adaptive control mechanism.

5.3.1 Moving Time Window

A simple approach to control optimistic execution is to set a bound on how far one logical process can advance ahead of others in simulation time. LPs that reach this bound are forced to block until the LPs lagging behind in simulation time have advanced. Operationally this can be accomplished by defining a window of simulation time extending from GVT to GVT + W, where W is the size of the time window. Logical processes are not allowed to advance beyond GVT + W. This time window advances forward whenever GVT advances.

The above idea is the essence of the Moving Time Window (MTW) parallel simulation protocol. The original MTW protocol called for a static window size, specified by the modeler, that does not change during the execution of the simulation. It is clear that adaptive versions of this algorithm are also possible where the runtime system automatically monitors the execution and adjusts the window size to maximize performance.

The central advantage of time windows is that they provide a simple, easy to implement mechanism to avoid "runaway LPs" from advancing far ahead of others. The central disadvantage of this approach is the cost of maintaining the window, which requires either frequent GVT computations or an efficient mechanism for estimating GVT. Another disadvantage of this approach is that the window does not distinguish correct computations from incorrect ones; that is, incorrect computations within the window would still be allowed to execute, while correct ones beyond the window are not allowed to execute. Further it is not immediately clear how the size of the window should be set; this is clearly dependent on the application, since the number of simulation events per unit of simulation time must be considered. Empirical data concerning this approach are mixed, with some studies indicating significant benefit but others reporting modest gain.

A variation on the time window approach is to define the window in terms of the number of processed, uncommitted events (NPUE) that may reside in a logical process rather than on simulation time. In the Breathing Time Warp protocol, the user must specify this NPUE parameter. An LP is blocked when the number of processed events in that LP with time stamp larger than GVT reaches NPUE. The LP becomes unblocked when GVT is advanced and some of these events become committed.

5.3.2 Lookahead-Based Blocking

The window-based approaches define blocking mechanisms that are not related to detailed dependencies between events in the simulation program. Another approach is to base blocking decisions on information obtained by applying a conservative synchronization protocol. This inevitably implies utilizing lookahead information to determine which events are safe to process. One can envision starting with a conservative synchronization protocol to determine which events are safe to process, and adding to it optimistic synchronization mechanisms such as rollback and anti-messages to allow processing of events that cannot be guaranteed to be safe to be processed. This leads to hybrid conservative/optimistic synchronization algorithms.

One such algorithm is the *filtered rollbacks* approach. This is an extension to the conservative Bounded Lag synchronization algorithm discussed in Section 3.5. Lookahead is used to determine the minimum distance (in simulation time between LPs). In the original Bounded Lag algorithm, the user provides a lower bound to the minimum amount of simulated time that must elapse for an event in one process to affect another. Such minimum "distances" are derived based on application specific information such as the minimum time stamp increment encountered by an event as it "passes through" a logical process. The minimum distance between processes is used as a basis for deciding which events are safe to process. In filtered rollbacks the simulator is allowed to violate this lower bound, possibly leading to violation of the local causality constraint. Such errors are corrected using a Time Warp like rollback mechanism. By adjusting the distance values, one can vary the optimism of the algorithm between the conservative bounded lag scheme and the optimistic moving time window approach.

5.3.3 Local Rollback

One can distinguish between two different types of rollback in Time Warp: primary rollbacks where a logical process received a straggler message in its past, and secondary rollbacks caused by receiving an anti-message that cancels an event that has already been processed. Simulation protocols that allow primary rollbacks are sometimes called aggressive protocols, while those that send messages that may later be canceled (thus creating the possibility of secondary rollbacks) are said to allow *risk.* Time Warp is aggressive and allows risk. It is the combination of these two different types of rollback that causes the cascaded rollback effect where rollbacks can be propagated among many processors. The "dog chasing its tail" effect described earlier is one possible consequence of the cascaded rollback effect.

Cascaded rollbacks can be eliminated without completely discarding the benefits of optimistic synchronization by allowing primary rollbacks but not secondary rollbacks. This approach gives rise to aggressive, no-risk (ANR) protocols. It is accomplished by not allowing messages to be sent until it can be guaranteed that they will not be rolled back. Operationally this means that when a logical process sends a message, the processor does not immediately send it but rather stores the message in a buffer. The message is not sent until GVT advances beyond the send time stamp of the message, thereby guaranteeing that the message will not be later canceled. Because rollbacks do not propagate to other processors, this mechanism is sometimes referred to as a *local rollback* mechanism. The local rollback mechanism avoids the need for anti-messages, but state-saving mechanisms are still required to allow recovery from rollbacks due to straggler messages.

5.3.4 Breathing Time Buckets

The Breathing Time Buckets (BTB) algorithm uses a combination of synchronous event processing with barriers (like that in Filtered Rollbacks, and its predecessor, Bounded Lag), time windows, and local rollback. The central idea in BTB is to compute a quantity called the *event horizon* that determines the size of the time window.

BTB can be viewed as an extension of the sequential event list mechanism that allows optimistic parallel processing; in this sense, it is an optimistic version of the synchronous conservative protocol discussed in Section 3.5.5. The key idea is determining the minimum time stamp among events that will be produced in the future. In the conservative protocol, lookahead is used to determine the minimum time stamp of future events. In BTB one optimistically processes events to compute this quantity.

Consider a sequential simulation that has advanced to simulation time T. There will be some number of events in the pending event list, all with time stamp of at least T. Let $H(T)$ denote the smallest time stamp of any new event that will be generated after simulation time T. $H(T)$ is referred to as the *event horizon*. If the parallel simulation has advanced to time T (i.e., GVT is T), all events in the pending event list with time stamp less than $H(T)$ can be processed without the possibility of being rolled back.

The BTB algorithm operates in cycles, where in each cycle, the parallel simulation will perform as follows (assume that GVT is at simulation time T at the beginning of the cycle):

1. *Optimistically process events in each processor in time stamp order.* During this phase local rollback is used so that new messages generated as the result

of processing an event are *not* sent but rather kept local in the sender in a message buffer. Also, as each processor optimistically processes events, it keeps track of the minimum receive time stamp among new events which were scheduled during this cycle. This quantity $H_i(T)$ is the local minimum in processor i; it represents the event horizon in processor i based only on local information. Each processor will only process events so long as their time stamp is less than the current value of $H_i(T)$ (recall that events are processed in time stamp order).

2. *Compute the global event horizon.* $H(T)$ is computed as the minimum of $H_i(T)$ over all of the processors.

3. *Send messages.* All messages with a send time stamp less than $H(T)$ can now be sent. It can be guaranteed that these messages will not later be rolled back.

4. *Advance simulation time.* GVT is advanced to $H(T)$.

The above steps are repeated until the simulation terminates.

An example illustrating the execution of BTB is shown in Figure 5.12. Here, there are three logical processes LP_A, LP_B, and LP_C, and each is mapped to a different processor. Figure 5.12(a) shows a snapshot of the system at simulation time T with the boxes representing unprocessed events within each LP that were generated in previous cycles. Each LP processes its events in time stamp order so long as the time stamp of the event is less than the minimum time stamp of any new event produced in this cycle. For example, as shown in Figure 5.12(b), LP_A processes events A1, A2, and A3, and A2 schedules a new event Y. It does not process A4 because A4 has a time stamp larger than Y. Similarly LP_B processes its two events B1 and B2, and then it stops because there are no more events for it to process. LP_C processes C1 but does not process C2 because C1 produced a new event X with a smaller time stamp than C2. The local event horizon for LP_A is computed as T_Y, the time stamp of event Y, while that of LP_C is T_X. The local event horizon of LP_B is ∞ because it did not schedule any new events.

After the optimistic event-processing phase is complete, the global event horizon is computed as the minimum of the three local event horizons, or T_X; see Figure 5.12(b). Like the GVT algorithms discussed in Chapter 4, some care must be taken here to ensure that there are no transient messages in the system. Simulation time (i.e., GVT) is advanced to $H(T)$, and the messages generated by the optimistic processing are sent to their destination processor. The events A1, A2, B1, B2, and C1 are now committed, and memory used by these events (log information) can now be reclaimed via the fossil collection mechanism. In this example, A3 was processed but not committed; one could roll back this event and reprocess it in the next cycle, or preserve this computation. In this example, the message X is sent to LP_A with time stamp less than that of A3, so A3 must be rolled back and reprocessed in the next cycle. Had A3 scheduled a new event, the message for this new event would *not* have been sent to the destination processor because A3 had not been committed, so the erroneous event can be canceled locally. The final state of the simulation at the end of this cycle is shown in Figure 5.12(c).

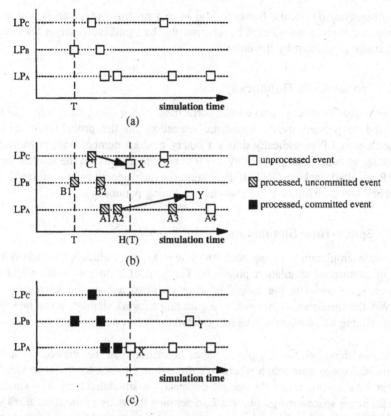

Figure 5.12   Example illustrating the execution of the Breathing Time Buckets algorithm. (a) Initial set of unprocessed event; (b) result of simulation phase and computation of the event horizon; (c) messages generated during the simulation phase are sent, and simulation time is advanced.

5.3.5   Wolf Calls

The "dog chasing its tail" effect discussed earlier can be avoided by blocking processors when a rollback is detected. In the Wolf Calls protocol, when a processor detects that it has received a straggler message, it broadcasts a special control message that causes the processors to stop advancing until the error has been erased (via anti-messages and rollbacks). The special control messages warning of "possible danger" are referred to as "wolf calls," in reference to the well-known fable.

Broadcasting has the disadvantage that it may unnecessarily block some LPs. This can be alleviated if the LP detecting the error can determine the set of processors to which the error may have spread. In this case the control messages need only be sent to this set of processors. This requires an upper bound on the speed in wallclock time that an erroneous computation may spread, as well as an upper bound on the latency of the control messages. Such bounds may be difficult to define on multiprocessor systems, however, and even with this optimization, the set of processors that *might* be affected by an error may be significantly larger than the set that actually is affected by the error.

5.3.6 Probabilistic Rollbacks

Besides rollbacks necessary to ensure correctness of the simulation, rollbacks may be added to prevent overly optimistic execution. In the probabilistic rollback approach each LP periodically draws a binary random number with probability p of coming up heads (and probability $1 - p$ of coming up tails). If the result is heads, the LP is rolled back to GVT. If it is tails, no such operation is performed. The frequency and probability p are user-defined tuning parameters.

5.3.7 Space-Time Simulation

Space-time simulation is an approach based on relaxation techniques similar to those used in continuous simulation problems. The goal of a discrete event simulation program is to compute the values of state variables across simulated time. For example, the simulation of a server in a queueing network simulation can be viewed as determining the number of jobs that exist in the server at every point in simulated time.

As was described in Chapter 2, the simulation can be viewed as a two-dimensional space-time graph where one dimension enumerates the state variables used in the simulation, and the second dimension is simulated time. The simulator must fill in the space-time graph, that is, determine the value of the simulator's state variables over simulated time in order to characterize the behavior of the physical system. In space-time simulation this graph is partitioned into regions, with one process assigned to each region. This process is responsible for filling in the portion of the space-time graph that is assigned to it. In order to accomplish this task, the process must be aware of boundary conditions for its region, and update them in accordance with activities in its own region. Changes to boundary conditions are passed among processes in the form of messages. Thus each process repeatedly computes its portion of the space-time graph, transmits changes in the boundary conditions to processes responsible for neighboring regions, and then waits for new messages indicating further changes to the boundary conditions. The computation proceeds until no more changes occur, that is, until the computation converges to a fixed point. Time Warp can be viewed as a special case of space-time simulation where the space-time region is defined as rectangles, one per LP, that span all of simulation time for the set of state variables mapped to that LP.

5.3.8 Summary

Building on the basic mechanisms defined for Time Warp, numerous synchronization protocols have been defined to circumvent the pitfalls that may occur with over-optimistic execution. Most provide control parameters that must be set by the user to tune performance. Some provide mechanisms to have the Time Warp system automatically set these parameters and, in some cases, change these parameters during execution to optimize performance. Space does not permit elaboration of all of the protocols that have been proposed. Pointers to additional information on this subject are provided at the end of this chapter.

At present, conventional wisdom within the parallel simulation community is that:

1. "Pure" Time Warp systems with no flow control mechanisms are not well suited as a general purpose parallel simulation executive because of the potential for extremely poor performance in certain situations.
2. The problem of overoptimistic execution in Time Warp is solvable. A number of protocols have been developed and have been demonstrated to achieve good performance.
3. There is no one protocol that is clearly better than all others in most cases that arise in practice. For any given simulation application containing an adequate amount of intrinsic parallelism, several approaches may be used that will be effective in controlling optimistic execution.

5.4 PUTTING IT ALL TOGETHER: GEORGIA TECH TIME WARP (GTW)

We conclude this chapter by examining a particular Time Warp executive called Georgia Tech Time Warp (GTW). GTW is a parallel simulation executive designed to execute on networked uniprocessor and multiprocessor machines. Here, we specifically discuss the version that executes on shared-memory multiprocessors. GTW includes a variety of algorithms and techniques designed specifically for this class of parallel computers that have not been discussed thus far.

5.4.1 Programmer's Interface

The GTW executive was designed to provide a modest set of basic simulation primitives, while allowing more sophisticated mechanisms to be implemented as library routines. For example, GTW supports an event-oriented world view. Mechanisms for more complex world views such as process-oriented simulation must be built on top of the GTW executive.

A GTW program consists of a collection of logical processes that communicate by exchanging time-stamped messages. The execution of each LP is entirely message driven; that is, any execution of application code is a direct result of receiving a message. LPs cannot "spontaneously" begin new computations without first receiving a message. Each LP has three procedures associated with it: The *IProc* procedure is called at the beginning of the simulation to initialize the LP and generate the initial messages, the *Proc* procedure (also called the *event handler*) is called to process each event received by the LP, and an optional *FProc* procedure is called at the end of the simulation, typically to output application specific statistics. These procedures, and the routines that they call, completely specify the behavior of the LP. Each LP is identified by a unique integer ID.

In addition the user must provide a procedure for global initialization of the simulation. This procedure is passed command line arguments and must specify the number of logical processes, the IProc, Proc, and FProc procedures for each LP, and the mapping of LPs to processors.

LPs may define four different types of state:

1. A state that is automatically checkpointed by the GTW executive.
2. A state that is incrementally checkpointed using GTW directives invoked by the application.
3. Local (sometimes called automatic) variables defined within the IProc, Proc, and FProc procedures.
4. Global variables that are not checkpointed.

The fourth category is intended to hold data structures that are not modified during the simulation. The state vector of each LP is an arbitrary data structure defined within the application program.

During initialization (typically in the IProc procedure), the application program must specify the memory locations that are automatically checkpointed. A copy of the LP's automatically checkpointed state is made prior to each invocation of its event handler, transparent to the application. Incrementally checkpointed variables must be individually copied through explicit calls to GTW primitives. A variable needs only to be checkpointed once in each event, but it must be checkpointed prior to any modification of the variable within the event. Any state that is dynamically allocated after the initialization phase of the simulation must be incrementally checkpointed. Incremental checkpointing by overloading the assignment operator in C++ is also provided in a layer above the GTW executive.

Two procedures are provided for message passing. The *TWGetMsg* procedure allocates a message buffer by storing a pointer to the buffer in a GTW-defined variable. The *TWSend* procedure sends the message.

5.4.2 I/O and Dynamic Memory Allocation

Application programs may also schedule events that will not be processed until GVT exceeds the time stamp of the event, guaranteeing that the computation will not be later rolled back. This allows application programs to perform irrevocable operations such as I/O. Such events are referred to as I/O events, although event handlers for I/O events may perform arbitrary computations and do not need to actually perform any I/O operations. A different event handler may be associated with each I/O event. An LP may schedule an I/O event for itself or for another LP.

The GTW executive provides two types of I/O events. *Blocking* I/O events do not allow optimistic execution of the LP beyond the time stamp of the I/O event. This is intended for I/O operations requiring input from external sources. In this case the LP cannot compute forward until it receives this input, so it is better to simply block the LP rather than optimistically execute it beyond the time of the I/O event. The LP is temporarily blocked once a blocking I/O event becomes its smallest time-stamped, unprocessed event. The LP remains blocked until it is either rolled-back (the LP will again block once the rolled-back events are reprocessed, if the I/O event has not been canceled), or until GVT advances to the time stamp of the blocking I/O event. Once the event handler for the I/O event is called, the LP resumes normal optimistic execution. The event handler for blocking I/O events can access the LP's state vector.

Nonblocking I/O events do not temporarily block LPs as described above. The event handler for these events cannot access the state vector of the LP, since the LP will typically have advanced beyond the time stamp of the I/O event when the I/O event handler is called. All data needed by the I/O event handler must be included within the message for the event. Output operations will typically use nonblocking I/O events.

Mechanisms are provided to attach handlers, called *rollback handlers*, to events that are executed when the event is rolled back or canceled. This, and I/O events, are used to implement dynamic memory allocation. Specifically, dynamic memory allocation in GTW must be performed by calling a GTW procedure called TW_malloc(). TW_malloc() calls malloc(), the memory allocation procedure in the C programming language, and attaches a rollback handler to the event that is now being processed. The rollback handler contains a call to the free() procedure to release the memory if the event is rolled back or canceled, avoiding memory leaks as was discussed in Chapter 4. Memory must be released by calling the TW_free() procedure which schedules a nonblocking I/O event. The I/O event handler contains a call to free(). This ensures that memory is not released until it is guaranteed the memory really is no longer needed. If the event calling TW_free() is rolled back or canceled, the I/O event will be automatically canceled via GTWs rollback mechanism.

5.4.3 GTW Data Structures

Each data structure in the GTW executive is said to be "owned" or "reside" on a specific processor. In principle, no such specification is required because all memory can be accessed by any processor in a shared-memory system. However, the GTW design assigns each data structure to a unique owner (in some cases the owner may change during execution) in order to ensure that synchronization (for example, locks) is not used where it is not needed and to maximize locality in memory references. Synchronization and nonlocal memory references are typically much more time-consuming than local memory references on most existing multiprocessor platforms.

Time Warp uses three distinct types of memory objects: events stored in the input queue, anti-messages stored in the output queue, and state history information stored in the state queue. In GTW these are, in effect, combined into a single object type, the event object. The event object includes a copy of the automatically checkpointed portion of the state of the LP, and pointers that are used to implement anti-messages, as will be described momentarily. Each processor contains a single event queue data structure that implements the functionality of the input, output, and state queues for the logical processes mapped to that processor.

The event queue data structure is shown in Figure 5.13. Each LP contains a list of the processed events for that LP. This list is sorted by receive time stamp and is implemented using a linear list. Unprocessed events for all LPs mapped to the same processor are stored in a *single* priority queue data structure. Using a single queue for all LPs eliminates the need for a separate "scheduling queue" data structure to enumerate the executable LPs, and this allows both the selection of the next LP to execute and location of the smallest time stamped unprocessed event in that LP to be implemented with a single dequeue operation. The single-queue approach reduces the overhead associated with "normal" event processing, and as discussed later, greatly simplifies the GVT computation. A drawback with this approach is that migration of an LP to another processor by a dynamic load management mechanism is more difficult because the events for a specific LP are intermixed with events for other LPs in the priority queue holding unprocessed events, requiring one to extract the events from this data structure. To circumvent this problem, GTW allows a processor to be configured with multiple priority queues, with each LP assigned to one queue. The set of LPs mapped to a single priority queue, referred to as a cluster,

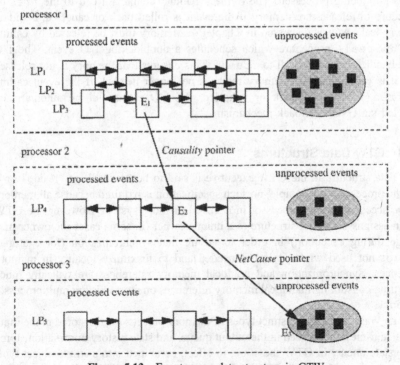

Figure 5.13 Event queue data structure in GTW.

is the atomic unit that is migrated between processors by the dynamic load management software.

In addition to the event queue shown in Figure 5.13, each processor maintains two additional queues to hold incoming messages from other processors. The message queue (*MsgQ*) holds incoming positive messages that are sent to an LP residing on this processor. Messages are placed into this queue by the *TWSend* primitive. The message cancellation queue (*CanQ*) is similar to the *MsgQ* except that it holds messages that have been canceled. When a processor wishes to cancel a message, it enqueues a pointer to the message being canceled into the *CanQ* of the processor to which the message was originally sent. Logically each message enqueued in the *CanQ* can be viewed as an anti-message; however, it is a pointer to the message itself rather than an explicit anti-message that is enqueued, as will be described momentarily. Separate queues are used to hold messages generated by other processors (as opposed to the processors directly manipulating the data structures shown in Fig. 5.13) to avoid using time-consuming synchronization locks to access the event queue.

Each processor also maintains another priority queue called the *I/O queue* which holds I/O events (as well as some non-I/O events) for LPs mapped to that processor. I/O events are scheduled in exactly the same way as ordinary events; that is, they are enqueued in the unprocessed event priority queue via the *MsgO* if the sender and receiver are on different processors. This simplifies cancellation of I/O events. Just prior to calling an event handler, the GTW executive first checks to see if the event is an I/O event. I/O events are placed in the I/O queue, and the call to the event handler is deferred until later. If the event is a blocking I/O event, the LP is also marked as "blocked." All events for blocked LPs, both I/O and non-I/O events, are similarly diverted to the I/O queue when they are removed from the unprocessed event queue. If a blocked LP is rolled back, it becomes unblocked, and the LP's events in the I/O queue are returned to the unprocessed event queue. The fossil collection procedure processes I/O events with time stamp less than or equal to GVT, and unblocks blocked LPs.

5.4.4 Direct Cancellation

As noted earlier, it is important that Time Warp systems provide a mechanism to rapidly cancel incorrect computations and prevent the "dog chasing its tail" effect described in Section 5.2.1. GTW uses a mechanism called direct cancellation to speed the cancellation of incorrect computations. Rather than using copies of messages to implement anti-messages, pointers are used. Whenever an event computation schedules (sends) a new event, a pointer to the new event is left behind in the sending event's data structure (see Fig. 5.13). Because the new event is often stored on a different processor than the event that scheduled it, this technique requires a pointer in a data structure in one processor to point to a data structure in another processor. This is easily implemented on shared-memory machine architectures where different processors have a common address space. A variation on this approach is implemented in the distributed-memory version of GTW, where arrays of pointers to events and array indices are used to implement pointers across processors with distinct address spaces.

To support direct cancellation, each event contains two pointer variables, called *Cause* and *NextCause*. The events scheduled while processing one event are stored as a linked list referred to as the causality list. The *Cause* field is a pointer to the first event in this list, and *NextCause* contains a pointer to the next event in the causality list. For example, in Figure 5.13 event E_1 scheduled two events, E_2 and E_3. E_2 has since been processed but E_3 has not. If E_1 is rolled back, E_2 and E_3 would be canceled by enqueueing them into the *CanQ* data structure in processors 2 and 3, respectively.

The principal advantages of direct cancellation are that it eliminates the need for explicit anti-messages and an output queue, thereby economizing on storage, and more important it eliminates the need to search queues to locate events that must be canceled. Direct cancellation can be used with either the lazy or aggressive cancellation policy.

5.4.5   Event-Processing Loop

After the simulator is initialized, each processor enters a loop that repeatedly performs the following steps:

1. All incoming messages are removed from the *MsgQ* data structure, and the messages are filed, one at a time, into the event queue data structure. If a message has a time stamp smaller than the last event processed by the LP, the LP is rolled back.

2. All incoming canceled messages are removed from the *CanQ* data structure and are processed one at a time. Storage used by canceled messages is returned to the free memory pool. Rollbacks may also occur here, and they are handled in essentially the same manner as rollbacks caused by straggler positive messages, as described above.

3. A single unprocessed event is removed from the priority queue holding unprocessed events for the processor and is processed by calling the LPs event handler (*Proc* procedure). A *smallest time stamp first* scheduling algorithm is used; that is, the unprocessed event containing the smallest time stamp is selected as the next one to be processed.

These steps continue until the simulation has been completed. The application specifies the simulation time at which execution completes. Events that are scheduled with a time stamp larger than the end time are discarded. The simulation ends where there are no unprocessed events remaining in the system.

5.4.6   Buffer Management

The principal atomic unit of memory in the GTW executive is a buffer. Each buffer contains the storage for a single event, a copy of the automatically checkpointed state, pointers for the direct cancellation mechanism and incremental state saving, and miscellaneous status flags and other information.

The original implementation of the GTW software (version 1.0) used *receiver-based* free pools. This means that the TWGetMsg() routine allocates a free buffer from the processor *receiving* the message. The sender then writes the contents of the message into the buffer and calls TWSend() to enqueue it in the receiving processor's *MsgQ*. This approach suffers from two drawbacks. First, locks are required to synchronize accesses to the free pool, even if both the sender and receiver LP are mapped to the same processor. This is because the processor's free list is shared among all processors that send messages to this processor. The second drawback is concerned with caching effects, as discussed next.

In cache-coherent multiprocessor systems using invalidate protocols, receiver-based free pools do not make the most effective use of the cache. Buffers in the free pool for a processor will likely be resident in the cache for that processor, assuming that the cache is sufficiently large. This is because in most cases, the buffer was last accessed by an event handler executing on that processor. Assume that the sender and receiver for the message reside on different processors. When the sending processor allocates a buffer at the receiver and writes the message into the buffer, a series of cache misses and invalidations occur as the buffer is "moved" to the sender's cache. Later, when the receiver dequeues the message buffer and executes the receiver's event handler, a second set of misses occurs, and the buffer's contents are again transferred back to the receiver's cache. Thus two rounds of cache misses and invalidations occur with each message send.

A better solution is to use sender-based free pools. The sending processor allocates a buffer from its local free pool, writes the message into it, and enqueues it at the receiver. With this scheme, the free pool is local to each processor, so no locks are required to control access to it. Also, when the sender allocates the buffer and writes the contents of the message into it, memory references will hit in the cache in the scenario described above. Thus only one round of cache misses and interprocessor communications occurs (when the receiving processor reads the message buffer).

The sender-based pool creates a new problem, however. Each message send, in effect, transfers the ownership of the buffer from the sending to the receiving processor, since message buffers are always reclaimed by the receiver during fossil collection or cancellation. Memory buffers accumulate in processors that receive more messages than they send. This leads to an unbalanced distribution of buffers, with free buffer pools in some processors becoming depleted while others have an excess. To address this problem, each processor is assigned a quota of N_{buf} buffers that it attempts to maintain. After fossil collection, the number of buffers residing in the processor is checked. If this number exceeds N_{buf}, the excess buffers are transferred to a global free list. On the other hand, if the number of buffers falls below $N_{buf} - \Delta$ (Δ is a user-defined parameter), additional buffers are allocated from the global pool. Counters associated with each event list allow determination of the number of buffers reclaimed on each fossil collection without scanning through the list of reclaimed buffers.

5.4.7 Flow Control

The flow control mechanism based on adaptively controlling memory allocation (described in Section 5.1.7) is used. Specifically, the policy described there is used to estimate the memory requirements of each processor. If an LP attempts to schedule a new event while processing an event E, and no memory buffers are available to hold the new event, then E is aborted (rolled back, and returned to the list of unprocessed events). The processor then returns to the main scheduling loop and, unless new events were received, attempts to reprocess the event. This "abort and retry" cycle repeats, creating a kind of "busy wait loop" until either a new event with a smaller time stamp is received or GVT advances and memory is reclaimed.

5.4.8 GVT Computation and Fossil Collection

GTW uses on-the-fly fossil collection (see Section 4.3.1) in order to reduce the time required to reclaim memory. Each processed event is threaded into both the free list and the processed event list for the LP after the event has been processed, and the time stamp of the event is checked to make sure it is less than GVT before the memory buffer is reused. A GVT algorithm developed specifically for shared-memory multiprocessors is used to compute GVT. This is described next.

An asynchronous algorithm (i.e., no barrier synchronizations) is used that is interleaved with "normal" event processing. The algorithm requires neither message acknowledgments nor special "GVT messages." All interprocessor communication is realized using a global flag variable *GVTFlag*, an array to hold each processor's local minimum, and a variable to hold the new GVT value.

Any processor can initiate a GVT computation by writing the number of processors in the system into *GVTFlag*. This flag is viewed as being "set" if it holds a nonzero value. A lock on this variable ensures that at most one processor initiates a GVT computation.

Let T_{GVT} be the instant in wallclock time that *GVTFlag* is set. As before, GVT is defined as a lower bound on the time stamp of all unprocessed or partially processed messages and anti-messages in the system at T_{GVT}. Messages are accounted for by requiring that (1) the *sending* processor is responsible for messages sent after T_{GVT}, and (2) the *receiving* processor is responsible for messages sent prior to T_{GVT}. To implement (1), each processor maintains a local variable called *SendMin* that contains the minimum time stamp of any message sent after *GVTFlag* is set. *GVTFlag* is checked *after* each message or anti-message send, and *SendMin* is updated if the flag is set. To implement (2), each processor checks *GVTFlag* at the *beginning* of the main event-processing loop and notes whether the flag was set. Then, as part of the normal event-processing procedure, the processor receives and processes all messages (anti-messages) in *MsgQ* (*CanQ*) and removes the smallest time-stamped event from the unprocessed event queue. If *GVTFlag* was set at the beginning of the loop, the time stamp of this unprocessed event is a lower bound on the time stamp of any event sent to this processor prior to T_{GVT}. The processor computes the minimum of this time stamp and *SendMin*, and writes this value into its entry of the global array. It then decrements *GVTFlag* to indicate that it has reported its local minimum, and resumes "normal" event processing. The set *GVTFlag* is now ignored until the new GVT value is received.

The last processor to compute its local minimum (the processor that decrements *GVTFlag* to zero) computes the global minimum and writes this new GVT value into a global variable. Each processor detects the new GVT and updates its local copy of this value.

The overhead associated with this algorithm is minimal. When GVT is *not* being computed, *GVTFlag* must be checked, but this overhead is small because the flag is not being modified and will normally reside in each processor's local cache. No synchronization is required. To compute GVT, the principal overheads are updating *GVTFlag* and *SendMin*, and the global minimum computation performed by one processor. Performance measurements indicate that even with frequent GVT computations (for example, every millisecond) the parallel simulator is only slightly slower than when GVT computations are infrequent.

5.4.9 Incremental State Saving

Incremental state saving is implemented by defining an array or words for each LP into which values of state variables are stored prior to modification by an event. Logically this array can be viewed as a single, large array, but it is actually implemented as a linked list of fixed sized arrays. Each state save operation advances a pointer into the array to the next location, and copies a word from the LPs state into the array. When rollback occurs, the old contents of state variables are restored, one after the other, until the point of rollback is reached.

5.4.10 Local Message Sends

The TWSend() routine first checks if the destination LP is mapped to the same processor as the sender. If they are the same, TWSend() simply enqueues the message in the unprocessed event queue, bypassing *MsGQ* and thus avoiding synchronization overheads. Thus local message sends are no more time-consuming than scheduling an event in a sequential simulation.

5.4.11 Message Copying

The GTW executive performs no message copying, neither in sending nor receiving messages. This allows efficient execution of applications using large messages. Software executing above the GTW executive must ensure that the contents of a message are not modified after the message it sent and that the contents of received messages are not modified by the event handler.

5.4.12 Batch Event Processing

The scheduling loop always checks *MsgQ* and *CanQ* prior to processing each event. Rather than checking these queues before each event, an alternative approach is to check these queues prior to processing a *batch* of B events, thereby amortizing the overhead of each queue check over many events. If there are no B events available to be processed, the queue is checked after processing those that are available.

The batch-processing approach reduces queue management overheads somewhat, but it may lead to more rolled back computation because, in effect, the arrival of straggler and anti-messages is delayed. Thus it is clear that B should not be set to too large a value. Setting the batch size is left to user.

5.4.13 Performance Measurements

GTW has been successfully applied to speeding up simulations of asynchronous transfer mode (ATM) networks, wireless networks, and commercial air traffic systems. It is currently being used extensively to model commercial air traffic both in the United States and around the world for development of future expansions of air transportation services. This work involves use of a simulation model called DPAT (Detailed Policy Assessment Tool) running on GTW that was developed by Mitre Corp. At the time of this writing, work is in progress by Mitre to install GTW in the Federal Aviation Administration's air traffic control center as an on-line tool to manage the air traffic space when new conditions develop in the air traffic space (for example, thunderstorms reducing capacity of certain airports).

Figure 5.14 shows GTW performance in simulating a wireless personal communication services (PCS) network. This simulation models a wireless network providing communication services to mobile PCS subscribers. The service area is partitioned into subareas or *cells*, with each cell containing a receiver/transmitter and a fixed number of channels. When a portable (cellular telephone) moves from one cell to another, it must stop using one transmitter/receiver, and begin using another. Thus a new radio frequency channel must be allocated in the new cell to maintain the call. If no channels are available, the call is dropped. It is important that the network be engineered so that the number of dropped calls remains below a certain level, such as 1% of calls transmitted through the system.

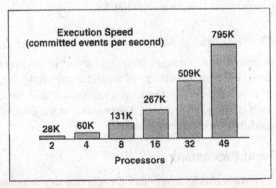

Figure 5.14 GTW performance in simulating a wireless personal communication services network.

The specific simulation used here consists of 2048 cells (each modeled by a logical process), and 50,000 portables. The simulation was executed on a Kendall Square Research KSR-2 multiprocessor; each KSR processor is approximately 20% faster than a Sun Sparc-2 workstation, based on measurements of sequential simulations. Figure 5.14 shows the average number of events committed by the simulator per second of wallclock time, referred to as the event rate, for different numbers of processors. The size of this model prevented execution on a sequential computer; however, based on measurements of smaller models, the event rate is estimated to be between 15,000 and 20,000 events per second. Thus this simulation yields approximately fortyfold speedup on 49 processors. One anomaly in these measurements is the simulation achieves super linear speedup, namely more than two times a performance improvement as the number of processors is doubled. This is because as the number of processors increases, the amount of cache memory provided to the simulation increases, so a larger fraction of the program resides in cache memory, leading to a disproportionate improvement in performance.

5.5 SUMMARY

While the previous chapter focused on fundamental mechanisms used in Time Warp systems, this chapter presented the techniques used to develop efficient optimistic parallel simulation systems. A principal concern with Time Warp, as originally proposed, is the amount of memory required to execute the simulation. It was seen that memory management protocols provide a means for Time Warp to execute within a constant factor of the amount of memory required for a sequential execution when executing on a shared-memory multiprocessor. More generally, an important problem that must be addressed in practical Time Warp systems is preventing over-optimistic execution. Controlling memory allocation is one approach to solving this problem. Several other synchronization protocols were discussed, most using fundamental concepts used in Time Warp (for example, rollback, anti-messages, GVT) that provide an effective means to control execution. Finally the implementation of the GTW system, a parallel discrete event simulation executive based on Time Warp, was described. Several techniques exploiting shared memory, such as buffer management techniques and GVT algorithms, were described.

Practical experience with optimistic parallel simulation indicates that runaway optimism can be controlled, and that efficient parallel simulation executives can be developed using these techniques. An intuitive explanation as to why runaway optimism tends not to be a severe problem is that erroneous computations can only be initiated when one processes a correct event prematurely; this premature event, and subsequent erroneous computations, must have time stamps that are larger than the correct, straggler computation. Also, the further the incorrect computation spreads, the larger its time stamp becomes, lowering its priority for execution since preference is normally given to computations containing smaller time stamps. Thus Time Warp systems automatically tend to slow the propagation of errors, allowing the error detection and correction mechanism to correct the mistake before too much damage has been done. A potentially more dangerous situation is when the erroneous computation propagates with smaller time stamp increments than the correct one. However, even here, a wide variety of solutions exist to control runaway optimism if it does appear.

5.6 COMPARING OPTIMISTIC AND CONSERVATIVE SYNCHRONIZATION

Unfortunately, the years of research in synchronization protocols do not reveal a clear winner for all applications. The fact remains that the optimal protocol for any particular situation is problem dependent. One can, however, give guidelines on which approach is appropriate for which situations. Important distinctions among these approaches are summarized in Table 5.1.

Simulation executives based on conservative protocols are generally less complex than those based on optimistic synchronization. If the simulation has large lookaheads, the synchronization mechanism will not have to be invoked very frequently in a well-designed system. This will result in lower runtime overheads than in optimistic executives because optimistic protocols must create and fossil collect history information. State saving is perhaps the most cumbersome among the optimistic overheads. But, as was seen in Chapter 4, relatively ordinary tasks such

TABLE 5.1 Comparing conservative and optimistic synchronization

Protocol	Conservative	Optimistic
Overheads	Simple simulation executive; may need special mechanism for dynamic LP topology; lower overheads if good lookahead	Complex simulation executive requires state saving, fossil collection; special mechanisms for dynamic memory allocation, I/O, runtime errors
Parallelism	Limited by worst-case scenario; requires good lookahead for concurrent execution and scalability	Limited by actual dependencies (rather than potential dependencies)
Application development	Potentially complex, fragile code to exploit lookahead	More robust; less reliant on lookahead; greater transparency of the synchronization mechanism
Legacy simulators	Straightforward inclusion in federations	Requires additional mechanisms (e.g., state saving) to support rollback

as dynamic memory allocation, runtime errors, and I/O that can be implemented using conventional programming methods in conservative systems require inclusion of special mechanisms in optimistic systems. While relatively straightforward solutions to these problems exist, they do add to the complexity of the simulation executive. One area where conservative systems do incur additional overheads that do not arise in optimistic systems is when the topology among logical processes changes during the execution. If the simulation protocol uses topology information, such as the distance between processes approach, an additional mechanism is required. But, on balance, optimistic systems are generally more complex than conservative ones.

But the Achilles's heel for conservative protocols is the need for lookahead to achieve good performance. As illustrated in Chapter 3, conservative protocols perform poorly if there is little or no lookahead, even if the model contains a large amount of parallelism. This is illustrated in Figure 5.15 where Time Warp performance is compared with the conservative null message and deadlock detection and recovery protocols in simulating a queueing network on eight processors. This application contains a fixed number of jobs cycling through the network. Figure 5.15 shows speedup as a function of the message density, defined as the number of jobs in the queueing network divided by the number of LPs. This particular queueing network includes a small number of high-priority jobs that preempt service of other jobs, resulting in very poor lookahead. As can be seen, Time Warp is able to successfully extract parallelism from this application, while both conservative algorithms yield speedup less than one; that is, they run slower than a sequential execution.

Conservative protocols cannot fully exploit the parallelism in the application because they must guard against a worst-case scenario, which may seldom actually occur in practice. A corollary to this observation is that no conservative protocol can scale unless certain assumptions are made regarding lookahead, except in relatively specialized circumstances such as large numbers of events containing exactly the same time stamp. By "scale" we mean that if the number of LPs and the number of processors increase in proportion, the parallel/distributed simulation is able to

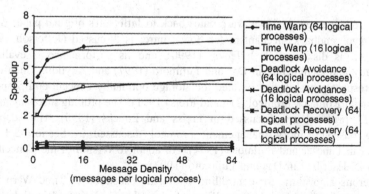

Figure 5.15 Performance of Time Warp and conservative protocols on an 8 processor system.

maintain approximately the same rate of advance in simulation time per second of wallclock time. By contrast, parallelism in optimistic protocols is not limited by potential dependencies between logical processes but rather by the actual dependencies as represented by event interactions. Thus optimistic approaches offer greater potential for scalability in the absence of lookahead.

As was noted in Chapter 3, not only must the physical system exhibit good lookahead characteristics, but the simulation must be programmed in a way that exposes the lookahead to the underlying simulation executive. This may require a relatively high level of expertise on the part of the simulation programmer. If changes to the model are included that affect the lookahead characteristics, such as the addition of preemptive behavior, substantial revisions to the model may be necessary. In the worst case, no revision yielding acceptable performance may be possible.

More important, exploiting lookahead can lead to simulation code that is complex; This leads to software that is difficult to develop and maintain. Constraints on dynamically changing the topology of logical processes can further aggravate this problem. If one's goal is to develop a "general purpose" simulation executive that provides robust performance across a wide range of models and does not require the model developer to be familiar with details of the synchronization mechanism, optimistic synchronization offers greater hope.

On the other hand, if one is retrofitting an existing (legacy) sequential simulation for parallel/distributed processing (for example, by "federating" it with other simulators, or even itself, in a distributed simulation environment), conservative synchronization offers the path of least effort. This is because there is no need to add state-saving mechanisms to the simulation code or to ensure that dynamic memory allocation and I/O are implemented to account for rollback. In the long run one may be able to automate many of these tasks for optimistic processing, but tools to support such automation do not yet exist.

5.7 ADDITIONAL READINGS

Memory management in Time Warp dates back to Jefferson's original paper where the message sendback mechanism for flow control is discussed (Jefferson 1985). Cancelback is discussed in Jefferson (1990), and its performance is evaluated empirically and analytically in Das and Fujimoto (1997) and Akyildiz, Chen et al. (1993), respectively. Lin first defined the storage optimality concept and proposed the Artificial Rollback protocol (Lin and Preiss 1991). The pruning mechanism and Pruneback protocol are discussed in Preiss and Loucks (1995). The adaptive, blocking based memory management protocol discussed in Section 5.1.7 is described in Panesar and Fujimoto (1997). An adaptive version of the Cancelback protocol is described in Das and Fujimoto (1997).

Numerous algorithms for controlling optimistic execution in Time Warp have been proposed. The Moving Time Window algorithm is described in Sokol and Stucky (1990). Breathing Time Warp is discussed in Steinman (1993). Risk-free execution was first proposed in the SRADS protocol (Dickens and Reynolds 1990) and was also utilized in the Breathing Time Buckets mechanism (Steinman 1991). Performance evaluations of this technique are described in Bellenot (1993), and Wonnacott and Bruce (1996). Risk-free execution is also used in a real-time simulation executive called PORTS (Ghosh, Panesar et al. 1994) because it offers favorable properties for predicting execution time in simulations. The Wolf Calls mechanism is described in Madisetti, Walrand et al. (1988), and a variation on this idea that avoids race conditions in locating LPs to roll back is described in Damani, Wang et al. (1997). Probabilistic rollbacks are described in Madisetti, Hardaker et al. (1993). The echo performance hazard was identified in Lubachevsky, Shwartz et al. (1991) where a blocking-based optimistic protocol is discussed. Several proposals for mixing conservative and optimistic LPs have appeared, including Arvind and Smart (1992), Rajaei, Ayani et al. (1993), and Jha and Bagrodia (1994).

Several proposals for adaptive synchronization mechanisms have appeared. In Ball and Hoyt (1990), and Ferscha (1995), processes may be blocked based on statistical estimates of the time stamp of the next event that will arrive from another processor. In Hamnes and Tripathi (1994), blocking intervals are based on recent simulation time advances by LPs. A class of protocols based on rapid dissemination of global state information is described in Srinivasan and Reynolds (1995). Space-time simulation is discussed in Chandy and Sherman (1989), Bagrodia, Liao et al. (1991). Other optimistic protocols include Prakash and Subramanian (1992), Turner and Xu (1992), Deelman and Szymanski (1997), Fabbri and Donatiello (1997), Tay, Teo et al. (1997).

The GTW executive is described in Das, Fujimoto et al. (1994). GTWs GVT algorithm, and on-the-fly fossil collection are described in Fujimoto and Hybinette (1997). The buffer management mechanism is described in Fujimoto and Panesar (1995). Air traffic simulations using GTW are described in Wieland (1997).

CHAPTER 6

Time Parallel Simulation

As discussed in Chapter 2, one can view the simulation computation as determining the values of a set of state variables across simulation time. The approaches discussed thus far accomplish this task by partitioning the state variables defined in the simulation among a set of logical processes. They assign each LP the responsibility of computing the evolution of its state variables over the duration of the simulation. As illustrated in Figure 6.1(a), this approach uses a *spatial decomposition* approach where the space-time diagram is partitioned into a set of horizontal strips, with each LP responsible for computing the values of the variables contained within that strip over simulation time.

Another approach is to use a *temporal decomposition* of the space-time diagram. Here, as shown in Figure 6.1(b), the space-time diagram is partitioned into a set of vertical strips, and a logical process is assigned to each strip. Each LP must perform a simulation of the entire system for the interval of simulation time covered by its strip of the space-time diagram.

Stated another way, the simulation computation constructs a *sample path* through the set of all possible states in which the system can reside across simulation time (see Fig. 6.2). A *time parallel* simulation partitions the simulation time axis into a sequence of nonoverlapping simulation time intervals $[T_0, T_1), [T_1, T_2), \ldots, [T_{n-1}, T_n)$. A logical process assigned to the ith window computes the portion of the sample path within that window.

This so-called time parallel approach to parallel simulation offers several attractive properties:

- *Massive parallelism.* The amount of parallelism in the simulation is potentially very large because simulations often extend over long periods of simulation time. Time parallel simulation algorithms typically run out of processors before they run out of parallelism within the simulation computation.
- *Independent logical processes.* Once a logical process begins the simulation of a vertical strip, it can proceed with this simulation independent of other logical processes, thereby avoiding expensive synchronization operations throughout much of the computation. Time parallel simulation algorithms typically only require coordination among the logical processes prior to beginning the computation of each strip. This is in sharp contrast to space-parallel algorithms

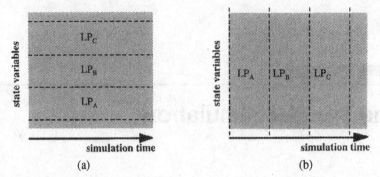

Figure 6.1 Space-time diagram of the simulation computation. (*a*) Space parallel approach; (*b*) time parallel approach.

which require continual synchronization among the logical processes throughout the entire computation.

The central problem that must be solved by the time parallel simulation algorithm is to ensure that the states computed at the "boundaries" of the time intervals match. This is referred to as the *state-matching problem*. Specifically, the state computed at the end of the ith interval must match the state at the beginning of the ith interval. But how can one compute the initial state of the ith interval without first performing the simulation computation for all prior intervals?

Several approaches to solving the state matching problem for specific simulation problems have been proposed. The three approaches to be discussed here are as follows:

- *Fix-up computations.* Logical process LP_i, responsible for the ith time interval, "guesses" the initial state of the simulation in its time interval and performs a simulation based on this guess. In general, the final state computed for the $i - 1$st interval will not match the initial guess, so LP_i must perform a "fix-up"

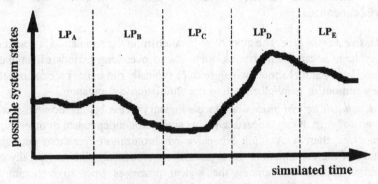

Figure 6.2 Sample path for a simulation computation.

computation to recompute the sample path for the ith interval using the final state computed by LP_{i-1} as the initial state for LP_i. The fix-up computation may be to simply repeat the simulation using the new initial state. This process is repeated until the final state computed by each interval matches the initial state of the next interval. When a state match occurs across all of the intervals, the simulation is completed.

- *Precomputation of state at specific time division points.* It may be possible to determine the state of the simulation at specific points in simulation time without performing a detailed simulation of everything preceding that time. For example, as will be seen later, one may be able to guarantee a buffer will overflow in simulating a queue based on the rate of traffic entering the queue relative to the maximum rate of traffic departing. If this is the case, one may define the simulation time intervals so that the state of the simulation is known at the beginning of each time interval, thereby solving the state matching problem.

- *Parallel prefix computations.* If one can formulate the state of the simulation as a linear recurrence equation, a parallel prefix computation can be used to solve the equation over simulation time.

As will be seen momentarily, the solution to the state matching problem requires detailed knowledge of the simulation application and the statistics that are being computed. Thus time parallel simulation techniques do not provide a general approach to parallel or distributed simulation but rather define a methodology that can be applied to develop parallel simulation algorithms for specific simulation problems.

In the following we describe three time parallel simulation algorithms for simulating a cache memory system, an asynchronous transfer mode (ATM) multiplexer, and a G/G/1 queue.

6.1   TIME PARALLEL CACHE SIMULATION USING FIX-UP COMPUTATIONS

The time parallel simulation approach using fix-up computations executes the following steps:

1. Logical process LP_i is assigned an interval of simulation time $[T_{i+1}, T_i)$ and selects an initial state $S^0(T_{i-1})$ for its interval. More generally, $S^j(T_i)$ denotes the state of the system at simulation time T_i computed after the jth iteration $(j = 1, 2, \ldots)$.

2. LP_i simulates the system over the time interval $[T_{i-1}, T_i)$, computing a final state $S^j(T_i)$ for this interval. Each logical process can execute on a separate processor, and no interprocessor communications is required during this step.

3. LP_i sends a copy of the final state it just computed $S^j(T_i)$ to LP_{i+1}.

4. If $S^j(T_{i-1})$ does not match the initial state $S^{j-1}(T_{i-1})$ used in the simulation for the interval $[T_{i-1}, T_i)$, then LP$_i$ sets its initial state to $S^j(T_{i-1})$ and recomputes the sample path for its interval. If during this recomputation the state of the new sample path that is being computed matches that of the previous iteration (i.e., $S^j(t)$ is identical to $S^{j-1}(t)$ for some simulation time t), the process can stop its computation because the remainder of its sample path will be identical to that derived from the previous computation.

5. Repeat steps 3 and 4 until the initial state used in each interval matches the final state computed for the previous interval for all logical processes.

This process is illustrated graphically in Figure 6.3. As shown in Figure 6.3(a), each logical process is assigned an interval in the simulation time axis, selects some initial state, and computes the sample path based on this initial state. The logical processes execute independent of each other during this phase. Only LP$_A$ computed a correct sample path because it is the only process that used the correct initial state (the initial state for the entire simulation). Each of the logical processes except LP$_A$ resets its initial state to the final state computed by the LP assigned the immediately preceding time window. In Figure 6.3(b), the new sample path converges to that

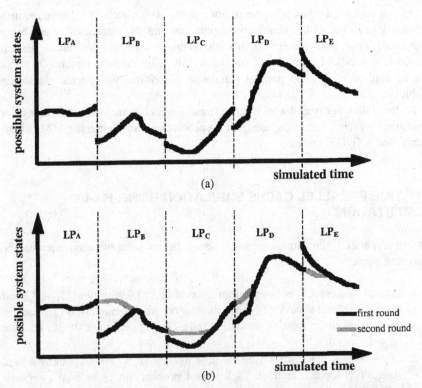

Figure 6.3 Time parallel simulation using fix-up computations. (a) Computation performed in first round; (b) fix-up computation in second round.

computed in the previous iteration for each logical process, so the computation completes after only two iterations. In general, however, more passes may be required to construct the complete sample path.

Using this approach, the computation for the first interval will always be completed by the end of the first iteration, the second interval computation will be completed after the second iteration, and so on. Thus, in the worst case, N iterations will be required to complete the sample path for N intervals, or approximately the same time for the sequential execution if overhead computations required in the time parallel execution are negligible. The algorithm will perform well if the final state for each interval computation does not depend on the initial state. When this is the case (as in Fig. 6.3), the final state computed in the first iteration for each interval computation will be correct despite the fact that an incorrect initial state was used.

This time parallel simulation approach can be applied to simulating a cache memory in a computer system using a least recently used (LRU) replacement policy. A cache is a high-speed memory that holds recently referenced memory locations (data and instructions). The goal is to store frequently used data and instructions in the cache that can be accessed very quickly, typically an order of magnitude faster than main memory. Because the cache memory has a low access time, it is expensive, so the computer system may only contain a limited amount of cache memory. If data or instructions are referenced by the CPU that do not reside in the cache, the information must be loaded into the cache, displacing other data/instructions from the cache if there is no unused memory in the cache. Main memory is partitioned into a collection of fixed-size blocks (a typical block size is 64 bytes), and some set of blocks are maintained within the cache. The cache management hardware includes tables that indicate which blocks are currently stored in the cache.

The cache *replacement policy* is responsible for determining which block to delete from the cache when a new block must be loaded. A commonly used policy is to replace the block that hasn't been referenced in the longest time, based on the premise that recently referenced blocks are likely to be referenced again in the near future. This approach is referred to as the *least recently used* (LRU) replacement policy. Due to implementation constraints, cache memories typically subdivide the cache into *sets* of blocks, and use LRU replacement within each set.

Time parallel simulation can be effective in simulating cache memories, particularly those using LRU replacement because the final state of the cache is seldom dependent on the cache's initial state for "reasonably long" strings of memory references. This is because subsequent references will tend to load new blocks into the cache, eventually displacing the cache's original contents.

The input to the cache simulation is a sequence of memory references. Each reference indicates which block of memory is being referenced. The sequence is partitioned into N subsequences, one for each logical process (i.e., each processor) participating in the simulation.

The state of the cache is a list of the blocks that are currently stored in the cache. These blocks are stored in a data structure known as the LRU stack. When a block is referenced, the LRU stack is searched to determine if the block already resides in the cache. If it does, a cache "hit" is said to occur, and the block is removed and placed on top of the stack. Removing a block from the stack causes the blocks above it to move down one position in the stack, much like removing a tray from the middle of a stack of trays in a cafeteria. Thus blocks that have been referenced recently will be near the top of the stack, while those that have not been referenced recently tend to sink toward the bottom of the stack. The block that has not been referenced for the longest time, that is, the least recently used block, will be at the bottom of the stack.

If the referenced block is not in the stack, the block does not reside in the cache and a miss is said to occur. The block must now be loaded into the cache. To make room, the block at the bottom of the stack (the LRU block) is deleted from the stack, causing all blocks to slide down one position. The newly referenced block is placed on top of the stack.

For example, Figure 6.4 shows the execution of a time parallel simulation for a single set of a cache memory system containing four blocks. The addresses listed across the top of the figure indicate the blocks that are referenced by successive memory references. A time parallel simulation using three logical processes is used. Each LP initially assumes the cache is empty as its initial state. LP_A first references blocks 1 and 2, with each causing a miss. Block 1 is then referenced again, causing it to be moved to the top of the LRU stack. Blocks 3 and 4 are referenced and loaded into the stack. When block 6 is referenced, the LRU block (block 2) at the bottom of the stack is deleted. The time parallel simulation divides the input trace of memory references into three segments, and each LP independently processes its trace, assuming that the cache is initially empty. Figure 6.4(a) shows the sample path computed by each LP during the first round of the simulation.

In the second round of this computation LP_A is idle because it correctly computed its portion of the sample path in the first pass. LP_B recomputes its sample path using the final state computed by LP_A as the initial state for its cache. Similarly LP_C

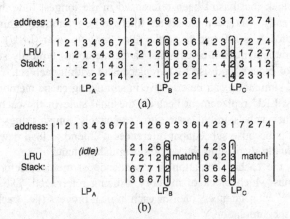

Figure 6.4 Example execution of time parallel cache simulation. (a) Execution during the first round using empty caches as the initial state; (b) execution during the second round.

recomputes its sample path using LP_B's final state after the first iteration. After simulating the fifth memory reference in its trace, LP_B observes that the state of the cache is now identical to what it had computed after the fifth memory reference in the first round. Therefore the remainder of its sample path will be identical to that computed in the first round, so there is no need to recompute it. Similarly LP_C's recomputation becomes identical to that computed in its first round after only four memory references, so it can also stop. LP_B and LP_C need only replace the first four and three stack states, respectively, in the first round simulation with the new values computed in the second round to reconstruct the entire sample path.

In general, the LRU replacement policy guarantees that if the number of blocks in the set is k, the state of the simulation will be independent of the initial state of the cache after k different blocks have been referenced. Thus, if each subsequence of memory references used by the logical processes references at least k different blocks, the time parallel simulation will require only two steps to compute the complete sample path.

6.2 SIMULATION OF AN ATM MULTIPLEXER USING REGENERATION POINTS

The points where the time axis was partitioned in the cache simulation could be made arbitrarily, so time intervals were defined with an equal number of memory references in each interval assigned to each logical process in order to balance the workload among the processors. The time parallel simulation algorithm described next selects the time division points at places where the state of the system can be easily determined. Specifically, the simulation time axis is broken at regeneration points; these are points where the system returns to a known state.

Asynchronous transfer mode (ATM)[25] networks are a technology that has been developed to better support integration of a wide variety of communication service— voice, data, video, and faxes—all within a single telecommunication network. These so-called Broadband Integrated Services Digital Networks (B-ISDN) are expected to provide high bandwidth and reliable communication services in the future. Messages sent into ATM networks are first divided into *fixed-size* cells that then form the atomic unit of data that is transported through the network.

A multiplexer, depicted in Figure 6.5, is a component of a network that combines (concentrates) several streams of incoming traffic (here, ATM cells) into a single output stream. The incoming lines might represent phone lines to individual customers, while the out-going line represents a high-bandwidth trunk line carry traffic for many customers. The bandwidth of the outgoing line is usually smaller than the sum of the bandwidths of the incoming lines. This means that cells will accumulate in the multiplexer if the total incoming traffic flow exceeds the capacity of the output link. For this purpose the multiplexer contains a certain amount of

---

[25] An unfortunate acronym. ATM networks are not to be confused with automated teller machines used by banks!

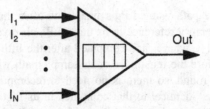

Figure 6.5 An ATM multiplexer with N inputs. The circuit contains a fixed sized buffer. Data (cells) are lost if the buffer overflows.

buffer memory to hold cells waiting to be sent on the outgoing link. To simplify its design, if the buffer memory overflows (i.e., a new cell arrives but the outgoing link is busy and there is no unused buffer space in which to store the cell), the cell is simply discarded. A goal in designing a multiplexer is to provide sufficient buffer memory to ensure that the expected number of lost cells is below some design goal, typically on the order of only one lost cell per 10^9 successfully transmitted cells. Since cell losses are rare, very long simulation runs are required to capture a statistically significant number of cell losses.

Assume that each of the incoming links can transmit B cells per second, and the outgoing link is of bandwidth $C \times B$ cells per second, where C is an integer. Link bandwidths are normalized so that the input link has unit bandwidth, and the output link has bandwidth C. Here, the unit of time that is used is the amount of time required to transmit a single cell over an input link. This quantity is referred to as a *cell time*. C cells may be transmitted by the output link during a single cell time.

A traffic generator (called a source) transmits cells on each incoming link. A separate source is attached to each incoming link of the multiplexer. The traffic produced by each source can be viewed as a sequence of "on" and "off" periods. When the source is on, it transmits cells, one per cell time, over the link. When the source is off, no cells are transmitted. This behavior is depicted in Figure 6.6.

The stream of incoming cells to the multiplexer can be characterized as a sequence of tuples $\langle A_i, \delta_i \rangle$ ($i = 1, 2, 3, \ldots$), where A_i denotes the number active or "on" (transmitting cells) sources, and δ_i denotes the length of time that exactly this number of sources remain active. For example, in Figure 6.6 the input is characterized by the tuples $\langle 1, 4 \rangle$, $\langle 4, 2 \rangle$, $\langle 3, 4 \rangle$, and so on, meaning initially one source is active for four units of time, then four are active for two units of time, then three for four units of time, and so on.

The simulation problem is formulated as follows: Consider a multiplexer with N input links of unit capacity, an output link with capacity C, and a FIFO queue containing K buffers, with each buffer able to hold a single cell. Any cells arriving when the queue is full are discarded. The simulation must determine the average utilization and number of discarded cells for incoming traffic characterized by the sequence of tuples $\langle A_i, \delta_i \rangle$, as depicted in Figure 6.6.

Let T_i denote the simulation time corresponding to the end of the ith tuple, with T_0 denoting the beginning of the simulation which is equal to zero. The state of the simulation model at any instant of simulation time is simply the number of cells

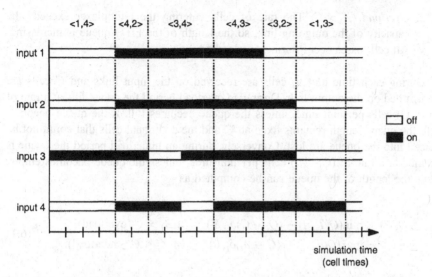

Figure 6.6 On/off periods of four sources. The input to the multiplexer is characterized by a sequence of tuples $\langle A_i, \delta_i \rangle$, where A indicates the number of on sources and δ_i indicates the duration (in cell times) that this number of sources are active.

stored in the queue. Let $Q(T_i)$ denote the number of cells stored in the queue at time T_i. Let $S(T_i)$ denote the total number of cells serviced (transmitted on the output link) and $L(T_i)$ denote the number of cells lost up to time T_i. The notation used for this simulation is summarized in Table 6.1. All of these quantities are integers.

During each time interval the multiplexer will be in one of two possible situations:

1. *Underload: $A_i \leq C$.* The number of active sources is less than or equal to the output link capacity; that is, the rate that cells are flowing into the multiplexer is less than or equal to the outgoing rate, so the length of the FIFO queue (Q_i) is either decreasing or remains the same. No cell losses can occur during an underload period.

TABLE 6.1 Symbols used in multiplexer simulation

N	Number of input links
C	Capacity of the output link
K	Number of buffers
A_i	Number of active sources during ith time interval
δ_i	Length of ith time interval
T_i	Time marking the end of the ith interval
$Q(T_i)$	Length of the queue at time T_i; $Q(T_0) = 0$
$S(T_i)$	Total number of cells transmitted on output at time T_i; $S(T_0) = 0$
$L(T_i)$	Total number of cell lost up to time T_i; $L(T_0) = 0$

2. *Overload:* $A_i > C$. The rate of cells entering the multiplexer exceeds the capacity of the outgoing link, so the length of the FIFO queue is increasing. All cell losses occur during overload periods.

During each time unit A_i cells are received on the input links and C cells are transmitted on the output link. During an overload period the queue fills at a rate of $(A_i - C)$ cells per unit time, unless the queue becomes full. If the queue becomes full, the queue length remains fixed at K, and the additional cells that could not be placed into the queue are lost. Conversely, during an underload period the queue is drained at a rate of $(C - A_i)$ cells per unit time, unless the queue becomes empty. Thus the length of the queue can be computed as

$$\begin{aligned} Q(T_i) &= \min(Q(T_{i-1}) + (Q_i - C)\delta_i, K) && \text{if } A_i > C \text{ (overload)} \\ &= \max(Q(T_{i-1}) - (C - A_i)\delta_i, 0) && \text{if } A_i \leq C \text{ (underload)}. \end{aligned} \tag{6.1}$$

The number of serviced and lost cells can be computed by accounting for all cells during each time period, which is the time represented by a single tuple. Specifically, at the beginning of the ith time period there are $Q(T_{i=1})$ cells buffered in the multiplexer. During this time period $A_i\delta_i$ additional new cells are received by the multiplexer. At the end of the time period, there are $Q(T_i)$ cells remaining. The difference between these two quantities, $(Q(T_{i-1}) + A_i\delta_i) - Q(T_i)$, corresponds to cells that were either serviced or lost during the time period.

First, let us compute the number of serviced cells. During an underload period no cells are lost. Thus all of the $(Q(T_{i-1}) + A_i\delta_i) - Q(T_i)$ cells derived in the previous paragraph represent cells that were serviced. Now consider an overload period. Observe that the output link transmits C cells per unit time so long as the queue is not empty. Because the queue cannot become empty during an overload period, the number of serviced cells increased by $C\delta_i$. In other words,

$$\begin{aligned} S(T_i) &= S(T_{i-1}) + C\delta_i && \text{if } A_i > C \text{ (overload)} \\ &= S(T_{i-1}) + ((Q(T_{i-1}) + A_i\delta_i) - Q(T_i)) && \text{if } A_i C \text{ (underload)}. \end{aligned} \tag{6.2}$$

The utilization of the output link is computed as the total number of cells serviced during the simulation divided the number of cells that could have been serviced during the length of the simulation. Specifically, if the simulation ends at time T_M (i.e., the simulation includes M intervals, or M tuples), the output link utilization is $S(T_M)/CT_M$.

Now consider lost cells. No cells are lost during underload. During overload, the number of cells either lost or serviced is $(Q(T_{i-1}) + A_i\delta_i) - Q(T_i)$, as discussed earlier. The number of serviced cells is easily computed because as was observed in computing $S(t_i)$, C cells will be serviced per unit time during overload. The difference between these two quantities is the number of lost cells during the ith time period. Thus we have

$$
\begin{aligned}
L(T_i) &= L(T_{i-1}) + (Q(T_{i-1}) + A_i\delta_i) - Q(T_i) - C\delta_i && \text{if } A_i > C \text{ (overload)} \\
&= L(T_{i-1}) && \text{if } A_i \leq C \text{ (underload)}.
\end{aligned}
\tag{6.3}
$$

These equations for computing $Q(T_i)$, $S(T_i)$, and $L(T_i)$ enable one to simulate the behavior of the multiplexer. To perform a *time parallel* simulation of the multiplexer, the sequence of tuples is partitioned into P subsequences, where P is the number of processors available to perform the simulation, and a subsequence is assigned to each one. The principal question that must be answered is again the state-matching problem, or here, What is the initial state (the initial length of the queue) for each subsequence assigned to each processor?

This state-matching problem can be solved if the length of the queue at certain points in simulation time can be computed during a (parallel) precomputation phase. One could then partition the tuple sequence at points in time where the state of the multiplexer is known. Two key observations are used to determine the state of the multiplexer at specific points in time:

1. *Guaranteed overflow.* Consider a tuple defining an overload period. If the length of the overload period is sufficiently long that even if the queue were empty at the beginning of the tuple's period, the buffer is guaranteed to be full by the end of the period, then it would be known that the length of the queue is K at the end of the tuple period. A tuple with this property is referred to as a *guaranteed overflow* tuple.

2. *Guaranteed underflow.* Similarly consider a tuple defining an underload period. In this case the queue is being drained. If the duration of the tuple is sufficiently long that the queue will be empty at the end of the tuple's period even if the queue were full at the beginning of the period, then the tuple is said to be a guaranteed underflow tuple, and the queue must be empty at the end of the tuple's period.

More precisely, the conditions for $\langle A_i, \delta_i \rangle$ to be a guaranteed overflow (underflow) tuple are

Guaranteed overflow:

$$
\begin{aligned}
&\text{if} && (A_i - C)\delta_i \geq K, \\
&\text{then} && Q(T_i) = K.
\end{aligned}
\tag{6.4}
$$

Guaranteed underflow:

$$
\begin{aligned}
&\text{if} && (C - A_i)\delta_i \geq K, \\
&\text{then} && Q(T_i) = 0.
\end{aligned}
$$

The time parallel simulation algorithm for the ATM multiplexer operates as follows. Given a sequence of tuples $\langle A_i, \delta_i \rangle$, $i = 1, 2, \ldots$:

1. Identify a set of guaranteed overflow or underflow tuples G by applying conditions (6.4). This can be accomplished by assigning an equal length subsequence to each processor, and by having each processor search from the beginning of its subsequence for a guaranteed overflow or underflow tuple. The tuples in G define the time division points at which the simulation time axis is broken, as shown in Figure 6.2.

2. For each processor, if the ith tuple is found to be a guaranteed overflow tuple, set $Q(T_i)$ to K; if the ith tuple is a guaranteed underflow tuple, set $Q(T_i)$ to 0.

3. For each processor, compute $Q(T_i)$, $S(T_i)$ and $L(T_i)$ using equations (6.1), (6.2), and (6.3) defined above for each tuple, starting with the tuple following the guaranteed overflow (or underflow) tuple. Assume that S and L are initially zero for each subsequence; that is, each processor only computes the number of serviced and lost cells for the subsequence assigned to it (not a cumulative total for the entire simulation). When this has been completed, send the queue length at the end of the subsequence to the processor assigned the next subsequence. Upon receipt of this information, the processor can simulate the tuples assigned to it that preceded the guaranteed overflow/underflow tuple.

4. Compute the total number of serviced and lost cells by summing the values computed for these quantities by each processor.

This algorithm relies on being able to identify a guaranteed overflow or underflow tuple in the subsequence assigned to each processor. The algorithm fails if any processor does not locate a guaranteed underflow or overflow tuple. In general, it is impossible to guarantee such a tuple will be found. In practice, because cell losses are so rare, there will usually be an abundance of guaranteed underflow tuples. An alternative approach to this problem is to examine short *sequences* of tuples in order to identify a sequence that results in a guaranteed underflow (overflow), even though individual tuples within the sequence could not be guaranteed to result in an underflow (overflow). There is again no guarantee, however, that such a sequence can always be identified.

The central advantage of this algorithm compared to the approach described in the previous section for cache memories is no fix-up computation is required. The central disadvantages are the need for a precomputation to compute the time division points, and the possibility the algorithm may fail if such time division points cannot be identified.

6.3 SIMULATION OF QUEUES USING PARALLEL PREFIX

A third approach to time parallel simulations utilizes parallel prefix computations to determine the state of the simulation across simulation time. A *prefix computation* computes the N initial products of N variables $X_1, X_2, \ldots, X_N$:

$$P_1 = X_1$$
$$P_2 = X_1 * X_2$$
$$P_3 = X_1 * X_2 * X_3$$
$$\vdots$$
$$P_N = X_1 * X_2 * \cdots * X_N$$

where the asterisk (*) is an associative operator. This set of equations can be rewritten more compactly as the linear recurrence $P_i = P_{i-1} * X_i$, $i = 1, 2, \ldots, N$, where P_0 is the identity element. As will be discussed momentarily, prefix computations are of interest because efficient algorithms exist for performing these computations on a parallel computer.

The simulation of a $G/G/1$ queue[26] where the service time does not depend on the state of the queue can be recast as a prefix computation. Specifically, let r_i denote the interarrival time of the ith job at the queue, and s_i denote the service time assigned to the ith job. These values can be trivially computed in parallel because they are independent random numbers. The simulation computation must compute the arrival time of the ith job A_i, and the departure time of the ith job D_i for $i = 1, 2, \ldots, N$. The arrival time of the ith job can immediately be rewritten as a linear recurrence:

$$A_i = A_{i-1} + r_i \ (= r_1 + r_2 + \cdots + r_i),$$

so it can be immediately solved using a parallel prefix computation. The departure times can also be written as a linear recurrence. Specifically, the ith job begins service either when it arrives, or when the i-1st job departs, which ever is later. Thus $D_i = \max(D_{i-1}, A_i) + s_i$. This can be rewritten as the following linear recurrence:

$$\begin{pmatrix} D_i \\ 0 \end{pmatrix} = \begin{pmatrix} s_i & A_i + s_i \\ -\infty & 0 \end{pmatrix} \cdot \begin{pmatrix} D_{i-1} \\ 0 \end{pmatrix},$$

where the matrix multiplication is performed using max as the additive operator (with identity $-\infty$), and + as the multiplicative operator (identity 0). Rewriting the departure time equation in this form puts it into the proper format for a parallel prefix computation.

Because the simulation computation can be specified as a parallel prefix computation, the only question that remains concerns the parallel prefix computation itself. The parallel prefix for N initial products can be computed in $O(\log N)$ time. Consider computation of the arrival times A_i. Suppose that the N data values r_1,

---

[26] The notation $G/G/1$ means a general distribution is used to select the interarrival time and service time of jobs arriving at the queue, and the 1 denotes the fact that there is one server.

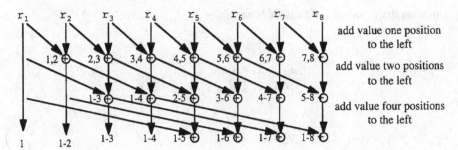

Figure 6.7   Binary tree for performing a parallel prefix computation.

$r_2, \ldots, r_N$ are assigned to different processors. The ith initial partial product A_i can be computed in parallel by defining a binary tree, as shown in Figure 6.7. In the first step, each data value r_i is added to the data value one position to the left (r_{i-1}). In the next step, a new cumulative sum is formed by adding in the value two elements to the left, then four to the left, eight, and so on. If each processor repeats these steps, all N initial products will be performed in $\lceil \log N \rceil$ steps, as shown in Figure 6.7.

More precisely, the parallel prefix computation is defined as follows:

```
FOR j=0 to ⌈log N⌉ - 1 DO
  FOR ALL i ∈ (2^j+1, 2^j+2, ..., N) DO IN PARALLEL
    NewR[i] := r[i-2^j] + r[i];
  END-FOR ALL
  FOR ALL i ∈ (2^j+1, 2^j+2, ..., N) DO IN PARALLEL
    r[i] := NewR[i];
  END-FOR ALL
END-FOR
```

The FOR ALL statement performs the iterations of the loop in parallel, one iteration per processor. The second FOR ALL loop is used to copy intermediate results back into the r array for the next iteration. When the above program completes, r[i] will hold the arrival time for the ith job.

In practice, there will usually be many more partial products than processors, so one would aggregate groups of the values onto individual processors and perform computations involving data values on the same processor sequentially. This will improve the efficiency of the parallel algorithm because there will be more local computation between interprocessor communications, which are time-consuming relative to the time to perform an addition.

6.4 SUMMARY

Time parallel algorithms are currently not as robust as space parallel approaches because they rely on specific properties of the system being modeled, such as specification of the system's behavior as recurrence equations and/or a relatively simple state descriptor. This approach is currently limited to a handful of important applications, such as queuing networks, Petri nets, cache memories, and statistical multiplexers. Space parallel simulations offer greater flexibility and wider applicability, but concurrency is limited to the number of logical processes. In some cases both time and space parallelism can be used together.

Time parallel algorithms do provide a form a parallelization that can be exploited when there isn't spatial parallelism available in the application. The three examples described in this chapter are all examples where there is very little space parallelism in the original simulation problem. The fact that the time parallel algorithms can exploit massive amounts of parallelism for these problems highlights the utility of the time parallel approach, provided suitable algorithms can be developed.

6.5 ADDITIONAL READINGS

Time parallel simulation for trace-driven simulations is described in Heidelberger and Stone (1990); this is perhaps the first proposal for using this technique. Extensions to this method to simulate caches are described in Nicol, Greenberg et al. (1992). The algorithm using regeneration points to simulate ATM multiplexers is described in Andradottir and Ott (1995) and Fujimoto, Nikolaidis et al. (1995), and extension of this method to simulate cascaded multiplexers is described in Nikolaidis, Fujimoto et al. (1994). Time parallel simulation of queues using parallel prefix algorithms were first reported in Greenberg, Lubachevsky et al. (1991). Related work in using time parallel simulation to simulate queues and Petri networks are described in Lin and Lazowska (1991), Ammar and Deng (1992), Wang and Abrams (1992), and Baccelli and Canales (1993). Other algorithms have been proposed to simulate telephone switching networks (Gaujal, Greenberg et al. 1993) and Markov chains (Heidelberger and Nicol 1991).

PART III

DISTRIBUTED VIRTUAL
ENVIRONMENTS (DVEs)

CHAPTER 7

DVEs: Introduction

We now shift attention to distributed simulation technologies intended to create computer-generated virtual environments into which users, possibly at geographically distant locations, can be embedded. Typical applications for this technology are training and entertainment. As discussed in Chapter 1, work in this field has progressed on a largely separate track from the work described in previous chapters concerning parallel discrete event simulation (PDES) technology. This can be traced to the fact that distributed virtual environments (DVEs) have different requirements than the analytic simulation applications to which PDES has historically been applied. We begin this discussion by contrasting these two technologies. General approaches for building DVEs are then discussed. The remainder of this chapter provides an overview of Distributed Interactive Simulation (DIS) and its successor, the High Level Architecture (HLA) to describe a typical approach to building distributed simulation systems for DVE applications.

7.1 GOALS

A principal goal in most virtual environments is concerned with achieving a "sufficiently realistic" representation of an actual of imagined system, as perceived by the participants embedded into the environment. What "sufficiently realistic" means depends on what one is trying to accomplish. In the context of training, this means that humans embedded into the environment are able to develop skills that would be applicable in actual situations they might later encounter. Thus the environment must be sufficiently realistic that the system with which the operator is working, such as an aircraft in the case of a flight simulator, behaves the way a real aircraft would behave in terms of its response to controls and other effects such as smoke or wind.

Fortunately, every aspect of the environment does not have to be absolutely accurate in its minutest detail. In reality, a human is often looking for certain cues that trigger some action, such as a target coming into view in a flight simulator. Other aspects of the environment, such as realistic looking trees, may not necessarily contribute very much to increasing the effectiveness of the environment as a training vehicle, depending on the scenario. This concept that certain parts of the environment must be more accurately reproduced than others is called *selective fidelity*.

An often discussed goal of many DVEs in the context of adversarial exercises (for example, military training or multi-user video games) is to achieve what is referred to as a *fair fight*. This means that the outcome (for example, success or failure of a user to accomplish some task) depends entirely on the skill of the player rather than on artifacts of the virtual environment. Success becomes more difficult to achieve if the players are using different types of computing equipment. For example, one player should not be able to see a target any sooner than a second player just because he is using a high-resolution graphics workstation, while the other is using an inexpensive personal computer.

Determining "how realistic is realistic enough?" is an important problem that must be addressed when constructing a virtual environment, but it is a problem that is beyond the scope of the discussion here. The important thing to note is that there is tolerance for error built into the application, typically more so than for analytic simulation applications. This affects the requirements of the underlying distributed simulation system.

7.2 CONTRASTING DVE AND PDES SYSTEMS

Driven primarily by differing requirements, key features that distinguish DVE from PDES systems are summarized below:

- *Paced versus unpaced execution.* Unlike PDES systems which are typically designed to achieve as-fast-as-possible execution of the simulation, advances of simulation time in DVEs are almost always paced with wallclock time.[27] This has important ramifications in the development of the simulation model and the underlying simulation executive. PDES models and the synchronization algorithms described in the previous chapters all operate correctly despite arbitrary message latencies. In general, large unpredictable latencies cannot be tolerated in DVEs.

- *Geographical distribution.* PDES systems are seldom executed in a geographically distributed fashion because of the difficulty in achieving speedup when communication latencies are high. However, it is not unusual for users and other resources (for example, data bases) in DVEs to be geographically distributed. Thus PDES systems are typically deployed on multiprocessors, while DVEs are more often deployed on networked workstations interconnected through a local area network (LAN) or wide area network (WAN).

---

[27] Not all PDES executions are unpaced, however. Execution may be paced if there are physical devices or human participants interacting with the simulation.

- *Repeatability.* Many analytic simulation applications must produce exactly the same results if the simulation program is re-executed with the same inputs. This is often not so essential in DVEs.

- *Synchronization requirements.* Because the goal of a DVE is to provide a sufficiently realistic environment as perceived by its users, synchronization requirements can often be relaxed. For example, if two or more events occur so close together in time that the humans viewing the environment cannot perceive which occurred first, it may be permissible for the distributed simulation to process those events in any order without compromising the goals of the training exercise (or entertainment session). This is in contrast to PDES systems where each event is assigned a precise time stamp, and the simulation executive guarantees that events are always processed in time stamp order.

The last observation is important because it suggests that one may not need to use sophisticated synchronization algorithms for much of the DVEs message traffic to ensure that events are always processed in time stamp order. Indeed, DVEs that are deployed today typically do not utilize these algorithms. This aspect will be discussed in greater detail in Chapter 9.

7.3 SERVER VERSUS SERVERLESS ARCHITECTURES

An important decision in the design of a DVE that includes geographically distributed participants and/or resources concerns the physical distribution of the simulation computations. Possible approaches include the following:

- *Centralized server architecture.* As shown in Figure 7.1(*a*), interactive users (clients) may "log into" a central computer (a server) that maintains the shared state of the virtual world. Machines at the user's site may perform local simulation computations pertaining to entities "owned" by the client, and generate one or more graphical displays for the user. For example, each local machine may be executing a flight simulator program in a multi-user game that periodically generates messages to the server to indicate the aircraft's current position. The server maintains the global state of the simulation (for example, the position of each aircraft) and is responsible for notifying each client simulator whenever some portion of the virtual world relevant to the client has changed. For example, the server might reflect a position update message it received to all other aircraft simulators that can "see" the aircraft whose position has changed. Such systems often also include computation-only entities (sometime referred to as synthetic forces in military contexts) that do not have an interactive user associated with them. An example of a computation-only entity is a computer-generated "enemy" aircraft in a human-versus-computer dogfight, whose movements are controlled by a

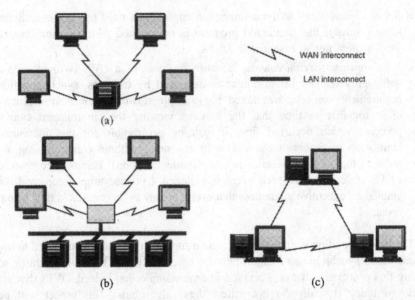

Figure 7.1 Three DVE architectures with geographically distributed users. (*a*) Centralized compute server architecture; (*b*) cluster of workstations server architecture; (*c*) distributed, serverless architecture.

computer program. Such computation-only entities may also be maintained within the compute server.

- *Distributed server architecture.* This is similar to the centralized server architecture, except that a multiprocessor or a collection of processors interconnected on a LAN is used to implement the server; see Figure 7.1(*b*). The shared state of the virtual world is now distributed among the processors within the compute server and must be maintained by exchanging messages among these processors. Computation-only entities are typically executed on the processors within the compute server to take advantage of the high-performance interconnection. Changes in the shared state must be transmitted among the processors within the compute server as well as "end user" processors that require updates to state information.

- *Distributed, serverless architecture.* Rather than utilize a server, the simulation computations are distributed among geographically distributed processors; see Figure 7.1(*c*). Computation-only entities may now be distributed among geographically distributed processors.

The centralized approach shown in Figure 7.1(*a*) is the simplest from an implementation standpoint because global information concerning the state of the simulation can be maintained on a single computer. The central drawback of this approach is, of course, that it does not scale to modeling large numbers of entities. As more entities are added, there will be insufficient compute cycles to service all of them.

The distributed server and distributed, serverless architectures allow one, in principle, to circumvent the scalability problem in the centralized architecture, since the number of CPUs can increase in proportion to the number of simulated entities. The cluster-of-workstations server architecture offers the advantage of low-latency, high-bandwidth communications among the processors within the server. If the majority of the communications is computer-to-computer communications as opposed to user-to-user communications, as would be the case if the DVE is populated by a large number of computational-only entities, this is a significant advantage. However, individual user-to-user communications may incur higher latencies in the server-based approach because two message transmissions are required, one from the user to the server, and then another from the server to the second user. Only a single transmission over the WAN is required in the serverless approach shown in Figure 7.1(*c*).

A second important consideration in deciding whether to use a server-based or server-less architecture is reliability and maintainability of the system. In one sense, server-based systems are less reliable because failure of the server (for example, a power failure at the location housing the server) will render the entire system unavailable to any user. But on the other hand, having all of the computers in one physical location affords the system operators much greater control over the server's physical environment. System administrators can more easily prevent clumsy users from tripping over cables or spilling coffee on vital components! Further, mundane tasks such as making sure all of the machines are configured properly and have the appropriate version of the software are simplified if all of the machines are in a single room under one system administrator.

The remainder of this chapter provides an introduction to DVEs by examining one class of systems. Specifically, design principles utilized in Distributed Interactive Simulation (DIS) systems are discussed next. The section that follows concerning the High-Level Architecture describes the types of services provided in a distributed simulation system infrastructure supporting DVEs.

7.4 DISTRIBUTED INTERACTIVE SIMULATION

Distributed Interactive Simulation (DIS) has been used extensively in building DVEs for training in the defense community. A principal objective of DIS (and subsequently the High Level Architecture effort) is to enable interoperability among separately developed simulators:

> The primary mission of DIS is to define an infrastructure for linking simulations of various types at multiple locations to create realistic, complex, virtual "worlds" for the simulation of highly interactive activities (DIS Steering Committee 1994).

Although DIS, per se, has been supplanted by the High-Level Architecture effort, HLA in fact builds upon and extends the DIS concept, so principles used in DIS still remain relevant to systems being deployed in the late 1990s.

A DIS exercise may include (1) human-in-the-loop systems such as tank or flight simulators (sometimes referred to as virtual simulators), (2) computation only elements such as wargame simulations (sometimes referred to as constructive simulations), and (3) live elements such as instrumented tanks or aircraft. Each simulator participating in the exercise is referred to as a DIS node.

7.4.1 DIS Design Principles

DIS utilizes the following design principles (DIS Steering Committee 1994):

- *Autonomous simulation nodes.* Autonomy is important because it simplifies development (developers of one simulator need not be overly concerned with details of other simulators in the DVE), it simplifies integration of existing (legacy) simulators into a DVE, and it simplifies allowing simulators to join or leave the exercise while it is in progress. A DIS node is responsible for maintaining the state of one or more entities during the simulation execution, as well as some representation of the state of other entities relevant to it, such as the position of other entities visible to a human operating the controls in a tank simulator. The simulator receives inputs from the user and models the behavior of the entity in response to those inputs. When this behavior causes actions that may be visible to other entities (for example, firing the canon), the simulator generates messages referred to as protocol data units (PDUs) to notify other nodes of this action. Autonomy among nodes is enhanced in DIS in two specific ways:
  1. DIS nodes are not responsible for identifying the recipients of messages. In contrast to typical PDES systems, it is the responsibility of the underlying distributed simulation infrastructure to determine which nodes should receive notification of the event, and/or receiving nodes to "filter" messages that do not impact entities assigned to that node. A simple solution used in SIMNET and early DIS systems was to broadcast the message to all simulators, forcing each node to determine which events are relevant to the entities it is modeling. The general problem of determining which simulators should receive what messages is referred to as *data distribution management* and will be discussed in greater detail in the Chapter 8.
  2. Each simulator in a DIS exercise advances simulation time according to a local (typically hardware) clock. Again, in contrast to PDES systems, no coordination among simulators is used to advance simulation time. With the exception of communications that may be necessary to keep these clocks synchronized (discussed in Chapter 9), each node advances simulation time autonomously from other nodes.
- *Transmission of "ground truth" information.* Each node sends absolute truth concerning the state of the entities it represents. This state information will usually be a subset of the state variables maintained by the node. Typical state

information transmitted to other nodes includes the location and orientation of the entity, the direction and velocity that it is moving, the position of subcomponents of the entity (for example, the direction the gun turret of a tank is pointed), and so on. Any degradation of this information, such as due to environment effects or sensor limitations, is performed at the receiver.

- *Transmission of state change information only.* To economize on communications, simulation nodes only transmit changes in behavior. Information concerning objects that do not change (for example, static terrain) does not need to be transmitted over the network. If a vehicle continues to "do the same thing" (for example, travel in a straight line with constant velocity), the rate at which state updates are transmitted is reduced. Simulators do transmit "keep alive" messages (referred to as "heart beat" messages), typically, every five seconds, so new simulators entering the exercise will be made aware of these entities. Periodic updates also improve the robustness of the system, by providing resistance to lost messages.

- *Use of "dead reckoning" algorithms to extrapolate entity state information.* Each node maintains information concerning other entities, such as those that are visible to it on the battlefield. This information is updated whenever the entities send new status information via PDUs. In between state updates, all simulators use common algorithms to extrapolate the current state (position) of other entities between state updates, based on previously reported information. This also enables one to reduce the amount of communication that is required among nodes because less frequent updates are required than if no such extrapolations were performed. Dead reckoning will be described in greater detail later in this chapter.

The principal components of a typical DIS simulator are depicted in Figure 7.2. This node includes a model of the dynamics of the vehicle manned by this node. Typically a continuous simulation is used to model the motion of the vehicle through

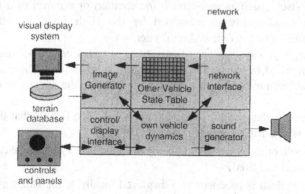

Figure 7.2 Principal components of a virtual simulator in a DIS system (reproduced from Miller and Thorpe 1995).

space. The image generator produces the visual image seen by the operator, using a database containing descriptions of the terrain visible to the vehicle. The control/display interface and sound generator provide additional inputs and output to the operator. The "other vehicle state table" maintains information concerning the state of other entities relevant to this vehicle, such as other vehicles within range of its sensors. State information concerning this vehicle is sent to other simulators via the network interface, and updates to state information for other vehicles are received from this interface.

7.4.2 DIS PDUs

A key ingredient in DIS to support interoperability among simulators is the definition of standard PDU types that are communicated among simulators. Several DIS PDUs are defined to transmit events of interest to entities in different DIS nodes, among which are the following examples:

- *Entity state PDUs* contain ground truth information indicating the appearance and location of an entity.
- *Fire PDUs* indicate a munition has been fired from an entity. This might cause a muzzle flash to be produced on the displays of entities that can view the entity firing the munition.
- *Detonation PDUs* indicate the trajectory of a munition has completed. Entities receiving this PDU must assess their damages and produce appropriate audio and visual effects from the detonation.

Other simulation events modeled by PDUs include requesting and receiving service (for example, resupplying the entity or repairing damages), generation of emissions (for example, electronic warfare), radio communications, and a variety of other functions. In addition to simulation events, still other PDUs are used to manage the simulation itself, such as to establish the creation or removal of a new entity. Much of this functionality is subsumed by the High Level Architecture, so discussion of this aspect is deferred until later.

For example, a typical sequence of operations in a DIS system between two tank simulators is depicted in Figure 7.3. This scenario is taken from Miller and Thorpe (1995). The circled numbers in this figure correspond to the actions listed below:

1. The first simulator (the upper diagram in Fig. 7.3) detects that the operator has pressed a trigger to fire the tank's cannon.
2. The simulator generates an audio signal to the tank's operator indicating that the cannon has fired.
3. A muzzel flash is produced and displayed locally to the tank's operator.
4. A *Fire PDU* is broadcast on the network, and received by the second simulator.

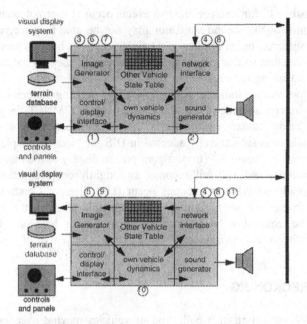

Figure 7.3 Sequence of actions between two simulators in DIS (reproduced from Miller and Thorpe 1995).

5. The muzzle flash for the first tank is displayed to the operator of the second tank.

6. Ballistic flyout calculations at the first simulator are used to display a tracer for the shell.

7. Impact of the shell at the target is displayed locally in the first simulator.

8. A *Detonation PDU* is broadcast over the network, and received at the second simulator.

9. The impact of the shell is displayed at the second tank.

10. Calculations assessing the damage are performed at the second tank.

11. Visible effects of the damage, if any, are broadcast to other simulators via an *Entity State PDU*.

7.4.3 Time Constraints

It is clear that the latency to transmit a message over the network will play an important role in determining the "realism" of the virtual environment. For example, if the Fire PDU is delayed in the network, it could be received by the second simulator *after* the detonation PDU is received so it could appear that the effect (the shell detonating) precedes the cause (the shell being fired) in the second simulator. While this may initially seem to be an unacceptable situation, anomalies such as this may be permissible. If, for instance, the two events occur at approximately the same time, the operator of the second simulator may not be able to perceive that they occurred in an incorrect order. Further, in a training exercise, humans may be able to "filter" such anomalies so that even if they are noticeable, they do not compromise the goals of the training exercise.

Human factors studies indicate that people begin noticing latencies when they exceed 100 milliseconds (Bailey 1982; Woodson 1987). In SIMNET, the goal was to keep latencies below human reaction times, or 250 milliseconds. A similar value (300 milliseconds) was subsequently adopted in DIS for "loosely coupled actions" such as that shown in Figure 7.3 (from trigger pull to display of the muzzle flash at the remote machine) and 100 milliseconds for "tightly coupled actions" where detailed, temporally sensitive interactions occur (DIS Steering Committee 1994). Fighter pilots flying in close formation is one example of the latter. Even lower latencies may be required in other situations, such as when hardware devices are embedded into the virtual environment.

7.5 DEAD RECKONING

Consider a DVE consisting of a collection of vehicles moving over some space. Assume that each simulator executes on a separate processor and models a single vehicle. Each simulator must generate a display for its driver indicating the position and orientation of the other vehicles within visual range. Assume that the display is updated at a rate of 60 times per second. Each simulator maintains locally the position of other vehicles, and every 17 milliseconds (1/60th of a second) generates a suitable graphical image. In order to keep other vehicles up to date, each simulator also broadcasts its current location to the other simulators every 17 milliseconds. Even if each incoming message requires only 0.1 milliseconds to process, a DVE containing 100 vehicles will require each simulator to consume almost two-thirds of its CPU cycles just to process incoming messages. Further, in computing environments with limited communication bandwidth (for example, users connected to the Internet via phone lines), the amount of information that must be exchanged is clearly prohibitive.

A technique called *dead reckoning* can be used to reduce interprocessor communication. The basic idea is that rather than send frequent state updates, each simulator estimates the location of remote entities from its last reported position, direction, velocity, and the like. For example, if it is known that the vehicle is traveling east at 50 feet per second, and its coordinate position at time 200 seconds into the simulation is (1000, 1000) where each unit corresponds to one foot, then it can be predicted that one second later it will be at position (1050, 1000) without transmitting a position update message (see Fig. 7.4).

The term "dead reckoning" comes from a technique used to determine the position of a ship at sea. A ship's position can be accurately determined by examining the position of stars relative to the horizon or from satellites. However, it is not always possible to do so because of weather conditions or malfunctioning

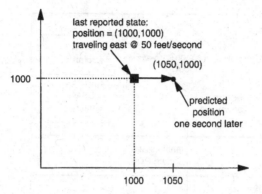

Figure 7.4 Predicting the location of a vehicle base in its last reported position, direction, and velocity.

navigational equipment. In such a case the ship's position can be estimated from its last recorded location and knowledge of its movements since then. This is the same problem in a DVE; one must extrapolate the position of other moving elements in the DVE based on recent reports of its location and movements.

In some cases, if information is available concerning the movement of the object, more sophisticated means can be used to project its future location. For example, if it is known that the object is a projectile, its position can be computed using trajectory calculations. More generally, the idea of replacing communications with local computations can be applied whenever a method is available to estimate the future state of a remote entity based on previous states.

To implement this technique, each simulator maintains a local model of remote vehicles called the *dead reckoning model* (DRM). If the display is updated 60 times per second, the DRM is interrogated every 17 milliseconds to determine the current location of each remote entity visible to this entity.

Of course, this approach breaks down if the vehicle's true motion deviates from the DRM used by other simulators. This might occur because the user steers the vehicle to move in a new direction, or because the DRM gives only an approximation to the vehicle's actual motion, as is typically the case to economize on DRM computations. Some mechanism is required to "resynch" the DRM if it becomes too inaccurate. This problem is addressed by having each vehicle simulator generate an update message if it detects the DRM other simulators are using has become too inaccurate with respect to its true position. To accomplish this, each simulator maintains a local copy of *its own* dead reckoning model (see Fig. 7.5). If the position predicted by the DRM and the true position of the vehicle as computed by the actual high-fidelity model differ by more than some threshold, a message is generated to provide new state information concerning the vehicle's true position and movement. The logical operation of this process is illustrated in Figure 7.5. Thus, if a vehicle continues to "do the same thing," the frequency of update messages that are generated is greatly reduced.

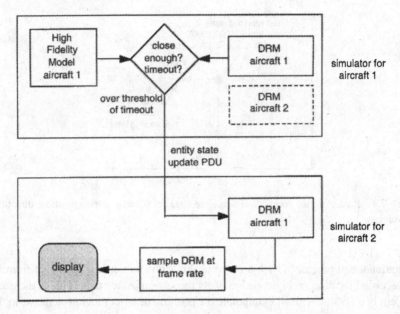

Figure 7.5 Logical operation of dead reckoning in DIS between two flight simulators. The high-fidelity model for aircraft 2 and its generation of state updates are not shown to simplify the figure.

In DIS, if the DRM continues to produce sufficiently accurate information, update messages do not stop completely. As discussed earlier, the update rate drops to some minimal frequency, such as once every five seconds, providing a means of notifying new simulators joining the virtual environment of other vehicles already in the environment.

An important advantage of the dead reckoning approach is that it provides resilience to lost messages. If a position update is lost, the simulator will continue to use dead reckoning to extrapolate its position (although the accuracy may exceed the prescribed threshold) until the next update is received. This allows the simulation application to utilize best effort message delivery, as opposed to services guaranteeing reliable delivery (by retransmitting lost messages) which introduce additional latency, and impose additional overheads on the network.

Dead reckoning was first used for distributed simulations in SIMNET. Local state updates were performed every 1/15th second. Messages were generated at approximately a rate of one per second in DVEs using manned vehicles, and slightly higher for aircraft (Miller and Thorpe 1995). Somewhat lower traffic rates are reported in DIS exercises, as will be discussed in the Chapter 8.

7.5.1 Dead Reckoning Models

Let $P(t)$ denote the true position of a remote entity at time t. Position updates are received at times $t_1, t_2, \ldots$ that indicate $P(t_1), P(t_2)$, and so on. The dead reckoning model produces an estimate $D(t)$ for times t. Let t_i denote the most recent state update earlier than time t, and Δt denote the quantity $t - t_i$. Three DRMs come to mind that differ according to the amount of information concerning the remote entity that is available:

1. Zeroth-order DRM: $D(t) = P(t_i)$. In the absence of any additional information, there is no basis for any other choice.
2. First-order DRM: $D(t) = P(t_i) + \mathbf{v}(\mathbf{t_i})\Delta t$, where $\mathbf{v}(\mathbf{t_i})$ is the velocity vector for the remote entity reported in the update at time t_i. This is the model used in the example in Figure 7.4.
3. Second order DRM: $D(t) = P(t_i) + \mathbf{v}(\mathbf{t_i})\Delta t + (\frac{1}{2})\mathbf{a}(\mathbf{t_i})(\Delta t)^2$ where $\mathbf{v}(\mathbf{t_i})$ is the velocity vector and $\mathbf{a}(\mathbf{t_i})$ is the acceleration vector reported in the state update at time t_i.

Extrapolations concerning the orientation of the remote entity can be derived based on periodic reports of its angular velocity and acceleration.

An example illustrating the use of dead reckoning is shown in Figure 7.6(a). The dark solid line denotes the true position of a remote vehicle in two-dimensional space, as determined by that vehicle's high-fidelity model. The thin solid lines tangent to the true position represents the local simulator's estimation of the remote vehicle's location, obtained from its local DRM for the remote vehicle. As discussed earlier, the DRM is sampled at regular intervals in order to generate updates to the simulator's display. Each such sample is represented by a square box in the figure, marked A, B, C, and so on. In this example, the local simulator has the correct position, velocity, and acceleration of the remote vehicle at time t_1. The DRM predicts the vehicle's position at points A, B, and C based on the information it had at

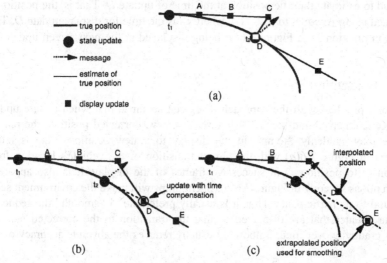

(a)

(b)   (c)

Figure 7.6 Example of dead reckoning scheme. (a) Basic scheme; (b) time compensation; (c) interpolation to smooth updates.

time t_1. Next, the remote vehicle detects that its DRMs error exceeds the threshold, so a state update message is generated at time t_2. This information is used the next time the DRM is sampled in the local simulator, resulting in the corrected position (point D) to be displayed. Continuing this example, the remote vehicle's position is next estimated to be at point E.

7.5.2 Time Compensation

One problem with the approach described thus far is that it does not take into account the latency to send the state update messages over the network. Thus the position reported in the message is out of date by the time the remote processor receives the message. If the processor updates its display based on the contents of the message, it will be displaying where the vehicle was L time units ago, where L is the latency to receive and process the message. The error introduced by not taking into account this latency could be significant if the vehicle is moving rapidly, or latencies are large. In a wide area network the latency could be hundreds of milliseconds, or more.

To address this problem, one can include a time stamp in the state update message indicating the simulation time[28] at which the update was generated. The receiver can then compensate for the message latency by using the dead reckoning model to project the vehicle's position when the message is received and processed. This time-compensated position information is then used to update the remote simulator's display.

For example, Figure 7.6(b) illustrates the use of this technique. A state update message is received soon after display update C. Rather than simply using this position information for the next display update as was done in Figure 7.6(a), the time stamp of the update message (t_2) and the new state information in that message are used to estimate the true position at the time of update D. That is, the position is estimated using Δt equal to ($t_D - t_2$), where t_D is the time for display update D. This results in position D in Figure 7.6(b) being displayed at the next screen update.

7.5.3 Smoothing

A second problem with the approach discussed so far is that when a state update message is received and the DRM is reset to a new, corrected position, the remote vehicle may suddenly "jump" in the display to a new position. This is rather apparent in Figure 7.6(a) with the abrupt transition of the vehicle's location from position C to position D in successive frames of the display. It is also apparent, though not as severely in Figure 7.6(b). Such jumps will make the environment seem unnatural to its participants. Thus it is usually preferable to "smooth" the sequence of state updates that are displayed so that the transition to the corrected position occurs gradually over time. Smoothing usually reduces the absolute accuracy of the

---

[28] Recall that simulation time is essentially synonymous with wallcock time in virtual environments.

displayed position relative to the true position immediately after an update message is received because one imposes a delay before the new information is fully utilized. But this is often preferable to causing sudden jumps in the display.

One approach to smoothing the display is shown in Figure 7.5(c). When the new update message arrives and is first used by the DRM (point D in Fig. 7.5(c), the DRM extrapolates the anticipated position of the vehicle some time into the future. In Figure 7.5(c) the DRM estimates the position of the vehicle at point E, the next time the display will be updated, using the correction information that was just obtained. It computes the current position by interpolating between the last displayed position (point C) and this predicted, future position (point E). It then displays this interpolated position (point D). When the next display time comes, it will show the vehicle at point E, the same as if no smoothing had been used; (see Figure 7.6 (b) and (c).

More generally, this technique can be extended to extrapolate the position K display update times into the future, and interpolating K intermediate positions that would result before reaching this final position. The example shown in Figure 7.6(c) uses $K = 1$. A larger value of K may result in a "smoother" transition to the corrected position. The disadvantage with this approach is that it increases the time until the simulator reaches its best estimate of the remote vehicle's location (i.e., the location indicated by its DRM). Thus the accuracy of the displayed position, averaged over time, may be reduced. This may be irritating to the operator trying to fire upon a vehicle when the simulator records a miss, even though the user's weapon was aimed directly at the displayed target! In any event, interpolation does smooth the transition to the updated state information and helps to produce a more natural looking display.

7.6   HIGH LEVEL ARCHITECTURE

The discussion thus far concerning DIS has focused on general design principles and modeling techniques such as dead reckoning to reduce interprocessor communication. We now examine the underlying support provided by a distributed simulation executive to support DVEs such as DIS. Like DIS, the principal goal of the High-Level Architecture is to support interoperability and reuse of simulations. Unlike DIS, HLA provides explicit support for simulations other than training. For example, explicit support for synchronizing analytic simulation models is provided.

In the HLA a distributed simulation is called a *federation*, and each individual simulator is referred to as a *federate*. A federate need not be a computer simulation; it could be an instrumented physical device (for example, the guidance system for a missile) or a passive data viewer.

We next give an historical perspective on the HLA, followed by discussion of technical aspects of HLA federations. We are specifically concerned with the interface to the distributed simulation executive, called the Run-Time Infrastructure (RTI) in the HLA, in order to identify the types of services that are provided to support DVEs.

7.6.1 Historical Perspective

The roots for the HLA stem from DIS aimed primarily at training simulations and the Aggregate Level Simulation Protocol (ALSP) which applied the concept of simulation interoperability to wargaming simulations. The HLA development began in October 1993 when the Defense Advanced Research Projects Agency (DARPA) awarded three industrial contracts to develop a common architecture that could encompass the DoD modeling and simulation community. The designs were received in January 1995 and, with inputs from the DoD community, were combined to form an initial architecture proposal. In early 1995 the Defense Modeling and Simulation Office (DMSO) formed a group called the Architecture Management Group (AMG) which included representatives from several sizable efforts in the DoD in modeling and simulation. The AMG was given the task of overseeing the development of the HLA. An initial architecture proposal was given to the AMG in March 1995, and the HLA began to take form.

The AMG formed several technical working groups to develop specific aspects of the HLA. These included definition of the Interface Specification and the Object Model Template, described below, as well as specific technical aspects such as the time management services dealing with synchronization issues such as those discussed in Part II of this book, and data distribution management for large-scale distributed simulations. At the same time, a team lead by Mitre Corp. was tasked with developing a prototype implementation of the RTI. This implementation was later merged with software developed at MIT Lincoln Laboratories to support large-scale federations. Several teams were formed to develop initial federations that would be representative of the DoD modeling and simulation community. Specifically, four so-called proto-federations (prototype federations) were formed:

- The platform protofederation including DIS-style training simulations; that is, real-time human-in-the-loop training simulations.
- The Joint Training protofederation including as-fast-as-possible time-driven and event-driven wargaming simulation models to be used for command-level training.
- The analysis protofederation including as-fast-as-possible event-driven wargaming simulations such as those that might be used in acquisition decisions.
- The engineering protofederation including hardware-in-the-loop simulations with hard real-time constraints.

Protofederation development was largely focused on adapting existing simulations for use in the HLA to verify the claims that such an infrastruture could successfully support model reuse.

Initial implementations of the RTI and protofederations began to appear in late 1995, with the AMG meeting approximately every six weeks to monitor progress of the HLA development, and to discuss various technical and administrative issues. Final experimentation was completed in June 1996, and the individual protofederations reported their results back to the AMG in July of that year. Based on these results, the AMG recommended the baseline High-Level Architecture that had been defined to the Executive Council for Modeling and Simulation (EXCIMS) in August 1996. The EXCIMS in turn, recommended the architecture to the undersecretary of defense (Acquisition and Technology) for approval and standardization. On September 10, 1996 the undersecretary of defense designated that the HLA become the standard high-level technical architecture for all modeling and simulation activities in the U.S. Department of Defense. This meant that all simulation programs in the DoD would be required to pass certain procedures to certify that they were "HLA compliant," or obtain a waiver from this rule. At time of this writing (1999) efforts to define an IEEE standard for the HLA are in progress. The discussion that follows is based on version 1.3 of the HLA that was proposed for standardization by the IEEE.

7.6.2   Overview of the HLA

Any real-world entity that is visible to more than one federate is represented in the HLA by an object. The HLA does not assume the use of object-oriented programming languages, however. Each object instance contains (1) an identity that distinguishes it from other objects, (2) attributes that indicate those state variables and parameters of an object that are accessible to other objects, and (3) associations between objects (for example, one object is part of another object).

The HLA includes a non-runtime and a runtime component. The non-runtime component specifies the object model used by the federation. This includes the set of object types chosen to represent the real world, the attributes and associations (class definitions) of these objects, the level of detail at which the objects represent the world (for example, spatial and temporal resolution), and the key models and algorithms (for example, for dead reckoning) that are to be used.

The runtime component is the RTI that provides facilities for allowing federates to interact with each other, as well as a means to control and manage the execution (see Fig. 7.7). Individual federates may be software simulations (combat models, flight simulators, etc.), live components (for example, an instrumented tank), or passive data viewers. The RTI can be viewed as a distributed operating system that provides the software environment necessary to interconnect cooperating federates. It provides several categories of services, as described below. The interface specification defines a standard set of services provided by the RTI, and application program interfaces (APIs) for different programming languages.

The state variables for the federation are stored within the federates rather than the RTI. The RTI has no knowledge of the semantics of the information that it is transmitting. This is necessary to make the RTI general purpose, not tied to detailed semantics of the simulation model. This means that the RTI cannot include optimizations that require knowledge of the semantics of the simulation. Dead reckoning is an example of one such optimization. Techniques such as this that

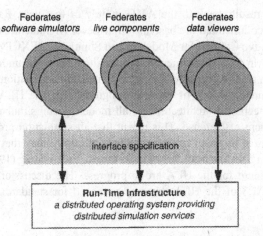

Figure 7.7 Components in an HLA federation.

require knowledge of the semantics of the simulation must be implemented within the federates.

Each object attribute has an owner that is responsible for notifying the RTI whenever the value of the attribute has been modified. An attribute can have at most one owner at any time. Federates that have indicated interest in the attribute are notified of such changes via *attribute reflections*. Reflections are implemented as calls from the RTI to the federate indicating which attributes have been modified and their new values. Different attributes for a single object can be owned by different federates. At any instant there can be at most one owner of an attribute; however, ownership of the attribute may pass from one federate to another during an execution. Any number of other federates may *subscribe* to receive updates to attributes as they are produced by the owner.

Federates may interact with each other by modifying object attributes that are then reflected to other federates that have expressed an interest in that object. A second way federates may interact is through HLA *interactions*. Interactions are used to model instantaneous events not directly associated with an object attribute. For example, weapon exchanges between combating units will be typically modeled using interactions rather than updates to attributes.

Each simulation must define a *simulation object model* (SOM) that identifies the objects used to model real-world entities in the simulation and specifies the public attributes, the attributes whose ownership may be transferred, and those attributes whose value may be received and processed. Using the SOMs for the simulations that are included in a particular federation, a *federation object model* (FOM) must then be developed that describes the common object model used by all simulations in the federation. The FOM specifies all shared information (objects, attributes, associations, and interactions) for a particular federation. The HLA includes an object model template (OMT) to provide a standard, tabular format for specifying objects, attributes, and the relationships among them.

More precisely, HLA consist of three components:

1. The *HLA rules* that define the underlying design principles used in the HLA.
2. An *object model template* (OMT) that specifies a common format for describing the information of common interest to the simulations in the federation.
3. An *interface specification* that defines the services provided by the Run-Time Infrastructure (RTI) for linking together individual federates.

Each of these is described next.

7.6.3 HLA Rules

The HLA rules summarize the key principles behind the HLA. The rules defined at the time of this writing are enumerated in Table 7.1. These principles were discussed in the previous section, so we do not elaborate upon them further.

7.6.4 Object Models and the Object Model Template

In any DVE composed of interacting, autonomous simulators, some means is required to specify aspects of the virtual world that are visible to more than one simulation. In the HLA, object models are used for this purpose because they

TABLE 7.1 HLA rules

1. Federations shalll have an HLA Federation Object Model (FOM) documented in accordance with the HLA Object Model Template.
2. In a federation, all simulation-associated object instance representation shall be in the federates, not in the runtime infrastructure (RTI).
3. During a federation execution, all exchange of FOM data among federates shall occur via the RTI.
4. During a federation execution, federates shall interact with the RTI in accordance with the HLA Interface Specification (IFSpec).
5. During a federation execution, an attribute of an instance of an object shall be owned by at most one federate at any time.
6. Federates shall have an HLA Simulation Object Model (SOM), documented in accordance with the HLA Object Model Template (OMT).
7. Federates shall be able to update and/or reflect any attributes of objects in their SOMs and send and/or receive SOM interactions externally as specified in their SOMS.
8. Federates shall be able to transfer and/or accept ownership of attributes dynamically during a federation execution, as specified in their SOMs.
9. Federates shall be able to vary the conditions (e.g., thresholds) under which they provide updates of attributes of objects, as specified in their SOMs.
10. Federates shall be able to manage local time in a way that will allow them to coordinate data exchange with other members of a federation.

Source: Defense Modeling and Simulation Office.

provide a convenient means of describing the real world. Each simulator "advertises" its capabilities with respect to the object attributes it can update and receive via its simulation object model (SOM). The federation object model (FOM) specifies the common objects used by the constituent simulators participating in a federation execution. Object models in the HLA are documented using a set of tables that are collectively referred to as the object model template (OMT). The OMT describes what is actually meant by an object model in the HLA, so the remainder of this section focuses on the information specified in the OMT.

The OMT specifies the class hierarchy for objects and interactions, and details concerning the type and semantics of object attributes. It is used to specify both SOMs and FOMs. Class definitions are similar to those used in object oriented design methodologies, as discussed in Chapter 2, but differ in several respects. In particular, HLA object models only specify object classes and properties of their attributes. They do not specify the methods or operations for manipulating the classes. In object-oriented programming the attributes for an instance of an object are usually encapsulated and stored in one location, while in the HLA attributes for a single object instance may be distributed across different federates. Moreover HLA object models are used for defining federations of simulations rather than an approach to software development.

The OMT (version 1.3) consists of the following tables:

- The *object model identification table* provides general information concerning the FOM or SOM such as its name, purpose, version, and point-of-contact information.
- The *object class structure table* specifies the class hierarchy of objects in the SOM/FOM.
- The *attribute table* enumerates the type and characteristics of object attributes.
- The *interaction class structure table* defines the class hierarchy defining the types of interactions in the SOM/FOM.
- The *parameter table* defines types and characteristics of interaction parameters.
- The *routing space table* specifies the nature and meaning of constructs called routing spaces that are used to efficiently distribute data throughout large federations; routing spaces and data distribution management are discussed in detail in Chapter 8.
- The *FOM/SOM lexicon* is used to describe the meaning of all terms used in the other tables, such as the meanings of object classes, attributes, interaction classes, and parameters.

The object and interaction class structure tables and their associated attribute and parameter tables form the heart of the object model template. These are described in greater detail next.

Object Class Structure Table   The object class structure table enumerates the classes used in the object model, and specifies class/subclass relationships. Class names are globally unique character strings. Subclasses can be defined that are specializations or refinements of the parent class (called the superclass). A subclass inherits the attributes and interactions of its superclass. For example, Table 7.2 shows a SOM for a hypothetical World War II flight simulator. Two classes are defined, one for moving vehicles, and one for bases. Three subclasses for the Vehicle class are defined, to distinguish between air, sea, and land vehicles. The Aircraft subclass is further refined into fixed wing aircraft and zeppelins, and fixed wing aircraft are refined further to include specific aircraft types (an American P-51 Mustang, a British Spitfire, and a German Messerschmitt ME-109). The aircraft subclass inherits the position attributes (shown in another table, as will be discussed momentarily) from the Vehicle superclass.

In the HLA OMT a class can have only a single parent class (single inheritance). Multiple inheritance is not supported at present. Thus the class hierarchy forms a set of trees (a forest), with the classes at the highest level (i.e., the first column in the object class structure table) defining the roots of the trees.

During the execution of the simulation each federate must be notified when objects "visible" to that federate change, such as when another aircraft being displayed by a flight simulator turns to move in a new direction. One mechanism provided in the HLA for this purpose is called declaration mangement which

TABLE 7.2 Example object class structure table

Vehicle (PS)	Aircraft (PS)	Fixed Wing (PS)	P-51 Mustang (S)
			Spitfire (PS)
			ME-109 (S)
		Zeppelin (S)	
	Naval vessle (S)	Submarine (S)	U-boat (S)
		Battleship (S)	Iowa class (S)
		Aircraft carrier (S)	
	Land vehicle (S)	Tank (S)	Panzer (S)
			Sherman (S)
		Jeep (S)	
Base (S)	Air field (PS)		
	Sea port (S)		
	Army post (S)		

implements *class-based subscription*. Specifically, a federate can subscribe to attributes of an object class, indicating it wishes to receive notification whenever that attribute of any object instance of that class is modified. For example, if a federate subscribes to the position attribute of the Spitfire class, it will receive a message for any update to the position attribute of any Spitfire object in the federation. Note that class-based subscription allows a federate to track changes to *all* spitfire objects. The federate must discard updates corresponding to spitfires that are not of interest to it, such as that are too far away to be visible to its pilot. A more sophisticated mechanism by which the RTI automatically eliminates these messages will be discussed in Chapter 8.

A federate may subscribe at any point in the class hierarchy. Attributes of a class are inherited by the subclasses of that class. Subscribing to an attribute of a class at a certain level in the hierarchy automatically subscribes the federate to that attribute as it is inherited by all the subclasses of that class. For example, in Table 7.2, a subscription to the position attribute of the *Fixed Wing* class will result in subscription to the position attribute of the *P-51*, *Spitfire*, or *ME-109* subclasses. If subclasses are later added, such as a *B-17* subclass of the *Fixed Wing* class to include bombers in the exercise, federates subscribed to the *Fixed Wing* class need not change their subscription to also receive position updates for this new type of aircraft.

The object class structure table also indicates a federate's (or federation's, in the case of FOMs) ability to publish (update) the value of attributes of an object class, or to subscribe to (and thus receive and react to) attribute updates. This is represented by *P* or *S* flags with each class.[29] Table 7.2, for instance, shows publication and subscription information for a flight simulator modeling a Spitfire. It is able to update attributes of the Spitfire class, and can process updates to attributes of other classes that it uses to update the display shown to the Spitfire's pilot.

Attribute Table Each object class includes a fixed set of attribute types. Attributes specify portions of the object state shared among federates during the execution. The object model template represents the following characteristics of attributes (corresponding to columns in the attribute table):

- *Object class*. This indicates the class in the object class structure table, such as Vehicle, and can be chosen from any level in the class hierarchy.
- *Attribute name*. This specifies the name of the attribute, such as position.
- *Data type*. This field specifies the type of the attribute and is not unlike type specifications in conventional programming languages. For basic data types, this field specifies one of a standard set of base data types, such as integer or floating point. Alternatively, user-defined data types can be specified. Records can be defined including multiple fields, such as the coordinate position and altitude of an aircraft. In this case individual fields are specified in a complex data-type table that includes information similar to the attribute table in that

---

[29] It is possible to define classes that are neither subscribable nor publishable. A federate may not be able to publish or subscribe to the object class, but it can publish or subscribe to a subclass of that object class.

units, accuracy, and the like, are specified. Enumerated types can also be defined, in which case another table is used to specify possible values and their representation.

- *Cardinality.* This field is used to record the size of an array or sequence.
- *Units.* This specifies the units for numeric values, such as meters or kilograms. This and the resolution and accuracy fields do not apply to complex and enumerated types.
- *Resolution.* This indicates the smallest difference between published values of the attribute. For example, if altitude is recorded to the nearest 100 meters, then the resolution is 100 meters.
- *Accuracy.* This indicates the maximum deviation of the attribute's value from the intended value (for example, recall the use of thresholds in dead reckoning schemes). This may be specified as "perfect" to indicate that there is no deviation between published values and the intended value. Note that this parameter does not specify the accuracy of the simulation model, only how close published values are to the true simulated value (which may or may not be very accurate to real-world systems).
- *Accuracy condition.* This allows one to specify conditions under which the accuracy specification applies. This may be specified as *always* to indicate the accuracy specification always applies.
- *Update type.* This indicates the policy used for updating the attribute. This is specified as *static* (meaning it is not updated), *periodic* if it is updated at regular intervals, or *conditional* if it is updated when certain conditions occur, such as when a dead reckoning threshold is exceeded.
- *Update condition.* This elaborates on the update type field. For example, if updates are periodic, it specifies the rate.
- *Transferable/acceptable.* This indicates whether the federate is able to transfer/accept ownership of the attribute to/from another federate.
- *Update/reflect.* This indicates whether the federate is able to update/reflect the attribute value.

Interaction Class Structure Table Interactions are actions taken by one federate that have an affect on another federate(s). A class hierarchy similar to that used for objects is used to document interaction types. For example, in Table 7.3

TABLE 7.3 Example interaction class structure table

Shoot	Aircraft cannon (IR)
	Bomb (IS)
	Torpedo (S)
	Anti-aircraft (R)

a shoot interaction is defined. Four subclasses of the interaction are specified corresponding to cannon fire, dropping a bomb, launching a torpedo, and anti-aircraft fire.

Entries in the interaction class structure table are annotated to indicate whether the federate can initiate (*I*), react (*R*), or sense (*S*) interactions. A federate can initiate an interaction if it is able to send that interaction class with appropriate parameters. For example, in Table 7.3 the Spitfire simulator can generate cannon fire and drop bombs but cannot fire a torpedo or generate anti-aircraft fire. A federate can react to interactions, if it can receive them, and produce appropriate changes in state; for example, it can generate appropriate attribute updates in response to the interaction. Table 7.3 indicates the Spitfire can react to cannon fire and anti-aircraft interactions, such as by producing damage and generating state updates to designate damage or destruction of the aircraft. The third category, sense, indicates that the object can receive interactions, but cannot produce suitable reactions to the interaction. In this example, the Spitfire can sense torpedo launches and bombs dropped by other aircraft and update its local display, if necessary, but it cannot (and should not) create attribute updates as the result of these interactions. Observers in the battlefield (called *Stealth viewers*) similarly can receive interactions and display them but cannot generate suitable actions from the interaction. The rules concerning inheritance of classes in interaction class structure tables are essentially the same as those of the object class structure table.

Parameter Table   Just as attributes provide state information for objects, parameters provide state information for interactions. Parameter types are specified in the parameter table. The parameter table includes many fields that are similar to attribute tables. Specifically, it includes columns to specify the interaction class, parameter name, and the data type, cardinality, units, resolution, accuracy, and accuracy condition for parameters. Their meaning is similar to that specified in the attribute table. The other entries in the attribute table that are not included in the parameter table concern state updates and ownership transfer, which do not apply to interactions.

7.6.5   Interface Specification

In the HLA there is a clear separation between the functionality of individual federates and the RTI. For example, all knowledge concerning the semantics and behavior of the physical system being modeled is within the federate. Further the actual state of the simulation model also resides within the federate. This allows the RTI to be a general software component that is applicable to any federation. The RTI could be used for general (i.e., nondefense) distributed virtual environments, although its functionality was derived primarily from requirements originating from the defense modeling and simulation community.

The interface specification defines a set of services provided by simulations or by the Run-Time Infrastructure (RTI) during a federation execution. HLA runtime services fall into the following categories:

- *Federation management.* This includes services to create and delete federation executions, to allow simulations to join or resign from existing federations, and to pause, checkpoint, and resume a federation execution.

- *Declaration management.* These services provide the means for simulations to establish their intent to publish object attributes and interactions, and to subscribe to updates and interactions produced by other simulations.

- *Object management.* These services allow simulations to create and delete object instances, and to produce and receive individual attribute updates and interactions.

- *Ownership management.* These services enable the transfer of ownership of object attributes during the federation execution; recall that only one federate is allowed to modify the attributes of an object instance at any time.

- *Time management.* These services coordinate the advancement of logical time, and its relationship to wallclock time during the federation execution.

- *Data distribution management.* These services control the distribution of state updates and interactions among federates, in order to control the distribution of information so that federates receive all of the information relevant to it and (ideally) no other information.

7.6.6 Typical Federation Execution

A typical federation execution begins with the invocation of federation management services to initialize the execution. Specifically, the *Create Federation Execution* service is used to start the execution, and each federate joins the federation via the *Join Federation Execution* service.

Each federate will then use the declaration management services to specify what information it can provide to the federation, and what information it is interested in receiving. The *Publish Object Class* service is invoked by the federate to indicate it is able to provide new values for the state of objects of a specific class, such as the position of vehicles modeled by the federate. Conversely, the *Subscribe Object Class Attribute* service indicates the federate is to receive all updates for objects of a certain class, such as the altitude attribute of all aircraft objects. Federates may use the data distribution management services to further qualify these subscriptions, such as to say that the federate is only interested in aircraft flying at an altitude greater than 1000 feet. The federate may then inform the RTI of specific instances of objects stored within it via the *Register Object Instance* (object management) service.

After the execution has been initialized, each federate models the behavior of the entities for which it is responsible. The federate may interact with other federates through object management services. The federate notifies other federates via the RTI of changes in the state of objects under its control via the *Update Attribute Values* object management service. This will cause the RTI to generate messages for all other federates that have expressed interest in receiving these updates via their subscriptions. Alternatively, the federate may issue interactions with other federates that are not associated with modifying the state of an object via the *Send Interaction* service. This might be used to exchange weapons fire, for example. As objects are registered and "become visible" to federates that have subscribed to their attribute values, the RTI notifies the federate of the existence of these objects via the *Discover Object Instance* service. Similarly this service is invoked as objects come "within range." For example, this service might be invoked as an aircraft reaches an altitude of 1000 feet in the previous example, or as new vehicles come within view of a tank simulator, causing the tank simulator to display the vehicle to the user, and to track and update its position.

Throughout the execution, analytic simulations invoke the time management services to ensure that events are processed in time stamp order and to advance simulation time. For example, the *Next Event Request* service requests the next smallest time-stamped event from the RTI and also causes the federate's simulation time to advance.

As mentioned earlier, an object can be updated by at most one federate, called the object's owner. A handoff protocol is provided in the RTI to transfer ownership from one federate to another. For example, a missile launch might be controlled by the army's simulation, but the trajectory of the missile's flight may be controlled by the air force's simulation. A federate can invoke the *Negotiated Attribute Ownership Divestiture* service to begin the process of transferring ownership to another federate. The RTI invokes the *Request Attribute Ownership Assumption* service in other federates to identify a federate that will take over ownership of the attribute. The federate taking on ownership responds by calling the *Attribute Ownership Acquisition* service. The RTI confirms the ownership transfer to both parties by invoking the *Attribute Ownership Divestiture Notification* and *Attribute Ownership Acquisition Notification* services in the federates giving up, and receiving ownership, respectively.

Finally, at the end of the execution, each federate invokes the *Resign Federation Execution* service. The execution is terminated by invoking the *Destroy Federation Execution* service.

7.7 SUMMARY

This chapter provided a bird's eye view of distributed simulations for DVEs. DIS is illustrative of a typical DVE. Although designed for military applications, it introduces design principles such as autonomy of simulation nodes and dead reckoning that apply to commercial applications, particularly those requiring many simulation nodes. A noteworthy observation in this discussion is that DVEs must appear realistic to participants embedded in the simulation environment, sometimes at the expense of absolute accuracy. Smoothing techniques used in conjunction with dead reckoning algorithms is one example. This is an important distinction between distributed simulations for DVEs and for analytic analysis.

While the discussion of DIS provides insight into the operation of simulator nodes in a DVE, the discussion of the High Level Architecture provides insight into the interface between simulators, and between simulators and the runtime infra-structure. In particular, the object model template provides some insight into the kind of information that simulations must agree upon in order to interoperate. The HLA interface specification provides an overview of the types of services one might expect to find in an RTI supporting DVEs. The chapters that follow focus on realization of RTI services.

7.8 ADDITIONAL READINGS

An overview of the SIMNET project by two of its principal architects is presented in Miller and Thorpe (1995). The DIS vision and underlying design principles are presented in DIS Steering Committee (1994). More detailed discussions are presented in Goldiez, Smith et al. (1993) and Hofer and Loper (1995), and its relationship to modeling and simulation in the Department of Defense is described in Davis (1995). Specifics concerning the DIS protocols, PDUs, formats, and the like, are described in IEEE standards documents (IEEE Std 1278.1-1995 1995; IEEE Std 1278.2-1995 1995). These references also include a description of the dead reckoning protocol used in DIS. An alternative approach to dead reckoning based on utilizing past position measurements to project current positions of remote objects is described in Singhal and Cheriton (1994).

Detailed documentation concerning the High Level Architecture is available from the Defense Modeling and Simulation Office (DMSO) through their Internet web site (http://hla.dmso.mil). This site includes documents concerning the HLA rules (Defense Modeling and Simulation Office 1996), object model template (Defense Modeling and Simulation Office 1996), and interface specification (Defense Modeling and Simulation Office 1998). An introduction to the HLA is presented in Dahmann, Fujimoto et al. (1997).

CHAPTER 8

Networking and Data Distribution

The network plays a critical role in distributed simulation systems. Simulator-to-simulator message latency can have a large impact on the realism of the virtual environment. One hundred to 300 milliseconds are considered adequate for most applications, though for some, latencies as low as a few tens of milliseconds may be required. Aggregate network bandwidth, the amount of data transmitted through the network per unit time, is also important because large-scale distributed simulations can easily generate enormous amounts of data. Thus it is important both to achieve maximal bandwidth and minimal latency in the network itself, as well as to control the amount of data that must be transmitted and still provide each participant a consistent view of the virtual world.

8.1 MESSAGE-PASSING SERVICES

All networks provide the ability to transmit messages between simulators. Having said that, there are a number of different characteristics that differentiate different types of network services. Some of the more important characteristics for DVEs are enumerated below. Simple DVEs may utilize only one type of communication service. Other DVEs, especially ones designed to handle a large number of participants, typically utilize a variety of different services.

8.1.1 Reliable Delivery

A reliable message delivery system is one where the service guarantees that each message will be received at the specified destination(s), or an exception will be raised for any message that cannot be delivered. Typically this means the networking software will retransmit messages if it cannot determine (for example, via an acknowledgment message) that the message has been successfully received. An *unreliable* or *best-effort* delivery service does not provide such a guarantee.

For many types of information, such as periodically generated position update messages, unreliable communication services are often preferred because they normally incur less latency and overhead than reliable services. An occasional lost message can be tolerated because a new update will be sent before long anyway. On

223

the other hand, reliable delivery is preferred in other cases, such as if a lost message causes a simulator to lock up, waiting for the lost message to arrive, or to enter an inconsistent state.

8.1.2 Message Ordering

An ordered delivery service guarantees that successive messages sent from one simulator to another will be received in the same order in which they were sent. This property may or may not be provided with the network delivery service. For example, if successive messages are routed along different paths through the network, they may not arrive in the same order that they were sent. On the other hand, if the network transmits messages along a single path and ensures that a message cannot jump ahead of other messages in message queues, ordered delivery is ensured. If the network does not provide ordered delivery and this property is required, the processor receiving the messages will have to ensure that they are correctly ordered before delivering them to the receiver. This is often accomplished by attaching a sequence number to each message and making sure the destination reorders messages according to the sequence number. As discussed later, this capability is often realized within the network communication software.

More sophisticated message ordering is sometimes important in DVEs, extending well beyond the ordering of messages sent between each pair of processors. Certain anomalies such as the effect of some action appearing to happen before the cause may occur unless precautions are taken. This will be discussed in greater detail in Chapter 9.

8.1.3 Connection-Oriented versus Connectionless Communication

In a connectionless (also called a *datagram*) service, the sender places the data it wishes to transmit into a message, and passes the message to the networking software for transmission to the destination(s). This is analogous to mailing a letter through the postal system. In a connection-oriented service, the sender must first establish a connection with the destination before data can be sent. After the data have all been sent, the connection must be terminated. Connection-oriented services are analogous to telephone services.

A connectionless service is often preferred for much of the information transmitted among simulators, such as for state updates, because of its simplicity. On the other hand, a connection-oriented service is better for streams of information, such as an audio or video channel established between a pair of simulators.

8.1.4 Unicast versus Group Communication

A unicast service sends each message to a single destination. A broadcast service sends a copy of the message to all possible destinations, while a multicast mechanism sends it to more than one, but not necessarily all, destinations. Multicast communication is important when realizing large-scale simulations. For example, a typical operation is a player needs to send a state update message to the other players that can see it. More will be said about how multicast can be used in DVEs later in this chapter.

8.1.5   Examples: DIS and NPSNet

The communication requirements in the DIS standard 1278.2 specify three classes of communication services, based in part on existing networking products:

1. Best-effort multicast
2. Best-effort unicast
3. Reliable unicast

These communication services are available in the Internet Protocol suite, discussed later in this chapter. There, best-effort communication is achieved using the connectionless User Datagram Protocol (UDP) and reliable communication is achieved using the Transmission Control Protocol (TCP) which provides a connection-oriented service.

Conspicuously missing from the DIS communication services is reliable multicast. Reliable multicast is considered important in many DVEs, but when the DIS protocols were defined, realization of this service was not sufficiently mature to enable inclusion in the DIS standard. At the time of this writing in the late 1990s, realization of reliable multicast services is still an active area of research in the networking community.

In DIS best-effort communication is typically used for entity state PDUs (ESPDUs). Loss of ESPDUs can be tolerated so long as they are not too frequent because new updates are generated at regular intervals. These PDUs make up the lion's share of communications in typical DIS exercises; one demonstration exercise reports 96% of the total DIS traffic was ESPDUs (Cheung 1994). Reliable communications are often used for nonrecurring events where losses are more problematic, such as fire and detonation PDUs.

A second example illustrating the communication services typically used in large DVEs is NPSNet. NPSNet is a project at the Naval Post Graduate School aimed at developing large-scale virtual environments containing thousands of users. The NPSNet communications architecture is described in Macedonia, Zyda et al. (1995). It provides four classes of communications:

1. *Light weight interaction.* This service provides a best-effort, connectionless group communication facility. State updates, interactions, and control messages will typically use this service. Each message must be completely contained in a maximum transfer unit (MTU), sized at 1500 bytes for Ethernet and 296 bytes for 9600 bits/second point-to-point links. It is implemented with a multicast communication mechanism.

2. *Network pointers.* These provide references to resources, analogous to links in the World Wide Web. They are somewhat similar to lightweight interactions (for example, both use multicast) but contain references to objects, while lightweight interactions contain the objects themselves.

3. *Heavy weight objects.* These provide a reliable, connection-oriented communication service.

4. *Real-time streams.* These provide real-time delivery of continuous streams of data, as well as sequencing and synchronization of streams. They are intended for transmission of video or audio streams.

8.2 NETWORKING REQUIREMENTS

The success of a DVE, especially large-scale DVEs containing many participants often depends critically on the performance of the underlying network infrastructure. For example, networking requirements for DIS are described in IEEE Std 1278.2-1995 (1995). Specific requirements include the following:

- *Low latency.* As discussed in the previous chapter, the DIS standard calls for simulator-to-simulator latencies of under 300 milliseconds for most (termed loosely coupled) interactions, and 100 millisecond latency for tightly coupled interactions, such as where a user is closely scrutinizing the actions of another participant in the DVE.

- *Low-latency variance.* The variance of delay between successive messages sent from one processor to another is referred to as *jitter*. Low jitter may be required in a DVE to maintain a realistic depiction of the behavior of remote entities. Jitter requirements can be alleviated somewhat by buffering messages at the receiver to smooth fluctuations in latency. Dead reckoning also provides some resilience to delay variance. The DIS standard specifies a maximum dispersion of arrival times for a sequence of PDUs carrying voice information to be 50 milliseconds.

- *Reliable delivery.* As discussed previously, best-effort communication is sufficient for much of the traffic generated in a DVE, but reliable delivery is important for certain, nonperiodic events. The DIS standard calls for 98% of the PDUs for tightly coupled interactions and 95% for loosely coupled interactions to be delivered within the specified latency requirement.

- *Group communication.* Group communication services are important for moderate to large DVEs, especially in geographically distributed systems where broadcast communication facilities are not readily available. A multicast group is the set of destinations that is to receive messages sent to the group, analogous to the set of subscribers to an Internet newsgroup. Large DVEs present a particularly challenging application for multicast protocols because they may require group communication services that support the following:

1. Large numbers of groups (for example, thousands).
2. A single simulator to belong to many different groups at one time.
3. Frequent changes to group composition that must be realized quickly (for example, within a few milliseconds) so that simulators do not miss important information.

Data distribution techniques are described later in this chapter, providing some insight into the usage of group communication services in large-scale DVEs.

- *Security.* Certain applications such as defense simulations have security requirements (for example, to prevent eavesdropping on classified information). Sensitive data must be encrypted at the source and decrypted at the destination. This of course affects the latency requirements, which must include the time to perform such operations.

8.3 NETWORKING TECHNOLOGIES

As discussed in Chapter 1, networks may be broadly categorized as local area networks (LANs) covering a limited physical extent (for example, a building or a campus), metropolitan area networks (MANs) covering a city, and wide area networks (WANs) that can extend across continents. Unlike parallel computing platforms which typically use proprietary interconnection networks, the distributed computers typically used to implement DVEs have standard networking technologies for interconnecting machines.

In general, LANs provide a much "friendlier" environment for distributed simulation systems than WANs (MANs are intermediate between these two). LANs often operate at link bandwidths, ranging from many megabits per second (for example, Ethernet operates at 10 MBits per second) up to a gigabit per second or more, and can achieve application-to-application latencies of a few milliseconds or less. They typically have error rates ranging from 10^{-8} to 10^{-12}. By contrast, links in WANs typically range in bandwidth from thousands of bits per second up to megabit per second, and they often incur latencies on the order of hundreds of milliseconds or more. Error rates are on the order of 10^{-5} to 10^{-7}. Bandwidth is important in distributed virtual environments because the different computers executing the distributed simulation must perceive a common state of the virtual world, and a substantial amount of interprocessor communication is required to keep this world consistent among the different participants.

8.3.1 LAN Technologies

Historically LAN interconnects have typically been based on either a shared bus or a ring interconnection scheme (see Fig. 8.1). A recent phenomenon is the appearance of switched LANs, such as those based on Ethernet or asynchronous transfer mode

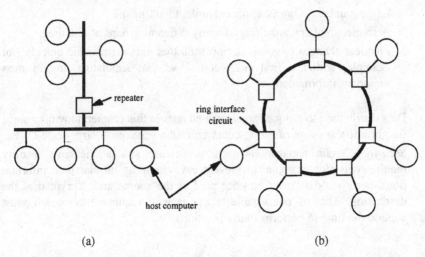

(a)   (b)

Figure 8.1   Typical LAN topologies. (*a*) Bus-based network; (*b*) ring network.

(ATM) switching technology. These are increasing in popularity, especially for applications requiring high bandwidth. Bus and ring topologies date back to the 1970s and have been in widespread use since then. Each is discussed next.

Bus-Based Networks   In a bus-based system each computer connects directly to the bus via a tap. Actually, as shown in Figure 8.1(*a*), the bus may consist of many bus segments that are interconnected by a circuit, called a *repeater*, that copies the signal from one segment of the bus to another, amplifying the signal to compensate for attenuation. Each message is broadcast over the bus. Processors connected to the bus must check the address of the message against their local address and read the message into their local memory if there is a match.

A complication arises concerning access to the bus. If more than one processor simultaneously places data onto the bus, the data will become garbled, and neither message will get through. This is not unlike two people trying to talk at the same time during a conversation. Thus it would be prudent to check that the bus is idle before beginning to transmit. However, suppose that while the bus is in use by some processor, *two* other processors decide they want to send a message. Both will wait until the bus becomes idle, then both will simultaneously begin transmitting. This will result in a *collision*; that is, the data on the bus will be garbled.

To address this problem, a *Medium Access Control* (MAC) protocol is required. A well-known example of a MAC protocol is the exponential back-off algorithm used in Ethernet. Each processor sending a message can detect that a collision has occurred by noticing that the data on the bus does not match the data it is sending. When this occurs, the processor stops transmitting and puts a jamming signal on the bus to make sure that all other processors have recognized that there is a collision. The processor then becomes idle for a certain, randomly selected amount of time ranging from 0 to $K - 1$ time periods, and it repeats the process by waiting until the bus becomes free before retransmitting the message. In Ethernet, K is initialized to 2 for each message but is doubled with each successive collision in trying to send that message. To prevent excessively long delays because K has become too large, the exponential growth is often stopped when it has reached a maximum value. At this point the retransmission interval is based on a random number drawn between 0 and K_{max}, where K_{max} is maximum value assigned to K. This retransmission algorithm is referred to as the *truncated binary exponential backoff algorithm*. The Ethernet MAC protocol is an example of what is commonly referred to as a *Carrier Sense Multiple Access with Collision Detection* (CSMA/CD) protocol.

Rings   Here, the processors are organized as a ring using point-to-point communication links (rather than a shared bus) between pairs of processors, as shown in Figure 8.1(*b*). Data circulate in one direction on the ring. When a message passes through a processor, the message's destination address is compared with that of the processor. If there is a match, the processor retains a copy of the message. In some rings the destination processor removes the message from the ring. In others, the message is allowed to circulate around the ring, in which case the source is responsible for removing the message. One node of the ring is designated as a monitor that prevents messages from cycling indefinitely around the ring, in case the processor responsible for removing the message has failed, as well as to perform other housekeeping functions. Some rings include a means to bypass a node, and/or additional links to protect against link failures which would otherwise cause the entire network to fail.

Like bus-based systems, a MAC protocol is needed to control access to the ring. Token ring and slotting ring protocols are most commonly used for ring networks.

In a token ring, a special message, called the *token*, circulates around the ring. The token contains a flag indicating whether it is *free* or *busy*. A processor can only transmit a message after it has received the token, and the token's flag is set to free. The processor then sets the token's flag to busy, attaches its message, and sends the token and message around the ring. The destination processor removes the message from the network and forwards only the busy token around the ring. The processor that sent the message will eventually receive the busy token, mark it free, and then forward the token on the ring to allow another processor to send a message. The monitor processor is responsible for ensuring that the token is not lost or duplicated. Unlike the CSMA/CD protocol used in Ethernet, one can bound the time to access the media using a token ring protocol. The Fiber-Distributed Data Interface (FDDI) is an example of a networking technology based on token rings.

In a slotted ring protocol, a fixed number of message slots continually cycle around the ring. Each slot is marked either full or empty. To send a message, the source processor first breaks the message up into pieces of size equal to the slot size. It then waits for an empty slot for each piece of the message it wants to send. When an empty slot occurs, it marks the slot full and inserts its message. Each receiver examines each slot to see if it contains a message destined for it. If it does, it marks the slot to indicate the message has been received and forwards the slot down the ring. When the slot completes a round-trip and arrives back at the sender, the sender processor marks the slot empty and forwards it around the ring.

Switched LANs Switched LANs are networks based on N-input, N-output switches. Recently these have seen greater use, especially with the advent of asynchronous transfer mode (ATM) technology which has resulted in several commercial products. A small switched LAN network topology is shown in Figure 8.2(a). Each link in this figure is bidirectional; it can carry traffic in both directions.

ATM networks use a connection-oriented approach where a path through the network (i.e., an ATM connection), must first be established before sending data. At any instant several connections may be mapped to a single physical communication link. For example, in Figure 8.2(a) the connection from host A to host B and the connection from X to Y both use the link from switch S1 to switch S2. The network must be able to distinguish between data traveling on these two different connections so that S2 can route incoming data to the appropriate destination. This is accomplished by defining a link as containing a number of *virtual channels* and by assigning each connection using the link a different channel number. A connection can be viewed as a sequence of channels from the source to the destination processor. For example, in Figure 8.2(a), the connection from A to B might use channel 1 to reach switch S1, then channel 3 to reach S2, and channel 4 to reach host B. The virtual circuit from X to Y might use channel 5 on the link from S1 to S2, enabling S2 to distinguish between data sent on the X-to-Y circuit from data on the A-to-B circuit.

Each data packet, or cell, includes a field that indicates the number of the channel it is using. This field changes from hop to hop as the cell moves through the network. Actually this channel number consists of two fields, a 12-bit Virtual Path Indicator (VPI) and a 16-bit Virtual Channel Indicator (VCI). The VPI is analogous to the

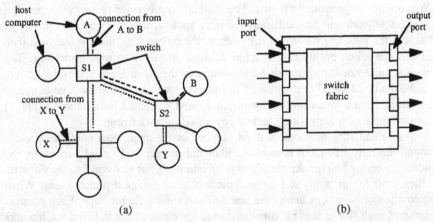

(a)   (b)

Figure 8.2 Switched LAN. (a) Typical topology; (b) four-input, four-output switch.

regional (or area code) portion of a telephone number, and the VCI to the local phone number within the region. This allows a two-level routing scheme where routing by "long-distance" switches can be done using only the VPI field without having to examine the VCI field, and routing within the region can be done using the VCI field.

A four-input, four-output switch is depicted in Figure 8.2(b). The switch contains tables that indicate for each input port and channel which output port and channel are used in the next hop of the connection. When a cell arrives, its incoming port number, VPI, and CPI are used to look up the outgoing port and channel number. The cell is routed through the internal switch fabric to the output link, and is sent on that link with the new VPI and VCI to identify the channel that is being used. The switch fabric contains a switching circuit, such as a crossbar switch, that allows simultaneous transmission of cells from different input links to different output links.

If cells arriving simultaneously on two different input links need to use the same output link, one is transmitted on that link and the other must be stored in a buffer. The latter is transmitted on the link at a later time. If the queue becomes full, the cell is dropped. If a reliable transmission service is provided, the host processor sending the cell must retransmit it.

Switched LANs are more expensive than bus or ring networks because of the need for switching hardware, compared to the cables and taps required in Ethernet. Switched LANs can provide higher bandwidth in applications where the bus/ring becomes a bottleneck, so they are becoming more widely used where high-bandwidth communications are required.

8.3.2 WAN Technologies

Historically communications in wide area networks have evolved from two distinct camps, the telephone industry and the computer data communications industry. In voice communication using telephones, the sound produced by the speaker is converted to an electrical signal that is then sampled at regular intervals. Each sample is transmitted through the network and converted back to sound at the receiver. Telephone voice traffic requires the network to provide a steady stream of voice samples flowing from the speaker to the listener with a minimal amount of latency. Ideally there will be little or no variance in the time between successive voice samples (recall that this is referred to as jitter), since this could cause unwanted distortions in the resulting audio signal.

To accommodate these requirements, telephone-switching networks usually use a technique called *circuit switching*. Circuit switching is a connection-oriented approach where a path or circuit is established from the source to the destination before data can be transmitted. The circuit is established while the caller dials the telephone number. In this respect it is similar to connections in ATM networks. There is an important difference, however. In circuit switching, link bandwidth is allocated to each circuit using the link, regardless of whether or not the circuit has any data to transmit. Because bandwidth is pre-allocated when the call is set up, this ensures that the bandwidth will be available during the conversation, enabling the network to provide a predictable latency and low jitter in transmitting information.

Operationally bandwidth allocation in circuit switching networks can be realized using a technique called time division multiplexing. Consider a multiplexer shown in Figure 8.3(a) that combines four low-bandwidth communication links into one high-speed link. With time division multiplexing, time on the output link is partitioned into successive slots, each able to transmit a single piece of data, such as a voice sample; see Figure 8.3(b). The slots are allocated in succession to each input link, much like dealing cards at a poker table. In this example, the first slot is allocated to link 1, the second to link 2, and so on, and this process repeats when all of the multiplexer's input links have received a slot. An input link to the multiplexer can only transmit data during a time slot allocated to that link. If link 1 is not carrying any data, its slot is not used. In general, a link that rotates among N slots can carry traffic for N different circuits at one time. The $N + 1$st circuit trying to use the link is not granted permission to do so when it is trying to set up a new call. If an alternate path through the network cannot be found, the call cannot be established, and the user is given a busy signal, usually using a tone different from the one given when the receiver's phone is engaged.

Data communications in computer networks such as the Internet typically use packet switching rather than circuit switching. While voice traffic tends to produce a steady stream of information, data traffic does not. Rather, data traffic tends to be very bursty. Two computers may exchange little or no information but then suddenly must transmit megabytes of data, for example, because a user has decided to

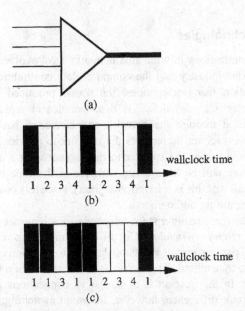

Figure 8.3 Link allocation techniques. (a) Multiplexer; (b) time division multiplexing; (c) statistical multiplexing.

download a large file through the network or has decided to send a lengthy electronic mail message. Further, data traffic in these networks usually does not have the strict latency and jitter requirements of voice traffic. Consider communication requirements for electronic mail. The time division multiplexing approach used in circuit switching is not well suited for transmitting bursty data. For example, as can be seen from Figure 8.3(*b*), if one link has a large data file to transmit, but the other links are idle, only one-fourth of the link's physical bandwidth can be used to transmit the file, and three-fourths of the link bandwidth is unused.

A more efficient approach is to allocate the link's bandwidth on demand, to whoever needs to use it. This approach, referred to as statistical multiplexing, is shown in Figure 8.3(*c*). Here, successive time slots can be allocated to any link that has data to send. Each packet contains an identifier (like the VPI and VCI fields in ATM networks) to identify the traffic being sent over the link. Buffers are required to hold data that cannot be immediately sent. This introduces delays, depending on traffic conditions, resulting in increased jitter, and more difficult to predict latencies.

In packet switching, a message is divided into some number of packets of some fixed, maximum length. The packets are then routed through the network, usually as individual units with no relationship to each other. Different packets for the same message may travel over different routes to reach the destination. The message must then be reassembled from the individual packets at the destination.

To summarize, data communication networks usually use packet switching because it is more efficient for bursty traffic than circuit switching. The price one pays for this is less predictable, and potentially long, latency due to queueing within the network. Further the jitter in transmitting a stream of information may be larger. This is the price one pays for better link utilization in packet-switched networks.

8.3.3 Quality of Service

Much current work in the networking community has been focused on trying to achieve both the predictable, low-latency properties in circuit switching and the efficient utilization of bursty traffic in packet switching. This is accomplished by segregating different types of traffic according to their bandwidth and delay requirements. The basic idea is to provide traffic requiring low latency and jitter certain amounts of guaranteed bandwidth, similar to the guarantees made in circuit switching. However, bandwidth (for example, time slots) not used by this traffic can be utilized by other traffic (for example, bursty, delay insensitive traffic such as file transfers or electronic mail), thereby enabling better link utilization. Much work in the networking community is currently focused on defining suitable resource allocation and reservation schemes to meet specific Quality of Service (QoS) requirements for different applications using the same networking infrastructure. This is a welcome development for DVEs because a single exercise can create diverse types of network traffic with different QoS requirements.

A network architecture designed to provide QoS guarantees to applications includes several important components (Zhang 1993):

- *Flow specification.* This is a language used to specify characteristics of the message flows produced by traffic sources and the QoS requirements of the application with respect to the flows.
- *Routing.* The routing algorithms specify the paths used to transmit messages through the network. This includes paths for point-to-point traffic as well as routing trees for multicast traffic. The routing algorithm can have a large effect on the QoS provided to the application; a poor routing algorithm will result in congestion in the network that might otherwise have been avoided.
- *Resource reservation.* These protocols provide a means to reserve resources in the network such as bandwidth and message buffers for traffic produced by the application. RSVP is one example of such a protocol that propagates resource reservation requests among nodes in the Internet to reserve resources for unicast and multicast traffic (Zhang 1993).
- *Admission control.* Since the network only has a finite amount of resources, some reservation requests must be rejected in order to ensure QoS guarantees for other traffic flows that have already been accepted can be maintained. Admission control algorithms determine which resource reservation requests are accepted and which are denied.
- *Packet scheduling.* This algorithms determines which packet is transmitted over each communication link next. As discussed in the previous section, this can significantly impact the QoS provided to each traffic flow.

8.4   COMMUNICATION PROTOCOLS

When dignitaries from two foreign countries come together, a protocol is necessary for the two to interact and communicate, but without each offending the other according to their own local customs and procedures. Similarly interconnecting two or more computers, particularly computers from different manufacturers, requires agreement along many different levels before communication can take place. For example, what cable and connectors should be used? What is the unit of data transmitted: a byte, a packet, a variable length message, or...? Where is the destination address stored in the message? What should happen if data transmitted over a link are lost or damaged by a transmission error? The set of rules and conventions that are used to precisely answer questions such as these are referred to as a *communication protocol*.

Networking protocols are usually specified as a sequence of layers in order to separate different concerns. For example, the error recovery procedure has little to do with the type of connector that is used, so there is no reason to bundle them together. Each layer provides functionality that is utilized by higher layers. For example, the type of connector, plus numerous other detailed specifications typically define the lowest level, providing the capability to transmit bits from one side of a communication link to another. Clearly this functionality is necessary to implement an error recovery protocol that involves the receiver asking the sender to retransmit corrupted data. An important advantage of this layered approach is that it allows separation of different functions in the network, allowing implementations of one function at one level to change, without affecting functions at other levels. The series of layered protocols in a specific implementation is often referred to as the protocol stack, a terminology that will be adopted here.

8.4.1 OSI Protocol Stack

The International Standards Organization (ISO) defined the Open System International (abbreviated OSI) reference model as a guide for protocol specification. It is intended as a framework into which specific protocol standards can be defined. Seven layers are defined, as depicted in Figure 8.4. Each of these layers is described briefly to convey the functionality provided by each layer.

Layer 1: Physical Layer The physical layer is concerned with defining the electrical signals (optical signals in the case of fiber optic links, or electromagnetic signals in the case of microwave or radio links) and mechanical interface to enable the transmission of a bit stream across a communication link. Detailed information such as the voltage levels for ones and zeros, timing information, the dimension of connectors, and the signal assigned to each wire of the link are specified here. RS-232-C is an example of a physical layer protocol that is often used to connect terminals to computers.

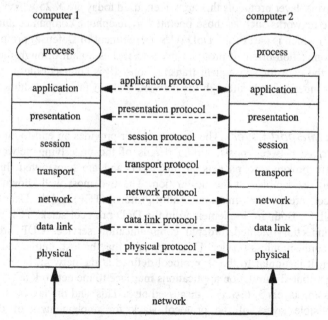

Figure 8.4   Seven-layer OSI protocol stack.

Layer 2: Data Link Layer The data link layer divides the stream of bits provided by the physical layer into *frames* and performs error checking on individual frames. Error checking is performed by combining all of the bits in the frame (for example, adding all of the bytes together, although more sophisticated techniques are often used) to produce a compact *checksum* which is appended to the end of the frame. The receiver performs the same operation on the bytes of the frame and compares the result with the *checksum* at the end. If they do not match, the frame is discarded, and a protocol to retransmit the corrupted frame comes into play. For example, the receiver might send a signal to the sender asking it to retransmit the frame.

Flow control across the link is also performed at this level so that a fast sender does not inundate a slow receiver with excessive amounts of data. This can be accomplished, for example, by having the receiver ask the sender to stop or resume transmitting frames.

Layer 3: Network Layer The network layer is responsible for creating a path through the network from the sender to the receiver. This requires a routing function to specify which outgoing link should be used at each hop as the data move through the network. Routing is not as straightforward as it might seem at first because it may be desirable to take into account loading on the network in order to route messages to bypass congested links. Also the routing function must consider failed links and/or processors. The network layer is not applicable to LANs based on buses or rings because each message is broadcast to all processors, so no routing function is needed.

Two network-layer protocols that are widely used today are X.25 which is used in many public networks such as those operated by telephone companies and Internet Protocol (IP) which is part of the DoD (U.S. Department of Defense) protocol stack. X.25 is a connection-oriented protocol that establishes a path through the network and retains the path for subsequent transmissions. IP is connectionless, and routes each packet independently through the network without first establishing a path.

Layer 4: Transport Layer The transport layer provides an end-to-end communication service between hosts, hiding details of the underlying network. Large messages are broken into packets in this layer, and are transmitted through the network and reassembled at the destination. The two most well-known transport layer protocols are the Transmission Control Protocol (TCP) and the User Datagram Protocol (UDP). Both are implemented in the DoD protocol stack. TCP provides a reliable, connection-oriented, ordered communication service. UDP provides an unreliable, connectionless service. UDP messages may be lost, duplicated, or arrive out of order. It is similar to the IP protocol defined at the network layer.

Many distributed simulation applications interface to the network at the transport level, bypassing layers 5, 6, and 7, discussed next. This, and the layers above it, are the most visible layers of the protocol stack for implementers of distributed simulation systems and applications.

Layer 5: Session Layer The session layer is applicable when connection-oriented communications are used. It enhances the transport layer by providing dialogue control to manage who's talking, and synchronization. For example, it allows two communicating systems to authenticate each other before beginning communication. Other services provide the ability to group a collection of messages so that they can be released as an atomic action (for example, for database management systems), and reordering messages, perhaps according to priority.

In distributed simulation standards such as DIS the session layer includes rules concerning what PDUs should be generated and when, and what classes of communication services should be used. This would include, for instance, the rules concerning which PDUs must be exchanged during an engagement.

Layer 6: Presentation Layer The presentation layer provides a means for parties to communicate without concern for low level details of the representation of data. For instance, data types, such as floating point numbers, may be represented differently on different machines, so some conversion is necessary if these numbers are transmitted across the network. A well-known problem is the byte-ordering problem. Different computers may use different conventions concerning whether the most significant byte of a word is stored at the first or last byte address of the word (referred to as the _machine Endian-ness_), so a byte-swapping operation is required if transmitting data between machines using a different ordering convention. These tasks are often accomplished by converting the data to a standard format called eXternal Data Representation (XDR) before transmission, and converting them to the desired format at the receiver. A disadvantage of using a standard format for data "on the wire" is unnecessary conversions will be performed if the sending and receiving machines use the same representations, but this representation is different from the standard. The presentation layer also packs and unpacks structured data, such as arrays and records, into/from messages.

Data may be encrypted/decrypted in this layer for security or privacy purposes. Along the same lines, data may be compressed (i.e., encoded into a smaller number of bits) by the sender and decompressed at the receiver to reduce the number of bytes that must be transmitted through the network. These functions are performed in the presentation layer.

In DIS the format of PDUs and their interpretation are defined in this layer. Formats for compressing data to reduce bandwidth requirements are also specified here.

Layer 7: Application Layer This layer defines a collection of protocols for various commonly used functions required by end users. Examples include protocols for file transfers, electronic mail, remote login, and access to directory servers. DIS protocols defined in this layer include specification of the kind of data exchanged (position, orientation, etc.), dead reckoning algorithms, and rules for determining when a hit or miss occurs, and the resulting damage.

8.4.2 ATM Protocol Stack

As discussed earlier, circuit switching is well suited for voice traffic but is inefficient for bursty data communications. Conversely, packet switching is more efficient for bursty traffic but suffers from unpredictable latencies and increased jitter, making it less attractive for voice communication. Asynchronous transfer mode (ATM) technology was developed as a means to efficiently handle both types of traffic, as well as a others such as video for teleconferencing and multimedia applications.

ATM uses a hybrid approach that features virtual circuits and cell switching. Unlike pure packet switching where packets are routed independently through the network, virtual circuits allow the network to more easily control allocation of resources to data belonging to a particular connection. This is necessary in order to ensure that Quality of Service guarantees are met. Unlike circuit switching where bandwidth is allocated to each circuit regardless of whether or not it is needed, cell switching and statistical multiplexing are used that allow more efficient utilization of network resources when traffic is bursty. Cell switching is also better suited for realization of multicast protocols which can be of great benefit to distributed simulation applications.

The protocol stack for ATM defines three layers, the ATM physical layer, the ATM layer, and the ATM Adaptation layer (AAL). Standard transport layer (level 4) protocols such as TCP can then be built on top of the ATM services.

Level 1: ATM Physical Layer The ATM physical layer protocols provide similar functionality to the physical layer in the OSI model. Data may be transferred between two locations by one of two means:

1. An ATM adapter board in a computer can put a stream of cells directly onto the wire or fiber. A continuous stream of cells is sent. If there are no data, empty cells are transmitted. This approach is usually used in switched LANs using ATM.
2. ATM cells may be embedded into another framing protocol. In particular, cells may be transmitted via the Synchronous Optical NETwork (SONET) protocol which is widely used in the telephone industry.

A SONET frame containing 810 bytes is transmitted every 125 microseconds to match the telephone industry's sample rate of 8000 samples per second. This yields a data rate (including overhead) of 51.840 Mbits per second. This data rate is called STS-1 (for Synchronous Transport Signal level 1) for electrical signals, or OC-1 (for Optical Carrier-1) for optical signals. Higher-rate signals are called STS/OC-n, where n indicates the number of OC-1 circuits that can be realized from the higher bandwidth. For example, an OC-12 signal is 622.08 Mbits/sec (12 times the OC-1 data rate) and can carry twelve independent OC-1 circuits, four OC-3 circuits or one 622.08 Mbits/sec channel. In the latter case where a single channel is supported, the signal is called OC-12c where the c stands for concatenated or clear channel.

Commonly used values for n are OC-1 (51.84 Mbits/sec), OC-3 (155.520 Mbits/sec), OC-12 (622.080 Mbits/sec), and OC-48 2,488.32 Mbits/sec).

Level 2: ATM Layer The ATM layer deals with cell transport through the network and routing. Each cell is 53 bytes including a 5 byte header and 48 byte payload (data). The 48 byte payload size was a compromise between 32 (promoted by Europe) and 64 (promoted by the United States). The functionality of the ATM layer can be seen from the fields of the header, shown in Figure 8.5. Two slightly different formats are used. The format in Figure 8.5(a) is used for cells first entering the network (at the user-network interface or UNI), and the format in Figure 8.5(b) is for cells passed between two ATM switches (at the network-network interface or NNI).

In the UNI format the General Flow Control field is intended for use for prioritized congestion control, such as to give voice traffic priority over video traffic. It is also used to limit the amount of traffic flowing into the network, such as to restrict input of additional traffic during periods of high utilization. The Virtual Path Identifier (VPI) and Virtual Channel Identifier (VCI) fields identify the path the cell is to follow in traveling through the network, as was discussed in Section 8.2.1.

The Payload Type Identifier (PTI) is used to distinguish between user data cells and control cells used in the network. The Cell Loss Priority (CLP) bit is used to identify cells that should be dropped first if a buffer overflow occurs. Finally the Cyclic Redundancy Checksum (CRC) is used to detect errors in the header field.

The NNI format is the same as the UNI format, except the GFC field is eliminated, and the four bits used by this field are instead used in the VPI field.

Level 3: ATM Adaptation Layer The adaptation layer is responsible for "adapting" specific types of data (for example, video frames, voice samples, data

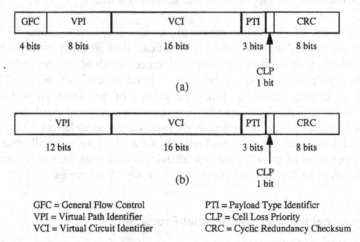

GFC = General Flow Control   PTI = Payload Type Identifier
VPI = Virtual Path Identifier   CLP = Cell Loss Priority
VCI = Virtual Circuit Identifier CRC = Cyclic Redundancy Checksum

Figure 8.5 Header format for ATM cells. (a) Format for cells at the user/network interface; (b) format for cells within the network.

packets) for transmission through the network. Specifically, this layer is responsible for dividing the data into cells, sending the cells into the network, and reassembling them at the destination. This task is typically done within the ATM interface card because cells arrive at too high a rate for the CPU to process them using interrupts. For example, at OC-3 data rates (155.520 Mbits/sec), a stream of incoming cells could generate an interrupt every 3 microseconds.

Several different adaptation layer protocols are defined, optimized for different types of traffic.

1. AAL1 supports constant bit rate (CBR) traffic such as that occurring in uncompressed voice and video. This traffic is usually connection oriented and sensitive to delays.

2. AAL2 supports variable bit rate (VBR) traffic that is connection oriented, and sensitive to delays. Some video and audio traffic belong to this category, such as video where the number of bits used to represent each video image is reduced using a compression algorithm, resulting in a varying number of bits from one video frame to the next.

3. AAL3/4 supports VBR traffic that is not delay sensitive, and may or may not be connection oriented. Computer-generated data (for example, file transfers or electronic mail) is often of this type. This is called AAL3/4 (rather than just AAL3) for historical reasons. Originally two different protocols were defined, one to support connection-oriented services, and the second for connectionless services. It was later discovered that the resulting mechanisms were very similar, so these were combined.

4. AAL5 also supports delay insensitive VBR traffic but is simpler than AAL3/4. This protocol is also called SEAL (Simple and Efficient Adaptation Layer); it was proposed after it was found that AAL3/4 was more complex than necessary to support computer-generated traffic.

Clearly much of the traffic generated by distributed simulations for virtual environments is delay sensitive. The amount of data transmitted at one time depends on the amount of state information that is changed, which in turn depends on how much activity there is in the portion of the virtual environment managed by the processor generating the traffic. Since the volume of data often varies from one message to the next, much of the traffic generated in a distributed simulation best fits the AAL2 category. On the other hand, uncompressed video or voice traffic transmitted during the exercise would fall into the AAL1 category. Still other traffic such as generation of message logs for afteraction review of the simulation is not delay sensitive and fits best into the AAL3/4 or AAL5 categories.

8.4.3 Internetworking and Internet Protocols

A wide variety of different networking technologies and protocols have been developed, each with different advantages and disadvantages. Many are in use today. The idea in internetworking is to be able to link together different types of networks to form a "network of networks" that appears to users as a single network. In this way, users connected to an Ethernet LAN can communicate with users connected to a token ring as if they were together on a single network. By convention, internetworking (with a lower case "i") refers to the practice of hooking together different networking technologies to create a new network, and the Internet (upper case "I") refers to the global network of networks in widespread use today.

One approach to internetworking is to use common higher-level protocols while allowing different subnetworks to utilize (as they must) different lower layers in the protocol stack. This is the approach used in the Internet. Specifically, the Internet uses the Internet Protocol (IP) developed by the U.S. Department of Defense at level 3 in the OSI reference model. IP is a connectionless protocol where the standard unit of data transmitted through the network is a datagram. To connect a new networking technology (e.g., ATM) to the Internet, one need only define how to encapsulate IP datagrams into that technology's framing protocol (cells, in the case of ATM), and specify a way of mapping IP network addresses to the addressing scheme used in that network (ATM addresses).

Separate subnetworks are connected through IP routers. For example, an Ethernet and ATM network connected by an IP router is shown in Figure 8.6(*a*). If host *A* on the Ethernet wishes to send a message to host *B* on the ATM network, the message is encapsulated into an IP datagram at host *A* and then placed into an Ethernet frame and sent to the router using Ethernet's CSMA/CD protocol, discussed earlier. The router extracts the datagram from the Ethernet and encapsulates it into ATM cells

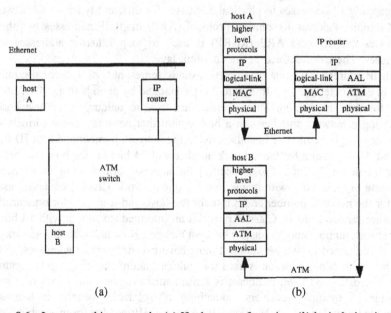

(a)   (b)

Figure 8.6   Internetworking example. (*a*) Hardware configuration; (*b*) logical view in terms of the protocol stacks.

that are then sent to host B through the ATM switch. Host B then recovers the datagram from the cells and passes it up to the user using higher-level protocols. A logical view of this operation in terms of the protocol stacks is shown in Figure 8.6(b).

More generally, a message may have to traverse several subnetworks before reaching its final destination. Thus a principal task for each router is to select the next router in the path to reaching the final destination. Each router maintains tables that indicate which direction to route datagrams, based on its IP address. Routers also communicate with other routers to try to maintain the best paths through the Internet by routing message around failed components and congested areas.

The suite of Internet protocols is the most popular in use today. It is an open standard governed by the Internet Engineering Task Force (IETF). The protocol stack consists of five layers, with several protocols defined within each layer, affording one the ability to pick and choose the protocol that best fits one's application. These protocols cover the physical, data link, network, transport, and application layers of the OSI reference model, or levels 1 through 4, and level 7.

Level 1: Internet Physical Layer   The internetworking concept suggests many different physical layer protocols, and indeed, many different physical layer protocols defined today use the Internet protocol stack. Ethernet is perhaps the most popular among users connected to a LAN. SLIP (Serial Line Internet Protocol) is used for serial lines, such as home access to the Internet via personal computers. Token ring protocols are also used, as well as many others.

Level 2: Data Link Layer   As mentioned earlier, standard protocols are needed for mapping IP addresses to physical addresses for different types of subnetworks. For example, Address Resolution Protocol (ARP) maps IP addresses to Ethernet addresses and Reverse ARP (RARP) is used to map Ethernet addresses to IP addresses. These are defined in the data link layer.

An IP address is 32 bits or 4 octets, usually represented as 4 decimal numbers, one for each octet (ranging from 0 to 255), separated by periods (e.g., 194.72.6.57). Four formats are defined. Three formats are used to uniquely specify a host by indicating a network number and a host within that network. These formats vary according to the number of bits allocated to the network number and host ID fields. Format A uses 7 bits for the network number and 24 bits for the host number (the other bit in the 32 bit address specifies the address format being used), accommodating organizations with many hosts on one network. Class C addresses use 21 bits for the network number and 8 bits for the host, and it is used for organizations requiring far fewer hosts. Class B provides an intermediate format with 14 bits for the network number and 16 bits for the host number. Note that with this scheme, if a host is connected to two networks, it must have two different IP addresses.

The fourth address format is used for multicast addresses for group communications. As discussed later, multicast is a mechanism to transmit copies of a single message to multiple receivers, something of particular benefit in large-scale distributed simulations. A Multicast Backbone (MBone) has been established on the Internet that is used for group communications.

Level 3: Network Layer   Three network layer protocols are defined. In addition to IP, two other protocols called ICMP (Internet Control Message Protocol) and IGMP (Internet Group Multicast Protocol) are defined. ICMP is used to send control messages between routers and hosts, such as to implement flow control and to indicate errors. IGMP is used for multicasting.

IP provides best effort delivery of datagrams to a host. Datagrams may be lost or corrupted before reaching their destination. No ordering guarantees are made concerning delivery; that is, datagrams do not need to be received in the same order in which they were sent. A Checksum is used in the datagram header, but none is provided for the data.

When IP is passed data to send, it adds a message header that includes the destination's IP address. If necessary, the datagram is broken up into IP packets, and the packets are sent separately to the destination. The receiver must collect the packets and reassemble the datagram before delivering it to the receiver.

Level 4: Transport Layer   Two transport layer protocols are defined, UDP (User Datagram Protocol) and TCP (Transport Control Protocol). These are sometimes denoted TCP/IP and UDP/IP to designate that the protocols operate using IP at the network layer.

IP provides delivery to a host computer. Both UDP and TCP provide for delivery to an application on the host. This is done be defining source and destination ports (designated by a 16 bit port number) within the host to uniquely identify the application. UDP does not provide much else besides application addressing beyond what IP provides. Specifically, delivery is unreliable and unordered.

On the other hand, TCP does provide a connection-oriented, reliable, ordered delivery service. It effectively provides a stream of bytes between applications. Reliable delivery means that the data will be delivered or an error will be flagged. Message acknowledgments are used to detect lost data. If an acknowledgment is not received after a certain time-out period, it must be retransmitted. Sequence numbers are used to order data.

Level 5: Application Layer   Several application protocols are defined at the top of the protocol stack. Some well-known protocols include File Transfer Protocol (FTP) and Trivial File Transfer Protocol (TFTP) for transferring files between remote hosts, TELNET for creating a login session on a remote host, Simple Mail Transfer Protocol (SMTP) for exchanging electronic mail, and Domain Name Service (DNS) which provides services for mapping easier to remember symbolic host names such as cc.gatech.edu to IP addresses.

8.5   GROUP COMMUNICATION

The discussion thus far has focused on point-to-point or unicast communication where there is one sender and one receiver of each message. Of particular interest to DVE applications are group communication facilities. For example, if a player in a

DVE moves to a new position, each of the other players that can "see" that the mobile player should be sent a message. Here, we describe the communication facilities that are often provided to support group communications. Later, we describe data distribution mechanisms to utilize these group communication facilities in DVE applications.

8.5.1 Groups and Group Communication Primitives

A group is a set of processes, or here, simulators, such that each receives a copy of every message sent to the group. Open groups are groups where the sender need not be a member of the group to send a message to the group. Closed groups only allow simulators that are part of the group to send a message to the group.

Groups may dynamically expand and contract during the execution of the distributed simulation. For example, if a vehicle moves to a position that makes it visible to another player, the latter should be added to the group to which the vehicle simulator is publishing position updates so that it can receive updates concerning the vehicle's position. A *join* operation is used to add a simulator to a group. Conversely, a *leave* operation is used to delete someone from a group. Minimally the group communications facilities will provide primitives to create, destroy, join, leave, and send a message to the group.

Separate send and receive primitives may be defined for group communications. Alternatively, the same primitives used for point-to-point communication may be used, with separate group destination addresses defined to distinguish between point-to-point and group communication.

An addressing scheme is required to uniquely identify the group on join, leave, send, and receive operations. This address may be an internal representation of the group address, such as a network multicast address used to implement the group. In addition an ASCII name is also often used. Assuming that groups are assigned unique names, a name server process can then be used to convert the ASCII address to the internal representation of the group address.

8.5.2 Transport Mechanisms

The actual mechanism used to transport messages to the simulators in the group depends on the mechanisms provided by the underlying network. In particular, group communication can be implemented by the following mechanisms:

- *Unicast.* Separate point-to-point communications are used to send messages to destinations in the group.
- *Broadcast.* If the underlying network provides an efficient broadcast medium, the message can be broadcast to all simulators, and destinations not in the group discard the message.
- *Multicast.* The network provides a mechanism to only deliver messages to members of the multicast group. This is often accomplished by constructing a

spanning tree that controls the generation and distribution of copies of the message among the members of the group. Alternatively, a flooding/pruning mechanism may be used where intermediate network nodes retransmit copies of incoming messages on outgoing links according to certain rules that guarantee distribution to all destination nodes but economize on bandwidth usage.

Broadcast was used in Simnet and many DIS systems. This is adequate for small systems, but it does not scale because communication increases by $O(N^2)$ for N simulators. In current systems the principal limitation is the amount of CPU time required to receive, examine, and discard messages that are not relevant to the local simulator.

Large-scale DVEs being constructed today usually use either multicast communication or unicast to implement group communication. At the time of this writing, unicast is typically used when reliable communication is required because reliable multicast is still an active research area. Multicast is often used when best-effort communication is adequate.

8.6 DATA DISTRIBUTION

Whatever communication facility is provided by the underlying network, some strategy must be developed to efficiently distribute state information among the simulators. The software in the distributed simulation executive to control this distribution of information is referred to as the data distribution (DD) system. The task of the DD software is to provide efficient, convenient to use services to ensure that each simulator receives all of the messages relevant to it, and ideally, no others.

8.6.1 Interface to the Data Distribution System

Whenever a simulator performs some action that may be of interest to other simulators, such as moving an entity to a new location, a message is generated. Some means is required to specify which other simulators should receive a copy of this message. Specifically, the distributed simulation executive must provide mechanisms for the simulators to describe both the information it is producing, and the information it is interested in receiving. Based on these specifications, the executive must then determine which simulators should receive what messages.

This situation is not unlike that in Internet newsgroups. Users express what information they are interested in receiving by subscribing to specific newsgroups. The information that is being published is described by the newsgroup(s) to which it is sent. For example, a recipe for a new cake would be published to a cooking newsgroup and not one concerning the weather. The newsgroup names are critical because they provide a common vocabulary for users to characterize both the information being published and the information they are interested in receiving.

The set of newsgroup names defines a *name space*, which is a common vocabulary used to describe data and to express interests. Each user provides an *interest expression* that specifies a subset of the name space, which is a list of newsgroups, that indicates what information the user is interested in receiving. A *description expression*, again a subset of the name space, is associated with each message that describes the contents of the message. Logically the software managing the newsgroups matches the description expression of each message with the interest expression of each user. If the two overlap (i.e., have at least one element of the name space in common), the message is sent to that user.

The newsgroup analogy is useful to specify how information should be disseminated in a DVE. There are three basic concepts:

- *Name space.* The name space is a set of values used to express interests and to describe information. The name space is a set of tuples $(V_1, V_2, \ldots, V_N)$ where each V_i is a value of some basic type, or another tuple. For example, a simulator modeling a radar might indicate it is interested in receiving a message whenever the location of any aircraft within one mile of the radar changes. The name space could be defined as a tuple (V_1, V_2), where V_1 is an enumerated type specifying the different types of vehicles in the DVE (for example, truck, aircraft, and ship), and V_2 is a tuple specifying the X and Y coordinate positions of a vehicle.

- *Interest expressions.* An interest expression provides the language by which the simulator specifies what information it is interested in receiving. An interest expression defines some subset of the name space. For example, the interest expression for all aircraft within 1 mile of location (X_0, Y_0) is all tuples (aircraft, (X, Y)) such that $(X_0 - X)^2 + (Y_0 - Y)^2 < 1$.

- *Description expressions.* A description expression is associated with each message. It specifies a subset of the name space that characterizes the contents of the message. For example, a simulator modeling an aircraft moving to location (151, 211) may generate a message indicating this is its new position, with description expression (aircraft, (151, 211)). Each simulator with an interest expression containing this point in the name space will receive the message.

The name space, interest expressions, and description expressions define the heart of the interface to the DD mechanisms. The DD software must map this interface to the primitives provided by the communication facilities such as joining, leaving, and sending messages to multicast groups. The challenging aspect of the DD interface is defining abstractions that are both convenient for the modeler to use, and provide an efficient realization using standard communication primitives. DD interfaces that are similar to basic communications primitives lend themselves to straightforward implementation but may be difficult for modelers to use. On the other hand, higher-level mechanisms such as those described above to specify the radar simulator's interests may be difficult to implement, leading to slow and/or inefficient mechanisms.

In the radar example the name space was defined in terms of the actual data fields of the message; that is, the position attributes of entities were used to define part of the name space. In general, the name space need not be defined directly in terms of the message's data fields. Instead, it may be defined to be completely distinct from the simulation state. For example, in the High-Level Architecture, a separate abstraction called *routing spaces* is used to define the name space. Separating the name space from the data within the message offers the advantage that it separates two different concerns, the state information necessary to model the virtual environment and the specification of the DD mechanisms in order to ensure efficient data distribution. Separating these concerns allows the simulator to more easily manipulate the DD mechanisms in order to ensure efficient realization. For example, if join and leave operations are time-consuming in the underlying implementation, one might define the interest and description expressions in a way that reduces the frequency that these operations will have to be invoked. If the name space is separate from the entity attributes in the simulation, this may be accomplished with minimal impact on the simulation model.

It is worth noting that although spatial proximity of simulated entities in the virtual world is an important criterion for data distribution, it is not the only one of practical interest. For example, if the virtual environment includes radio transmissions, the frequency to which a transmitter is tuned may be used to derive interest expressions. Thus, while physical proximity is a useful example to illustrate these concepts, it may be inappropriate to design the data distribution system to rely on properties that are only relevant in the context of physical distances.

Finally the interface to the DD system may also include some means for allowing a simulator to discover or forget entities in the DVE. For example, when a radar is switched on, the simulator modeling the radar must discover those vehicles within range. Similarly, when a vehicle moves out of range, it must become invisible (i.e., forgotten) by the radar simulator. This is equivalent to providing notifications to the simulator whenever it becomes eligible or ineligible to receive messages from another simulator. This can be realized by associating a set of description expressions characterizing the data that *could* be produced by that simulator in the future. By matching the interest expressions of a simulator with these *possible description expressions* of other simulators one can determine when a simulator is eligible or ineligible to receive messages from another simulator. Changes to either the set of possible description expressions or a simulator's interest expressions could result in entities becoming discovered or forgotten.

8.6.2 Example: Data Distribution in the High Level Architecture

To illustrate these concepts, consider the interface to the data distribution system in version 1.3 of the High Level Architecture (Defense Modeling and Simulation Office 1998). The HLA provides two mechanisms for controlling the distribution of data:

1. Class-based data distribution.
2. Value-based data distribution via routing spaces.

The name space consists of the tuple (V_1, V_2) where V_1 enumerates all object class/attribute pairs specified in the federation object model (FOM), and V_2 enumerates the routing spaces that are defined by the federation.

Class-Based Data Distribution

Recall that in the HLA the federation must define a FOM that specifies the classes of objects of common interest to the federation. The FOM specifies a hierarchy indicating object classes and their interrelationships, and object attributes. For example, a class may be defined called *vehicle*, with separate subclasses called *aircraft, tank,* and *truck*. These class definitions are used for data distribution. Specifically, each federate invokes the *Subscribe Object Class Attributes* service to indicate it is to receive notification of updates to attributes of a specific class in the class hierarchy tree. For example, a federate might invoke this service to subscribe to the *position* attribute of the *vehicle* class to be notified whenever a vehicle's location is updated.

Each attribute defined within a class is automatically inherited by the subclasses derived from that class. For example, the *aircraft* subclass inherits the *position* attribute defined in the *vehicle* class. Recall that when a federate subscribes to an attribute in the class hierarchy tree, it automatically subscribes to that attribute inherited by the subclasses in the subtree rooted at that class. Thus a subscription to the *position* attribute of the *vehicle* class will cause the federate to be notified whenever the *position* attribute of any *aircraft, tank,* or *truck* object is modified via the *Update Attribute Values* service.

In the class-based data distribution scheme the name space is the set of ⟨class, attribute⟩ tuples, specified in the FOM. In our simple example, the name space consists of the tuples ⟨*vehicle, position*⟩, ⟨*aircraft, position*⟩, ⟨*tank, position*⟩, and ⟨*truck,* position⟩. Class-based data distribution can be realized as follows: A subscription to an attribute A within class C becomes an interest expression enumerating a set of tuples ⟨C_0, A⟩, ⟨C_1, A⟩, ⟨C_2, A⟩, ..., ⟨C_N, A⟩ where $C_0 = C$ and C_i ($i = 1, 2, ..., N$) are the subclasses (and subclasses of these subclasses, etc.) of C. For example, a subscription to ⟨*vehicle, position*⟩ turns into the interest expression ⟨*vehicle, position*⟩, ⟨*aircraft, position*⟩, ⟨*tank,* position⟩, and ⟨*truck, position*⟩. The description expression for an update to attribute A of an object of class C is simply ⟨C, A⟩, such as ⟨*tank, position*⟩ when the position of a tank object is updated. Federates subscribed to ⟨*vehicle, position*⟩ and ⟨*tank, position*⟩ will be notified of this update because their interest expressions overlap with the description expression, but those only subscribed to ⟨*aircraft, position*⟩ and/or ⟨*truck, position*⟩ will not.

This approach to defining interest and description expressions is not unique. An alternative approach that yields the same results is to define a subscription to attribute A of class C as an interest expression containing a *single tuple* ⟨C, A⟩. An update to attribute A of class C carries a description expression ⟨C_0, A⟩, ⟨C_1, A⟩,

$\langle C_2, A \rangle, \ldots, \langle C_N, A \rangle$, where $C_0 = C$ and C_i $(i = 1, 2, \ldots, N)$ are the classes along the path from C up the class hierarchy tree to the class where A was originally defined, that is, not inherited. Here, a subscription to $\langle vehicle, position \rangle$ turns into the interest expression $\langle vehicle, position \rangle$. An update to the position attribute of a tank object contains the description expression $\langle tank, position \rangle$, $\langle vehicle, position \rangle$. Again, federates subscribed to $\langle vehicle, position \rangle$ and $\langle tank, position \rangle$ will be notified of this update, but those only subscribed to $\langle aircraft, position \rangle$ and/or $\langle truck, position \rangle$ will not.

Class-based data distribution allows a federate to subscribe to, for example, all aircraft objects. It does not provide the ability to discriminate based on values computed during the federation execution. For example, class-based distribution does not allow a federate to specify that it is only interested in aircraft within 10 miles of its current location. Routing spaces are provided for this purpose. The central distinction between these two mechanisms is the name space in class-based data distribution only includes information that is known prior to the execution of the federation, so class-based distribution can only distinguish between statically defined characteristics of objects. On the other hand, routing spaces extend the name space to include information computed during the execution, thereby allowing federates to discriminate based on dynamic information. For this reason the routing space mechanism is sometimes referred to as *value-based data distribution*.

Routing Spaces Routing spaces are an abstraction defined separately from objects and attributes, solely for the purpose of data distribution. A routing space is a multidimensional coordinate system. The name space for a single N-dimensional routing space is a tuple $(X_1, X_2, \ldots, X_N)$ with $X_{min} \leq X_i \leq X_{max}$, where X_{min} and X_{max} are federation-defined values. For example, Figure 8.7 shows a two-dimensional routing space with axis values ranging from 0.0 to 1.0. The relationship of the routing space to elements of the virtual environment is left to the federation designers. For example, a two-dimensional routing space might be used to represent the geographical area covered by the virtual environment; however, the data distribution software is not aware of this interpretation.

Interest and description expressions in the HLA define areas,[30] called *regions*, of a routing space. Specifically, each region is a set of one or more *extents*, where each extent is a rectangular N-dimensional area defined within the N-dimensional routing space. Four extents are shown in Figure 8.7. Each extent is specified as a sequence of N ranges $(R_1, R_2, \ldots, R_N)$, where range R_i is an interval along dimension i of the routing space. For example, the extent labeled S1 in Figure 8.7 is denoted ([0.1, 0.5], [0.2, 0.5]), using the convention R_1 corresponds to the horizontal axis, and R_2 corresponds to the vertical axis.

A region is the union of the set of points in the routing space covered by its extents. Interest expressions are referred to as *subscription regions*, and description expressions are referred to as *update regions*. For example, the routing space in

---

[30] Areas are line segments in one-dimensional routing spaces, volumes for three or more dimensional spaces.

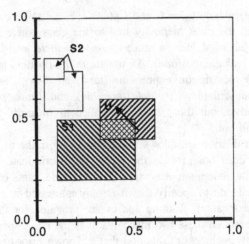

Figure 8.7 Update region U and subscription regions S1 and S2 in a two-dimensional routing space.

Figure 8.7 includes one update region U and two subscription regions S1 and S2. S1 includes a single extent, and S2 consists of two extents. The extents defining a single region need not overlap.

Each federate can qualify a subscription to an object class by associating a subscription region with the subscription, for example to only get updates for vehicles within a certain portion of the routing space. Similarly an update region may be associated with each instance of an object. If a federate's subscription region for an object class overlaps with the update region associated with the instance of the object being modified, then a message is sent to the federate.

For example, suppose the routing space in Figure 8.7 corresponds to the geographic area (i.e., the playbox) of a virtual environment that includes moving vehicles. Suppose that the update region U is associated with an aircraft object that contains attributes indicating the aircraft's position. The region defined by U indicates the aircraft is within this portion of the playbox. Suppose that S1 and S2 are the subscription regions created by two distinct federates F1 and F2, each modeling a sensor. The extents of these subscription regions are set to encompass all areas that the sensors can reach. If the aircraft moves to a new position within U, thereby updating its position attribute, a message will be sent to F1 because its subscription region S1 overlaps with U, but no message will be sent to F2 whose subscription region does not overlap with U.

This example illustrates that certain compromises must usually be made in defining a DD system. First, the range of the sensors is in general, not a collection of rectangular areas. In principal, one can approximate any area with many such rectangles, but this may degrade the performance of the DD system, offsetting the advantage of using routing spaces at all. Thus federates may receive some messages corresponding to positions the sensor cannot detect, so the sensor federate must check incoming messages and discard those that are not relevant to it. The advantage of using rectangular regions is it simplifies the implementation of the data distribution mechanism without requiring the RTI to understand the semantics of the simulation models.

Further the update region only specifies that the aircraft is *somewhere* within that region, but does not pinpoint its exact location. In particular, the aircraft may lie in the part of *U* that *does not overlap with S1*. In this case the sensor federate will receive a message, even though the aircraft cannot be detected by the sensor. Again, the federate must filter incoming messages and discard the ones that are not relevant.

One could achieve more precise filtering by reducing the size of the update region, for example the update region might be defined as a single point that is modified each time the aircraft's position is updated. However, this introduces other difficulties. Successive updates may lie outside the subscription region, although the path of the aircraft actually passes within range of the sensor. This is illustrated by the arrow within the update region in Figure 8.7; the head and tail of the arrow indicate successive position updates, and the line segment indicates its path. If the update region were a point that is modified with each position update, the sensor federate would not be notified of the aircraft's position because its update region never actually intersects the subscription region. To avoid this problem, the aircraft's update region at any instant in the execution should include at least all positions the aircraft could occupy from the most recent to the next position that will be reported by the aircraft simulator.

Definition of subscription regions also involves certain compromises, particularly if the subscription region changes, as would be the case for a sensor mounted on a moving vehicle. Changing a subscription region can be a time consuming operation involving joining and leaving multicast groups, as will be seen momentarily. Defining large subscription regions will result in less frequent region modifications, but will result in the federate receiving more messages that are not relevant to it. Small regions yield more precise filtering but more frequent changes. The region size should be set to strike a balance between these two extremes.

Finally the HLA interface includes services for notifying when an object becomes discovered or forgotten. The latter is called *undiscovery* in HLA terminology. In this regard, update regions serve a dual role as defining both the *possible description expression* as well as the description expressions themselves. An object instance becomes discovered by a federate when its update region overlaps with the federate's subscription region (and no overlap existed previously). The object is undiscovered when one or both regions are modified, resulting in no overlap when there previously was overlap.

8.6.3 Implementation Issues

The data distribution software must map the name space, interest expressions, and description expressions to the communications services provided by the underlying network. Here, we will assume a group communication facility is available. Even if the underlying network does not support group communications, this provides a convenient abstraction that can be built on top of a unicast facility.

Implementing the data distribution mechanism requires one to do the following:

1. Map the name space to multicast groups; here, we assume each point in the name space maps to a single group.
2. Convert each interest expression, which expresses a subset of the name space, to one or more groups according to the mapping defined in (1); the simulator declaring the interest expression must subscribe to these groups.
3. Convert each description expression to a set of groups according to the mapping defined in (1); messages should be sent to these groups.

To illustrate this approach, consider an implementation of a data distribution system for the HLA routing space approach. To simplify the discussion, we only consider a single routing space, and ignore class-based data distribution. The routing space defines a name space. One can partition the routing space into a checkerboard grid and assign each grid sector to a different multicast group. For example, in Figure 8.8 the routing space is partitioned into 25 grid cells. Federate F1 subscribes to groups 6, 7, 8, 11, 12, and 13 because these groups include portions of the name space specified by F1s subscription region (interest expression) S1. Similarly F2 subscribes to 11, 12, 16, and 17, corresponding to region S2. When an attribute is updated that is associated with publication region (description expression) U, a message is sent to multicast groups 12 and 13.

This approach will guarantee that each federate will receive all information that it had requested via its interest expressions. However, federates may receive additional messages:

1. A federate may receive messages, even though its subscription region did not overlap with the publication region. For example, in Figure 8.8 F2 will receive

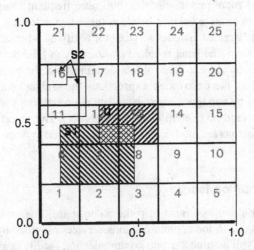

Figure 8.8   Example mapping an HLA routing space, subscription regions, and publication regions to multicast groups.

a message sent with publication region U because U posts a message to multicast group 12, and F2 is subscribed to that group.

2. A federate may receive multiple copies of the same message. For example, federate F1 will receive two copies of the message, one via group 12 and a second via group 13.

These duplicate messages can be eliminated at the receiver by checking that the update and subscription regions overlap.

Extra messages such as those described above are not unique to this particular example. In the first case, a simulator receives a message even though its interest expression does not overlap with the message's description expression. This can happen whenever the part of the name space covered by a multicast group overlaps with the interest (description) expression and part of it does not. For example, it can be seen in Figure 8.8 that part of the name space corresponding to multicast group 12 includes portions of F2 (U), but parts do not. More precisely, let N_i be the part of the name space covered by the interest expression, let N_d be the part of the name space covered by the description expression, and N_g the part covered by the multicast group. The simulator could receive messages outside of its interest expression if

1. the interest expression overlaps with the group ($N_i \cap N_g \neq \varnothing$) and
2. the description expression overlaps with the group ($N_d \cap N_g \neq \varnothing$), but
3. the interest expression does not overlap with the description expression ($N_i \cap N_d = \varnothing$).

Further a simulator may receive duplicate copies of messages if the intersection of its interest expression and the description expression used to send the message spans more than one multicast group. In other words if there exist two multicast groups covering portions of the the name space N_{g1} and N_{g2}, where

1. $N_i \cap N_{g1} \neq \varnothing$ and $N_d \cap N_{g1} \neq \varnothing$, and
2. $N_i \cap N_{g2} \neq \varnothing$ and $N_d \cap N_{g2} \neq \varnothing$,

then duplicate messages will be received.

Extra messages result from an imperfect mapping of the name space to multicast groups where part of the name space covered by a group lies within the interest/description expression, and part does not. One could eliminate these messages by requiring interest and description expressions to be defined so that each maps to exactly the name space covered by a single group (for example, one might constrain each routing region to cover exactly one grid cell in Fig. 8.8). This does not really solve the problem. In practice, the simulator would still receive unwanted messages because its desired interest and declaration expressions most likely do not exactly match the group definitions.

Finally one remaining aspect concerns the operations that must be performed when a simulator's interest expressions change (for example, as the result of a simulator for a sensor moving to a new location). This will, in general, result in the simulator leaving certain multicast groups, and joining others. The steps required to realize this change are as follows:

1. Identify the multicast groups that cover the portion of the name space specified by the new interest expression. Let G_{new} be the set of groups that cover the new interest expression. Let G_{old} be the set of groups covered by the old interest expression.
2. Issue a join operation to add the simulator to each group in the set $G_{new} - G_{old}$.
3. Issue a leave operation to remove the simulator from each group in the set $G_{old} - G_{new}$.

For example, Figure 8.9 depicts a situation where the subscription region of a federate changes. The new region includes multicast groups 13, 21, 27, 28, and 29 which were not included in the previous region, so joins must be issued for these groups. Similarly leave operations must be issued for groups 2, 3, 4, 10, and 18.

8.6.4   Dynamic Group Management

A challenging task in designing the data distribution mechanism is to define an effective mapping of the name space to the available multicast groups. Thus far we have been assuming this mapping was static, namely it does not change during the

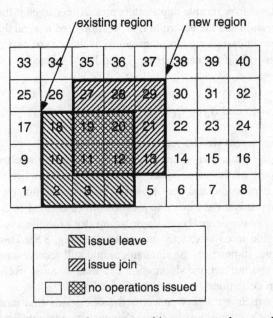

Figure 8.9 Example illustrating changes to multicast groups when a subscription region changes.

execution of the distributed simulation. A static approach is simple, and straightforward to implement. The disadvantage of this approach is it can lead to certain inefficiencies, particularly if the number of groups supported by the underlying communication services is limited.

In many networks only a limited number of multicast groups are available. The distributed simulation executive must make effective use of the groups that are provided. Approaches such as the static grid scheme discussed above may not make efficient use of the groups. For example, it is often the case that entities in the virtual environment are not uniformly distributed across the playbox but rather are clustered in certain "hot spots." For example, areas of the virtual environment containing mountainous terrain are unlikely to contain many land vehicles. Other areas where intensive activities are occurring, such as combat in a military DVE, may contain many entities. Thus multicast groups in "quiet" areas of the virtual environment where few state updates occur will be underutilized, while those in "busy" areas will see heavy use.

Dynamic group management schemes change the mapping of the name space to the multicast groups during the execution of the simulation in order to achieve more efficient usage of the groups. This is not unlike utilizing a personal address book that can hold only a limited number of entries. Just as the personal address book provides fast access relative to a general telephone directory, but can include information for only a small number of people, multicast groups provide more efficient communications but are in limited supply. The goal of the group management system is to reserve allocation of groups to only those portions of the name space that are heavily utilized, such as portions of the name space carrying a large amount of traffic. For example, using the grid-based scheme described earlier in the HLA, one might map those cells of the grid containing the most messages to the available multicast groups, and implement communication in other grid cells using some other (i.e., unicast or broadcast) mechanism. If a cell assigned to a group becomes underutilized, the group can be reallocated to another cell with a higher level of activity, just as infrequently used entries in a personal address book can be erased and overwritten by more frequently referenced addresses. A policy is required to determine which addresses are kept in the address book (i.e., which sections of the name space are stored in multicast groups).

As with the address book scheme, changing the mapping of the name space to groups does incur a certain amount of overhead computation. Remapping a group to another grid cell (or, more generally, to another portion of the name space) requires simulators that are subscribed to the remapped group to leave, and simulators with interest expressions overlapping the part of the new name space assigned to the group to join. Thus care must be taken to ensure that the overhead of remapping the multicast group does not exceed the benefit.

8.6.5 Wide-Area Viewers and Fast-Moving Entities

Another challenge associated with efficient utilization of multicast groups is the so-called wide-area viewer problem. A wide-area viewer is a simulator that can "see" large portions of the virtual environment, though usually not in great detail. For example, aircraft can view much broader geographic areas than ground vehicles but typically require much less detailed information concerning each portion of its viewing area than entities with a much narrower field of view. In using grid structures such as that described earlier for the HLA, wide-area viewers will have interest expressions spanning large portions of the name space. The viewer will have to join many multicast groups and receive large quantities of information, much of which will be discarded because the viewer often will not be able to utilize so much detailed information.

A solution to the wide-area viewer problem is to cover the playbox with multiple grids of different resolutions. For example, in addition to the five-by-five grid shown in Figure 8.8, another routing space might be established using a coarser, two-by-two grid structure. Less detailed information could be published using description expressions that refer to the routing space with the coarse structure. For example, position updates might be generated less frequently than on the original routing space. Interest expressions for wide-area viewers would refer to the coarse routing space in order to obtain less detailed information of the entities.

A related problem concerns rapidly moving entities, such as high-speed aircraft. The interest expressions for such entities may change very rapidly. This can place high demands on the data distribution and network communication software, especially if the data distribution software is also remapping groups, because joins and leaves to multicast groups are often time-consuming operations.

Coarse grid schemes also help solve the fast-moving entity problem. Because the multicast groups cover a broader portion of the name space, as the fast-moving entity changes its interest expression, each change will usually result in less frequent join and leave operations.

Another approach to dealing with fast-moving entities is to use a lookahead prediction scheme. This is essentially a latency hiding technique where one issues join operations in advance so that they will be completed by the time the entity actually moves into a new area of the playbox. For example, suppose that an entity in Figure 8.8 currently has a subscription region covering grid cell 2 and is moving directly east. It can subscribe to the information in grid cell 3 before actually entering that cell, in anticipation of its entry in the not too distant future. The subscription must be issued far enough in advance so that it is in place before the entity actually moves into cell 3. Once the entity moves into cell 3, it can drop its subscription to cell 2.

8.7   SUMMARY

The DVE must ensure a suitable view of the virtual world is maintained for each participant. The network providing communication services plays a critical role in realization of this function. DVEs, especially large-scale DVEs containing many participants, present very challenging requirements with respect to latency, jitter, bandwidth, and reliability. These requirements coupled with the dynamic, rapidly changing communication interconnectivity among participants distinguish DVEs from more traditional networking applications such as data and telephone communications or even more recent multimedia applications such as teleconferencing and video on demand.

This chapter examined networking technologies and how they affect the design of DVEs. Techniques such as circuit switching and time division multiplexing are well suited for transmitting continuous streams of traffic while guaranteeing fulfillment of latency and jitter requirements. Packet switching and statistical multiplexing enable efficient transmission of bursty traffic. DVEs often require both of these types of traffic. Technologies such as ATM, which are designed to efficiently handle both traffic types on a single networking, infrastructure may provide the best solution for DVEs.

Protocol stacks provide a useful means of organizing the functionality realized in modern networks. Because DVEs must often rely on commercially available networking technology not designed specifically for DVEs, stacks such as ATM and the Internet Protocol are often used to implement DVEs today. Group communications provide a particularly useful service and are essential for large DVEs.

The DVE must include data distribution software above the communication layer to ensure that each participant receives updates to the state of the virtual world that are relevant to it. Interest expressions are used to specify what information is relevant to each participant, and data description expressions characterize the information being generated. A name space provides the vocabulary for these expressions. Developing an efficient realization of the data distribution system can be a challenging task, trading off efficiency with ease of use. In practice, compromises must often be made to define a data distribution system that is both efficient and provides sufficient expressiveness in defining interest and description expressions.

8.8 ADDITIONAL READINGS

There are several excellent textbooks devoted to computer networks. Some examples are Partridge (1993), Tanenbaum (1996), and Walrand and Varaiya (1996). Several other books discuss networks in the context of distributed operating systems, such as Tanenbaum (1994), Sinha (1996), and Chow and Johnson (1997). Network requirements for DIS are discussed in Pullen and Wood (1995) as well as in IEEE Std 1278.2-1995 (1995). The architecture of NPSNet for realizing large-scale DVEs is described in Macedonia, Zyda et al. (1995). Surveys of group communications and local area networks are presented in Diot, Dabbous et al. (1997) and Abeysundara and Kamal (1991), respectively.

Several data distribution management (DD) mechanisms are described in Morse (1996). Data distribution based on routing spaces was used in the Synthetic Theater of War (STOW) program (Van Hook, Calvin et al. 1994), a large-scale military training exercise resulting in a demonstration conducted in the fall of 1997. Use of routing spaces in the HLA is described in Defense Modeling and Simulation Office (1996). Another approach to data distribution used in the Joint Precision Strike Demonstration is to define interest expressions as predicates on entity attributes

(Powell, Mellon et al. 1996). Gridding schemes have long been used for military applications. Examples include ModSAF (Russo, Shuette et al. 1995), CCTT (Mastaglio and Callahan 1995), and NPSNET (Macedonia, Zyda et al. 1995). Approaches to ensure proper time synchronization of the data distribution mechanism (discussed in Part II of this book) are described in Steinman and Wieland (1994), Blanchard and Lake (1997), and Tacic and Fujimoto (1997).

CHAPTER 9

Time Management and Event Ordering

The goal of the data distribution system is to ensure that the simulators perceive a common view of the virtual environment. Some differences in the views perceived by different simulators is permissible, so long as they do not compromise the objectives of the DVE, whether it be effective training or satisfied customers in an entertainment system. The goal of the time management system in the DVE is to ensure that participants perceive a common view of temporal aspects of the DVE. For example, it may be important for two participants observing a common set of events to perceive them in the same sequence.

9.1 THE PROBLEM

To illustrate why a DVE might need a time management system, consider a collection of real-time simulators interconnected via a network. Each simulator sends messages to the other simulators when it performs some action of interest to the other simulators. Consider a scenario involving three simulators in a simulated battlefield, a tank, a target, and a command post containing observers monitoring engagements (see Fig. 9.1). Suppose that the tank fires on the target, causing it to be destroyed, while the observers watch this engagement. In the distributed simulator this engagement unfolds by the tank simulator first generating a message indicating that it is firing upon the target. This message is sent to both the target and the observer simulators. Upon receiving this message, the target simulator models the detonation of the round, and determines that it has been destroyed. The target simulator then generates a new message indicating this fact. The observer simulator receives both the original tank-firing message and the target-destroyed message. However, suppose that the tank-firing message is delayed in the network, causing the observer simulator to receive the target-destroyed message first. In other words, the observer might see the target being destroyed before it sees that the tank has fired upon it!

This problem occurs because in the physical world, timing delays are governed by natural phenomena, such as the speed of light. However, in the simulated world, delays are affected by artificial phenomenon such as the latency a message

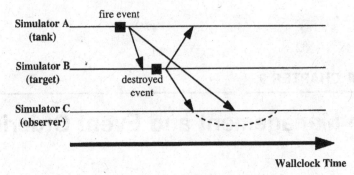

Figure 9.1 Scenario leading to a temporal anomaly. The anomaly can be eliminated by delaying delivery of the "destroyed" event to simulator *C*.

encounters as it is transmitted through the network. Thus timing relationships may be distorted in the simulated world, causing anomalies such as impossible orderings of events.

It may be noted that this problem is an instance of the synchronization problem that was studied in detail in Part II of this book, in the context of analytic simulation environments. Indeed, the synchronization algorithms described there are directly applicable to DVEs. However, it will be seen that other ordering mechanisms may be used to eliminate at least certain classes of temporal anomalies. The remainder of this chapter discusses these approaches, as well as the problem of synchronizing wallclock time across different simulators. In the discussions that follow, we assume that a reliable message delivery mechanism is used; in other words, every message that is sent is eventually delivered to its destination.

It is important to note that temporal anomalies may or may not represent a significant problem in a DVE. For example, it could be that the exchange described in Figure 9.1 happens so rapidly that the tank-firing and target-destroyed events appear to happen simultaneously, in which case it may be perfectly acceptable to display them in the incorrect order. Similarly, if these anomalies do not occur very frequently, and can be easily ignored by users of the system without compromising the goals of the DVE, the computation and communication resources required to eliminate them may not be justified. Indeed, most DVEs today do not provide protection against temporal anomalies.

On the other hand, a more serious problem is temporal anomalies may lead to divergence in different portions of the virtual environment. For example, if two simulators observe different orderings of the same set of events, they may attempt to evolve the virtual world in inconsistent ways, leading to impossible outcomes or other types of errors. An example illustrating this phenomenon will be described later. Thus a reasonable approach might be to use unordered communication services in situations where temporal anomalies cannot occur, or are not important, but to use some type of time management mechanism where ordering is important.

9.2 MESSAGE-ORDERING SERVICES

Here, we are concerned with ensuring the distributed simulation executive "correctly" orders messages before delivering them to each simulator. A message is said to be *sent* when a simulator invokes a primitive instructing the simulation executive to transmit a message, for example, invoking the Update Attribute Values service in the High Level Architecture. A message is *received* when it is passed to the distributed simulation executive at the destination, typically by the operating system. The message is said to be *delivered* when the simulation executive passes the message to the receiving simulator, such as invoking the Reflect Attribute Values service in the HLA. In general, messages received by the distributed simulation executive may not be deliverable until correct ordering can be guaranteed. Thus one disadvantage of ordering services is that they may introduce additional latency.

We next describe three different types of ordering services: causal order, causal and totally ordered (CATOCS), and time stamp order. The algorithms used to implement time stamp order are identical to those described in Chapters 3, 4, and 5. In particular, the conservative synchronization algorithms described in Chapter 3 are most relevant because they do not require each simulator to realize a rollback capability.

9.2.1 Causal Order

Causal ordering can be used to eliminate certain types of temporal anomalies. If the simulation executive can determine that there is a dependency between two events, it will ensure that these events are delivered to each simulator in an ordering consistent with the dependence relationships.

More precisely, causal ordering is based on Lamport's "happens before" relationship (Lamport 1978). The execution of each simulator[31] is viewed as an ordered sequence of actions. For example, execution of a single machine instruction can be viewed as an action. Two specific actions of particular interest are sending and receiving a message. The "happens before" relationship (denoted by an arrow, $\rightarrow$) is defined by the following rules:

1. If actions A and B occur in the same simulator, and A appears before B in the ordered sequence of actions within that simulator, then $A \rightarrow B$ (read "A happens before B"),
2. If A is a message send, and B is receiving the same message, then $A \rightarrow B$.
3. If $A \rightarrow B$, and $B \rightarrow C$, then $A \rightarrow C$ (transitivity).

For example, Figure 9.2 shows a space-time graph (where time is wallclock time) for three simulators. Each box represents an event, and each arc a message transmission. In this figure $E_1 \rightarrow E_2$, $E_2 \rightarrow E_4$, and by the transitive property

---

[31] More generally, causal ordering is usually defined for each process; however, we use the terms *process* and *simulator* synonymously here to simplify the discussion.

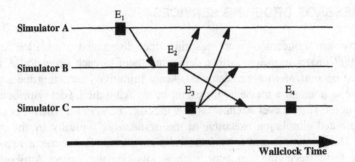

Figure 9.2 The "happens before" relationship. Here $E_1 \rightarrow E_4$, but E_1 and E_3 are concurrent events.

$E_1 \rightarrow E_4$. Intuitively, if there is a left-to-right path from an event E_x to another event E_y in the space-time graph, then $E_x \rightarrow E_y$. Two events that are not related by the $\rightarrow$ relationship (i.e., two events where no left-to-right path exists from one to the other) are referred to as *concurrent events*. In Figure 9.2, E_1 and E_3 are concurrent events. If there is a path between two events in the space-time graph, then this implies the first event might affect the second; that is, there is a potential dependence between these two events.

A causal order delivery service guarantees that if $E_1 \rightarrow E_2$, then each simulator receiving both messages will have E_1 delivered to it before E_2 is delivered. Concurrent events may be delivered to the simulator in any order.

It is important to note that the "happens before" relationship is independent of the semantic meaning of the events in the simulation. It is possible that E_1 and E_4 in Figure 9.2 are independent events that have no relationship to each other so far as the simulation is concerned. In this case the causal ordering mechanism will infer a causal relationship exists for the purpose of message ordering, even though none actually exists. Thus causal ordering may be overconservative in ensuring events are properly ordered.

The "happens before" relationship can be extended to describe relationships between messages. In particular (1) if a message M_1 is sent by a simulator before the same simulator sends another message M_2, then $M_1 \rightarrow M_2$; (2) if M_1 is delivered to a simulator before that simulator sends another message M_2, then $M_1 \rightarrow M_2$; (3) if $M_1 \rightarrow M_2$, and $M_2 \rightarrow M_3$, then $M_1 \rightarrow M_3$.

Causal ordering will eliminate temporal anomalies such as that shown in Figure 9.1. Specifically, because the tank-fires event happens before the target-destroyed event, the distributed simulation executive will delay delivery of the target destroyed event until after it has delivered the tank fired event. This is illustrated by the dashed line in Figure 9.1.

Causal order can be implemented for messages sent to a multicast group using a construct called a *vector clock*. Consider a closed group containing N simulators. Assign each simulator in the group a number $(1, 2, \ldots, N)$. Each simulator i maintains a vector of counters C_i where

1. $C_i[i] =$ the number of messages simulator i has sent to the group, and

2. $C_i[j]$ ($j \neq i$) indicates the number of group messages that have been delivered to simulator i that were sent by j.

When simulator i sends a message M, it increments $C_i[i]$ by one and places a vector clock time stamp on the message with its new (i.e., just incremented) clock value. The vector clock time stamp indicates what messages had been delivered to the sender and what other messages the sender has sent, prior to sending M. The time stamp therefore provides a summary of the number of messages sent by each simulator that causally precede (i.e., happen before) M. For example, a vector clock time stamp (5, 9, 6) on a message M sent by simulator 1 indicates that prior to sending M:

1. Simulator 1 had sent 4 messages to the group.
2. Nine messages from simulator 2 were delivered to simulator 1.
3. Six messages from simulator 3 were delivered to simulator 1.

These 19 messages $(4 + 9 + 6)$ causally precede (i.e., happen before) M, so for any simulator belonging to the group, all 19 messages must be delivered before M is delivered in order to maintain the causal ordering property.

For example, Figure 9.3 illustrates the example depicted in Figure 9.1 when causal ordering is used. Simulators A, B, and C in Figure 9.1 have been renamed 1, 2, and 3, respectively, to be consistent with the notation used in this section. There are three simulators, so each initializes its vector clock to (0, 0, 0). When simulator 1 sends a message to indicate that it has fired, it increments its vector clock to (1, 0, 0) and places this vector into the time stamp field of the message.

Consider the distributed simulation executive implementing causal ordering for simulator 2. When the message arrives, the executive must decide whether or not it

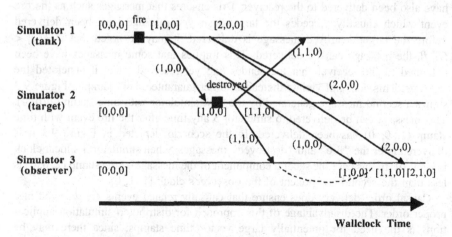

Figure 9.3 Implementation of causal ordering using vector clocks. Vector time stamps are indicated in parentheses, and vector clocks are indicated in brackets.

can deliver this message. In this case, simulator 2's local clock is $(0, 0, 0)$, and T, the time stamp on the incoming message, is $(1, 0, 0)$. The fact that $T[1] = C_2[1] + 1$ indicates that all messages generated by simulator 1 (in this case there are no such messages) preceding this one have already been delivered to simulator 2. The fact that $T[2] = C_2[2]$ and $T[3] = C_2[3]$ indicates that all of the messages for this group that had been delivered to simulator 1 when it sent the "fire" message have already been delivered to simulator 2. Thus this message is not causally dependent on any other messages that had not already been delivered to simulator 2, and the message may be delivered. Simulator 2's vector clock can be advanced to $(1, 0, 0)$.

Next, simulator 2 generates a new message and advances its clock from $(1, 0, 0)$ to $(1, 1, 0)$. When this message arrives, the executive for simulator 3 notices the sender had previously received a message from 1 (because $T[1] = 1$), but simulator 3 had not yet received this message (because $C_3[1] = 0$). Indeed, this is the message for the fire event. Thus the "destroyed" message cannot be delivered to simulator 3 yet. When the message for the fire event with time stamp $(1, 0, 0)$ arrives, this event is delivered to simulator 3, and 3's clock is advanced to $(1, 0, 0)$. The message carrying the "destroyed" event with time stamp $(1, 1, 0)$ can now be delivered to simulator 3.

In general, if a simulator r has local vector clock C_r, then a message from simulator s with vector time stamp T can only be delivered to r if:

1. $T[s] = C_r[s] + 1$, and
2. $T[j] \leq C_r[j]$ for all $j \neq s$.

The first condition guarantees this is the next message from simulator s. Successive messages from the same simulator are clearly causally dependent, so they must be delivered in the order in which they were sent. The second condition guarantees that any messages delivered to the sender before sending this message have also been delivered to the receiver. This ensures that messages such as the fire event which causally precedes the target-destroyed message have been delivered before the target-destroyed message is delivered. It may be noted that if $T[j] < C_r[j]$, the message can be delivered. This implies that some messages have been delivered to the receiver that the sender had yet received when it generated the message. This does not violate the causal order guarantee. For example, Figure 9.3 shows a second message generated by the tank simulator with time stamp $(2, 0, 0)$. This message can be delivered to simulator 3 any time after the fire event with time stamp $(1, 0, 0)$ has been delivered. In the scenario depicted in Figure 9.3 it is delivered after the "fire" and "destroyed" messages, when simulator 3's local clock is $[1, 1, 0]$. In this case the second component of the message's time stamp $(2, 0, 0)$ is less than the second component of the observer's clock $[1, 1, 0]$.

Causal order delivery does ensure that causally related events are received in a proper order. The disadvantage of this approach for distributed simulation applications is the need for potentially large vector time stamps, since there may be thousands of simulators in a distributed simulation exercise. The algorithms for ensuring causal ordering also become much more complex when one must consider many multicast groups (large distributed simulations may contain thousands of groups) and one must ensure causal order among messages sent to different groups. Further, causal ordering does not prevent all temporal anomalies, as will be described next.

9.2.2 Causal and Totally Ordered

While causal ordering prevents certain temporal anomalies, it does not eliminate others. One problem is that causal order does not guarantee any order concerning concurrent events. In particular, it is possible for two different simulators to see the same set of events in a different order. This can lead to other temporal anomalies.

To illustrate this problem, consider the scenario depicted in Figure 9.4. Here, there are four flight simulators, two on the red team about to take off from an airport and two on the blue team flying overhead. The blue team has devised a strategy whereby blue aircraft 1 will attack the first red aircraft to take off and blue aircraft 2 will attack the second. Suppose that red aircraft 1 takes off first, followed by red aircraft 2. The simulator for each aircraft generates a message indicating that it has taken off. Because the two aircraft take off, events are concurrent (there is no path between them in the space-time diagram); the message delivery system is free to deliver them in any order to the receiving simulators. In the example depicted in Figure 9.4, blue aircraft 2 correctly sees red aircraft 1 take off first. However, blue aircraft 1 sees the incorrect order. Thus, both blue aircraft move to attack aircraft 2, a situation which is impossible with the strategy that they had devised.

This problem could be solved if the causal order delivery service were strengthened so that not only are events delivered in causal order but all simulators are also guaranteed to receive messages for a common set of events in the same order. In other words, a *total order* of all events must be defined; that is, some ordering relationship is specified for every two events. By contrast, Lamport's happens before

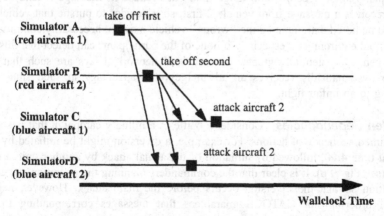

Figure 9.4 Temporal anomaly resulting from two simulators seeing the same sets of events, but in a different order.

relationship only defines a *partial ordering* because no ordering relationship is specified for concurrent events. A causal and totally ordered communication service (CATOCS) ensure that (1) if $E_1 \rightarrow E_2$ and a simulator receives messages for both E_1 and E_2, then E_1 will be delivered before E_2 and (2) if two simulators both receive messages for any two events E_1 and E_2, both will receive them in the same order. Note that CATOCS still does not specify what order concurrent events will be delivered to each simulator, only that all simulators will receive the messages in the same order.

CATOCS will eliminate the anomaly shown in Figure 9.4 because it will ensure that both blue aircraft observe the red aircraft taking off in the same order. Thus it will prevent the two blue aircraft from attacking the same opponent.

A simple approach to realizing CATOCS[32] is to send each message to a central sequencer, that then sends the message to the group. If each receiver ensures it receives messages from the sequencer in the order that they were sent, it is guaranteed that all messages are received in the same order. Ensuring that messages received from the sequencer are received in a correct order can be accomplished by maintaining a counter in the sequencer that is incremented with each message send. The counter is included in each message sent by the sequencer. Each destination simulator can only deliver a message with sequence number i when it has delivered all of the messages with smaller sequence numbers.

While causal ordering and CATOCS are sufficient to avoid certain anomalies, neither is sufficient in other situations. Specifically, causal order is not sufficient if ordering relationships among *concurrent* events are important, or if there are "hidden dependencies" between events, as elaborated upon below.

Ordering Concurrent Events CATOCS ensures that the simulators observe the *same* ordering of concurrent events but does not guarantee that they will see the *correct* ordering of these events. Consider the example shown in Figure 9.5. Here, simulator A modeling a tank has orders to pursue the first vehicle it "sees." In this example, vehicle 1 comes into range first, but because its message is delayed, the tank receives a message from vehicle 2 first, so it decides to pursue that vehicle. It should be noted that pursuing the "wrong" vehicle may not necessarily compromise the virtual environment, especially if none of the participants can detect that this has happened. Of potentially greater concern is if network delays are such that one player systematically receives an advantage or disadvantage in such situations, leading to an unfair fight.

Hidden Dependencies Consider a battle in a military campaign that is staged as a timed sequence of actions. For example, a diversion might be initiated by one unit at time 4:00, followed by initiation of the actual attack by another unit at time 4:10 (see Fig. 9.6). It is clear that the commanders planning the operation staged its execution so that the diversion occurs before the main attack. However, neither causal ordering nor CATOCS guarantees that messages corresponding to the

---

[32] Clearly any mechanism for implementing CATOCS trivially also realizes causal order.

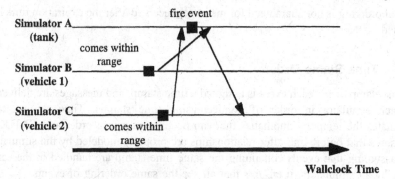

Figure 9.5 Example illustrating an incorrect event ordering.

diversion reach federates representing the opposing force before messages corresponding to the main attack! The problem is that all message ordering in CATOCS is based *only* on messages passed between federates. Thus, as noted earlier, semantic relationships between events are not visible to the distributed simulation executive.

9.2.3 Delta Causality

Delta causality is a variation on causal ordering that was developed for real-time applications. It is based on the idea that in applications such as DVEs, information that is "old" (for example, because it has been delayed in the network for an excessively long time) is no longer useful. This concept was used in DIS, for example; PDUs that exceed the 100 (or 300) millisecond latency constraint can be ignored by the receiver.

With delta causality, messages are assigned a certain expiration time, defined as the time the message was sent plus some time value *delta*. Messages received at the destination before the expiration time has elapsed are delivered in causal order.

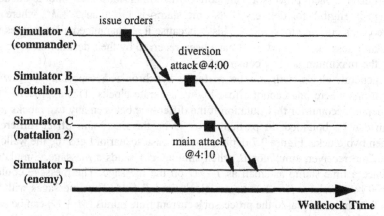

Figure 9.6 Example illustrating hidden dependencies between events.

Causal ordering is not guaranteed for messages received after the expiration time has elapsed.

9.2.4 Time Stamp Order

In time stamp order, each event is assigned a time stamp, and messages are delivered to each simulator in order of nondecreasing time stamps. Time stamp order eliminates the temporal anomalies that can occur with causal order and CATOCS. It ensures that before-and-after relationships are properly modeled by the simulator, and assuming that events containing the same time stamp are handled in the same order by all simulators, it ensures that all see the same ordering of events.

The fundamental difference between the causal and timestamp ordered services is concerned with their respective definition of the "happens before" relationship. In a time-stamped order service, an event is said to happen before another event if it has a smaller time stamp than the second, following one's intuitive notion of event ordering in physical systems. Simulators can precisely specify which events happen before which other events by assigning appropriate time stamps. For example the "fire" event might be assigned a time stamp of 102, and the "destroy" event a time stamp of 103 to specify that "the fire event happens before the destroy event."

One approach to realizing time stamp order is to utilize synchronization algorithms such as those discussed in Part II of this book. The central disadvantages of using this approach are (1) the reliance on lookahead, or optimistic processing which requires simulators to implement a rollback capability, and (2) the computation and communication overhead necessary to realize these algorithms.

Another approach to realizing the time stamp order delivery service can be used if the maximum message latency can be bounded. Assume that each processor contains a synchronized wallclock time clock, and the maximum message latency is M. Each processor assigns a time stamp on each message it sends equal to its current wallclock time. Assume for a moment that the clocks are perfectly synchronized. Each processor can collect incoming messages into a queue. A message is eligible for delivery if its time stamp is less than $T + M$, where T is the receiver's current clock value. This is because it is guaranteed all messages with time stamp less than $T + M$ must have been received by their destination processor, under the maximum latency constraint.

In general, clocks will not be perfectly synchronized, especially in low-cost applications where one cannot afford highly accurate clocks. This approach can be extended to account for this situation if the difference between any two clocks in the system can be bounded. In particular, let O be the maximum offset (difference) between two clocks. Figure 9.7 depicts a worst-case scenario. Let T be the wallclock time of the receiver, simulator B, when simulator A sends a message. Simulator A can place a time stamp as small as $T - O$ on the message. The message could be received by simulator B as late as wallclock time $T + M$. Thus messages with time stamp less than or equal to the processor's current time minus $(M + O)$ can be safely delivered while maintaining time stamp order.

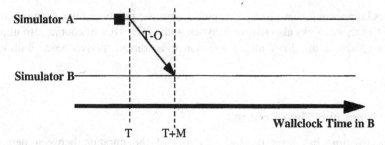

Figure 9.7 Implementing time stamp order in a DVE with maximum latency M and clock offset O.

The disadvantages of this approach relative to the synchronization mechanisms developed for analytic simulations are (1) the requirement of a guaranteed maximum latency and clock offset and (2) message delivery may be delayed longer than necessary. Regarding (1), if a bound on latency and offset cannot be determined, one can dictate that messages exceeding this maximum latency may be delivered out of order, similar to the delta causality approach. If this is infrequent and simulators can be guaranteed not to diverge should they receive certain messages late, this is a reasonable and practical approach.

Regarding (2), this scheme in effect enforces a maximum latency M on every message, even if the network could deliver the message with a latency smaller than M. Conservative synchronization protocols use lookahead to circumvent this problem. On the other hand, if M is sufficiently small, this drawback may be acceptable. For example, recall that it has been observed latencies lower than 100 to 300 milliseconds are beyond what humans can perceive. This suggests that if the network can maintain latencies below this level, the system will perform satisfactorily.

9.3 SYNCHRONIZING WALLCLOCK TIME

Each processor in a distributed computing environment usually maintains a local, hardware clock indicating the time of day (wallclock time). This clock may be used to assign time stamps to events. Thus it is important to ensure that the clocks in different processors remain in relatively close synchrony with one another, or confusion will result concerning event time stamps.

There are two forms of the clock synchronization problem. If the distributed simulation is self contained and does not need to interact with external elements that are tightly synchronized to "true time" (or UTC, as discussed below), then it is usually sufficient to ensure that the hardware clocks used by the different processors remain in synchrony with each other. These clocks may drift with respect to UTC without noticeable consequences. On the other hand, if the simulation does interact with devices synchronized to UTC, such as a hardware-in-the-loop simulation which includes components that produce outputs at specific points in time, then one must ensure that these clocks also remain in synch with UTC. This, of course, also implies that the clocks in the distributed simulation must remain in synchrony with each other.

9.3.1 Time and Time Sources

Historically time has been defined in terms of the duration between periodic, astronomical events. A *solar day* is defined as the amount of time that elapses between successive times when the sun is at the highest point in the sky. The solar day is divided into 24 hours, which is, in turn, divided into 3600 seconds. Thus a solar second is 1/86400 of a solar day. Greenwich Mean Time is the mean solar time at the Greenwich meridian that passes through the Greenwich observatory near London, England.

Today, atomic clocks are used to define standard sources of time. Time duration is based on transitions of the cesium atom. One slight complication is this time source does not take into account the fact that the earth's rotation is gradually slowing down, so the length of a day as defined by astronomical phenomena is actually increasing slightly as time progresses. To compensate for this, extra *leap seconds* are periodically added to the values produced by the atomic clocks, giving rise to an international standard for time called Universal Time [Coordinated] (UTC), usually spoken Coordinated Universal Time. Without the introduction of these extra ticks, "noon" would gradually occur earlier and earlier in the day (i.e., with the sun at a lower point in the sky), creating obvious problems. UTC is widely accepted as the international standard with respect to defining the current time.

UTC can be obtained from various standards organizations via radio, satellite, and telephone links. For example, in the United States, the National Institute of Standards and Technology (NIST) maintains a shortwave radio broadcast that disseminates UTC, and the Geostationary Environment Operational Satellites (GEOS) also provide UTC. Other services provide telephone access via a modem. Radio broadcasts allow time estimates to be accurate within about 10 milliseconds. Satellite broadcasts offer better accuracy, often within 0.5 millisecond, or less. The principal limitation in achieving perfectly accurate time is uncertainty in the propagation delay from the time source to the receiver.

There are essentially two sources of time that can be used by a computer:

- An internal hardware oscillator, derived from a quartz crystal, that produces an electrical signal of some known, fixed, frequency.
- An external "time service" providing UTC; one can purchase devices called *time providers* to receive and interpret UTC signals.

The internal hardware clock within a computer usually contains a counter that is decremented once per clock cycle. When the counter reaches zero, it is reset to some fixed value stored in a hardware register, and an interrupt is generated to the CPU.

Each such interrupt is referred to as a *clock tick*. The constant register is set to hold a value to produce interrupts at some fixed known frequency, such as every sixtieth of a second.

9.3.2 Clock Synchronization Algorithms

The problem with hardware clocks derived from oscillators is that they drift; that is in practice, they run slightly faster or slower than UTC. Ideally the hardware clock C would increase at a rate dC/dt equal to one, where one second on the hardware clock corresponds to one second of UTC. In practice, the clock advances at a rate dC/dT where $1 - \rho \le dC/dT \le 1 + \rho$, with ρ defined as the maximum drift (error) per unit of UTC. If all clocks operate with this specification, in the worst case, two clocks may drift apart at a rate of 2ρ per unit UTC. This could be a problem, particularly if the distributed simulation exercise has a long duration. Thus some mechanism is required to resynchronize the hardware clocks to correct for drift, and if necessary, to maintain synchronization with UTC.

The clock offset δ refers to the maximum difference between two clocks that is allowed. If two clocks drift apart at a rate of 2ρ per unit UTC time, after $\delta/2\rho$ UTC time units they will have drifted δ time units apart, so resynchronization must be done at least once every $\delta/2\rho$ time units.

There are three classes of clock synchronization algorithms:

1. *Centralized, pull time service.* Each processor requests the current time from a central time server, and receives a value in response. These are also sometimes called passive server algorithms because the time service is only invoked upon request.

2. *Centralized, push time service.* Here, a central time server periodically sends new time values to the processors without them having to request it.

3. *Distributed algorithms.* No central server is used, but rather the processors use a distributed computation to synchronize their clocks.

The centralized approaches are particularly well suited when an external UTC time service is utilized. In this case the processor with the UTC connection is assumed to have the correct time, and the problem becomes one of distributing estimates of the UTC to other processors. Distributed algorithms tend to be geared toward making sure that the clocks in different processors do not drift too far apart. In both cases a principal challenge in distributing time among the processors is the difficulty of measuring and predicting delays in transmitting messages over the network. In the case where there is no UTC server, an additional problem is defining the "correct" time value, since there is no standard reference time source. Averaging techniques are usually used for this purpose.

Centralized, Pull Algorithms The processor requests a time value by sending a message to the server and then waits for a reply. Assume that the time of the

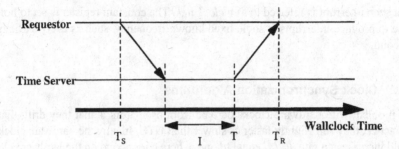

Figure 9.8 Centralized, pull algorithm.

requestor's clock is T_S when the message is sent, and the reply is received at time T_R (see Fig. 9.8). The problem is if the time value provided by the server is T, and the latency to transmit this information from the server to the requestor is L, then the time when the message was received is $T + L$, but L is unknown. Without any additional information, one might assume the latency through the network for the request and response messages are the same.[33] Using this assumption, if I is the amount of time required by the server to receive and process the time request message, the requestor can estimate the time at which the message was received is $T + (T_R - T_S - I)/2$. The latter term is an estimate of the latency for the response message returned from the time server.

To obtain a better estimate of the network latency, one can collect several measurements of $T_R - T_S$, discard those above a certain threshold as being outliers that are not representative measurements, and then average the remaining measurements (Cristian 1989). This will give a better estimate of the actual latency, at the cost of requiring additional message traffic to produce the estimate.

Centralized, Push Algorithms Rather than have each processor poll the time server to request time values, the server can simply broadcast new time values on a regular basis. Each processor receiving the new time value must compensate by adding an estimate of the latency for the value to travel through the network. This must be known a priori because each processor does not have a means for estimating the latency, without generating additional messages.

If there is no UTC connection providing a standard time reference, a "true" value of time must be derived from some other means. Using one processor's clock makes the entire distributed simulation reliant on the accuracy of one machine. A better approach is to average the clocks from several machines.

The algorithm used in Berkeley Unix uses such an approach. A central time server polls each of the other processors to get their current time value. It then averages the values that are received and notifies the other processors that should resynchronize their clocks to add or remove a certain amount of time.

---

[33] Latencies tend to be symmetric in local area networks, but are often asymmetric in wide area networks such as the Internet.

Distributed Algorithms The centralized approaches suffer from the usual problems of centralization, namely having a single point of failure and lack of scalability to large numbers of processors. Distributed time synchronization algorithms alleviate this problem.

A simple approach is to have each processor broadcast its time at a certain, agreed-upon frequency, much like the way radio stations broadcast the time at the beginning of each hour. More precisely, each processor broadcasts its time every R time units, starting from some agreed upon initial time T_0. Thus each broadcast is made at time $T_0 + iR$ for integer values of i. The broadcasts will not actually occur simultaneously because the clocks in different processors are not identical. After issuing a broadcast, each processor collects time messages from other processors over a certain time interval and then computes a new time value by averaging the values received from other processors. The highest and lowest m values may be discarded from this averaging process to protect against unreliable values. One can also compensate for network latency by using an estimate of message delays, defined a priori or through measurements.

Broadcasting time estimates in this way does not scale to a large number of processors. An alternative approach is to limit each processor's broadcast to some set of processors. The processors can be organized into a virtual topology, such as a mesh. Each processor would then only send its time message to its nearest neighbors in the mesh and perform the averaging on values received from its neighbors.

9.3.3 Correcting Clock Synchronization Errors

Once the clocks have been synchronized, the processor's local clock must be corrected to reflect the newly computed time value. Simply resetting the local clock to the new time value is usually not a very good idea because this could cause time to go backward; which could result in problems in the simulation computations. For example, simulators using dead reckoning algorithms to compensate for latency may not expect a negative time duration. Actually it is undesirable for time to make abrupt changes forward as well. For example, if the user in a training simulator has three seconds to respond before the aircraft goes into an uncontrollable spin, a sudden increase in time could prematurely cause the user's allowed reaction period to end, not providing adequate opportunity to respond. If one were to simply reset the clock whenever a new value is computed, there would be abrupt changes, or time could actually move backward.

To prevent problems such as these, the new time value should be gradually phased in. For example, if the clock is 10 milliseconds too fast, and a clock tick interrupt is generated every 30 milliseconds, one could reset the interrupt software to increment time by 29 milliseconds on each interrupt for 10 successive interrupts. This will avoid abrupt changes and backward movement of time.

9.3.4 Network Time Protocol

The Network Time Potocol (NTP) is used in the Internet to provide a synchronized clock service. It is built on top of the user datagram protocol (UDP) and the Internet Protocol (IP). NTP uses a self-organizing, hierarchical (tree-based), subnetwork of clock servers. A set of *primary servers* reside at the top (level 1) of the hierarchy that are synchronized with national time servers. Servers at lower levels (levels 2, 3, etc.) of the tree are called *secondary servers*. Clock synchronization information flows down the tree in order to determine the offset between primary and secondary server clocks.

To determine the offset between clocks, a message is sent from a server at level i of the hierarchy to a peer at the next level, and returned. Four time stamps are assigned to the message (see Fig. 9.9). T_1 holds the local clock of the server when it sends the message. The time of the peer at this instant is $T_1 + \delta$, where δ is the offset between the two clocks. The second time stamp T_2 represents the time of the peer when the message is received, or $T_1 + \delta + L$, where L is the message latency from server to peer. The third time stamp T_3 is the peer's clock when it returns the message to the server. At this instant, the server's local clock is $T_3 - \delta$, assuming that the offset has not changed. The final time stamp T_4 is the local time of the server when it receives the message, or $T_3 - \delta + L'$, where L' is the message latency from peer to server.

Let A be equal to $T_2 - T_1$ (i.e., $\delta + L$) and B be equal to $T_3 - T_4$ (i.e., $-L'$). Then the round-trip delay $L + L'$ is $A - B$. Further, since L must be greater than zero, $A = \delta + L > \delta$; that is, A provides an upper bound on the clock offset. Similarly $B = \delta - L' < \delta$; that is, B is a lower bound on the offset. The estimated offset δ_e is computed to be the midpoint between these two bounds:

$$\delta_e = A + B/2.$$

The width of the interval is the round-trip latency $(L + L')$, so the maximum error in this estimate for the offset is half the round-trip latency.

Offset and delay estimates are collected from several clock sources. NTP uses a *clock selection algorithm* that selects a suitable subset of these sources with which the peer synchronizes. Clock selection is accomplished using two sub-algorithms.

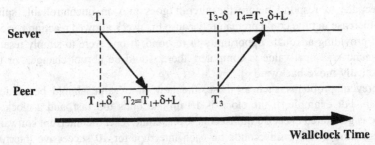

Figure 9.9 Message exchange to determine offset and round-trip latency in NTP.

The first is called the *interval intersection algorithm*. This algorithm is designed to detect and discard from the set unreliable clocks that are called *falsetickers*. The interval intersection algorithm determines a confidence interval for the offset of each clock based on the measured offset and various error estimates. The actual offset lies with very high probability within this confidence interval. The intersection algorithm determines a subset containing at least K clocks where it attempts to ensure the confidence intervals of all K clocks have at least one point in common, and the size of the overlapping interval is minimized. Clocks with intervals falling outside this overlapping interval are designated as falsetickers and are discarded.

The second sub-algorithm of the clock selection algorithm is called the *clustering algorithm*. This algorithm is applied to the clocks that survive the interval selection algorithm. It performs a computation to identify and reject the outlier among the measured offsets, taking into account the level of the clock source in the hierarchy and the size of its interval. This process is repeated until either a specified minimum number of clocks is reached or the estimated error is determined to be sufficiently small. Details of these calculations are somewhat involved and are beyond the scope of the current discussion, but are described in (Mills 1995).

Once the clock selection algorithm whittles down the set of available clocks to a set of trusted clocks, another computation called the *clock combining algorithm* computes a weighted average of the remaining clock estimates. The value resulting from this computation is used to adjust the frequency of the local oscillator which is used to generate a time reference for producing the time stamps used by the clock synchronization algorithm.

9.4   SUMMARY

Time management and event-ordering mechanisms are used to reduce or eliminate temporal anomalies such as the effect appearing to happen before the cause. Causal order and causal and totally ordered message delivery based on Lamport's happens before relationship can be used to ensure correct ordering of messages that may be dependent on each other. Delta causality takes into account the timely nature of information in a DVE. Time stamp order eliminates anomalies that cannot be addressed with causal-ordering mechanisms.

Wallclock time must be synchronized among different machines in DVEs to ensure that a consistent notion of time is maintained across the system. Several clock synchronization algorithms are available for this purpose. In some cases wallclock time must also be synchronized with international time standards such as UTC.

9.5   ADDITIONAL READINGS

The happens before relationship used to define causal ordering is defined in Lamport (1978). Several approaches to realizing causal ordering have been proposed. For example, see Fidge (1988), Schiper, Eggli et al. (1989), Birman, Schiper et al.

(1991), Meldal, Sankar et al. (1991), Raynal, Schiper et al. (1991), Singhal and Kshemkalyani (1992), and Schwarz and Mattern (1994). Delta causality is described in Yavatkar (1992) and Adelstein and Singhal (1995). Message-ordering alternatives that were considered in the High-Level Architecture are described in Fujimoto and Weatherly (1996). Clock synchronization algorithms are described in Kopetz and Ochsenreiter (1987), Srikanth and Toueg (1987), Lundelius-Welch and Lynch (1988), Cristian (1989), Gusella and Zatti (1989), Ramanathan, Kandlur et al. (1990), and Drummond and Babaoglu (1993); a survey is presented in Ramanathan, Shin et al. (1990). The network time protocol is described in Mills (1991).

REFERENCES

Abeysundara, B. W. and A. E. Kamal (1991). High-speed local area networks and their performance: A survey. *ACM Computing Surveys* **23**(2): 221–264.

Adelstein, F. and M. Singhal (1995). Real-time causal message ordering in multi-media systems. *Proceedings of the 15th International Conference on Distributed Computing Systems*, IEEE: 36–43.

Agrawal, D., M. Choy, et al. (1994). Maya: A simulation platform for distributed shared memories. *Proceedings of the 8th Workshop on Parallel and Distributed Simulation*, Society for Computer Simulation: 151–155.

Ahuja, M. (1990). Flush primitives for asynchronous distributed systems. *Information Processing Letters*: 5–12.

Akyildiz, I. F., L. Chen, et al. (1993). The effect of memory capacity on Time Warp performance. *Journal of Parallel and Distributed Computing* **18**(4): 411–422.

Ammar, H., and S. Deng (1992). Time Warp simulation using time scale decomposition. *ACM Transactions on Modeling and Computer Simulation* **2**(2): 158–177.

Andradottir, S., and T. Ott (1995). Time-segmentation parallel simulation of networks of queues with loss or communication blocking. *ACM Transactions on Modeling and Computer Simulation* **5**(4): 269–305.

Arvind, K., and C. Smart (1992). Hierarchical parallel discrete event simulation in composite Elsa. *Proceedings of the 6th Workshop on Parallel and Disributed Simulation* **24**: 147–158.

Avril, H., and C. Tropper (1995). Clustered Time Warp and logic simulation. *Proceedings of the 9th Workshop on Parallel and Distributed Simulation* 112–119.

Ayani, R. (1989). A parallel simulation scheme based on the distance between objects. *Proceedings of the SCS Multiconference on Distributed Simulation*, B. Unger and R. M. Fujimoto, Society for Computer Simulation **21**: 113–118.

Baccelli, F. and M. Canales (1993). Parallel simulation of stochastic petri nets using recurrence equations. *ACM Transactions on Modeling and Computer Simulation* **3**(1): 20–41.

Bagrodia, R., Y. Chen, et al. (1996). Parallel simulation of high speed wormhole routing networks. *Proceedings of the 10th Workshop on Parallel and Distributed Simulation*, IEEE Computer Society: 47–56.

Bagrodia, R., W.-T. Liao, et al. (1991). A unifying framework for distributed simulation. *ACM Transactions on Modeling and Computer Simulation* **1**(4).

Bagrodia, R., and W.-T. Liao (1994), Maisie: A language for the design of efficient discrete-event simulations, *IEEE Transactions on Software Engineering* **20**(4): 225–238.

Bailey, M. L., J. V. Briner, et al. (1994). Parallel logic simulation of VLSI systems. *ACM Computing Surveys* **26**(3): 255–294.

Bailey, M. L., M. A. Pagels, et al. (1993). How using buses in multicomputer programs affects conservative parallel simulation. *Proceedings of the 7th Workshop on Parallel and Distributed Simulation*, SCS Simulation Series **23**: 93–100.

Bailey, R. W. (1982). *Human Performance Engineering: A Guide for System Designers.* Englewood Cliffs, NJ, Prentice Hall.

Bain, W. L. and D. S. Scott (1988). An algorithm for time synchronization in distributed discrete event simulation. *Proceedings of the SCS Multiconference on Distributed Simulation*, SCS Simulation Series **19**: 30–33.

Ball, D. and S. Hoyt (1990). The adaptive Time Warp concurrency control algorithm. *Proceedings of the SCS Multiconference on Distributed Simulation* **22**: 174–177.

Banks, J., J. S. Carson II, et al. (1996). *Discrete–Event System Simulation.* Upper Saddle River, NJ, Prentice Hall.

Bellenot, S. (1990). Global virtual time algorithms. *Proceedings of the SCS Multiconference on Distributed Simulation*, Society for Computer Simulation: 122–127.

Bellenot, S. (1992). State skipping performance with the Time Warp operating system. *Proceedings of the 6th Workshop on Parallel and Distributed Simulation* **24**: 53–64.

Bellenot, S. (1993). Performance of a risk free Time Warp operating system. *Proceedings of the 7th Workshop on Parallel and Distributed Simulation*: 155–158.

Biles, W. E., D. M. Daniels, et al. (1985). Statistical considerations in simulation on a network of microcomputers. *Proceedings of the 1985 Winter Simulation Conference*: 388–393.

Birman, K., A. Schiper, et al. (1991). Lightweight causal and atomic group multicast. *ACM Transactions on Computer Systems* **9**(3): 272–314.

Blanchard, T. D. and T. Lake (1997). A light-weight RTI prototype with optimistic publication. *Proceedings of the Spring Simulation Interoperability Workshop.*

Blanchard, T. D., T. W. Lake, et al. (1994). Cooperative acceleration: Robust conservative distributed discrete event simulation. *Proceedings of the 1994 Workshop on Parallel and Distributed Simulation.* Edinburgh, Scotland: 58–64.

Briner, J., Jr. (1991). Fast parallel simulation of digital systems. *Advances in Parallel and Distributed Simulation*, SCS Simulation Series, **23**: 71–77.

Bruce, D. (1995). The treatment of state in optimistic systems. *Proceedings of the 9th Workshop on Parallel and Distributed Simulation*: 40–49.

Bryant, R. E. (1977). Simulation of Packet Communication Architecture Computer Systems. *Computer Science Laboratory.* Massachusetts, Massachusetts Institute of Technology, Cambridge.

Cai, W., and S. J. Turner (1990). An algorithm for distributed discrete-event simulation—The carrier null message approach. *Proceedings of the SCS Multiconference on Distributed Simulation*, SCS Simulation Series **22**: 3–8.

Carothers, C., R. M. Fujimoto, et al. (1995). A case study in simulating PCS networks using Time Warp. *Proceedings of the 9th Workshop on Parallel and Distributed Simulation*, IEEE Computer Society: 87–94.

Chai, A., and S. Ghosh (1993). Modeling and distributed simulation of a broadband-ISDN network. *IEEE Computer* **26**(9).

Chamberlain, R. D., and M. A. Franklin (1990). Hierarchical discrete event simulation on hypercube architectures. *IEEE Micro* **10**(4): 10–20.

Chamberlain, R. D., and C. D. Henderson (1994). Evaluating the use of pre-simulation in VLSI circuit partitioning. *Proceedings of the 8th Workshop on Parallel and Distributed Simulation*, Society for Computer Simulation: 139–146.

Chandrasekaran, S., and M. Hill (1996). Optimistic simulation of parallel architectures using program executables. *Proceedings of the 10th Workshop on Parallel and Distributed Simulation*, IEEE Computer Society: 143–150.

Chandrasekaren, S., and M. D. Hill (1996). Optimistic simulation of parallel architectures using program executables. *Proceedings of the 10th Workshop on Parallel Simulation*: 143–150.

Chandy, K. M., and L. Lamport (1985). Distributed snapshots: Determining global states of distributed systems. *ACM Transactions on Computer Systems* **3**(1): 63–75.

Chandy, K. M., and J. Misra (1978). Distributed simulation: A case study in design and verification of distributed programs. *IEEE Transactions on Software Engineering* **5**(5): 440–452.

Chandy, K. M., and J. Misra (1981). Asynchronous distributed simulation via a sequence of parallel computations. *Communications of the ACM* **24**(4): 198–205.

Chandy, K. M., and R. Sherman (1989). The conditional event approach to distributed simulation. *Proceedings of the SCS Multiconference on Distributed Simulation*, B. Unger and R. M. Fujimoto, Society for Computer Simulation **21**: 93–99.

Chandy, K. M., and R. Sherman (1989). Space, time, and simulation. *Proceedings of the SCS Multiconference on Distributed Simulation*, SCS Simulation Series **21**: 53–57.

Chen, Y., V. Jha, et al. (1997). A multidimensional study on the feasibility of parallel switch-level circuit simulation. *Proceedings of the 11th Workshop on Parallel and Distributed Simulation*, IEEE Computer Society: 46–54.

Cheung, S. (1994). Analysis of I/ITSEC 1993 DIS Demonstration Data. Institute for Simulation and Training, Orlando, FL.

Chow, R., and T. Johnson (1997). *Distributed Operating Systems and Algorithms*. Reading, MA: Addison Wesley.

Chung, M., and Y. Chung (1991). An experimental analysis of simulation clock advancement in parallel logic simulation on an SIMD machine. *Advances in Parallel and Distributed Simulation*, SCS Simulation Series **23**: 125–132.

Cleary, J., F. Gomes, et al. (1994). Cost of state saving and rollback. *Proceedings of the 8th Workshop on Parallel and Distributed Simulation*: 94–101.

Cleary, J., B. Unger, et al. (1988). A distributed and-parallel backtracking algorithm using virtual time. *Proceedings of the SCS Multiconference on Distributed Simulation*, Society for Computer Simulation **19**: 177–182.

Cleary, J. G., and J. J. Tsai (1997). Performance of a conservative simulator of ATM networks. *Proceedings of the 11th Workshop on Parallel and Distributed Simulation*, IEEE Computer Society: 142–145.

Comfort, J. C. (1984). The simulation of a master-slave event set processor. *Simulation* **42**(3): 117–124.

Concepcion, A., and S. Kelly (1991). Computing global virtual time using the multi-level token passing algorithm. *Advances in Parallel and Distributed Simulation*. **23**: 63–70.

Costa, A., A. DeGloria, et al. (1994). An evaluation system for distributed-time VHDL simulation. *Proceedings of the 8th Workshop on Parallel and Distributed Simulation*, Society for Computer Simulation: 147–150.

Cota, B. A., and R. G. Sargent (1990). A framework for automatic lookahead computation in conservative distributed simulations. *Proceedings of the SCS Multiconference on Distributed Simulation*, SCS Simulation Series **22**: 56–59.

Cristian, F. (1989). Probabilistic clock synchronization. *Distributed Computing* **3**: 146–158.

D'Souza, L. M., X. Fan, et al. (1994). pGVT: An algorithm for accurate GVT estimation. *Proceedings of the 8th Workshop on Parallel and Distributed Simulation*: 102–110.

Dahmann, J. S., R. M. Fujimoto, et al. (1997). The Department of Defense High Level Architecture. *Proceedings of the 1997 Winter Simulation Conference*.

Damani, O. P., Y.–M. Wang, et al. (1997). Optimistic distributed simulation based on transitive dependency tracking. *Proceedings of the 11th Workshop on Parallel and Distributed Simulation*: 90–97.

Das, S., R. M. Fujimoto, et al. (1994). GTW: A Time Warp system for shared memory multiprocessors. *Proceedings of the 1994 Winter Simulation Conference*: 1332–1339.

Das, S. R., and R. M. Fujimoto (1997). Adaptive memory management and optimism control in Time Warp. *ACM Transactions on Modeling and Computer Simulation* **7**(2): 239–271.

Das, S. R., and R. M. Fujimoto (1997). An empirical evaluation of performance memory tradeoffs in Time Warp. *IEEE Transactions on Parallel and Distributed Systems* **8**(2): 210–224.

Davis, C. K., S. V. Sheppard, et al. (1988). Automatic development of parallel simulation models in Ada. *Proceedings of the 1988 Winter Simulation Conference*: 339–343.

Davis, P. K. (1995). Distributed interactive simulation in the evolution of DoD warfare modeling and simulation. *Proceedings of the IEEE* **83**(8): 1138–1155.

Deelman, E., and B. K. Szymanski (1997). Breadth-first rollback in spatially explicit simulations. *Proceedings of the 11th Workshop on Parallel and Distributed Simulation*, IEEE Computer Society: 124–131.

Defense Modeling and Simulation Office (1996). Data Distribution and Management Design Document, V0.2. Washington, DC.

Defense Modeling and Simulation Office (1996). High Level Architecture Object Model Template. Washington, DC.

Defense Modeling and Simulation Office (1996). High Level Architecture Rules, V1.0. Washington, DC.

Defense Modeling and Simulation Office (1998). High Level Architecture Interface Specification, V1.3. Washington, DC.

DeVries, R. C. (1990). Reducing null messages in Misra's distributed discrete event simulation method. *IEEE Transactions on Software Engineering* **16**(1): 82–91.

Dickens, P., P. Heidelberger, et al. (1996). Parallelized direct execution simulation of message-passing programs. *IEEE Transactions on Parallel and Distributed Systems* **7**(10): 1090–1105.

Dickens, P. M., and J. Reynolds, P. F. (1990). SRADS with local rollback. *Proceedings of the SCS Multiconference on Distributed Simulation*. **22**: 161–164.

Dijkstra, E. W., and C. S. Scholten (1980). Termination detection for diffusing computations. *Information Processing Letters* **11**(1): 1–4.

Diot, C., W. Dabbous, et al. (1997). Multipoint communication: A survey of protocols, functions, and mechanisms. *IEEE Journal on Selected Areas in Communications* **15**(3): 277–290.

DIS Steering Committee (1994). The DIS Vision, A Map to the Future of Distributed Simulation. Institute for Simulation and Training, Orlando, FL.

Drummond, R., and O. Babaoglu (1993). Low-cost clock synchronization. *Distributed Computing* **6**: 193–203.

Earnshaw, R. W., and A. Hind (1992). A parallel simulator for performance modeling of broadband telecommunication networks. *Proceedings of the 1992 Winter Simulation Conference*: 1365–1373.

Ebling, M., M. DiLorento, et al. (1989). An ant foraging model implemented on the time Warp operating system. *Proceedings of the SCS Multiconference on Distributed Simulation*, SCS Simulation Series **21**: 21–26.

Fabbri, A., and L. Donatiello (1997). SQTW: A mechanism for state dependent parallel simulation: Description and experimental study. *Proceedings of the 11th Workshop on Parallel and Distributed Simulation*: 82–89.

Felderman, R., and L. Kleinrock (1991). Two processor Time Warp analysis: Some results on a unifying approach. *Advances in Parallel and Distributed Simulation*. **23**: 3–10.

Ferscha, A. (1995). Probabilistic adaptive direct optimism control in Time Warp. *Proceedings of the 9th Workshop on Parallel and Distributed Simulation*: 120–129.

Fidge, C. (1988). Time stamps in message-passing systems that preserve the partial order. *Proceedings of the 11th Australian Computer Science Conference*.

Fishwick, P. A. (1994). *Simulation Model Design and Execution: Building Digital Worlds*. New York: McGraw–Hill.

Fleischmann, J., and P. A. Wilsey (1995). Comparative analysis of periodic state saving techniques in Time Warp simulators. *Proceedings of the 9th Workshop on Parallel and Distributed Simulation*: 50–58.

Flynn, M. J. (1995). *Computer Architecture: Pipelined and Parallel Processor Design*. Boston: Jones and Bartlett.

Franks, S., F. Gomes, et al. (1997). State saving for interactive optimistic simulation. *Proceedings of the 11th Workshop on Parallel and Distributed Simulation*: 72–79.

Frohlich, N., R. Schlagenhaft, et al. (1997). A new approach for partitioning VLSI circuits on transistor level. *Proceedings of the 11th Workshop on Parallel and Distributed Simulation*, IEEE Computer Society: 64–67.

Fujimoto, R. M. (1983). Simon: A simulator of multicomputer networks, ERL, University of California, Berkeley.

Fujimoto, R. M. (1989). Performance measurements of distributed simulation strategies. *Transactions of the Society for Computer Simulation* **6**(2): 89–132.

Fujimoto, R. M. (1989). Time Warp on a shared memory multiprocessor. *Transactions of the Society for Computer Simulation* **6**(3): 211–239.

Fujimoto, R. M. (1989). The virtual time machine. *International Symposium on Parallel Algorithms and Architectures*: 199–208.

Fujimoto, R. M. (1990). Performance of Time Warp under synthetic workloads. *Proceedings of the SCS Multiconference on Distributed Simulation* **22**: 23–28.

Fujimoto, R. M., and M. Hybinette (1997). Computing global virtual time in shared memory multiprocessors. *ACM Transactions on Modeling and Computer Simulation* **7**(4): 425–446.

Fujimoto, R. M., I. Nikolaidis, et al. (1995). Parallel simulation of statistical multiplexers. *Journal of Discrete Event Dynamic Systems* **5**: 115–140.

Fujimoto, R. M., and K. Panesar (1995). Buffer management in shared memory Time Warp systems. *Proceedings of the 9th Workshop on Parallel and Distributed Simulation*: 149–156.

Fujimoto, R. M., J. J. Tsai, et al. (1992). Design and evaluation of the roll back chip: Special purpose hardware for Time Warp. *IEEE Transactions on Computers* **41**(1): 68–82.

Fujimoto, R. M., and R. M. Weatherly (1996). Time management in the DoD High Level Architecture. *Proceedings of the 10th Workshop on Parallel and Distributed Simulation*.

Gafni, A. (1988). Rollback mechanisms for optimistic distributed simulation systems. *Proceedings of the SCS Multiconference on Distributed Simulation.* **19**: 61–67.

Gaujal, B., A. G. Greenberg, et al. (1993). A sweep algorithm for massively parallel simulation of circuit-switched networks. *Journal of Parallel and Distributed Computing* **18**(4): 484–500.

Ghosh, K. and R. M. Fujimoto (1991). Parallel discrete event simulation using space-time memory. *Proceedings of the 1991 International Conference on Parallel Processing.* **3**: 201–208.

Ghosh, K., K. Panesar, et al. (1994). PORTS: A parallel, optimistic, real-time simulator. *Proceedings of the 8th Workshop on Parallel and Distributed Simulation*: 24–31.

Glass, K., M. Livingston, et al. (1997). Distributed simulation of spatially explicit ecological models. *Proceedings of the 11th Workshop on Parallel and Distributed Simulation*, IEEE Computer Society: 60–63.

Glynn, P. W. and P. Heidelberger (1991). Analysis of parallel replicated simulations under a completion time constraint. *ACM Transactions on Modeling and Computer Simulation* **1**(1): 3–23.

Goldiez, B., S. Smith, et al. (1993). Simulator Networking Handbook. Institute for Simulation and Training. Orlando, FL.

Greenberg, A. G., B. D. Lubachevsky, et al. (1991). Algorithms for unboundedly parallel simulations. *ACM Transactions on Computer Systems* **9**(3): 201–221.

Groselj, B., and C. Tropper (1986). Pseudosimulation: An algorithm for distributed simulation with limited memory. *International Journal of Parallel Programming* **15**(5): 413–456.

Groselj, B., and C. Tropper (1988). The time of next event algorithm. *Proceedings of the SCS Multiconference on Distributed Simulation*, Society for Computer Simulation **19**: 25–29.

Gupta, A., I. F. Akyildiz, et al. (1991). Performance analysis of Time Warp with multiple homogeneous processors *IEEE Transactions on Software Engineering* **17**(10): 1013–1027.

Gusella, R., and S. Zatti (1989). The accuracy of the clock synchronization achieved by TEMPO in Berkeley UNIX 4.3BSD. *IEEE Transactions on Software Engineering* **15**(7): 847–853.

Hamnes, D. O., and A. Tripathi (1994). Investigations in adaptive distributed simulation. *Proceedings of the 8th Workshop on Parallel and Distributed Simulation*: 20–23.

Hao, F., K. Wilson, et al. (1996). Logical process size in parallel ATM simulations. *Proceedings of the 1996 Winter Simulation Conference*: 645–652.

Heidelberger, P. (1986). Statistical analysis of parallel simulations. *Proceedings of the 1986 Winter Simulation Conference*: 290–295.

Heidelberger, P., and D. Nicol (1991). Simultaneous parallel simulations of continuous time Markov chains at multiple parameter settings. *Proceedings of the 1991 Winter Simulation Conference*: 602–607.

Heidelberger, P., and H. Stone (1990). Parallel trace-driven cache simulation by Time partitioning. *Proceedings of the 1990 Winter Simulation Conference*: 734–737.

Hennessy, J. L., and D. A. Patterson (1996). *Computer Architecture: A Quantitative Approach.* San Mateo, CA: Morgan Kaufmann.

Hering, K., and R. Haupt (1996). Hierarchical strategy of model partitioning for VLSI— Design using an improved mixture of experts approach. *Proceedings of the 10th Workshop on Parallel and Distributed Simulation*, IEEE Computer Society: 106–113.

Hiller, J. B., and T. C. Hartrum (1997). Conservative synchronization in object-oriented parallel battlefield discrete event simulations. *Proceedings of the 11th Workshop on Parallel and Distributed Simulation*, IEEE Computer Society 12–19.

Hofer, R. C., and M. L. Loper (1995). DIS today. *Proceedings of the IEEE* **83**(8): 1124–1137.

Hwang, K. (1993). *Advanced Computer Architecture: Parallelism, Scalability, and Programmability.* New York: McGraw–Hill.

IEEE Std 1278.1–1995 (1995). *IEEE Standard for Distributed Interactive Simulation— Application Protocols.* New York: Institute of Electrical and Electronics Engineers.

IEEE Std 1278.2–1995 (1995). *IEEE Standard for Distributed Interactive Simulation— Communication Services and Profiles.* New York: Institute of Electrical and Electronics Engineers.

Jefferson, D. R. (1985). Virtual time. *ACM Transactions on Programming Languages and Systems* **7**(3): 404–425.

Jefferson, D. R. (1990). Virtual time II: Storage management in distributed simulation. *Proceedings of the Ninth Annual ACM Symposium on Principles of Distributed Computing*: 75–89.

Jefferson, D. R., B. Beckman, et al. (1987). The Time Warp operating systems. *11th Symposium on Operating Systems Principles.* **21**: 77–93.

Jha, V., and R. Bagrodia (1994). A unified framework for conservative and optimistic distributed simulation. *Proceedings of the 8th Workshop on Parallel and Distributed Simulation:* 12–19.

Jones, D. W., C.-C. Chou, et al. (1989). Experience with concurrent simulation. *Proceedings of the 1989 Winter Simulation Conference*: 756–764.

Kapp, K. L., T. C. Hartrum, et al. (1995). An improved cost function for static partitioning of parallel circuit simulations using a conservative synchronization protocol. *Proceedings of the 9th Workshop on Parallel and Distributed Simulation*, IEEE Computer Society: 78–85.

Keller, J., T. Rauber, et al. (1996). Conservative circuit simulation on shared-memory multiprocessors. *Proceedings of the 10th Workshop on Parallel and Distributed Simulation*, IEEE Computer Society: 126–134.

Kim, H. K., and J. Jean (1996). Concurrency preserving partitioning (CCP) for parallel logic simulation. *Proceedings of the 10th Workshop on Parallel and Distributed Simulation*, IEEE Computer Society: 98–105.

Knight, T. (1986). An architecture for mostly functional programs. *Proceedings of the Lisp and Functional Programming Conference*. Cambridge, MA: ACM.

Konas, P. and P.-C. Yew (1992). Synchronous parallel discrete event simulation on shared memory multiprocessors. *Proceedings of the 6th Workshop on Parallel and Distributed Simulation*, SCS Simulation Series **24**: 12–21.

Konas, P., and P.-C. Yew (1994). Improved parallel architectural simulations on shared-memory multiprocessors. *Proceedings of the 8th Workshop on Parallel and Distributed Simulation*, Society for Computer Simulation: 156–159.

Kopetz, H., and W. Ochsenreiter (1987). Clock synchronization in distributed real-time systems. *IEEE Transactions on Computers* **36**(8): 933–940.

Krishnaswamy, D., P. Banerjee, et al. (1997). Asynchronous parallel algorithms for test set partitioned fault simulation. *Proceedings of the 11th Workshop on Parallel and Distributed Simulation*, IEEE Computer Society: 30–37.

Krishnaswamy, V., and P. Bannerjee (1996). Actor based parallel VHDL simulation using Time Warp. *Proceedings of the 10th Workshop on Parallel and Distributed Simulation*, IEEE Computer Society: 135–142.

Kumar, P., and S. Harous (1990). An approach towards distributed simulation of timed petri nets. *Proceedings of the 1990 Winter Simulation Conference*: 428–435.

Kumaran, K., B. Lubachevsky, et al. (1996). Massively parallel simulations of ATM systems. *Proceedings of the 10th Workshop on Parallel and Distributed Simulation*, IEEE Computer Society: 39–46.

Kung, H. T., and J. T. Robinson (1981). On optimistic methods of concurrency control. *ACM Transactions on Database Systems* **6**(2).

Lamport, L. (1978). Time, clocks, and the ordering of events in a distributed system. *Communications of the ACM* **21**(7): 558–565.

Lavenberg, S., R. Muntz, et al. (1983). Performance analysis of a rollback method for distributed simulation. *Performance '83*. Amsterdam: North Holland, Elsevier Science, pp. 117–132.

Law, A. M., and D. Kelton (1991). *Simulation Modelling and Analysis*. New York: McGraw-Hill.

Lin, Y.-B. (1994). Determining the global progress of parallel simulation with FIFO communication property. *Information Processing Letters* (50): 13–17.

Lin, Y.-B., and E. Lazowska (1990). Determining the global virtual time in distributed simulation. *Proceedings of the International Conference on Parallel Processing*: 201–209.

Lin, Y.-B., and E. D. Lazowska (1990). Exploiting lookahead in parallel simulation. *IEEE Transactions on Parallel and Distributed Systems* **1**(4): 457–469.

Lin, Y.-B., and E. D. Lazowska (1990). Optimality considerations of Time Warp parallel simulation. *Proceedings of the SCS Multiconference on Distributed Simulation*. **22**: 144–149.

Lin, Y.-B. and E. D. Lazowska (1991). A time-division algorithm for parallel simulation. *ACM Transactions on Modeling and Computer Simulation* **1**(1): 73–83.

Lin, Y.-B., E. D. Lazowska, et al. (1990). Comparing synchronization protocols for parallel logic simulation. *Proceedings of the 1990 International Conference on Parallel Processing*. **3**: 223–227.

Lin, Y.-B., and B. R. Preiss (1991). Optimal memory management for Time Warp parallel simulation. *ACM Transactions on Modeling and Computer Simulation* 1(4).

Lin, Y.-B., B. R. Preiss, et al. (1993). Selecting the checkpoint interval in Time Warp simulations. *Proceedings of the 7th Workshop on Parallel and Distributed Simulation*: 3–10.

Lipton, R. J. and D. W. Mizell (1990). Time Warp vs. Chandy–Misra: A worst-case comparison. *Proceedings of the SCS Multiconference on Distributed Simulation*. **22**: 137–143.

Liu, L. Z., and C. Tropper (1990). Local deadlock detection in distributed simulations. *Proceedings of the SCS Multiconference on Distributed Simulation*, SCS Simulation Series **22**: 64–69.

Lomow, G., S. R. Das, et al. (1991). Mechanisms for user invoked retraction of events in Time Warp. *ACM Transactions on Modeling and Computer Simulation* 1(3): 219–243.

Lubachevsky, B. D. (1989). Efficient distributed event-driven simulations of multiple-loop networks. *Communications of the ACM* **32**(1): 111–123.

Lubachevsky, B. D., A. Shwartz, et al. (1991). An analysis of rollback-based simulation. *ACM Transactions on Modeling and Computer Simulation* 1(2): 154–193.

Lundelius–Welch, J., and N. Lynch (1988). A new fault-tolerant algorithm for clock synchronization. *Information and Computation* **77**(1): 1–36.

Macedonia, M., M. Zyda, et al. (1995). Exploiting reality with multicast groups: A network architecture for large-scale virtual environments. *1995 IEEE Virtual Reality Annual Symposium*: 11–15.

Madisetti, V., J. Walrand, et al. (1988). WOLF: A rollback algorithm for optimistic distributed simulation systems. *Proceedings of the 1988 Winter Simulation Conference*: 296–305.

Madisetti, V. K., D. A. Hardaker, et al. (1993). The MIMDIX operating system for parallel simulation and supercomputing. *Journal of Parallel and Distributed Computing* 18(4): 473–483.

Manjikian, N., and W. M. Loucks (1993). High performance parallel logic simulation on a network of workstations. *Proceedings of the 7th Workshop on Parallel and Distributed Simulation*, SCS Simulation Series **23**: 76–84.

Mastaglio, T. W., and R. Callahan (1995). A large-scale complex environment for team training. *IEEE Computer* **28**(7): 49–56.

Mattern, F. (1993). Efficient algorithms for distributed snapshots and global virtual time approximation. *Journal of Parallel and Distributed Computing* 18(4): 423–434.

Mehl, H. (1992). A deterministic tie-breaking scheme for sequential and distributed simulation. *Proceedings of the Workshop on Parallel and Distributed Simulation*. Society for Computer Simulation **24**: 199–200.

Mehl, H., and S. Hammes (1993). Shared variables in distributed simulation. *Proceedings of the 7th Workshop on Parallel and Distributed Simulation*: 68–75.

Meldal, S., S. Sankar, et al. (1991). Exploiting locality in maintaining potential causality. *Proceedings of the ACM Symposium on Distributed Computing*: 231–239.

Merrifield, B. C., S. B. Richardson, et al. (1990). Quantitative studies in discrete event simulation modeling of road traffic. *Proceedings of the SCS Multiconference on Distributed Simulation*, SCS Simulation Series **22**: 188–193.

Miller, D. C., and J. A. Thorpe (1995). SIMNET: The advent of simulator networking. *Proceedings of the IEEE* **83**(8): 1114–1123.

Mills, D. L. (1991). Internet time synchronization: The network time protocol. *IEEE Transactions on Communications* **39**(10): 1482–1493.

Mills, D. L. (1995). Improved algorithms for synchronizing computer network clocks, *ACM/IEEE Transactions on Networking* **3**(3): 245–254.

Misra, J. (1986). Distributed discrete event simulation. *ACM Computing Surveys* **18**(1): 39–65.

Mitra, D., and I. Mitrani (1984). Analysis and optimum performance of two message passing parallel processors synchronized by rollback. *Performance '84*. Amsterdam: North Holland, Elsevier Science, pp. 35–50.

Mitre Corp. (1997). DPAT: Detailed policy assessment tool, brochure. Center for Advanced Aviation System Development (CAASD). McLean, Virginia.

Morse, K. (1990). Parallel distributed simulation in Modsim. *Proceedings of the 1990 International Conference on Parallel Processing*. **3**: 210–217.

Morse, K. (1996). Interest management in large scale distributed simulations, University of California, Irvine.

Morse, K. and J. Steinman, (1997). Data Distribution Management in the HLA: Multi-dimensional regions and physically correct routing, *Proceedings of the Spring Simulation Interoperability Workshop*, Orlando, Florida.

Mouftah, H. T., and R. P. Sturgeon (1990). Distributed discrete event simulation for communication networks. *IEEE Journal on Selected Areas in Communications* **8**(9): 1723–1734.

Nandy, B., and W. Loucks (1992). An algorithm for partitioning and mapping conservative parallel simulations onto multicomputers. *Proceedings of the 5th Workshop on Parallel and Distributed Simulation*, SCS Simulation Series **24**: 139–146.

Nicol, D., A. Greenberg, et al. (1992). Massively parallel algorithms for trace-driven cache simulation. *Proceedings of the 6th Workshop on Parallel and Distributed Simulation* **24**: 3–11.

Nicol, D. M. (1988). Parallel discrete-event simulation of FCFS stochastic queueing networks. *SIGPLAN Notices* **23**(9): 124–137.

Nicol, D. M. (1991). Performance bounds on parallel self-initiating discrete-event simulations. *ACM Transactions on Modeling and Computer Simulation* **1**(1): 24–50.

Nicol, D. M. (1993). The cost of conservative synchronization in parallel discrete event simulations. *Journal of the Association for Computing Machinery* **40**(2): 304–333.

Nicol, D. M. (1995). Noncommittal barrier synchronization. *Parallel Computing* **21**: 529–549.

Nicol, D. M., and X. Liu (1997). The dark side of risk. *Proceedings of the 11th Workshop on Parallel and Distributed Simulation*: 188–195.

Nicol, D. M., and P. F. J. Reynolds (1984). Problem oriented protocol design. *Proceedings of the 1984 Winter Simulation Conference*: 471–474.

Nicol, D. M., and S. Roy (1991). Parallel simulation of timed petri nets. *Proceedings of the 1991 Winter Simulation Conference*: 574–583.

Nikolaidis, I., R. M. Fujimoto, et al. (1994). Time parallel simulation of cascaded statistical multiplexers. *Proceedings of the 1994 ACM SIGMETRICS Conference on Measurement and Modeling of Computer Systems*: 231–240.

Nitzberg, B., and V. Lo (1991). Distributed shared memory: A survey of issues and algorithms. *Computer* 24(8): 52–60.

Palaniswamy, A. C., and P. A. Wilsey (1993). An analytical comparison of periodic checkpointing and incremental state saving. *Proceedings of the 7th Workshop on Parallel and Distributed Simulation*: 127–134.

Panesar, K., and R. M. Fujimoto (1997). Adaptive flow control in Time Warp. *Proceedings of the 11th Workshop on Parallel and Distributed Simulation*.

Partridge, C. (1993). *Gigabit Networking*. Reading, MA: Addison Wesley.

Peacock, J. K., J. W. Wong, et al. (1979). Distributed simulation using a network of processors. *Computer Networks* 3(1): 44–56.

Phillips, C. I. and L. G. Cuthbert (1991). Concurrent discrete event simulation tools. *IEEE Journal on Selected Areas in Communications* 9(3): 477–485.

Powell, E. T., L. Mellon, et al. (1996). Joint precision strike demonstration (JPSD) simulation architecture. *14th Workshop on Standards for the Interoperability of Distributed Simulations*. Orlando, FL, pp. 807–810.

Prakash, A., and R. Subramanian (1992). An efficient optimistic distributed scheme based on conditional knowledge. *Proceedings of the 6th Workshop on Parallel and Distributed Simulation*. 24: 85–96.

Preiss, B. (1990). Performance of discrete event simulation on a multiprocessor using optimistic and conservative synchronization. *Proceedings of the 1990 International Conference on Parallel Processing*. 3: 218–222.

Preiss, B., W. Loucks, et al. (1991). Null message cancellation in conservative distributed simulation. *Advances in Parallel and Distributed Simulation*, SCS Simulation Series 23: 33–38.

Preiss, B., I. MacIntyre, et al. (1992). On the trade-off between time and space in optimistic parallel discrete event simulation. *Proceedings of the 6th Workshop on Parallel and Distributed Simulation*. 24: 33–42.

Preiss, B. R., and W. M. Loucks (1995). Memory management techniques for Time Warp on a distributed memory machine. *Proceedings of the 9th Workshop on Parallel and Distributed Simulation*: 30–39.

Pullen, J. M. and D. C. Wood (1995). Networking technology and DIS. *Proceedings of the IEEE* 83(8): 1156–1167.

Rajaei, H., R. Ayani, et al. (1993). The local Time Warp approach to parallel simulation. *Proceedings of the 7th Workshop on Parallel and Distributed Simulation*: 119–126.

Ramanathan, P., D. D. Kandlur, et al. (1990). Hardware-assisted software clock synchronization for homogeneous distributed systems. *IEEE Transactions on Computers* 39(4): 514–524.

Ramanathan, P., K. G. Shin, et al. (1990). Fault tolerant clock synchronization in distributed systems. *IEEE Computer* 23(10): 33–42.

Raynal, M., A. Schiper, et al. (1991). Causal ordering abstraction and a simple way to implement it. *Information Processing Letters* 39(6): 343–350.

Reed, D. A., and R. M. Fujimoto (1987). *Multicomputer Networks: Message-Based Parallel Processing.* Cambridge: MIT Press.

Reed, D. A., A. D. Malony, et al. (1988). Parallel discrete event simulation using shared memory. *IEEE Transactions on Software Engineering* **14**(4): 541–553.

Reiher, P., F. Wieland, et al. (1990). Providing determinism in the Time Warp operating system—Costs, benefits, and implications. *Proceedings of the Workshop on Experimental Distributed Systems.* Huntsville, AL: IEEE, pp. 113–118.

Reiher, P. L., R. M. Fujimoto, et al. (1990). Cancellation strategies in optimistic execution systems. *Proceedings of the SCS Multiconference on Distributed Simulation.* **22**: 112–121.

Reinhardt, S. K., M. D. Hill, et al. (1993). The Wisconsin wind tunnel: Virtual prototyping of parallel computers. *Proceedings of the 1993 SIGMETRICS Conference on Measurement and Modeling of Computer Systems.* **21**: 48–60.

Reynolds, P., Jr., C. Pancerella, et al. (1993). Design and performance analysis of hardware support for parallel simulations. *Journal of Parallel and Distributed Computing* **18**(4): 435–453.

Reynolds, P. F., Jr. (1982). A shared resource algorithm for distributed simulation. *Proceedings of the 9th Annual Symposium on Computer Architecture* **10**: 259–266.

Reynolds, P. F., Jr. (1988). A spectrum of options for parallel simulation. *Proceedings of the 1988 Winter Simulation Conference*: 325–332.

Rich, D. O., and R. E. Michelsen (1991). An assessment of the Modsim/TWOS parallel simulation environment. *Proceedings of the 1991 Winter Simulation Conference*: 509–518.

Ronngren, R., and R. Ayani (1994). Adaptive checkpointing in Time Warp. *Proceedings of the 8th Workshop on Parallel and Distributed Simulation*: 110–117.

Ronngren, R., M. Liljenstam, et al. (1996). Transparent incremental state saving in Time Warp parallel discrete event simulation. *Proceedings of the 10th Workshop on Parallel and Distributed Simulation*: 70–77.

Ronngren, R., H. Rajaei, et al. (1994). Parallel simulation of a high speed LAN. *Proceedings of the 8th Workshop on Parallel and Distributed Simulation*, Society for Computer Simulation: 132–138.

Russo, K. L., L. C. Shuette, et al. (1995). Effectiveness of various new bandwidth reduction techniques in ModSAF. *Proceedings of the 13th Workshop on Standards for the Interoperability of Distributed Simulations*: 587–591.

Samadi, B. (1985). Distributed simulation, algorithms and performance analysis. *Computer Science Department*, PhD Thesis, University of California, Los Angeles.

Schiper, A., J. Eggli, et al. (1989). A new algorithm to implement causal ordering. *Proceedings of the International Workshop on Distributed Algorithms.* Berlin: Springer-Verlag.

Schwarz, R., and F. Mattern (1994). Detecting causal relationships in distributed computations: In search of the Holy Grail. *Distributed Computing* 7: 149–174.

Shah, G., U. Ramachandran, et al. (1994). Timepatch: A novel technique for the parallel simulation of multiprocessor caches. *Proceedings of the 4th Workshop on Scalable Shared Memory Multiprocessors.*

Singhal, M., and A. Kshemkalyani (1992). An efficient implementation of vector clocks. *Information Processing Letters* **43**: 47–52.

Singhal, S. K., and D. R. Cheriton (1994). Using a position history-based protocol for distributed object visualization. Computer Science Department, Stanford University, Palo Alto.

Sinha, P. (1996). *Distributed Operating Systems*. Piscataway, NJ: IEEE Press.

Sokol, L. M. and B. K. Stucky (1990). MTW: Experimental results for a constrained optimistic scheduling paradigm. *Proceedings of the SCS Multiconference on Distributed Simulation*. **22**: 169–173.

Soule, L. and A. Gupta (1991). An evaluation of the Chandy-Misra-Bryant algorithms for digital logic simulation. *ACM Transactions on Modeling and Computer Simulation* **1**(4): 308–347.

Sporrer, C., and H. Bauer (1993). Corolla partitioning for distributed logic simulation of VLSI circuits. *Proceedings of the 7th Workshop on Parallel and Distributed Simulation*, SCS Simulation Series: 85–92.

Srikanth, T. K., and S. Toueg (1987). Optimal clock synchronization. *Journal of the ACM* **34**: 626–645.

Srinivasan, S., and J. Reynolds, P. F. (1995). NPSI adaptive synchronization algorithms for PDES. *Proceedings of the 1995 Winter Simulation Conference*: 658–665.

Steinman, J. (1991). SPEEDES: Synchronous parallel environment for emulation and discrete event simulation. *Advances in Parallel and Distributed Simulation*, SCS Simulation Series **23**: 95–103.

Steinman, J. (1993). Breathing Time Warp. *Proceedings of the 7th Workshop on Parallel and Distributed Simulation*: 109–118.

Steinman, J. S., and F. Wieland (1994). Parallel proximity detection and the distribution list algorithm. *Proceedings of the 8th Workshop on Parallel and Distributed Simulation*. Edinburgh, Scotland: 3–11.

Stone, H. S. (1990). *High Performance Computer Architecture*. Reading, MA, Addison-Wesley.

Su, W. K. and C. L. Seitz (1989). Variants of the Chandy-Misra-Bryant distributed discrete event simulation algorithm. *Proceedings of the SCS Multiconference on Distributed Simulation*, Society for Computer Simulation **21**: 38–43.

Sunderam, V. S., and V. J. Rego (1991). EcliPSe, a system for high performance concurrent simulation. *Software Practices and Experiences* **21**(11): 1189–1219.

Tacic, I., and R. M. Fujimoto (1997). Synchronized data distribution management in distributed simulations. *Proceedings of the Spring Simulation Interoperability Workshop*. Orlando, FL, pp. 303–312.

Tallieu, F. and F. Verboven (1991). Using Time Warp for computer network simulations on transputers. *Proceedings of the 24th Annual Simulation Symposium*, IEEE Computer Society **21**: 112–117.

Tanenbaum, A. S. (1994). *Distributed Operating Systems*. Upper Saddle River, NJ: Prentice Hall.

Tanenbaum, A. S. (1996). *Computer Networks*, Upper Saddle River, NJ: Prentice Hall.

Tay, S. C., Y. M. Teo, et al. (1997). Speculative parallel simulation with an adaptive throttle scheme. *Proceedings of the 11th Workshop on Parallel and Distributed Simulation*: 116–123.

Thomas, G. S., and J. Zahorjan (1991). Parallel simulation of performance petri nets: Extending the domain of parallel simulation. *Proceedings of the 1991 Winter Simulation Conference*: 564–573.

Tinker, P. (1989). Task scheduling for general rollback computing. *Proceedings of the 1989 International Conference on Parallel Processing* **2**: 180–183.

Tinker, P., and M. Katz (1988). Parallel execution of sequential scheme with ParaTran. *Proceedings of the Lisp and Functional Programming Conference*. Snowbird, UT: ACM.

Tomlinson, A. I., and V. K. Garg (1993). An algorithm for minimally latent global virtual time. *Proceedings of the 7th Workshop on Parallel and Distributed Simulation*: 35–42.

Turner, S., and M. Xu (1992). Performance evaluation of the bounded Time Warp algorithm. *Proceedings of the 6th Workshop on Parallel and Distributed Simulation*, SCS Simulation Series: 117–128.

Unger, B. W., F. Gomes, et al. (1995). A high fidelity ATM traffic and network simulator. *Proceedings of the 1995 Winter Simulation Conference*: 996–1003.

Van Hook, D. J., J. O. Calvin, et al. (1994). An approach to DIS scalability. *Proceedings of the 11th Workshop on Standards for the Interoperability of Distributed Simulations*: 347–356.

Varghese, G., R. Chamberlain, et al. (1994). The pessimism behind optimistic simulation. *Proceedings of the 8th Workshop on Parallel and Distributed Simulation*: 126–131.

Voss, L. (1993). *A Revolution in Simulation: Distributed Interaction in the 90s and Beyond*. Arlington, VA: Pasha Publications.

Wagner, D. (1991). Algorithmic optimizations of conservative parallel simulations. *Advances in Parallel and Distributed Simulation*, SCS Simulation Series **23**: 25–32.

Wagner, D. B., and E. D. Lazowska (1989). Parallel simulation of queueing networks: Limitations and Potentials. *Proceedings of the 1989 ACM Sigmetrics Conference on the Measurement and Modeling of Computer Systems and Performance '89* **17**: 146–155.

Walrand, J., and P. Varaiya (1996). *High Speed Communication Networks: Building the Superhighway*, San Mateo, CA: Morgan Kaufmann.

Wang, J. J., and M. Abrams (1992). Approximate time-parallel simulation of queueing systems with losses. *Proceedings of the 1992 Winter Simulation Conference*: 700–708.

Waters, R. C., and J. W. Barrus (1997). The rise of shared virtual environments. *IEEE Spectrum* **34**(3): 20–25.

West, D. (1988). Optimizing Time Warp: Lazy rollback and lazy re-evaluation. *Computer Science Department*, University of Calgary, Alberta Canada.

West, D., and K. Panesar (1996). Automatic incremental state saving. *Proceedings of the 10th Workshop on Parallel and Distributed Simulation*: 78–85.

Wieland, F. (1997). Limits to growth: Results from the detailed policy assessment tool. *Proceedings of the 16th Annual IEEE Digital Avionics Systems Conference*. Irvine, CA.

Wieland, F., E. Blair, et al. (1995). Parallel discrete event simulation (PDES): A case study in design, development, and performance using SPEEDES. *Proceedings of the 9th Workshop on Parallel and Distributed Simulation*, IEEE Computer Society: 103–110.

Wieland, F., L. Hawley, et al. (1989). Distributed combat simulation and Time Warp: The model and its performance. *Proceedings of the SCS Multiconference on Distributed Simulation*, SCS Simulation Series **21**: 14–20.

Willis, J. C., and D. P. Siewiorek (1992). Optimizing VHDL compilation for parallel simulation. *IEEE Design and Test of Computers*: 42–53.

Wilson, A. L., and R. M. Weatherly (1994). The aggregate level simulation protocol: An evolving system. *Proceedings of the 1994 Winter Simulation Conference*: 781–787.

Wonnacott, P., and D. Bruce (1996). The APOSTLE simulation language: Granularity control and performance data. *Proceedings of the 10th Workshop on Parallel and Distributed Simulation*: 114–123.

Woodson, W. E. (1987). *Human Factors Reference Guide for Electronics and Computer Professionals*. New York: McGraw–Hill.

Xiao, Z., J. Cleary, et al. (1995). A fast asynchronous continuous GVT algorithm for shared memory multiprocessor architectures. *Proceedings of the 9th Workshop on Parallel and Distributed Simulation*.

Yavatkar, R. (1992). MCP: A protocol for coordination and temporal synchronization in multimedia collaborative applications. *Proceedings of the 12th International Conference on Distributed Computing Systems*, IEEE: 606–613.

Yu, M.-L., S. Ghosh, et al. (1991). A non-deadlocking conservative asynchronous distributed discrete event simulation algorithm. *Advances in Parallel and Distributed Simulation*, SCS Simulation Series **23**: 39–46.

Zeigler, B. P., and D. Kim (1996). Design of high level modelling/high performance simulation environments. *Proceedings of the 10th Workshop on Parallel and Distributed Simulation*, IEEE Computer Society: 154–161.

Zhang, L., S. Deering, S, et al. (1993). RSVP: a new resource ReSerVation Protocol, IEEE Network, **7**(5): 8–18.

AAL, *see* ATM adaptation layer protocol
Ada language, 111
Adaptation Layer Protocol, *see* ATM adaptation
   layer protocol
Adaptive control policy, 155
Address Resolution Protocol (ARP), 242
Addressing schemes, 241, 244
Adventure, 10–11
Aggregate Level Simulation Protocol (ALSP), 10,
   210
Aggregate network bandwidth, 223
Aggregated simulations, 12
Aggressive cancellation, 131–132
Aggressive No-risk Protocol (ANR), 157
Aggressive protocols, 156–157
Air traffic control, *see* Applications
ALSP, *see* Aggregate Level Simulation Protocol
AMG, *see* Architecture Management Group
Analytic simulations, 6–8, 23–24, 29, 51, 91,197,
   220, 269
ANR, *see* Aggressive No-risk Protocols
API, *see* Application Program Interfaces
Anti-messages, 97, 102–106, 109–110, 112–114,
   116–117 124–125, 129–135, 152, 156–157,
   159, 163–166, 168, 171
Application Program Interfaces (API), 211
Applications
   air traffic control, 3–6, 9, 14, 23, 33, 36, 40–42,
     45, 47, 52, 55, 57–59, 75, 80, 82, 87–88,
     128, 130, 170
   entertainment, 9, 11, 13, 23, 195–197, 259
   military, 11, 24, 85, 220
   training, 5–10, 12–14, 23, 28–29, 195–197, 199,
     204, 209–210, 257, 259, 273
Architecture Management Group (AMG), 210–211
ARP, *see* Protocols, address resolution
Artificial rollback, 144–146, 148–150, 155, 174
As-fast-as-possible simulation, 7, 29, 51, 196,
   210

Asynchronous Transfer Mode (ATM), 14–15, 23,
   170, 179, 183, 188, 191, 227–228, 230–231,
   233, 238–242, 257
   ATM adaptation layer (AAL), 238, 240
   ATM Protocol stack, 238
ATM, *see* Asynchronous Transfer Mode
ATM adaptation layer protocol (AAL), 240
Atomic clocks, 270
Attribute reflections, 212
Attribute table, 216
Autonomy of simulation nodes, 220
Avatar, 7

Backward transient messages, 141
Bandwidth, 11, 183–184, 199, 204, 223, 227–228,
   231–234, 237–238, 245, 256
Barrier synchronizations, 65–66, 168
Baseline definition, 10
Batch fossil collection, *see* Fossil collection
Battlefield simulations, *see* Applications, military
Benchmarks, 9, 15, 132, 136
B-ISDN, *see* Broadband Integrated Services
   Digital Networks
Blocking, 66, 112, 138, 140, 144, 148, 155–156,
   159, 162–163, 165, 174–175, 276
Bounded Lag Synchronization Algorithm, 80, 92,
   95, 156
Breathing Time Buckets Algorithm (BTB),
   157–158, 175
Breathing Time Warp Algorithm, 156, 174
Broadband Integrated Services Digital Networks
   (B-ISDN), 14–15, 183
Broadcast service, 224
BTB, *see* Breathing Time Buckets Algorithm
Buffers, 56, 88, 144–146, 148–150, 154, 157–158,
   162, 166–168, 171, 175, 179, 184, 187, 231,
   239
Butterfly barriers, 68, 70–72, 95

Cache memory, *see* Memory, cache
Cancelback, 144–150, 155, 174
Carrier Sense Multiple Access with Collision Detection (CSMA/CD), 229, 241
Cascaded rollback, 157
CATOCS, *see* Causal And Totally Ordered Communication Service
Causal And Totally Ordered Communication Service (CATOCS), 261, 266–268
Causal ordering, 261–262, 268
Causality errors, 51–53, 82–83, 97
Cause pointer variable, 166
Cell Loss Priority (CLP), 239
Chandy/Misra/Bryant Algorithm, 12, 57, 60, 81–82, 92
Checkpointing, 112, 125–128, 135, 162, 219
Checksum, 239
Circuit switching, 231–233, 238, 257
Class-based subscription, 216, 248–249, 252
Clock synchronization (wallclock time)
  centralized, pull algorithm, 271
  centralized, push algorithm, 272
  clock combining algorithm, 275
  clock selection algorithm, 274–275
  clustering algorithm, 275
Clock ticks, 271, 273
Closed groups, 244
CLP, *see* Cell Loss Priority
Coast-forward, 124, 154
Collisions, 228–229
Colored messages, 119–121
Communication latency, *see* Latency
Communication protocol, 3, 18, 234
Computation-only entities, 197
Concurrency control algorithm, 97, 135
Concurrent events, 262, 265–266
Concurrent Theater Level Simulation (CTLS), 12
Conditional information, 81–82, 95, 98, 217
Connection Transfer Protocol, 83
Conservative synchronization, 51, 58, 65, 87, 92–93 97–98, 112, 156, 174, 261
Consistency protocols, 19
Consistent cut, 117–119
Continuous simulation, 30–31, 160, 201
Copy state saving, 100–101, 123–124, 126, 140, 147, 150, 153–154
Cray T3D, 20
CRC, *see* Cyclic Redundancy Checksum
CSMA/CD, *see* Carrier Sense Multiple Access with Collision Detection
CTLS, *see* Concurrent Theater Level Simulation
Cut point, 117–119
Cyclic Redundancy Checksum (CRC), 239

DARPA, *see* Defense Advanced Research Projects Agency
Data distribution management, 200, 210, 219, 257
Data Distribution systems (DD), 245–247, 250, 257
Datagrams, 224, 241–243, 274
DD, *see* Data Distribution systems
Dead Reckoning Algorithms, 201, 204, 206, 208–209, 217, 220–221, 237, 273
Dead Reckoning Model (DRM), 205–209
Deadlock, 54–56, 58, 60–66, 79, 89–90, 94, 106, 138–139, 173
Deadlock detection, 60, 64–65, 79, 89, 94, 173
Deadlock Detection and Recovery Algorithm, 64–65, 79, 89, 94, 173
Declaration management, 215, 219
Defense Advanced Research Projects Agency (DARPA), 9, 210
Defense Modeling and Simulation Office (DMSO), 25, 210, 221, 247, 257
Delta causality, 267, 275
Derived types, 45–46
Description expression, 246–249, 251–253, 256–257
Detailed Policy Assessment Tool (DPAT), 170
Diamond Park, 13
Diffusing computation, 60–61
Direct execution, 15, 24
Direct Memory Access (DMA), 21
DIS, *see* Distributed Interactive Simulation
DIS nodes, 200, 202
Discrete event simulation, 16, 18, 30–32, 34, 36, 40, 46–48, 52, 160, 171
Distance between processes, 64, 75, 156, 173
Distance matrices, 76, 78
Distributed algorithms, 273
Distributed computers, 4–5, 8, 17–19, 22–23, 30, 36, 38, 46, 51, 91, 227
Distributed Interactive Simulation (DIS), 10, 13–14, 22, 25, 195, 199–202, 204, 206, 209–210, 220–221, 225–226, 237, 245, 257, 267
Distributed memory multicomputers, 17, 19, 21
Distributed shared-memory (DSM), *see* Memory
Distributed Virtual Environments (DVEs), 8, 10–11, 13–14, 19, 23, 25, 193, 195–197, 199–200, 204–206, 209, 213, 215, 218, 220, 223–227, 233, 243, 245–247, 255–257, 259–260, 267, 275
DMA, *see* Direct Memory Access
DMSO, *see* Defense Modeling and Simulation Office
DNS, *see* Domain Name Service
DoD, *see* United States Department of Defense

Dog-chasing-its-tail-effect, 151–152, 157, 159, 165

Domain Name Service (DNS), 243

Domino effect, 106, 125

DPAT, *see* Detailed Policy Assessment Tool

Drift (error), 269, 271

DRM, *see* Dead Reckoning Model

DSM, *see* Memory, distributed-shared

Dungeons and Dragons, 10–11

DVE, *see* Distributed Virtual Environments

Electronic mail, 3, 233, 237, 240, 243

Encapsulation, 45

Endian-ness, 237

Entertainment, *see* Applications, entertainment

Entity State PDUs (ESPDU), 225

Error rates, 227

ESPDU, *see* Entity State PDUs

Ethernet, 23, 225, 227–229, 231, 241–242

Event cancellation, 47, 107, 129–132, 146, 151–152, 165–167

Event horizon, 157–158

Event list, 34–35, 38–39, 43–44, 48, 74, 94, 99, 110, 129, 142–143, 150, 157, 167–168

Event retraction, 47, 128–129, 136

Event-driven simulations, 33, 210

Event-oriented simulations, 33, 41, 43–45, 161, 210

EXCIMS, *see* Executive Council for Modeling and Simulation

Executive Council for Modeling and Simulation (EXCIMS), 211

Extents (routing spaces), 249–250

eXternal Data Representation (XDR), 237

Fair fight, 196

Falsetickers, 275

Fault tolerance, 5

FDDI, *see* Fiber-Distributed Data Interface

Federation management services, 219

Federation Object Model (FOM), 212, 214, 248

Federations, 209, 211–220, 248–252, 253–254

Fiber-Distributed Data Interface (FDDI), 229

FIFO, *see* First-In-First-Out

File Transfer Protocol (FTP), 243

Filtered rollbacks, 156

First-In-First-Out (FIFO), 54, 61, 110, 184–186

Flight simulators, 4–5, 195, 197, 200, 211, 215–216, 265

Flow analysis, 127–128

Flow specification, 234

FOM, *see* Federation Object Model

Fossil collection, 109–110, 123, 135–136, 145, 147–149, 158, 165–168, 172, 175

FProc procedure, 161–162

Free( ) procedure, 122–123, 163

FTP, *see* File Transfer Protocol

Games, *see* Applications, entertainment

GAO, *see* General Accounting Office

Gate-level logic simulation, 15

General Accounting Office (GAO), 84

Georgia Tech Time Warp (GTW), 150, 161–171, 175

GEOS, *see* Geostationary Environment Operational Satellites

Geostationary Environment Operational Satellites (GEOS), 270

Global clock, 21, 34

Global control mechanisms, 66, 98, 122

Global Virtual Time (GVT), 74, 97, 109–110, 112–121, 123, 125, 134–135, 138–139, 141–142, 144–145, 147, 149, 154–158, 160, 162–165, 168–169, 171, 175

asynchronous algorithm, 115, 119

GMT, *see* Greenwich Mean Time

Greenwich Mean Time (GMT), 28, 270

GTW, *see* Georgia Tech Time Warp

GVT, *see* Global Virtual Time

Hardware-in-the-loop simulation, 7, 210, 269

High Level Architecture (HLA), 9–10, 12, 25, 195, 199, 202, 209–215, 218, 220–221, 247–249, 251–252, 255–257, 261, 276

compliance, 10, 211

interactions, 212

HLA, *see* High Level Architecture

Human-in-the-loop, 7, 200, 210

IBM, *see* International Business Machines

ICMP, *see* Internet Control Message Protocol

IETF, *see* Internet Engineering Task Force

IGMP, *see* Internet Group Multicast Protocol

ILAR, *see* Lookahead, inverse lookahead ratio

Inconsistent cut, 117, 119

Incremental state saving, 100–101, 123–124, 126–128, 133, 135, 153–154, 167, 169

Infrequent state saving, 124–125, 135, 140, 147–148, 154

Input queue, 102, 104, 139–140, 147, 153, 163

Intel Paragon, 20

Interest expression, 246–249, 251–257

Interface Specification, 210, 218, 221

International Business Machines (IBM), 22

International Standards Organization (ISO), 235

Internet, 3, 5, 8, 10–11, 13, 17, 23, 204, 221, 225–226, 232, 234, 236, 240–243, 245, 257, 272, 274

Internet Control Message Protocol (ICMP), 243
Internet Engineering Task Force (IETF), 242
Internet Group Multicast Protocol (IGMP), 243
Internet Protocol (IP), 225, 236, 240–243, 257, 274
Internetworking, 241–242
Interval intersection algorithm, 275
Inverse LookAhead Ratio (ILAR), *see* Lookahead
IP, *see* Internet Protocol
IProc procedure, 161–162
ISO, *see* International Standards Organization

Jet Propulsion Laboratory (JPL), 9, 108, 136
Jitter, 226, 231–233, 238, 256–257
Join operation, 244, 254, 256
JPL, *see* Jet Propulsion Laboratory

LAN, *see* Networks, local area
Latency, 3, 11, 17–18, 23–24, 112, 159, 196, 199, 203–204, 206, 208, 223, 226–227, 231–233, 238, 256–257, 259, 261, 267–269, 272–274
Lazy cancellation, 129–133, 136
Lazy re-evaluation, 132–133
LBTS, *see* Lower Bound Time Stamp
Leap seconds, 270
Least Recently Used replacement policy (LRU), 181–183
Leave operation, 244, 247, 254, 256
Links, 15, 53–54, 56–57, 61, 75–76, 78, 81, 92, 183–186, 227, 229–236, 241–242
Livelock, 134
Local area networks (LAN), *see* Networks
Local causality constraint, 52–55, 59, 91–93, 97–99, 156
Local control mechanism, 98, 108–109
Local minimum computation, 115–116
Local rollback, 157
Lock-step, 21
Logical Processes (LP), 39–40, 46–47, 51–65, 70, 74–86, 88–89, 91–94, 97–102, 104–108, 111–112, 122–124, 128–134, 137–141, 143–148, 150–169, 171–175, 177–183, 191
Logs, 133, 240
Lookahead, 57–60, 64–66, 74–76, 78–79, 81–84, 86–88, 90–94, 98, 105–106, 112, 156–157, 172–174, 256, 268–269
   inverse lookahead ratio (ILAR), 91
   zero, 58, 64, 86, 88, 93, 98, 106, 108, 112, 136
Lookahead prediction scheme, 256
Lower Bound Time Stamp (LBTS), 78–79, 81–83, 92, 112
LP, *see* Logical Processes
LRU, *see* Least Recently Used replacement policy

MAC, *see* Medium Access Control
Malloc( ) procedure, 122–123, 163
MAN, *see* Networks, metropolitan area
MBone, *see* Multicast Backbone
Medium Access Control (MAC), 228–229
Memory, 16–22, 25, 34, 46, 48, 52, 66, 89, 92, 97–98, 100, 102, 109–112, 122–124, 126–127, 132–140, 142–149, 150–151, 154–155, 158, 162–163, 165–168, 171–174, 181–184, 228
   cache, 19–20, 134, 171, 179, 181–182
   distributed shared (DSM), 21
   leaks, 122–123, 163
   management, 21, 138–139, 142–144, 148–149, 154–155, 171, 174
   memory-based flow control, 144, 148
MERL, *see* Mitsubishi Electric Research Laboratory
Message annihilation, 102, 139–140
Message sendback, 140–141, 143–145, 174
Metropolitan area network (MAN), 23, 227
Military applications, *see* Applications, military
MIMD, *see* Multiple-Instruction stream, Multiple Data stream
MIT Lincoln Laboratories, 25, 210
Mitre Corporation, 25, 170, 210
Mitsubishi Electric Research Laboratory (MERL), 13
Moving Time Window (MTW), 155, 174
MTW, *see* Moving Time Window
MUD, *see* MultiUser Dungeons
Multicast Backbone (MBone), 242
Multicast service, 225
Multiple-Instruction stream, Multiple Data-stream (MIMD), 21–22
Multiplexer, 179, 183–188, 232
MultiUser Dungeons (MUD), 11

Name space, 246–249, 251–257
National Institute of Standards and Technology (NIST), 270
Naval Post Graduate School, 225
NCube/Ten, 20
Network Time Protocol (NTP), 274
Network–Network Interface (NNI), 239
Networks
   local area (LAN), 13, 23, 196, 198, 227, 230–231, 236, 238, 241–242, 257, 272
   metropolitan area (MAN), 23, 227
   ring, 229, 231
   wide area (WAN), 23, 196, 199, 208, 227, 231, 272
Newsgroups, 13, 245–246
NextCause pointer variable, 166

NIST, *see* National Institute of Standards and
Technology
NonUniform Memory Access (NUMA), 20
NPSNet, 225, 257. *See also* Naval Postgraduate
School
NTP, *see* Network Time Protocol
Null messages, 12, 54, 56–58, 60, 64–65, 78,
81–82, 91–92, 94, 136, 173
NUMA, *see* NonUniform Memory Access

Object Model Template (OMT), 210, 213–215,
221
Object-oriented simulation, 41, 45–46, 127, 211,
214
OC-1, *see* Optical Carrier-1
OMT, *see* Object Model Template
On-the-fly fossil collection, *see* Fossil collection
Open groups, 244
Open System International (OSI), 235, 238,
241–242
Optical Carrier-1 (OC-1), 238–239
Optimistic barriers, 73
Optimistic synchronization, 51, 74, 97, 135, 138,
142, 145, 150–151, 154–157, 160–163,
171–172, 174
OSI, *see* Open System International
Output queue, 102, 129, 131, 139, 163, 166

Packet scheduling, 234
Packet switching, 232–233, 238
Parallel Discrete Event Simulation (PDES), 4–5, 9,
12, 15, 18–19, 22, 24–25, 39–40, 53, 59, 64,
66, 74, 80, 83, 85, 97–98, 122, 143, 154–155,
157, 161, 171, 177, 179, 182, 191, 195–197,
200
Parameter table, 218
Partial ordering, 266
Payload Type Identifier (PTI), 239
PDES, *see* Parallel Discrete Event Simulation
PDU, *see* Protocol Data Units
Physical time, 27–28
Pipelining, 97
Pointer variables, 166
Pointers, 112, 122, 164–167, 226
Polymorphism, 46
Prefix computation, 179, 188–190
Probabilistic rollback, 160
Proc procedure, 38, 41, 44, 46, 161–163, 165–167,
169
Process-oriented simulation, 41–45, 133, 161
Protocol Data Units (PDU), 200–203, 221,
225–226, 237, 267
detonation, 202
entity state (ESPDU), 225

fire, 202
Protocol stack, 235–236, 238, 241–243
Protocols
ATM adaptation layer (AAL), 240
address resolution (ARP), 242
aggregate level simulation (ALSP), 10, 12, 210,
291
aggressive, 131–132, 136, 156–157, 166
aggressive no-risk (ANR), 157
breathing time buckets (BTB) 157–158, 175
breathing time warp, 156, 174
Chandy/Misra/Bryant 12, 57, 60, 81–82, 92
communication, 3, 18, 234
connection transfer, 83
conservative synchronization, 51, 58, 65, 87,
92–93, 97–98, 112, 156, 174, 261
consistency, 19
file transfer (FTP), 243
Internet (IP), 225, 236, 240–243, 257, 274
Internet control message (ICMP), 243
Internet group multicast (IGMP), 243
network time (NTP), 274
optimistic synchronization, 51, 74, 97, 135, 138,
145, 151, 154, 156–157, 172, 174
ReSerVation (RSVP), 234
reverse address resolution (RARP), 242
serial line internet (SLIP), 242
simple mail transfer (SMTP), 243
slotted ring, 229
synchronous execution, 10, 70, 76, 82, 84, 92,
98, 118–119, 132, 138, 155, 160, 171–172,
269
token ring, 229, 242
transmission control (TCP), 225, 236, 238, 243
trivial file transfer (TFTP), 243
user datagram (UDP), 225, 236, 243, 274
wolf calls, 159, 175
YAWNS, 92, 95
Protofederations
analysis, 210
engineering, 210
joint training, 210
platform, 210
Pruneback, 144, 147–148, 155, 174
Pruning, 140, 144, 147–148, 174, 245
PTI, *see* Payload Type Identifier
Publication regions, 249
Pull processing, 47
Push processing, 47

QoS, *see* Quality of Service
Quality of Service (QoS), 233–234, 238
Query events, 46–47, 133
Queuing networks, 9, 191

Radar, 246–247
RARP, *see* Reverse Address Resolution Protocol
Real-time execution, 29
Receive time stamp, 140–142, 158, 164
Reduced-Instruction-Set-Computers (RISC), 127
Reflect attribute values service, 261
Regions (routing spaces), 160, 249–251
Release messages, 67
Repeaters, 228
Replacement policy, 181, 183
Replicated trials, 48
ReSerVation Protocol (RSVP), 234
Resource reservation, 234
Retraction, 129
Reverse Address Resolution Protocol (RARP), 242
Ring networks, *see* Networks
RISC, *see* Reduced-Instruction-Set-Computers
Rollback, 73, 97, 99–100, 102–104, 106–113,
    122–127, 129–133, 135–136, 138, 140–148,
    150–157, 159–160, 163, 166, 169, 171–172,
    174–175, 261, 268
  cascaded, 157
  cycles, 107–108
  echoes, 152
  handlers, 163
  local, 157
  probabilistic, 160
  secondary, 103, 106, 125, 131, 141, 156–157
  thrashing, 138
Routing, 234, 236, 249, 276
Routing spaces, 214, 247–249, 250, 257
RS-232-C, 235
RSVP, *see* ReSerVation Protocol
RTI, *see* Run-Time Infrastructure
Run-Time Infrastructure (RTI), 10, 209–213, 216,
    218–221, 251

Salvage parameter, 145
Scalability, 172, 174, 199, 273
Scaled real-time execution, 29
Scheduling (an event), 34–35
Secondary rollback, 103, 106, 125, 131, 141,
    156–157
Secondary servers, 274
Selective fidelity, 196
Send time stamp, 131, 139–142, 145, 157–158
Sequential discrete event simulation, 34
Serial Line Internet Protocol (SLIP), 242
Server architecture, 197–199
Serverless architecture, 197
Shared-memory multiprocessor, 17, 19, 21, 161
Silicon Graphics, 22
SIMD, *see* Single Instruction stream, Multiple
    Data stream

SIMNET, *see* SIMulator NETworking Project
Simple Mail Transfer Protocol (SMTP), 243
Simula, 46
Simulation executive, 12, 35–36, 38, 41, 44–45,
    60, 63, 66, 80–86, 93–94, 99, 129, 131–133,
    135, 150, 171–175, 196–197, 209, 245, 255,
    261–263, 267
Simulation Object Model (SOM), 212, 214
Simulation time, 7, 27–29, 33, 39, 43, 75, 106,
    109, 153, 156, 158, 160, 171
Simulation time creep, 82
Simulations
  aggregated, 12
  analytic, 6–10, 12, 14, 23–24, 29, 51, 91,
      195–197, 209, 220, 260, 269
  as-fast-as-possible, 7, 29, 51, 196, 210
  continuous, 30–31, 160, 201
  discrete event, 16, 18, 30–32, 34, 36, 40, 46–48,
      52, 160, 171
  distributed interactive (DIS), 10, 13–14, 22, 25,
      195, 199–202, 204, 206, 209–210,
      220–221, 225–226, 237, 245, 257, 267
  event-oriented, 33, 41, 43–45, 161, 210
  gate-level logic, 15
  hardware-in-the-loop, 7, 210, 269
  object-oriented, 41, 45–46, 127, 211, 214
  parallel discrete event, 4–5, 9, 12, 15, 18–19, 22,
      24–25, 39–40, 53, 59, 64, 66, 74, 80, 83,
      85, 97–98, 122, 143, 154–155, 157, 161,
      171, 177, 179, 182, 191, 195–197, 200
  process-oriented, 41–45, 133, 161
  sequential discrete event, 34
  space parallel, 191
  space-time, 160, 175
  time parallel, 177–179, 181–183, 187–188, 191
  time-stepped, 31–33, 41
  war games, 9–10, 12
SIMulator NETworking Project (SIMNET), 9–10,
    200, 204, 206, 221, 245
Simultaneous events, 53, 85–86, 94, 106–108
Simultaneous reporting problem, 113, 115–116,
    135
Single Instruction stream, Multiple Data stream
    (SIMD), 17–19, 21–22
SLIP, *see* Serial Line Internet Protocol
Slotted ring protocols, 229
Smallest Time stamp First policy (STF), 134
Smoothing, 208, 220
SMP, *see* Symmetric MultiProcessor
SMTP, *see* Simple Mail Transfer Protocol
Snapshots, 135, 151–152
Solar days, 270
SOM, *see* Simulation Object Model
SONET, *see* Synchronous Optical NETwork

Space parallel simulation, 191
Space-time simulation, 160, 175
Spanning tree, 63–64, 245
Spatial decomposition, 177
Speedup, 79, 90–91, 94, 171, 173, 196
State queue, 101–102, 133, 139, 147, 163–164
State variables, 27, 30–36, 38–39, 45, 51–52, 58,
    93, 98, 100–101, 105, 111, 122–124, 126,
    128, 133, 136, 138–139, 153, 160, 169, 177,
    200, 211
Static control policy, 82, 92, 155, 201, 217,
    254–255
Statistical multiplexing, 233, 238, 257
Stealth viewers, 218
STF, *see* Smallest Time stamp First policy
Storage optimality, 139, 142–144, 146, 148, 174
Straggler events, 99, 133
Straggler messages, 99, 157
STS-1, *see* Synchronous Transport Signal Level 1
STS/OC-n, 238
Subscription, 212, 216, 219–220, 248–249, 252,
    256
Subscription regions, 249–251, 253
Sun Enterprise System, 19, 22, 171
Switched LANs, 230–231
Symmetric MultiProcessor (SMP), 19–20
Synchronization problem, 51, 91, 94, 260
Synchronization protocols, 8, 10, 12, 51–56,
    66–69, 71–73, 79–80, 82, 84, 91–92, 94–95,
    97–98, 115, 122, 132, 135, 138, 155–156,
    160, 163, 165, 169, 171–172, 174–175,
    177–178, 196–197, 210, 226, 237, 258, 260,
    268–269, 271, 273–274, 276
Synchronous execution, 10, 70, 76, 82, 84, 92, 98,
    118–119, 132, 138, 155, 160, 171–172, 269
Synchronous Optical NETwork (SONET), 238
Synchronous Transport Signal Level 1 (STS-1),
    238
Synthetic environments, 9
Synthetic forces, 197

TCP, *see* Transmission Control Protocol
Telephone industry, 15, 191, 224, 231, 236, 238,
    255, 257, 270
Temporal decomposition, 177
Test and Evaluation, 12
TFTP, *see* Trivial File Transfer Protocol
Threading mechanisms, 44
Time
  atomic clocks, 270
  clock combining algorithms, 275
  clock selection algorithms, 274–275
  clock synchronization algorithms, 79, 269, 271,
    275
  clock ticks, 271, 273
  falsetickers, 275
  Greenwich Mean Time, 28, 270
  interval intersection algorithms, 275
  leap seconds, 270
  physical, 27–28
  simulation, 7, 27–29, 33, 39, 43, 75, 106, 109,
    153, 156, 158, 160, 171
  solar days, 270
  universal time (coordinated) (UTC), 269–272,
    275
  wallclock, 27, 275
Time creep, 82
Time division multiplexing, 232–233, 257
Time flow mechanism, 30–31
Time parallel simulation, 177–179, 181–183,
    187–188, 191
Time providers, 270
Time Warp, 12, 97–102, 104, 106, 108–112, 117,
    122–123, 125–145, 148–152, 154, 156–157,
    160–161, 163, 165, 171, 173–174, 276
Time Warp Logical Process (TWLP), 99–100,
    102–104, 106–107, 109–111, 122–124, 132,
    134
Time Warp Operation System (TWOS), 9, 108,
    288
Time windows, 78, 81, 84, 155, 157
Time-stepped simulations, 31–33, 41
Token ring protocols, 229, 242
Tokens, 120, 229, 241
Training, *see* Applications, training
Transient messages, 66, 70–73, 77, 92, 95,
    113–121, 135, 141, 158
Transmission Control Protocol (TCP), 225, 236,
    238, 243
Transport mechanisms, 244
Trees, 61–64, 67–72, 74, 108, 190, 245, 248–249,
    274
Trivial File Transfer Protocol (TFTP), 243
Truncated binary exponential backoff algorithm,
    229
TWfree( ) procedure, 123
TWGetMsg procedure, 162, 167
TWLP, *see* Time Warp Logical Process
TWmalloc( ) procedure, 123
TWOS, *see* Time Warp Operation System
TWSend procedure, 162, 165, 167, 169

UDP, *see* User Datagram Protocol
UMA, *see* Uniform Memory Access
Unconditional information, 81–82
Undiscovery, 251
UNI, *see* User-Network Interface
Unicast service, 224–225, 234, 243, 245, 251, 255

Uniform Memory Access (UMA), 20
United States Department of Defense (DoD), 9–10, 210–211, 236
Universal Time (Coordinated) (UTC), 269–272, 275
Unix, 22, 111, 272
Unreliable delivery service, 223, 236, 243, 273, 275
Update attribute values service, 219, 248, 261
Update regions, 251
User Datagram Protocol (UDP), 225, 236, 243, 274
User-Network Interface (UNI), 239
UTC, *see* Universal Time (Coordinated)

Value-based data distribution, 248–249
VCI, *see* Virtual Channel Indicator
Vector clock, 262–264
Virtual Channel Indicator (VCI), 230–231, 233, 239
Virtual circuits, 238

Virtual environment, 5–14, 19, 23, 25, 28, 30, 48, 195–196, 203–204, 206, 208, 223, 225, 240, 247, 249–250, 255, 259–260, 266
Virtual Path Indicator (VPI), 230–231, 233, 239
VPI, *see* Virtual Path Indicator

Wallclock time, 27, 275
WAN, *see* Networks, wide area
War game simulations, 9–10, 12
Weapons systems, 11, 85, 220
Wide area network (WAN), 23, 196, 199, 208, 227, 231, 272
Wolf Calls protocol, 159, 175

X.25, 236
XDR, *see* eXternal Data Representation
Xerox Palo Alto Research Center, 10

YAWNS protocol, 92, 95

Zero lookahead, *see* Lookahead